MW01622048

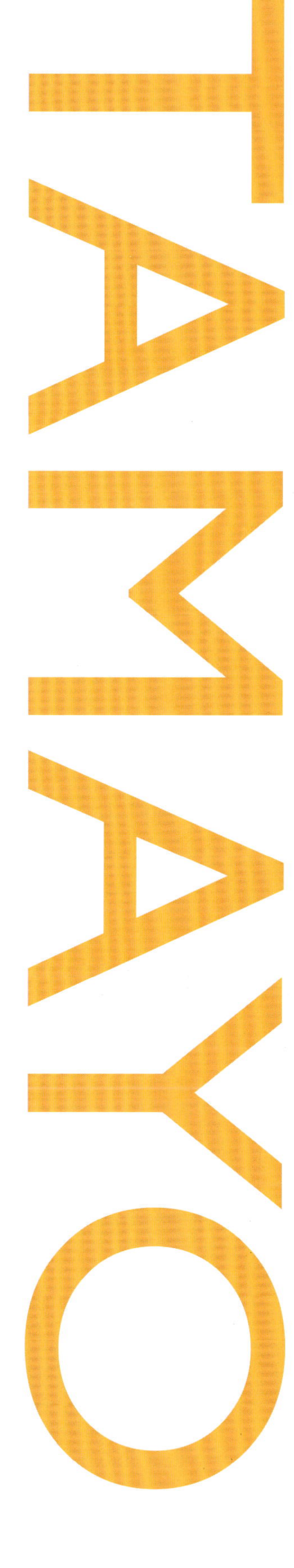

THE

NEW YORK

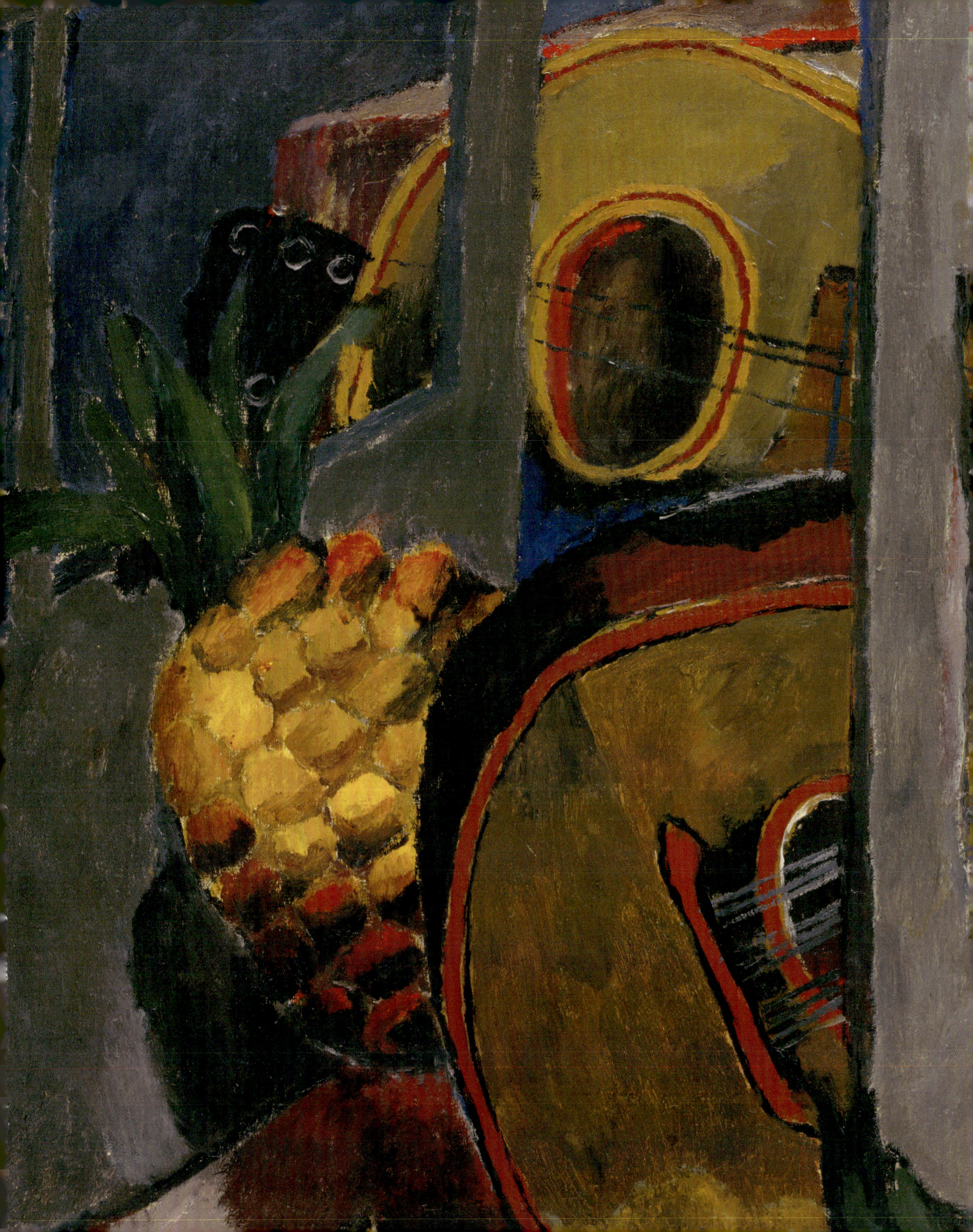

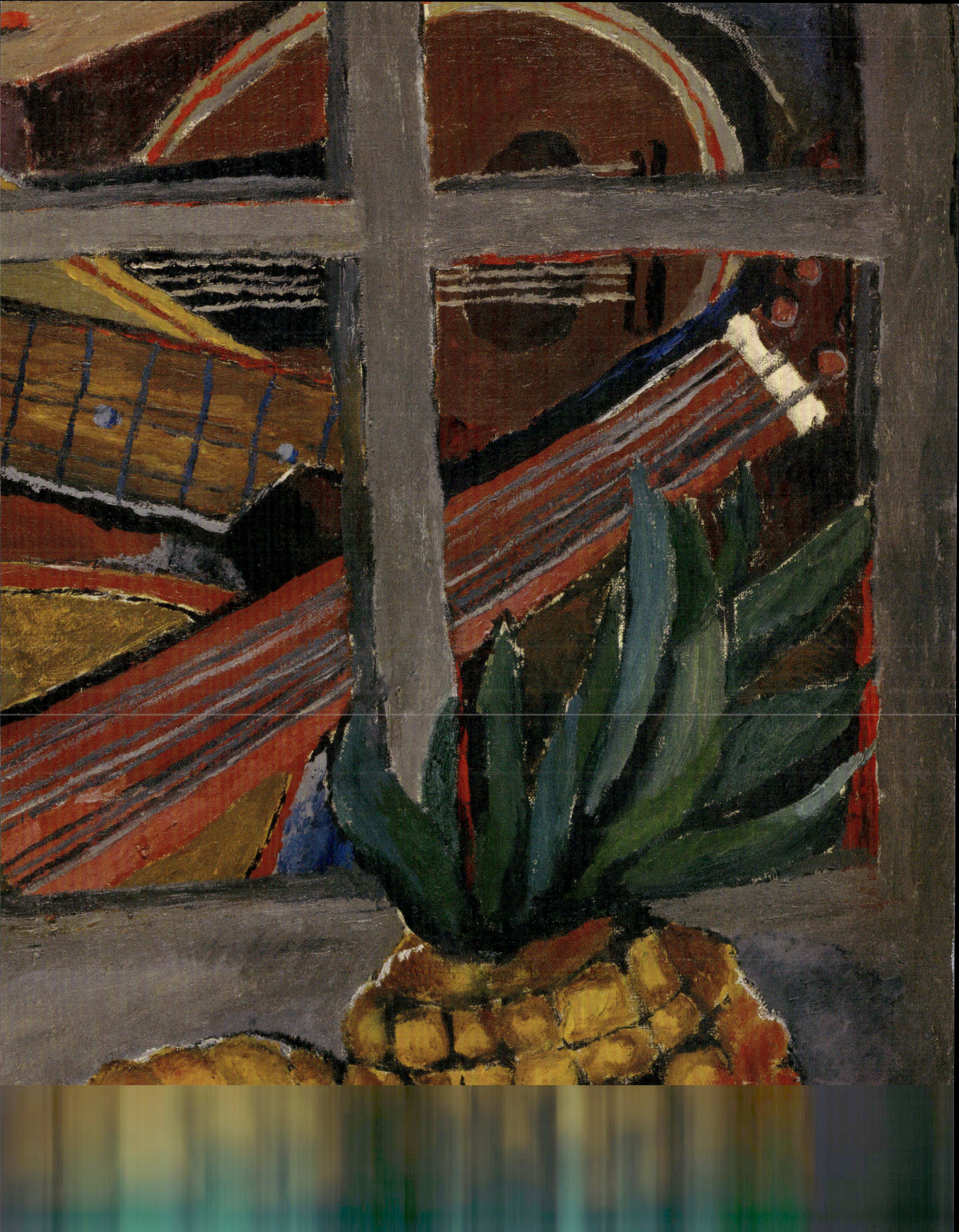

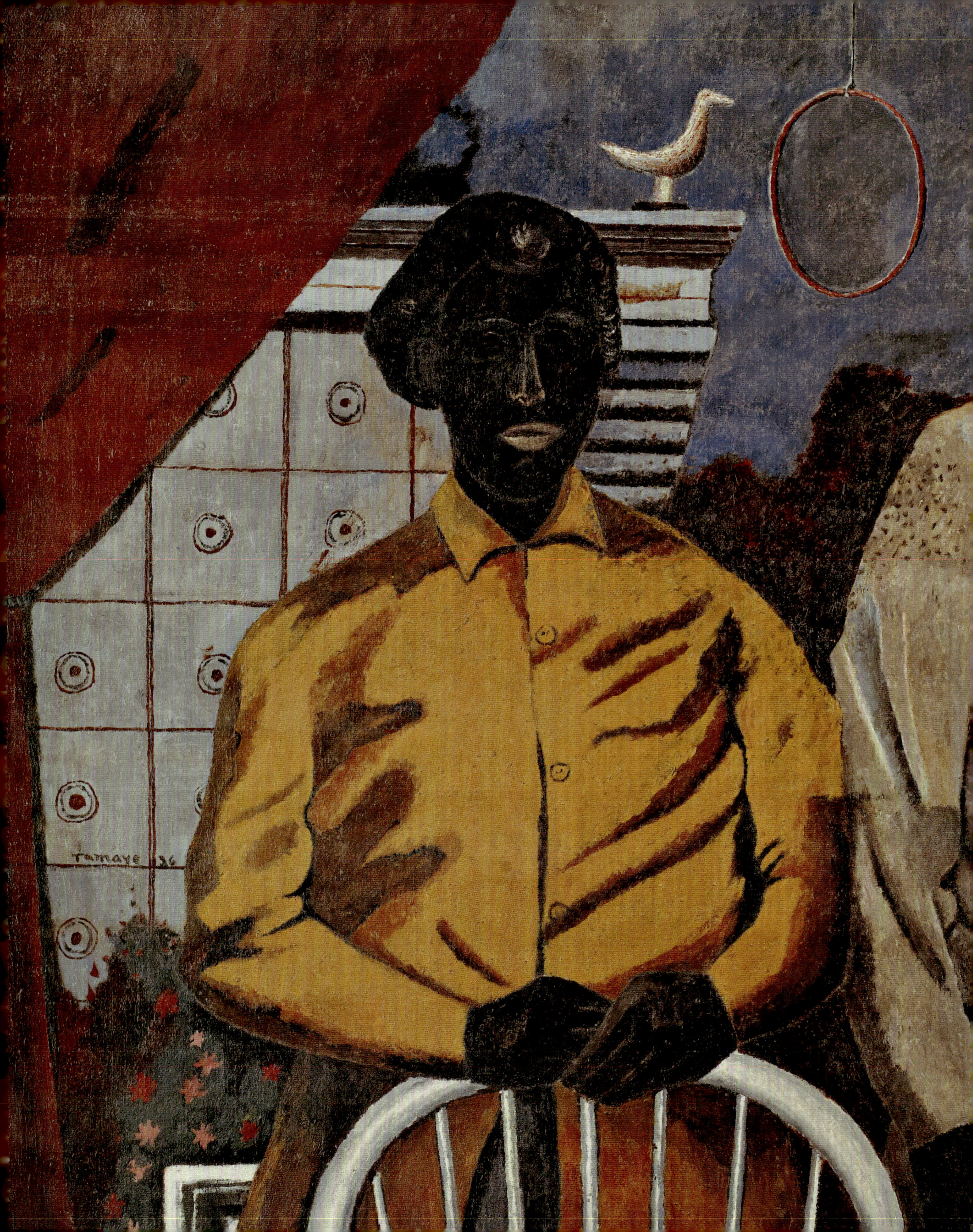

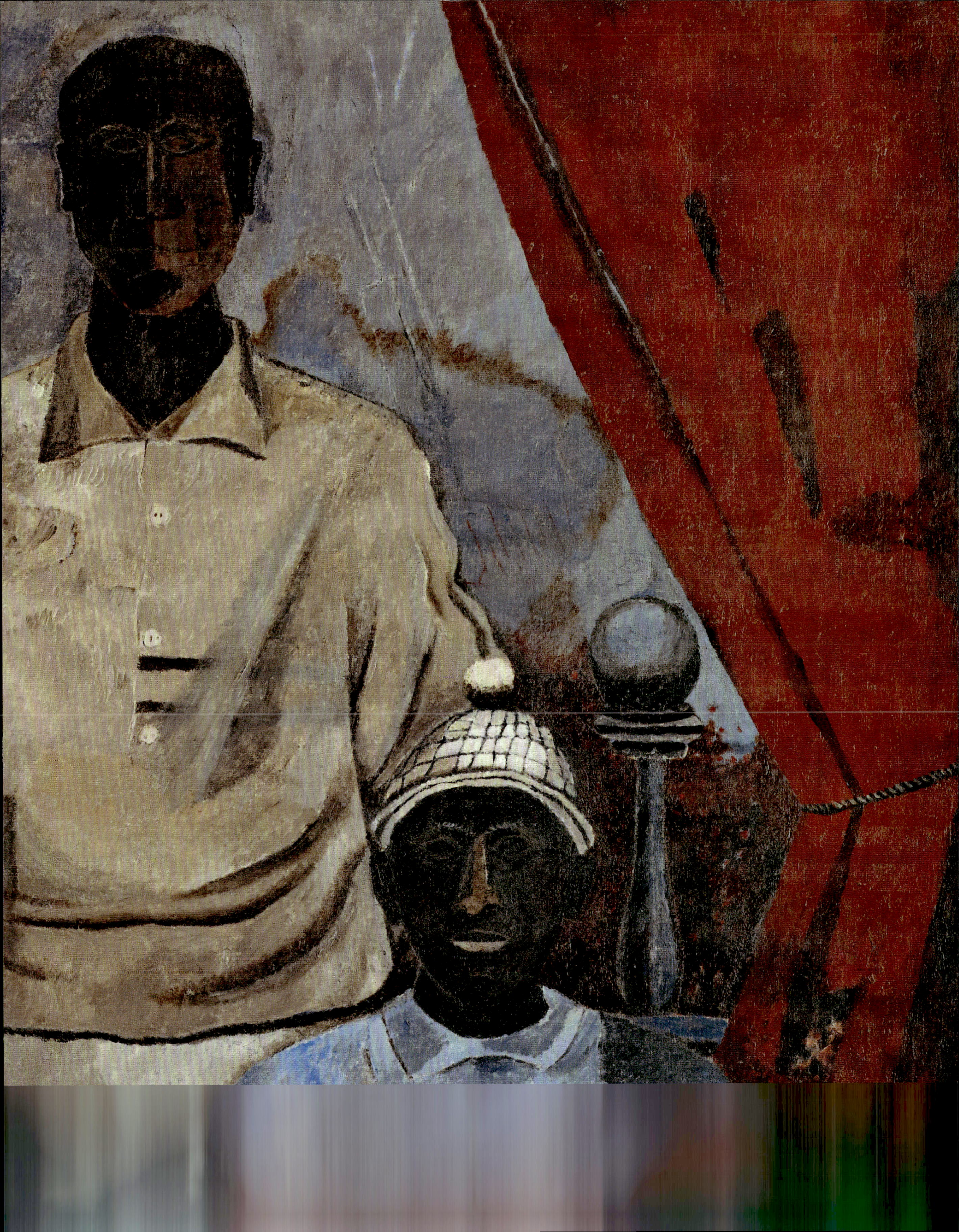

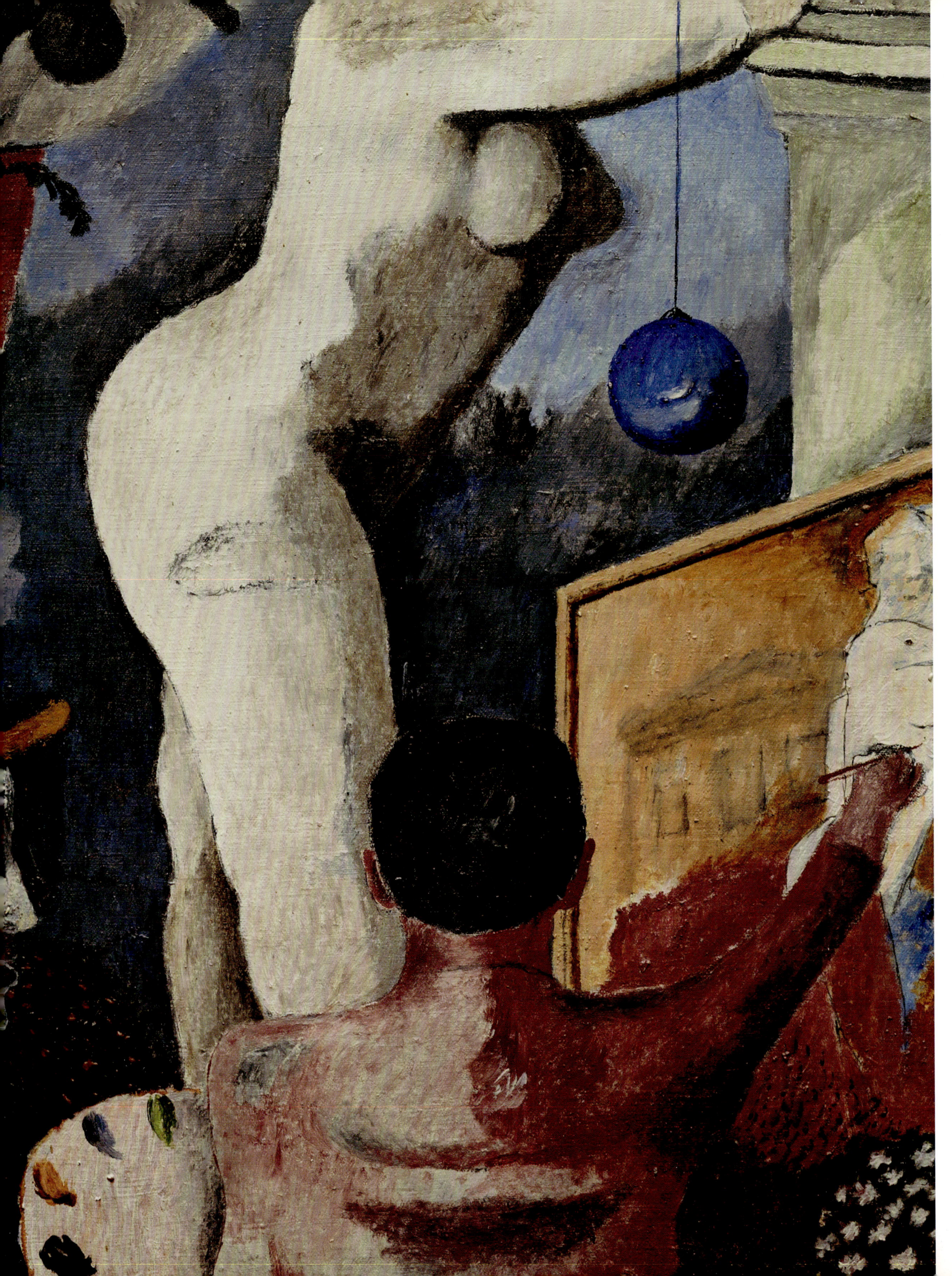

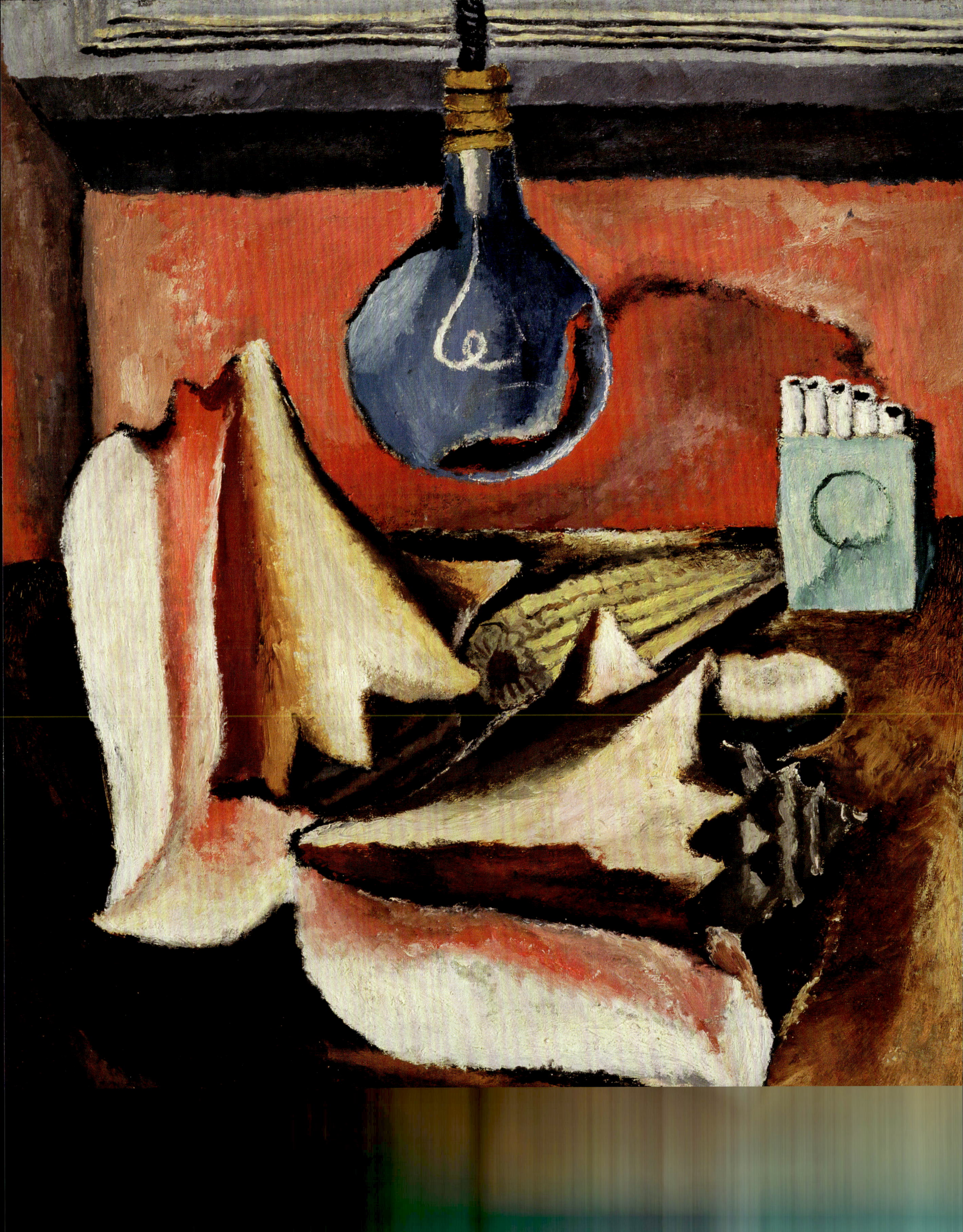

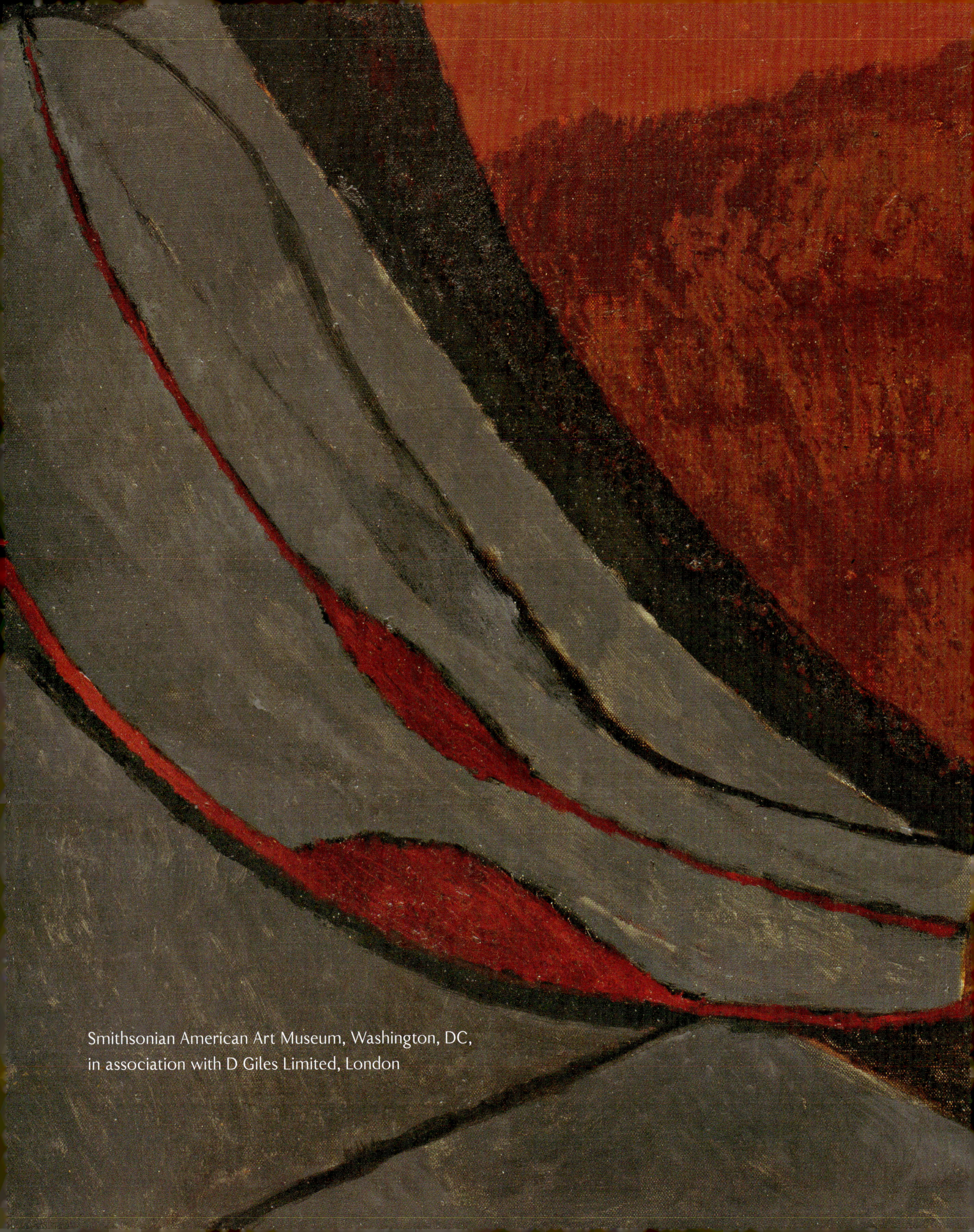

Smithsonian American Art Museum, Washington, DC,
in association with D Giles Limited, London

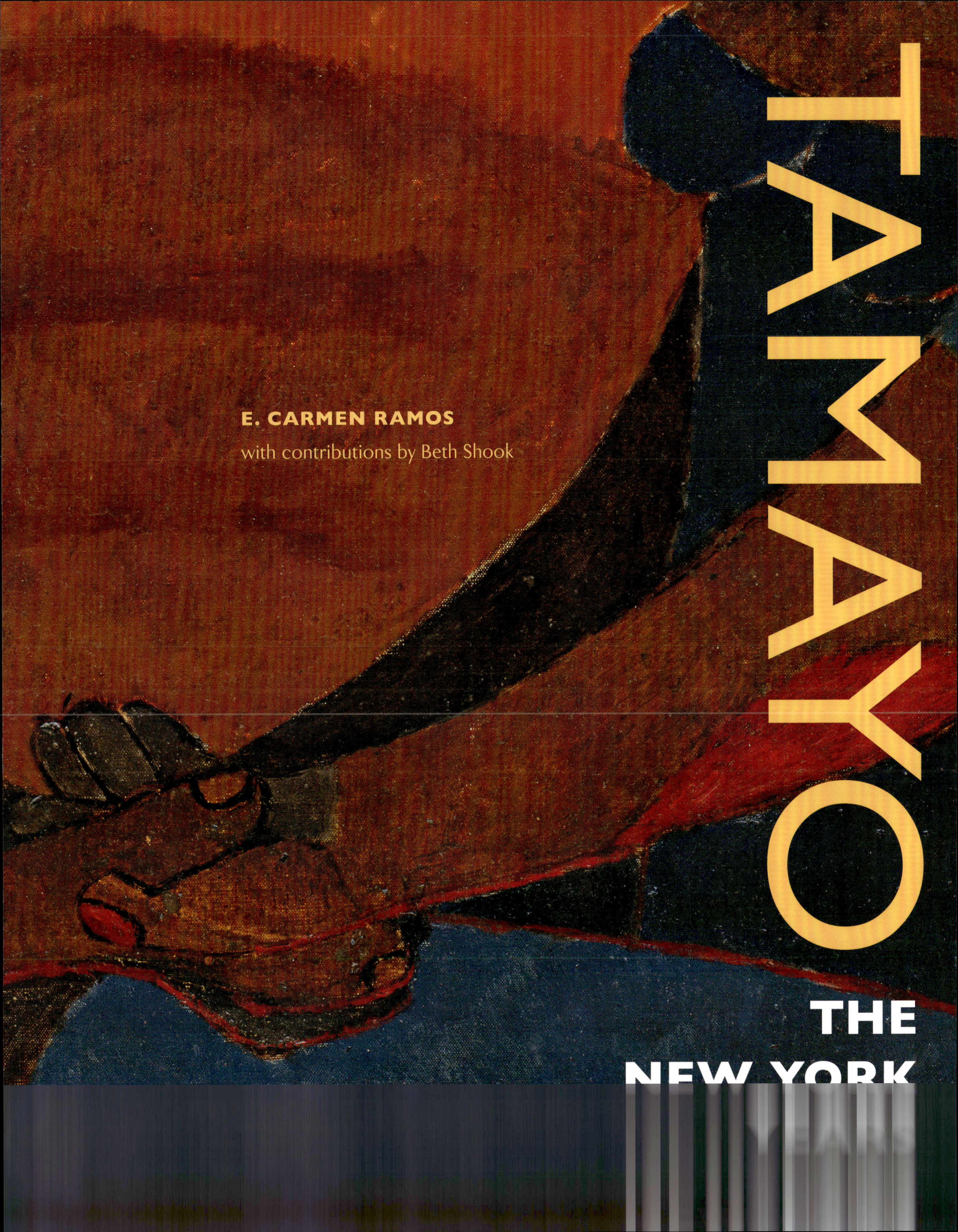
TAMAYO
E. CARMEN RAMOS
with contributions by Beth Shook
THE
NEW YORK

TAMAYO: THE NEW YORK YEARS
By E. Carmen Ramos

Published in conjunction with the exhibition of the same name, on view at the Smithsonian American Art Museum, Washington, DC, November 3, 2017–March 18, 2018.

Theresa J. Slowik, Chief of Publications
Karen Siatras, Designer
Mary J. Cleary, Editor
Amy Doyel, Permissions Coordinator
Julianna White and Jenny Wilson, Proofreaders

Published by the Smithsonian American Art Museum in association with

GILES
An imprint of D Giles Limited
4 Crescent Stables
139 Upper Richmond Road
London
SW15 2TN
UK

Typeset in Gill Sans and Gill New Antique. Printed and bound in Italy by Conti Tipocolor on 150 gsm Condat matt Périgord paper.

The Smithsonian American Art Museum is home to one of the largest collections of American art in the world. Its holdings—more than 43,000 works—tell the story of America through the visual arts and represent the most inclusive collection of American art of any museum today.

It is the nation's first federal art collection, predating the 1846 founding of the Smithsonian Institution. The Museum celebrates the exceptional creativity of the nation's artists, whose insights into history, society, and the individual reveal the essence of the American experience.

Visit us at AmericanArt.si.edu.

Image details:

Cover: *Carnival* [*Carnaval*], 1936. See p. 97.

pp. ii–iii: *Mandolins and Pineapples* [*Mandolinas y piñas*], 1930. See p. 89.

pp. iv–v: *The Family* [*La familia*], 1936. See pp. 104–105.

p. vi: *Academic Painting* [*Pintura académica*], 1935. See p. 95.

p. vii: *Seashells* [*Los caracoles*], 1929. See p. 88.

pp. viii–ix: *The Lovers* [*Amantes*], 1943. See pp. 118–19.

pp. xii–xiii: *Three Ice Creams* [*Tres helados*], 1938. See p. 103.

p. xiv: *Dog Barking at the Moon* [*Perro ladrando a la luna*], 1942. See p. 122.

p. xvi: *Total Eclipse* [*Eclipse total*], ca. 1946. See p. 130.

Library of Congress Cataloguing-in-Publication Data

Names:
Ramos, E. Carmen, author.
Smithsonian American Art Museum organizer, host institution.

Title:
Tamayo: the New York years / E. Carmen Ramos; with contributions by Beth Shook.

Description:
Washington, DC: Smithsonian American Art Museum; London: in association with D Giles Limited, 2017.
"Published in conjunction with the exhibition of the same name, on view at the Smithsonian American Art Museum, Washington, DC, November 3, 2017–March 18, 2018."
Includes bibliographical references and index.

Identifiers:
LCCN 2017020583
ISBN 9781911282150 (hardcover)

Subjects:
LCSH: Tamayo, Rufino, 1899–1991—Exhibitions.
BISAC: ART / Individual Artists / Monographs.
ART / American / Hispanic American.
ART / Collections, Catalogs, Exhibitions / General.
ART / History / Contemporary (1945–).

Classification:
LCC N6559.T36 A4 2017
DDC 700.92—dc23 LC record available at https://lccn.loc.gov/2017020583

CONTENTS

TAMAYO: THE NEW YORK YEARS
is organized by the Smithsonian American Art Museum.

We are especially grateful to
His Excellency Gerónimo Gutiérrez-Fernández,
the Mexican Ambassador to the United States,
for serving as the honorary patron for the exhibition.

The Mexican Cultural Institute of Washington, DC,
has provided invaluable advice and support.

The Latino Initiatives Pool,
administered by the Smithsonian Latino Center,
provided major support.

Additional generous contributions
have been provided by the following:

Mrs. J. Todd Figi
Robert S. Firestone Foundation
Wolf Kahn and Emily Mason Foundation
William R. Kenan Jr. Endowment Fund
Sara Roby Foundation
Sam Rose and Julie Walters
Smithsonian Scholarly Studies Grant Program

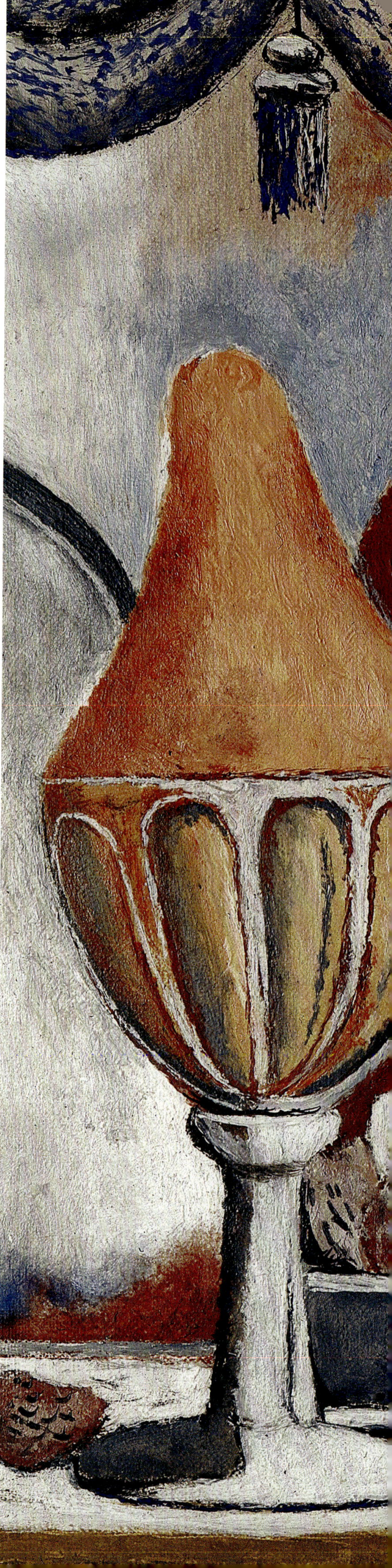

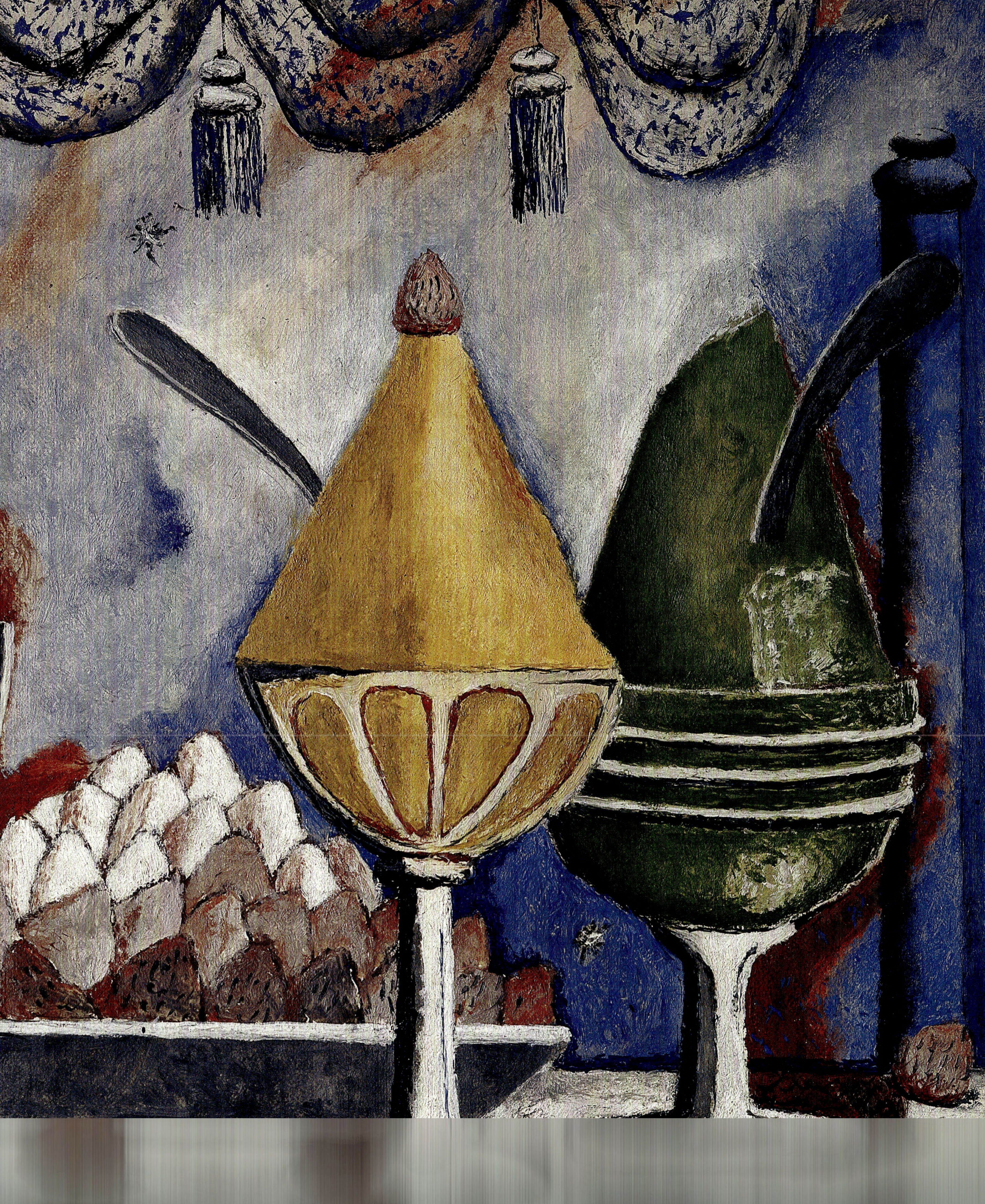

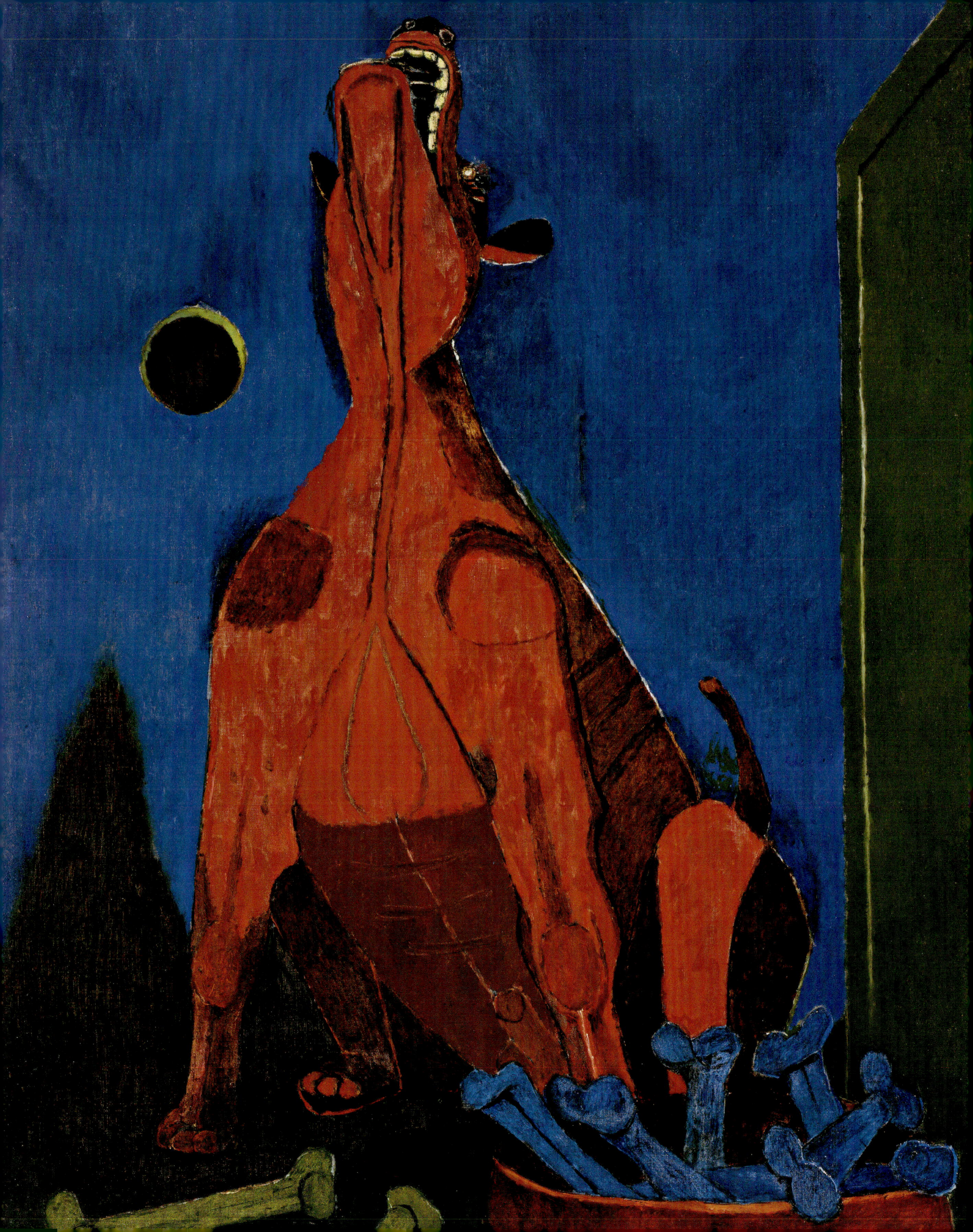

LENDERS TO THE EXHIBITION

Albright-Knox Art Gallery, Buffalo, New York
Gianfranco Arnoldi
The Art Institute of Chicago
Blanton Museum of Art, The University of Texas at Austin
William and Christopher Brumder Collection
Dallas Museum of Art
FEMSA Collection
Mrs. J. Todd Figi
John Fox and Sandy Allen
Stanley and Pearl Goodman
Peggy Guggenheim Collection, Venezia (Solomon R. Guggenheim Foundation, New York)
Harvard Art Museums
Hirshhorn Museum and Sculpture Garden, Smithsonian Institution, Washington, DC
Mildred Lane Kemper Art Museum, Washington University in St. Louis, Missouri
Brian and Florence Mahony
The Metropolitan Museum of Art, New York
The Minneapolis Institute of Art
Museo de Arte Moderno—INBA
Museum of Fine Arts, Boston
The Museum of Modern Art, New York
Philadelphia Museum of Art
The Phillips Collection, Washington, DC
Private collectors
Museum of Art, Rhode Island School of Design
San Francisco Museum of Modern Art

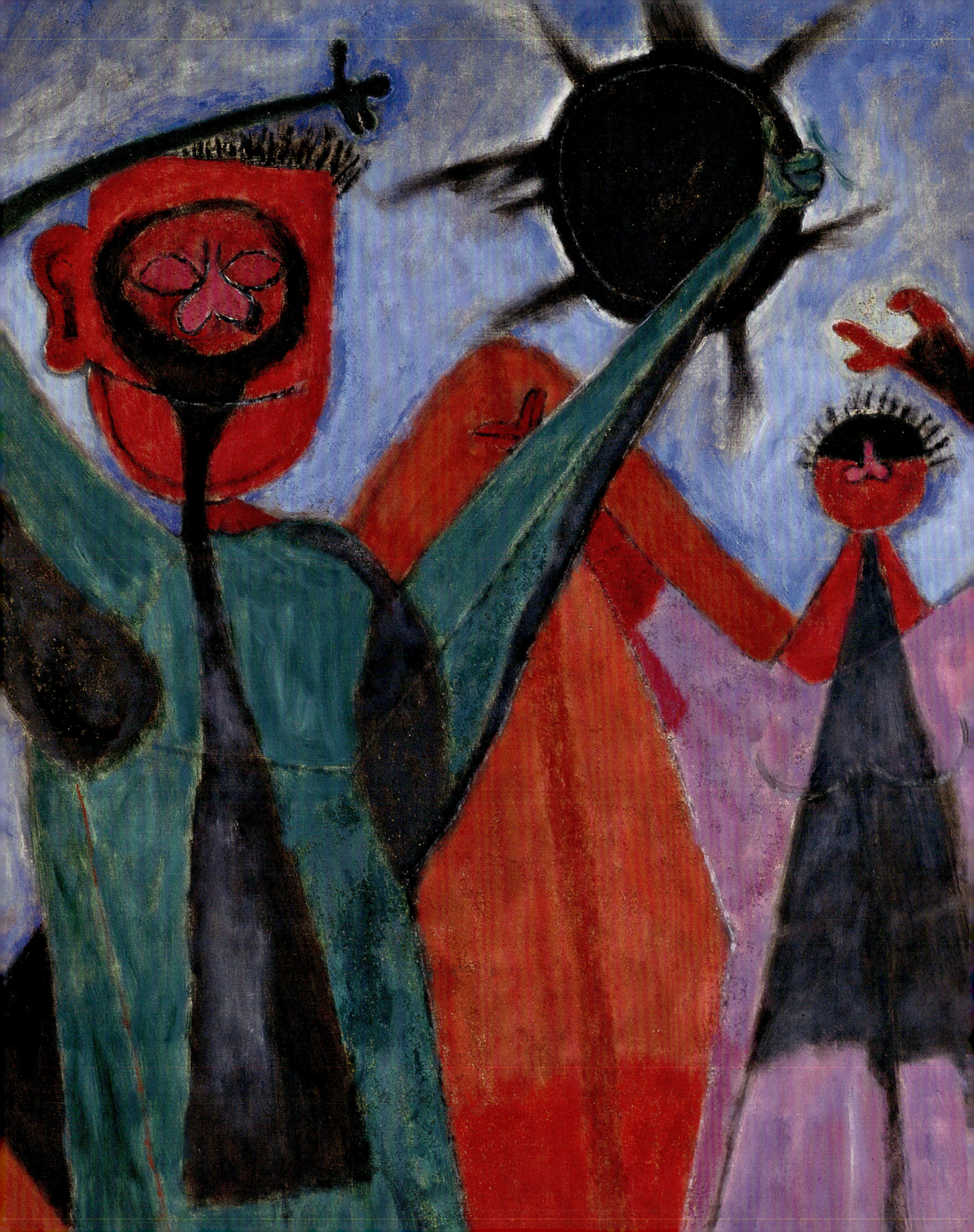

DIRECTOR'S FOREWORD

IN THE SPRING OF 1926, WHEN HE WAS ONLY twenty-six and eager to establish his reputation as a painter, Rufino Tamayo organized a successful solo exhibition in Mexico City. The venue was a storefront he rented on Avenida Madero, where he hung twenty canvases. The reviews were positive, discussing Tamayo's work in nationalist terms; but even at this early stage in his career, critics acknowledged his engagement with modernist ideas and the concerns current in the global art world. Five months later, in September of that year, he traveled to New York. By October—just one month after his arrival—his work was on view at the Weyhe Gallery on Lexington Avenue. When we look at the images in the present exhibition (and the catalogue in our hands), Tamayo's meteoric journey from that storefront on Avenida Madero to the gallery scene at a rising center of the modern art world appears, in retrospect, inevitable.

Once in New York, Tamayo reveled in the cross-cultural exchange that flourished there, visiting galleries and museums and meeting artists and intellectuals from Europe and New York, as well as others from Mexico and Latin America. Wherever he went he absorbed as much as he could, from works on the walls in exhibitions to those on easels in studios. He saw paintings by Diego Velázquez and El Greco at the Metropolitan Museum of Art and work by Henri Matisse at an exhibition in Brooklyn. Simultaneously, artists working in and visiting New York—including Marcel Duchamp, Stuart Davis, Yasuo Kuniyoshi, Berenice Abbott, Reginald Marsh, and others—interacted with Tamayo and took in the visual vocabulary that he, along with Frida Kahlo, José Clemente Orozco, and Diego Rivera, brought to the United States. Tamayo also crossed paths with younger American artists including Jackson Pollock, Adolph Gottlieb, and Helen Frankenthaler (his student at the Dalton School) who, like him, would break ground with new modes of representation befitting the seismic social transformation of the midcentury period. He was known as a great colorist but came to believe in restraint, saying that a restricted palette gave a painting greater power. He continued to live in New York intermittently from the late 1920s until 1949, painting prolifically and producing a rich trove of work that was exhibited at some of the city's premier galleries—the Valentine, Pierre Matisse, and Knoedler—and bought by eager collectors.

In *Tamayo: The New York Years,* E. Carmen Ramos exposes and analyzes the complex web of influences, ideas, and visual material circulating in New York during the decades when Tamayo worked there. The exhibition includes forty-two of his finest artworks, with subjects ranging from the classic—portraits and still lifes—to urban scenes, including factory floors, the New York skyline, and Luna Park at Coney Island. Over time, he began to incorporate archetypal themes into his work, asking us to confront our own dreams and nightmares with scenes of serene beauty or depictions of pain and despair. A dog howls at a blood-red moon, a bird attacks a child, or a horse struggles to escape the jaws of a lion; in other works, a woman reaches for the stars, a pale moon floats above a peacefully sleeping city, mermaids sing to the sounds of the sea and a guitar, or lovers clasp hands in contentment. This exhibition brings these symbolic works, especially those of the 1940s, into focus, showing how they not only broke crucial ground for Tamayo's later work and powered his increasing stature as a modernist but also established directions that were pursued by the generation that followed him.

The depth of E. Carmen Ramos's research and her keen insight have laid a critical foundation for scholars who will follow her. Her groundbreaking essay adds new perspectives to Tamayo scholarship and brings subtlety and nuance to the often-told tale of modernism and its evolution; the works she has assembled for the exhibition place Tamayo at the center of a major shift in the history of twentieth-century art. We are delighted that one of these works will remain in the Museum's collection after the exhibition; Ramos saw and pursued the opportunity to acquire *Carnival* (1936), a work that exemplifies the best of Tamayo's creative vision. The most complex of his Coney Island scenes, it features dramatic shifts in scale that entice the eye to linger on the dense, colorful composition.

One of the joys of museum work is seeing artworks from far-flung places assembled in our galleries and in conversation with each other. While curators are in the research phase of an exhibition they are often lucky enough to see the paintings "in the flesh"; they see them again when they are shipped in for the exhibition and they become something new and different—more than the sum of their parts. The rest of the museum staff waits, looking at flat images on computer screens and listening with growing anticipation to descriptions of the work that is coming. We know all too well that our pleasure at being in the gallery with the "real thing" is possible only through the generosity of those who agree to part (temporarily) with their treasures. So on behalf of the Smithsonian American Art Museum and its visitors, I thank all the lenders to the exhibition. I am also very grateful to our honorary patron His Excellency Gerónimo Gutiérrez-Fernández, the ambassador of Mexico, and Alberto Fierro, executive director of the Mexican Cultural Institute of Washington, DC, for enthusiastically embracing this project. Together, we are delighted that this exhibition sheds light on a flourishing period of cultural exchange between Mexican and US artists. And we are indebted to the Smithsonian Latino Center, especially its dynamic director, Eduardo Díaz. They have been the Museum's companions in developing this exhibition and, more broadly, its partner as we have envisioned and built the Museum's Latino program over more than two decades. I look forward to future collaborations that will enrich our museum, our city, and our nation.

Stephanie Stebich
The Margaret and Terry Stent Director
Smithsonian American Art Museum

ACKNOWLEDGMENTS

EVER SINCE MY FIRST LATIN AMERICAN ART CLASS at New York University, under the great Edward Sullivan, Mexican art has long held my fascination. While my own scholarship has focused primarily on Caribbean and Latino art, all Latin Americanists are aware of the foundational status of the Mexican Renaissance in the history of modern art in the Americas. The impact of Mexican muralism in particular on the art of the United States is widely understood, not only because the muralists were active stateside, but also because many scholars have unpacked the ripple effects of muralism and the muralists on the art of this country. *Tamayo: The New York Years* started as I pondered a "second wave" of Mexican influence that unfolded in the late 1930s and early 1940s, as the lure of muralism and social realism began to decline and Rufino Tamayo's art became representative of a new direction in Mexican art.

My interest in Tamayo grew after two recent exhibitions: *Nexus New York: Latin/American Artists in the Modern Metropolis* (2009), organized by Deborah Cullen for El Museo del Barrio, and *Nueva York* (2010), organized by City Lore for the New-York Historical Society, both of which called attention to his presence in New York during the first half of the twentieth century. These important exhibitions, and their catalogues, piqued my interest in Tamayo's lengthy but lesser-known New York tenure. I saw no contradiction in undertaking this project at a museum dedicated to the art of the United States. The Smithsonian American Art Museum (SAAM) has long presented and collected works by foreign artists who are not permanent residents or naturalized citizens. Major figures outside the United States like David Hockney, the English artist whose work is indelibly linked to the city of Los Angeles, are represented in our collection and their works showcased in major exhibitions. For over a decade, thanks to the Terra Foundation for American Art and its support of our fellowships and academic programs, including the symposium "*Encuentros:* Artistic Exchange between the U.S. and Latin America" (2011), SAAM has been at the forefront of investigating the global dimensions of the art of the United States. These efforts not only acknowledge that US art is part of a broader field of the art of the Americas, they also make evident that the flow of artists and ideas across borders is a foundational pillar of our national art history. Above all, our sustained commitment to Latino art naturally spurred a turn toward the Latin American presence in the United States. In our broad effort to re-envision a more accurate and dynamic picture of American art we cannot disregard that many Latin American artists—whether they stayed permanently here or not—have made and continue to make important work in this national context and form part of a US art world. SAAM's curatorial program is invested in making this history better understood and appreciated.

The Smithsonian American Art Museum is especially indebted to His Excellency Gerónimo Gutiérrez-Fernández, the ambassador of Mexico, for serving as honorary patron for this exhibition. We are honored to have his enthusiastic endorsement and that of Alberto Fierro and Gustavo Morales of the Mexican Cultural Institute of Washington, DC. Along with His Excellency Andrés Rozental, former ambassador of Mexico to the United Kingdom, they warmly embraced this exhibition and provided pivotal support that helped this project flourish.

This exhibition would not be possible without the generous contributions of individuals, foundations, and Smithsonian Institution grants. The Latino Initiatives Pool, administered by the Smithsonian Latino Center, provided major support. Early research for this project was underwritten by two Smithsonian Scholarly Studies grants. I deeply appreciate the contributions of Mrs. J. Todd Figi and Stanley and Pearl Goodman, who served as both lenders and funders. The Robert S. Firestone Foundation, the Wolf Kahn and Emily Mason Foundation, the William R. Kenan Jr. Endowment Fund, and the Sara Roby Foundation provided essential support. I am forever grateful to all the private collectors and institutions in Mexico and the United States that entrusted their works to us. Special thanks to Carmen Melian, Mary-Anne Martin, Marysol Nieves, Ramis Barquet, Axel Stein, Katrina Robelo, and Ana Sokoloff, who helped facilitate key loans. I offer my heartfelt thanks to Valerie Franklin, who for years cared for the beautiful Tamayo gouache (featured on our catalogue's cover) that is now proudly part of SAAM's collection.

I thank the institutions in the United States and Mexico that shared their archives and resources with me. I am eternally grateful to Juan Carlos Pereda, knowledgeable custodian of the Rufino Tamayo Archive at the Museo Tamayo in Mexico City. María Eugenia Bermúdez de Ferrer, niece of Olga and Rufino Tamayo, was gracious and generous. Other staff members at the Museo Tamayo, especially Iliana Sánchez Gallegos and Julio Álvarez, were instrumental in securing images for this catalogue. Mariana Pérez Amor, director of the Galería de Arte Mexicano, generously opened the Gallery's rich archives to us. Antonio Saborit, director of the Museo Nacional de Antropología in Mexico City, facilitated access to the museum's archive. Ana Luisa Madrigal Limón of the Instituto Nacional de Bellas Artes and Luis Felipe Crespo Oviedo of the Museo Nacional de las Culturas assisted with our research into Tamayo's production in Mexico. The delightful Alicia Pesqueira de Esesarte, director of the Museo de Arte Prehispánico de México Rufino Tamayo in Oaxaca, offered valuable insights into Tamayo's deep regard for pre-Columbian art.

I am grateful to scholars whose work provided the essential foundation for this project. I am especially indebted to Edward Sullivan, who wrote one of the first essays to explore Tamayo's New York years and who encouraged my interest and provided early feedback. I appreciate the generosity of Diana du Pont. Her groundbreaking exhibition and catalogue *Tamayo: A Modern Icon Reinterpreted* (2007) served as inspiration for this focused study. The expert guidance, encouragement, and camaraderie of Alejandro Anreus, Emilie Boone, Monica Bravo, Karen Cordero Reiman, Ingrid Elliott, Ray Hernández-Durán, Anna Indych-López, Fabiola Martínez-Rodríguez, Luis Pérez-Oramas, Ana María Reyes, Breanne Robertson, and Luis Vargas Santiago were instrumental to my thinking. I am grateful to the anonymous peer reviewers whose feedback strengthened this catalogue.

I've been extremely fortunate to work on this project during the tenure of two supportive directors: Elizabeth Broun, who championed the exhibition from the beginning, and our new director, Stephanie Stebich, who enthusiastically took the mantle when she arrived in April 2017. Chief Curator Virginia Mecklenburg has been a keen supporter, always believing in me and this project and finding solutions to obstacles big and small. Eduardo Díaz, director of the Smithsonian Latino Center, is a key member of SAAM's extended Smithsonian family. I've been fortunate to have had his backing since my first day at SAAM. The Museum is blessed to have the guidance of Commissioner Aída Álvarez, whose intelligence and strategic perseverance have strengthened our Latino art program in innumerable ways.

Every day I feel fortunate to work with SAAM's professional and dedicated staff, and this project was no exception. Deputy Director Rachel Allen, Chief Development Officer Donna Rim, Kate Earnest, and Elizabeth Daoust ensured financial resources. Jean Lavery processed the paperwork for my numerous research trips with grace and efficiency. My curatorial colleagues were always ready with encouragement and moral support. I am grateful to interns Laura Augustin (now one of our curatorial assistants) and Rochelle Safo, who conducted early research on this exhibition, as did my overqualified volunteer Norma Rosso. I am forever grateful to our talented Publications staff, especially Mary Cleary, Karen Siatras, and

Following pages:
New York Seen from the Terrace [*Nueva York desde la terraza*], 1937. See pp. 100–101.

Theresa Slowik, whose hard work and creativity made this elegant publication possible; thanks also to Dan Giles and his staff at D Giles Limited, London, our publishing partner. The Registrars office, headed by Melissa Kroning, was a constant source of support: special thanks to Heather Delemarre, who oversaw all loan requests; Craig Pittman, who oversaw packing and shipping arrangements; and Amy Doyel, who managed image rights and permissions. Exhibition designer Eunice Park Kim and graphic designer Grace Lopez created the perfect environment for our audience to encounter Tamayo's work. My colleagues in Research and Scholars and External Affairs, including Amelia Goerlitz, Nona Martin, Laura Baptiste, Kara Fikse, and Amy Hutchins, spearheaded public outreach and ensured that we had great programs. I also extend my deepest thanks to colleagues across the Smithsonian who provided encouragement and assistance, including Adrián Aldaba, Diana Bossa Bastidas, Taína Caragol, Ariana Curtis, Michelle Delaney, Joanne Flores, Josh Franco, Emily Key, Leslie Ureña, and Ranald Woodaman. Above all, I have relied on Beth Shook, my indispensable research assistant and partner on this venture. Her professionalism, dedication, keen research, optimism, and good humor were essential to the success of this project. Her thoroughly researched timeline is an important addition to this catalogue.

I owe my deepest gratitude to my supportive husband and partner, Steven Alfred, and our boys, Esteban and Miles. This project entailed many research trips and late nights when I could not be with them. They will always have my profound appreciation and love.

It has been a special privilege to study Mexican art and culture. I hope this exhibition serves as a potent reminder of the deep cultural links between Mexico and the United States, and the flourishing relationships among artists that have enriched our intertwining national art histories.

E. Carmen Ramos
Curator of Latino Art
Smithsonian American Art Museum

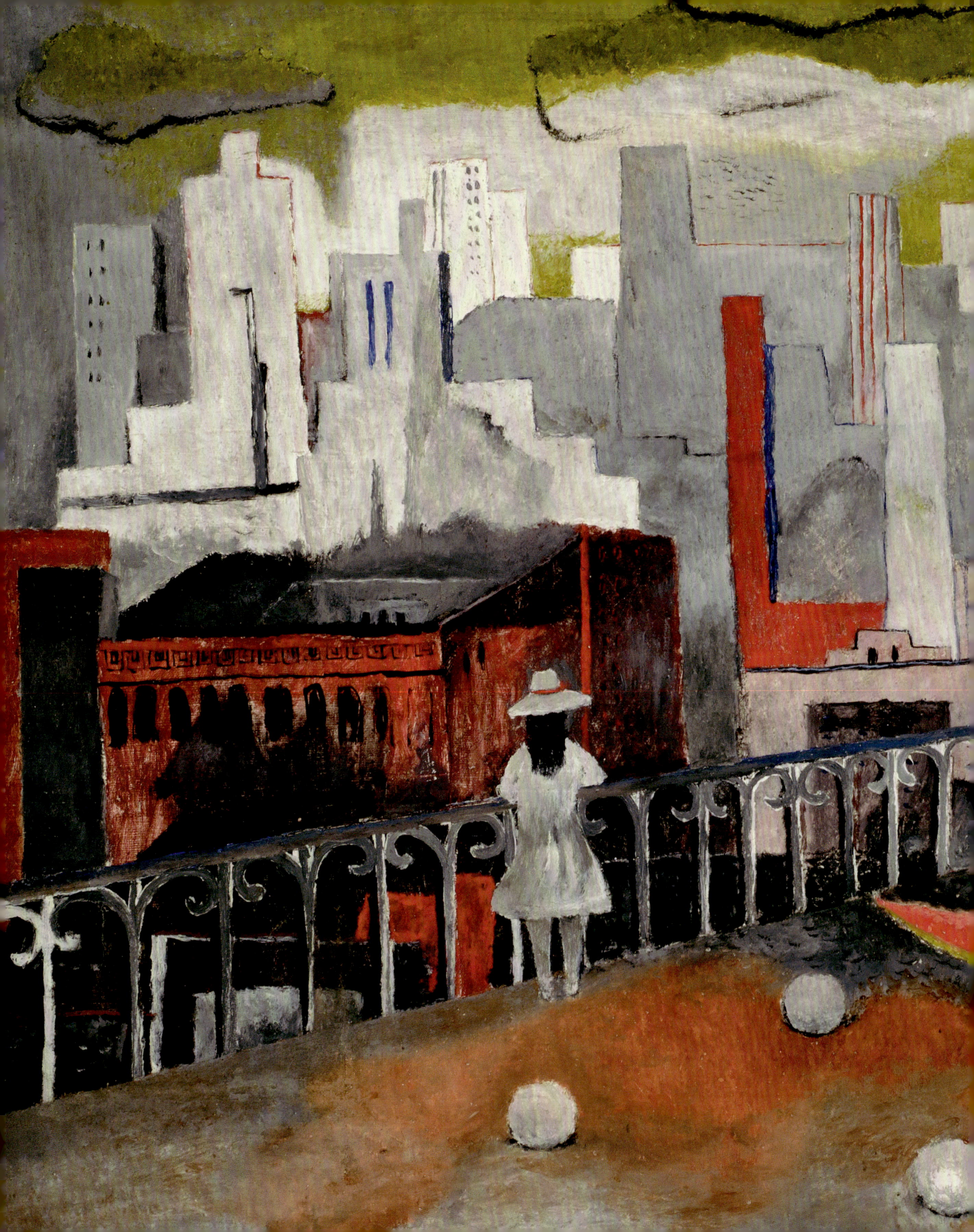

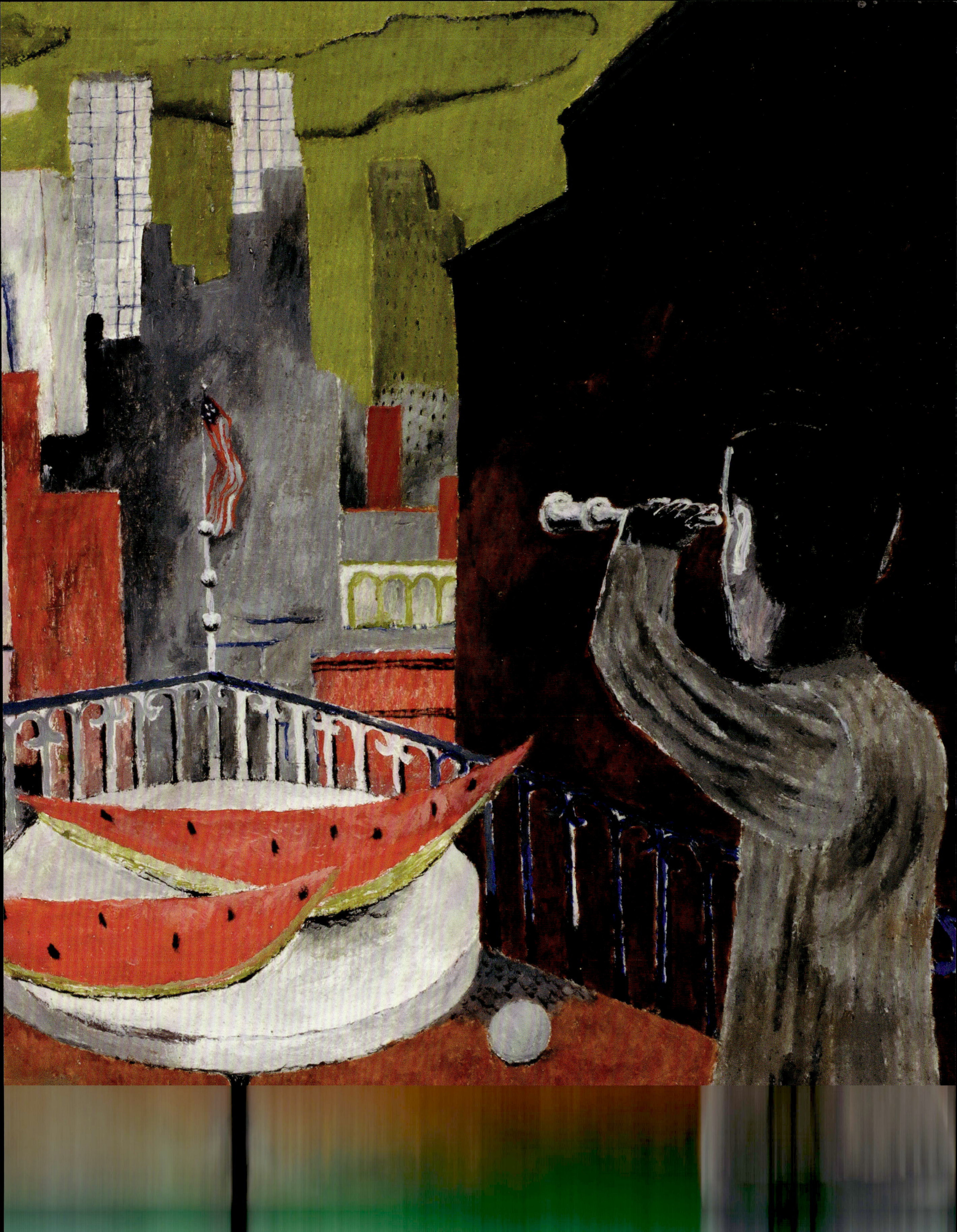

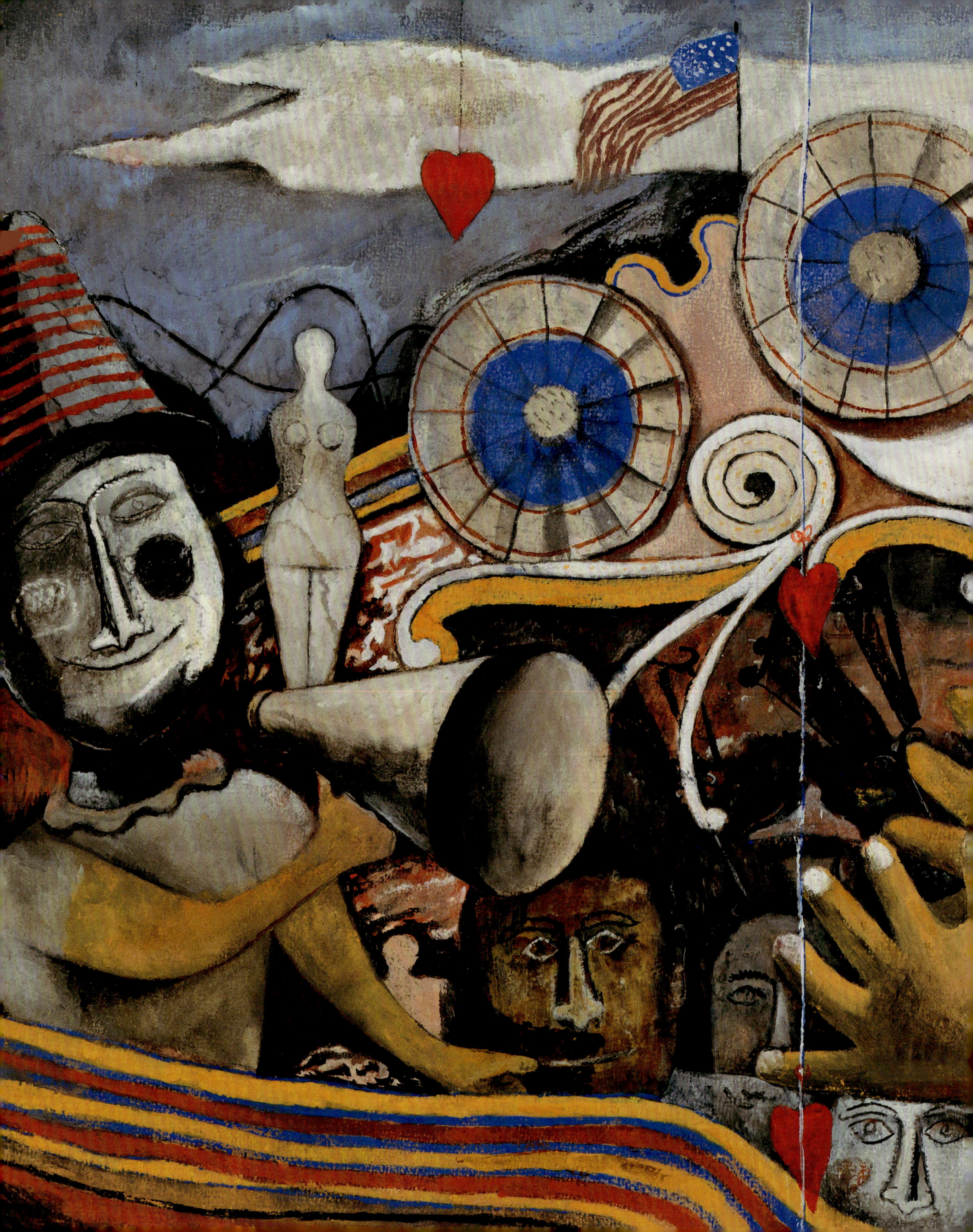

E. Carmen Ramos

TAMAYO

THE NEW YORK YEARS

DURING HIS INITIAL TRIPS TO NEW YORK CITY IN THE 1920S AND 1930S, MEXICAN ARTIST RUFINO TAMAYO visited Coney Island. The experience inspired at least three works, among which *Carnival* (1936; pl. 16) is the most visually complex. The painting captures a dense scene of parkgoers, parading clowns, rides, and the distinctive architecture of the park. He specifically homes in on Luna Park, an amusement park within Coney Island known for its crescent moon and heart-shaped decorations, and its electric lights that allowed it to be an evening destination (FIG. 1). Why was Tamayo attracted to Coney Island? Tamayo had been interested in popular entertainments in his native Mexico. Along with fellow artists Manuel Álvarez Bravo, Lola Álvarez Bravo, and María Izquierdo, he frequently visited *carpas*, urban tent shows that presented vaudeville acts, acrobatics, and puppet shows, which they saw as expressions of contemporary Mexican culture. In New York, Tamayo sought out parallel cultural expressions, and, like other artists of the period, including Joseph Stella and Reginald Marsh, he found in Coney Island a unique locus of modernity and the American experience.

Unlike Stella, however, Tamayo never came to permanently reside in the United States. He had two extended stays in New York between the mid-1920s and the late 1940s, and very much identified as Mexican.[1] But he still had an American experience, if we understand this to be the ways in which individuals are shaped by their immersion in the United States and how they, in turn, leave their mark on US

Frontispiece:
Carnival [*Carnaval*], 1936;
detail. See p. 97.

culture. By situating Tamayo's art and career in its New York context, we gain insight into the global exchanges that fueled the modern art of the Americas during the twentieth century. Before New York's ascendancy as a major international art center during the mid-twentieth century, and the hardening of divisions between Latin American, European, and US art that ensued, artists flowed between national contexts, taking in influences and contributing to artistic debates that shaped the art of the era. Tamayo's contributions to the period's dynamism are lesser known, and only by reconsidering his New York context can we more fully understand what he absorbed and advanced through his art.

Tamayo was one of several Mexican artists who established a foothold in New York City during the so-called Mexican vogue, a period of widespread US interest in Mexican art, history, and culture that followed the end of the Mexican Revolution (1910–20). Between the mid-1920s and early 1940s, Mexican culture held major appeal for Americans seeking an exotic and premodern world that they believed was the antithesis of American society.[2] For many American artists and cultural elites, Mexico's post-revolutionary art scene exemplified the kind of thriving national artistic tradition that Americans had long desired. Americans read about Mexico in books and journals, encountered murals by Mexican muralists in cities such as New York and Detroit, and traveled to Mexico or experienced its culture through exhibitions presented at leading cultural institutions in the United States. While the dissemination of knowledge about Mexican art and culture relied on collaborations between artists and promoters on both sides of the border, these exchanges also contributed to a steady Mexican presence in the United States.

Tamayo was an important member of this loosely organized Mexican cultural community in New York, which writer Jaime Torres Bodet once referred to as a "pequeña familia mexicana."[3] In fact, of all the well-known Mexican visual artists who spent time in New York—Jean Charlot, Miguel Covarrubias, Frida Kahlo, Adolfo Best Maugard, José Clemente Orozco, Diego Rivera, and David Alfaro Siqueiros—among critics and fellow artists, Tamayo was likely the most identified with the United States, an assessment buoyed by the fact that Tamayo was actually living in, and not visiting, New York.[4] Tamayo's Mexican identity was always a central feature of his artistic persona no matter where he resided. Yet his fifteen-year presence in New York urges us to consider his tenure as more than just a passing sojourn. In the words of one critic, Tamayo was "a fixed star in New York's art world."[5] What was the impact of this lengthy residence on Tamayo and his New York artistic milieu?

Tamayo: The New York Years is the first exhibition to explore the contours and repercussions of Tamayo's New York tenure. By carefully examining his artistic unfolding, associations, and critical reception in the United States, the exhibition reveals the formative role the city played in shaping Tamayo's vision of modern Mexican art, and that the circulation of his art and ideas contributed to the cross-cultural milieu that transformed New York into a leading center of postwar avant-garde art. Like his Latin American peers Siqueiros and Roberto Matta, whose contributions to US art have received more scholarly attention, Tamayo was an active participant in the postwar formulation of a new American art, one that turned away from social realism and earlier formulations of abstraction, in favor of boldly emotive and increasingly nonmimetic works that engaged American culture and the existential crisis of the time.[6]

Why is Tamayo's story still lesser known today? In part, knowledge about his New York

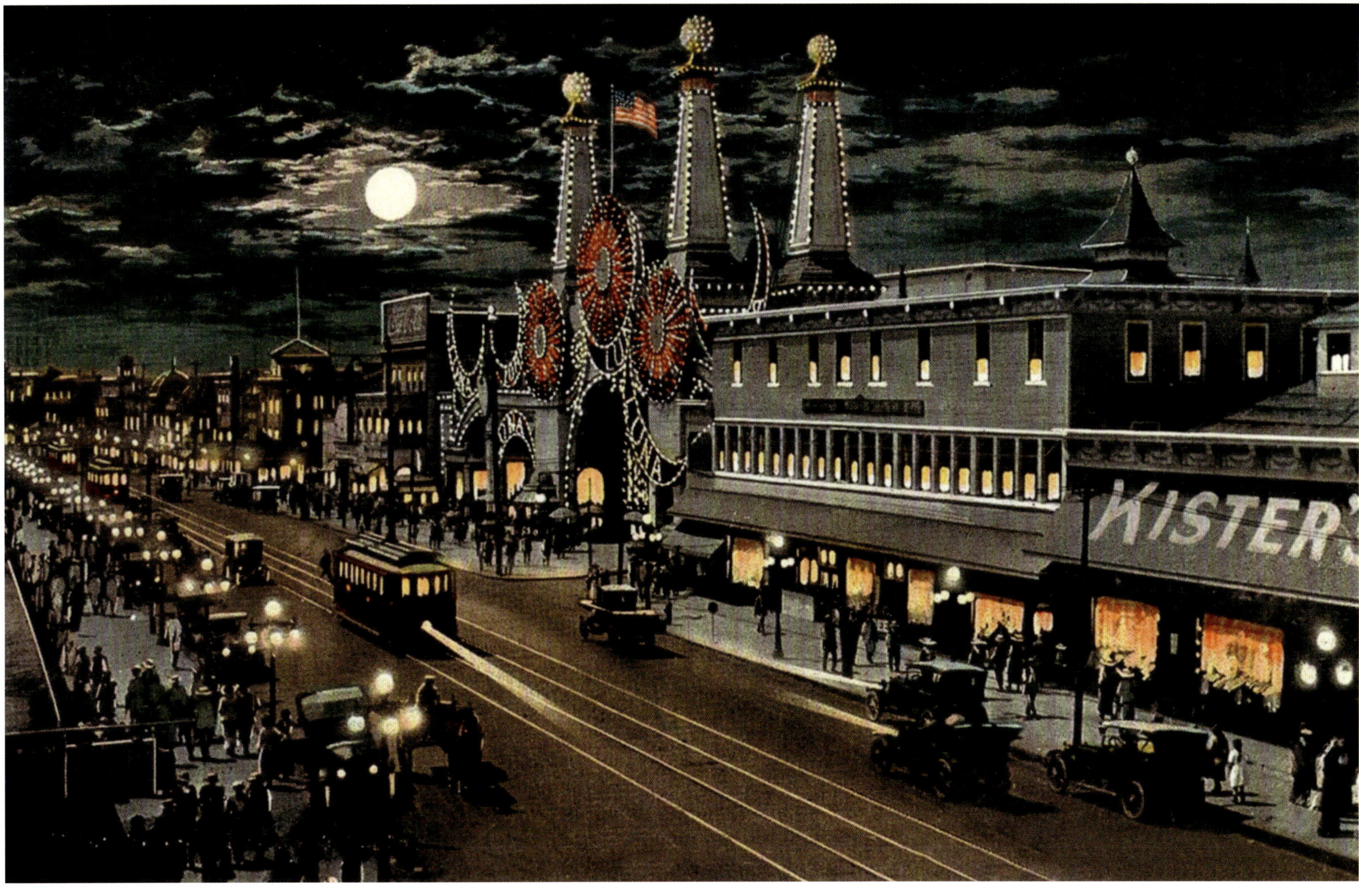

FIG. 1 1920s postcard showing Luna Park and Surf Avenue at night, Coney Island, New York

career has been inaccessible, compartmentalized, or too diffuse. In the late 1980s, Edward Sullivan and Rita Eder, who knew the artist during his lifetime, published important essays that considered Tamayo's New York career against the major artistic tendencies, events, and debates taking place there from the late 1920s through the 1940s.[7] These essays, which remain key sources to the present day, were published abroad in Spanish, making this history less accessible for non-Spanish-speaking scholars. More recent scholarship has taken a segmented approach, focusing on specific aspects of Tamayo's New York production and career.[8] At the same time, larger monographic studies encompass so many phases of the artist's career that the nuances of the New York years can be lost in such broad surveys. Most importantly, Tamayo's contributions have historically been overshadowed by the confluence of two factors: the extraordinary impact of Mexican muralism on the art of the United States, and Tamayo's complex relationship to other Mexican artists who, like him, came of age in the years surrounding the Mexican Revolution.

It is difficult to overstate the impact of Mexican muralism and the Mexican Renaissance on American art during the first half of the twentieth century. The various US federal arts programs of the Depression era would not have existed without the example of Mexican state-sponsored cultural programs of the 1920s and 1930s.[9] Early murals by Rivera, Orozco,

Siqueiros (*Los tres grandes*, or the three greats) and other artists were painted in government buildings and drew on subjects tied to Mexico's indigenous, colonial, and modern history, including the tumult and aftermath of the Mexican Revolution. The mural movement became one of the most influential, overtly national artistic movements of the modern era. The vocal example of renowned leftist Mexican artists like Rivera emboldened social-realist tendencies in American art. In 1931, Rivera had the honor of being the second artist (after Henri Matisse) to be given a major solo exhibition at New York's Museum of Modern Art (MoMA). American artists avidly studied and followed his work and that of other Mexican muralists, who were very active in the United States and whose careers were extensively covered in the press and artist-affiliated journals like *New Masses*.[10] The ways in which African American artists, including Romare Bearden, Jacob Lawrence, and Hale Woodruff, processed post-revolutionary Mexican art deeply shaped their alternative visions of American history.[11] Enthusiasts and scholars of Native American art in the United States advanced their cause by encouraging American institutions to follow Mexico's lead and promote indigenous art as a key element of "American" heritage.[12] Grace L. McCann Morley, director of the San Francisco Museum of Art in the 1940s and a key promoter of Latin American art in the United States, expressed the Mexican influence in these terms: "The Mexican Movement has been the most original and successful nationally developed school in the Western Hemisphere up to the present, and has had an influence in other Latin American countries, as well as in the United States."[13] Between the late 1920s and the early 1940s, Mexico led the Western Hemisphere in the arts, and US artists and cultural leaders digested and emulated its remarkable achievements.

The art historical literature does acknowledge the Mexican impact on American art; yet because of the intense focus on the muralists and their radical politics, Tamayo is rarely mentioned in these narratives.[14] Tamayo was equally shaped by and a contributor to the Mexican Renaissance, yet his approach was markedly different from that of the muralists, who received the lion's share of attention in the United States. From the outset of his career, Tamayo sought to create a modern art by integrating Western artistic currents and the particularities of Mexican culture, which did invoke notions of "Mexican" subjects, but which especially entailed studying and assimilating the formal properties of pre-Columbian and Mexican popular (folk) art. Unlike Siqueiros, Rivera, or Kahlo, he never joined the Communist Party. Tamayo embraced notions of *arte puro*, or pure art, which circulated in some Mexican avant-garde artistic circles that championed artists' individual, rather than sociopolitical and collective, approaches to modern Mexican art. His aesthetic position led him to vocally contest—both in Mexico and the United States—the work of the muralists, which he rejected as folkloric and nationalist paintings of Mexican subjects rather than Mexican painting.[15] While Tamayo's dismissive assessments of Mexican muralism must be taken with a grain of salt—and considered in relation to the contentiousness of this period in Mexican art and Tamayo's own desire to position his work as more relevant than that of the muralists—his work nevertheless posed a challenge to the narrative, revolutionary, proletarian thrust of classic Mexican muralism. Together with the critical establishment, Tamayo increasingly sought to distinguish himself from Rivera, Orozco, and Siqueiros, a perspective that gained traction as interest in Mexican muralism and social realism, and its implied socialist agenda, began to wane in the World War II era. Tamayo's star especially rose during these years, when he birthed what he would call "a new modality in Mexican painting."[16]

Tamayo's New York experiences played a fundamental role in shaping his art. It was in New York that Tamayo not only gained exposure to European and American art that expanded his understanding of the contemporary art landscape but also found a more receptive environment for his own work. He modeled an aestheticized approach to the art of the Americas grounded in the study of non-Western art and the idea that artists should creatively respond to their times. During the 1930s and 1940s, Tamayo exhibited actively in New York and attracted the support of collectors, cultural institutions, and critics who proselytized modernism and increasingly embraced abstraction. His orbit overlapped with a rising generation of abstract expressionists, including Adolph Gottlieb, Jackson Pollock, and Mark Rothko, who turned away from the figurative modernist approaches to forge a different aesthetic language able to represent the existential crisis unleashed by World War II. For this group, Tamayo's vocal disavowal of Mexican muralism and embrace of indigenous art reinforced their own developing aesthetic positions. *Tamayo: The New York Years* aims to bring this history to light, thereby expanding our knowledge of a second wave of Mexican influence on the art of the United States.

BEGINNINGS Tamayo's eventual acclaim in New York hinged on his difference from the reigning Mexican muralists. Much as he and others would set him apart from his Mexican peers, Tamayo was undoubtedly shaped within the broad flowering of modern art that emerged before and after the Mexican Revolution. Born to parents of Zapotec ancestry in the state of Oaxaca in 1899, Tamayo moved to Mexico City as a young boy and lived through the civil war that ended the dictatorship of Porfirio Díaz and addressed some of the class and racial divisions in Mexican society. When the war came to an end in 1920, the populist and leftist administration of Álvaro Obregón initiated broad economic and social reforms aimed at integrating disparate sectors of Mexican society. Culture played a central role. The Mexican state developed wide-reaching initiatives to educate all sectors of Mexican society about the country's indigenous, colonial, and modern history. Mexican muralism, an ambitious program of state-sponsored murals in public buildings, was the most visible manifestation of these efforts. The philosophical basis for post-revolutionary cultural programs emerged before and after the civil war in the writings of intellectuals like José Vasconcelos and Manuel Gamio, whose books *La Raza Cósmica* (1925) and *Forjando Patria* (1916) repositioned Mexico's indigenous and mestizo heritage as the foundation of Mexican identity, or *mexicanidad*. These ideas were nonetheless replete with contradictions, not the least of which was how the state sought to assimilate the Indian into modern Mexican culture while stamping out indigenous traditions they deemed "backward." As problematic as some of these ideas were, notions of *indigenismo* and *mestizaje* were incredibly influential among Mexican artists.[17] Many artists did not necessarily question the hierarchy or even the violence of these contradictions, but rather reified the idea that Mexico's indigenous heritage was a central feature of its national identity. Tamayo, who at this time identified as a person of indigenous descent, deeply internalized this post-revolutionary vision of Mexican national culture and identity—and later pointed out some of its blind spots—which shaped not only his art and ideas but also the ways he and his art would be framed in New York.

FIG. 2 Saturnino Herrán, *Tehuana*, 1914, oil on canvas, 59 1/16 × 29 1/2 in. Museo de Aguascalientes, INBA, Aguascalientes, Mexico

Notions of *mestizaje* and *indigenismo* were especially important to the early mural movement. In their manifesto, the Sindicato de Obreros Técnicos, Pintores y Escultores de México (SOTPE or the Technical Workers, Painters, and Sculptors Union of Mexico), which was formed in 1922 by many of the muralists, including Siqueiros, Rivera, and Orozco, expressed their thoughts this way:

> *The fact that our people are at the root of even the smallest expression of the physical and spiritual existence* ***of our race as an ethnic force*** *and, what's more, of its admirable and most particular ability to* ***create beauty; the art of the people of Mexico is the greatest, healthiest spiritual expression in the whole world,*** *and its indigenous tradition is simply the best of them all. The reason for this greatness is that, being a popular expression, it is collective. And this is why our basic aesthetic goal must be to socialize these individual artistic expressions that are in grave danger of vanishing completely under the influence of the bourgeoisie.*[18]

This strident declaration is often taken as defining the concerns of Mexican artists as a whole, yet not all Mexican artists embraced this socialist and collective view of Mexican society and culture. Indeed, as a young artist coming of age in the 1920s, Tamayo witnessed the indigenous- and revolutionary-themed murals of *Los tres grandes* and the development of other avant-garde movements like *estridentismo* (Stridentism) that embraced futurist and Dadaist perspectives.[19] Mexican artists debated the nature of Mexican art, formed avant-garde collectives, organized exhibitions, and spearheaded journals, which cumulatively posited a variety of perspectives about national art and culture. This wider field of activity informed Tamayo's emergent artistic concerns, which he later built upon in New York.

Though he later discounted the impact of his studies at the Escuela Nacional de Bellas Artes (ENBA) between 1917 and 1921, Tamayo's time there placed him in the center of Mexico's contemporary art scene. He considered the school and its teaching methods outmoded, yet he still praised some of his instructors like Saturnino Herrán, whose celebrated works like *Tehuana* visually codified icons of Mexico's indigenous identity in an introspective, symbolist style (FIG. 2).[20] Roberto Montenegro, another one of

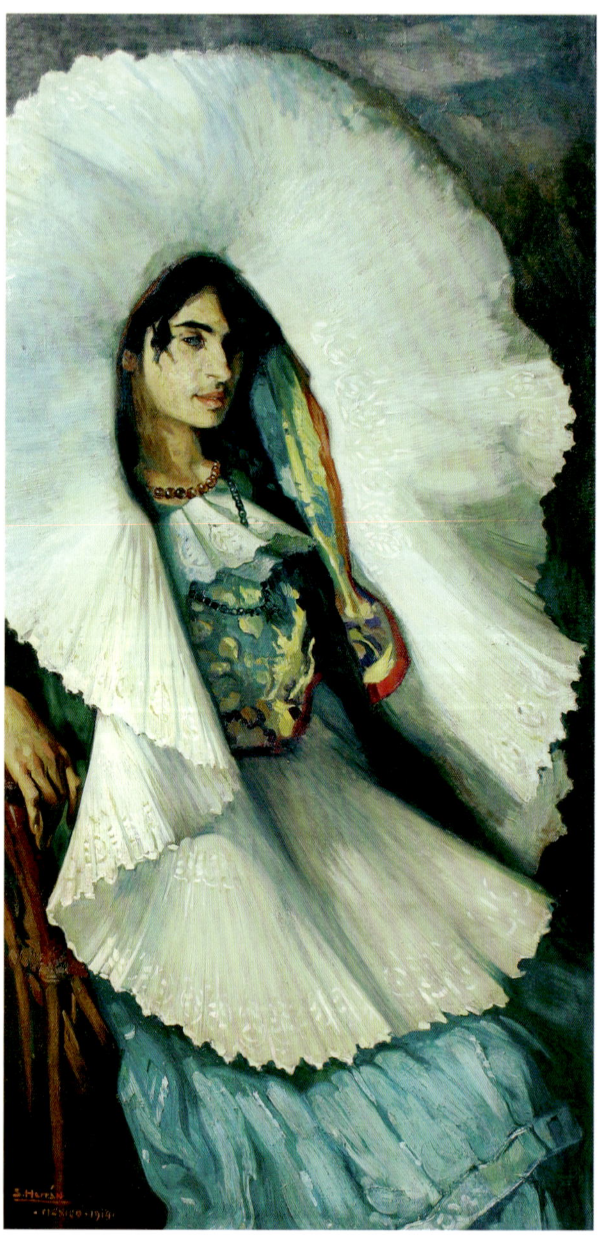

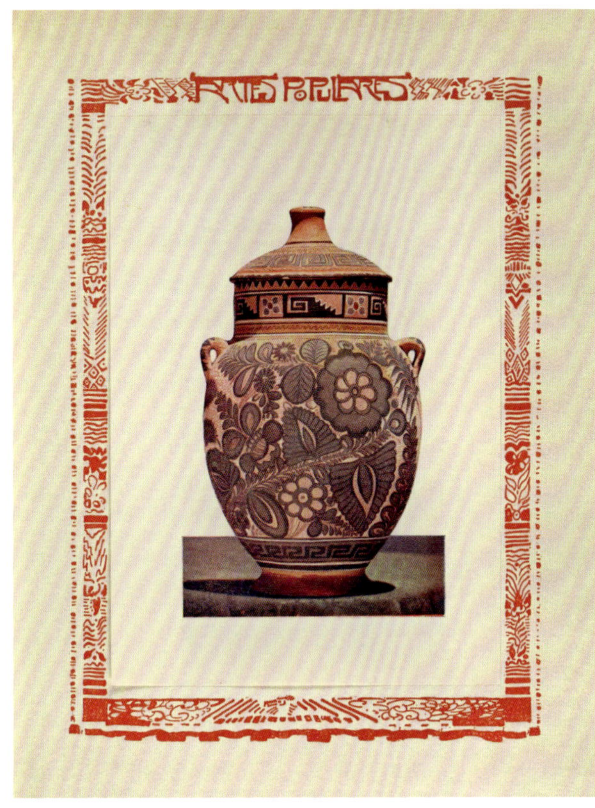

FIG. 3 "Los grandes decoradores de vasijas de Tonalá, zacarias jimon, tinja," illustration from *Las Artes Populares en México*, vol. 1, 1922

his professors, often took his students on plein-air painting expeditions. The school spread knowledge of French currents, and Tamayo himself acknowledged that his first artistic phase was impressionism.[21] Tamayo of course was not alone in his dissatisfaction with the academy. His cohort, which included artists like Leopoldo Méndez, Gabriel Fernández Ledesma, Julio Castellanos, and Agustín Lazo, went on to rebel in their own ways, forming avant-garde groups in Mexico City in subsequent years. For this group, the arrival of Rivera was a momentous event. "Everything changed when Diego Rivera returned to Mexico from Europe in 1921," Tamayo recalled. "In the face of so much mediocrity, Diego was our salvation."[22] Tamayo was deeply impressed by Rivera's articulate discourses about art. In spite of his own deep ties to cubism, Rivera encouraged students to shift their attention away from "overseas magazines" and toward their own national art—be it pre-Hispanic, colonial, or folk art.[23] That same year, Tamayo abandoned his studies at ENBA.

Mexico City's flourishing cultural events and new institutions afforded Tamayo ample opportunities to learn about his country's artistic heritage and contemporary art scene, putting him in the flow of ideas about national culture, which he would slowly start to reformulate in his art. In 1921, as part of the official centennial celebration of Mexican independence from Spain, Montenegro and artists Jorge Enciso and Dr. Atl organized the *Exposición de arte popular* (Exhibition of Popular Arts). The exhibition, which featured folk art from throughout Mexico, including ceramics, lacquerware, toys, textiles, leatherwork, basketry, and painted wood furniture, was a revelation to Mexican artists like Tamayo and to the public at large. The exhibition challenged the idea that these objects were mere curiosities or the disparaged material culture of the lower classes; rather, the organizers presented Mexican folk art as embodying Mexico's most innate and authentic national culture.[24] The two-volume catalogue written by Dr. Atl was an incredible visual resource (**FIG. 3**) that framed popular art as an example of the supposed intuitive creativity of Mexico's indigenous people, notions that would soon be applied to Tamayo's art as well.

Later in the 1920s, Tamayo became reacquainted with similar ideas when he was hired as an instructor of the Best Maugard Drawing Method, a national art curriculum for public schools designed by Tamayo's former teacher Adolfo Best Maugard and built largely around the "intuitive" design patterns of Mexican popular art.[25] Tamayo later rejected the importance of the program to his art, but indeed his works in the later 1920s and 1930s, which incorporate the use of patterning not tied to mimetic representation, owe something to this training.[26]

FIGS. 4, 5 Rufino Tamayo, undated drawings: *Study of Mask* (left), pencil, and *Drawing after a Figurine* (right), crayon; illustrated in Robert Goldwater's *Rufino Tamayo* (1947)

While the *Exhibition of Popular Arts* allowed Tamayo to experience firsthand a vast sampling of Mexican popular art, he soon had the opportunity to intimately study pre-Columbian art. In 1921, Vasconcelos hired Tamayo as the first draftsman in the Ethnographic Drawing Department at the Museo Nacional de Arqueología, Historia y Etnografía (now the Museo Nacional de Antropología), a position Tamayo held until 1926.[27] His task was to sketch faithful copies of works in the museum's pre-Columbian and Mexican popular art collections. His drawings would be shared with artisans across the country in an effort to stimulate the production of folk art. Tamayo recalled this experience as transformational:

> *[My] office was in the middle of the great pre-Columbian collections. There I was surrounded by objects that were a revelation to me. They made me realize that everything I had been taught at school was useless, at least for me. The technical facility was useless. I had to forget all that I had been taught and learn to do things in a new way.... I realized there was a great beauty in those objects, and it had nothing to do with what we had been taught in school.*[28]

Examples of Tamayo's early sketches have not surfaced, but drawings that appear in a 1947 publication may relate to these early works (**FIGS. 4, 5**). The drawings reveal Tamayo's interest in small objects, like the masks and clay sculptures he would later collect.[29] Making these sketches allowed Tamayo to appreciate the gestures, facial expressions, forms, color, and proportions of pre-Hispanic art. The act of direct observation

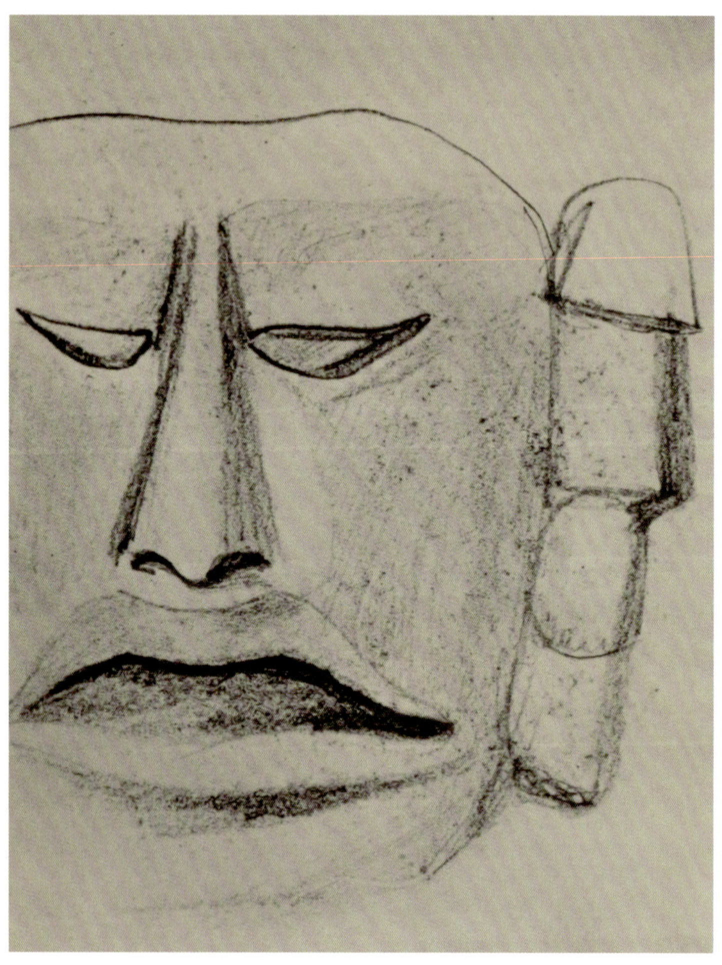

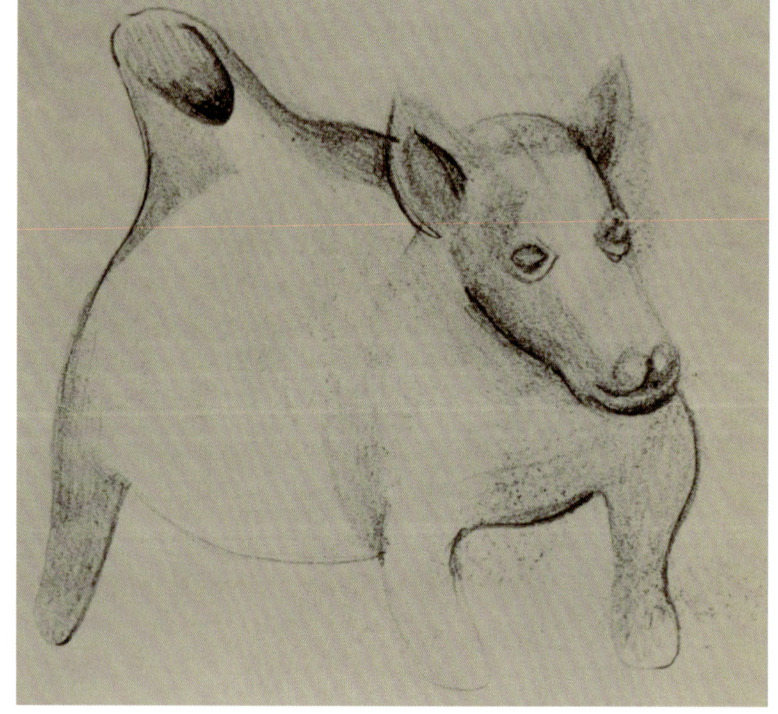

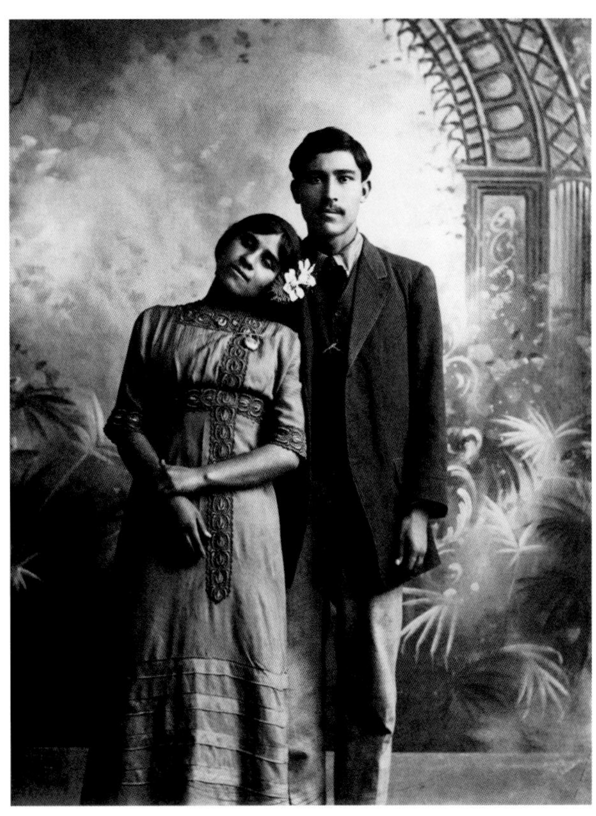

FIG. 6 Romualdo García, studio portrait, 1905–14. Collection unknown

and the fluid relationship between the artist's eye and hand had a profound impact on Tamayo's artistic development. The experience of processing pre-Columbian art through his own creative faculties—in the shadow of the indigenist discourses of the Mexican Renaissance—solidified his artistic and personal connection to indigenous art.

Tamayo's early work from the mid-1920s shows him uniting subjects considered national and experimenting with modernist styles. Perhaps recalling his plein-air excursions through Mexico City, *The Family* (1925; pl. 1) depicts a young family standing in front of a verdant mountainous environment and what may be a baptismal fountain. Ever since the nineteenth century and through Tamayo's era, Mexican artists such as José Velasco and Dr. Atl represented mountains and volcanoes as signs of Mexico's unique geography. Tamayo repeats the gesture here, in a painting that combines landscape and portraiture. The figures' reddish complexion indicates a conscious attempt to depict a particular shade of nonwhite skin, suggesting that the family before us is mestizo. The formality of the couple's posture and attire—the woman wears a flower in her hair, the man a suit and tie—echoes the conventions of Mexican studio photography, where couples posed in front of painted landscapes (FIG. 6). Here Tamayo is beginning to depict the national scene on a number of levels: the natural environment that recalls parts of Mexico, the mestizo couple, and the artist's own interest in referencing the popular traditions of the Mexican middle class who embraced photography.

Tamayo's works also homed in on indigenous subjects that were explored by the Mexican muralists, especially Diego Rivera, who in 1926 received most of the state mural commissions. *Woman with Fruit Basket* of 1926 (FIG. 7), presents a brown-skinned female fruit seller within an arch, recalling the architectural context of Mexican muralism and anticipating the trompe-l'oeil murals Rivera would complete in 1928.[30] The painting was alternatively titled *India frutera* (Indian Fruit Seller), indicating Tamayo's intent to focus on an Indian subject.[31] The figure holds a large tray of fruit near her hips and stands in front of a background painted in various shades of brown. The painting recalls Rivera's mural *Tehuanas*, which he completed in 1923 at the Secretaría de Educación Pública (FIG. 8). Tamayo, who at the time admired Rivera and was also employed by the Secretaría, was undoubtedly familiar with this mural. While both artists associate Indian subjects with the natural bounty of Mexico, Tamayo's composition is sparingly minimal in comparison to Rivera's lush, tropical environment. Rather than invoke the subject's indigeneity through context, Tamayo turns instead to the figure's skin color and facial features, which he modeled after pre-Columbian art. With her almond-shaped eyes, oval face, and open mouth, Tamayo's *Woman with Fruit Basket*

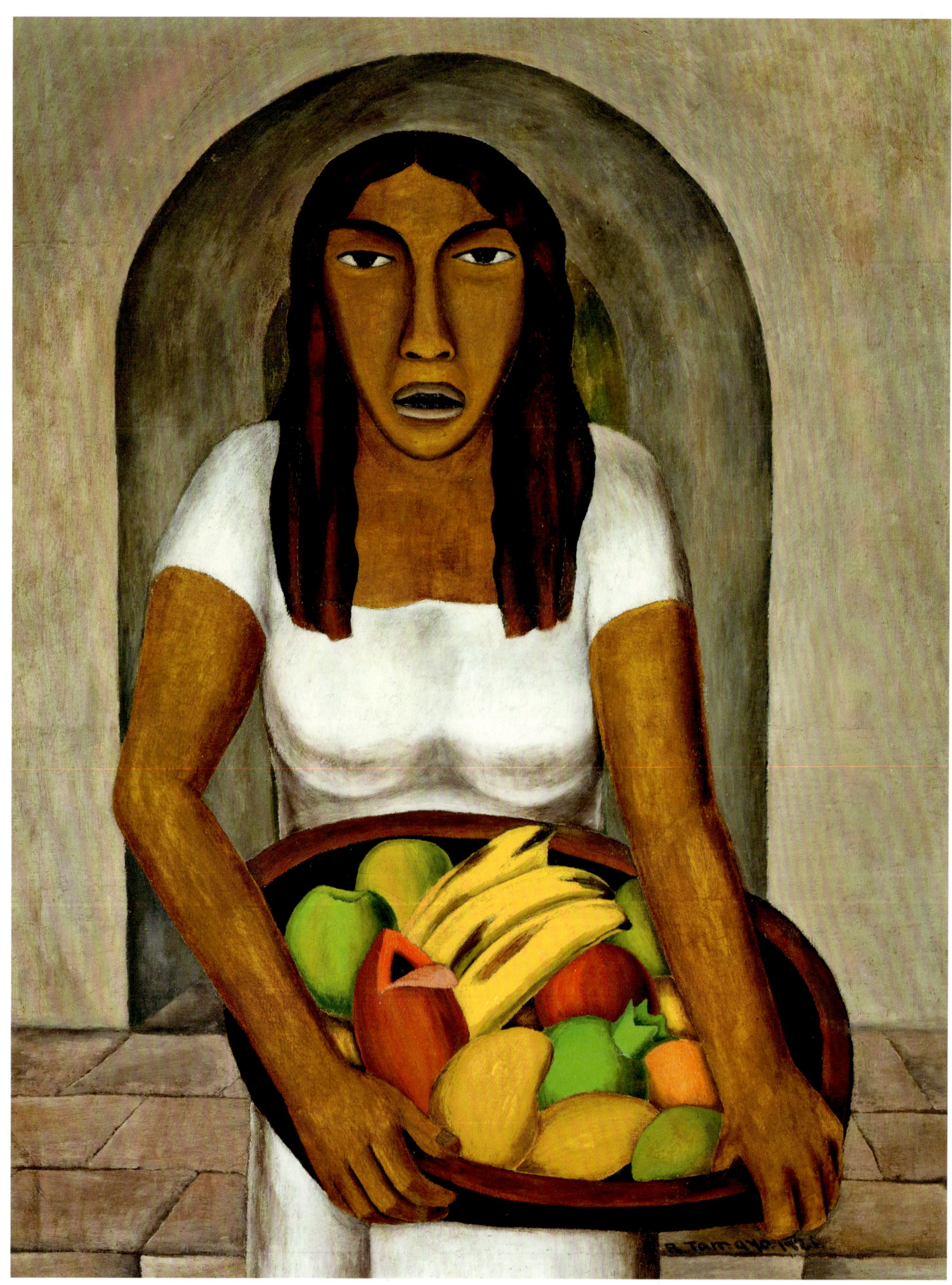

FIG. 7 Rufino Tamayo, *Woman with Fruit Basket* [*Mujer con canasta de frutas*], 1926, oil on canvas, 34 ¾ × 26 ¾ in. Los Angeles County Museum of Art, The Bernard and Edith Lewin Collection of Mexican Art

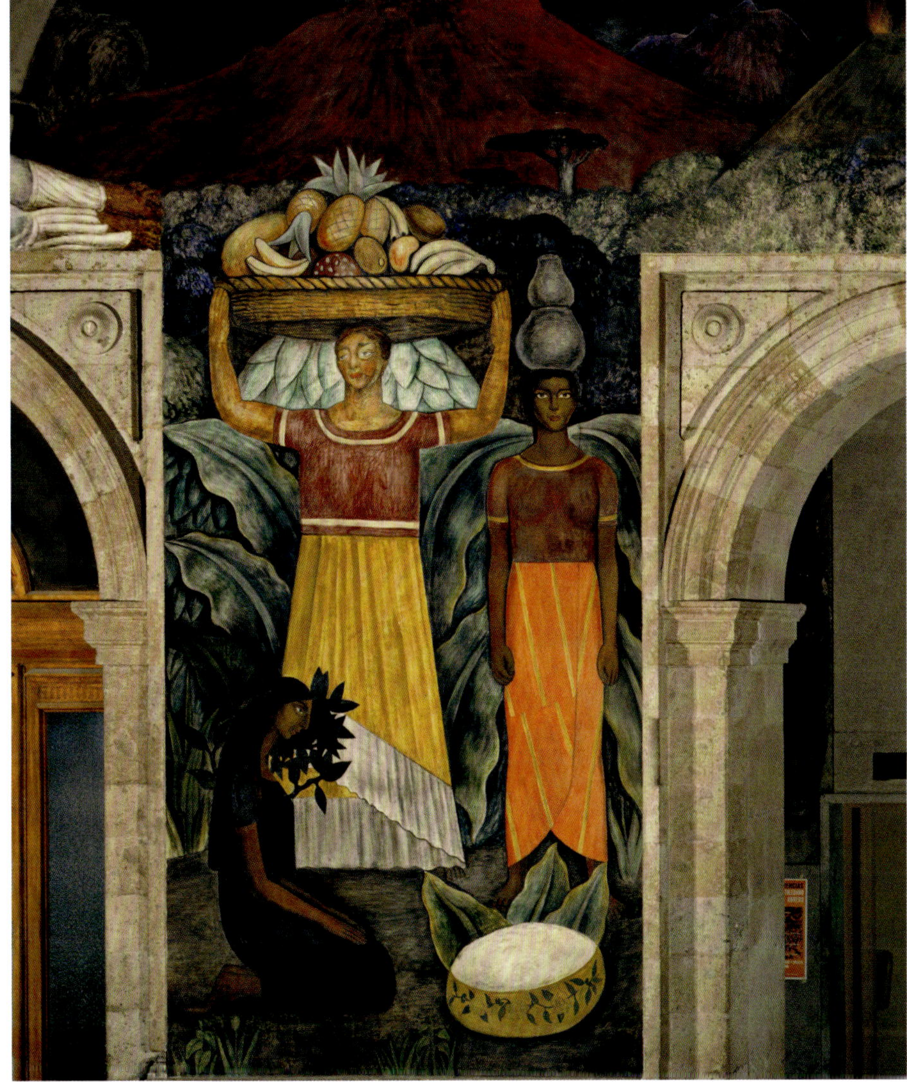

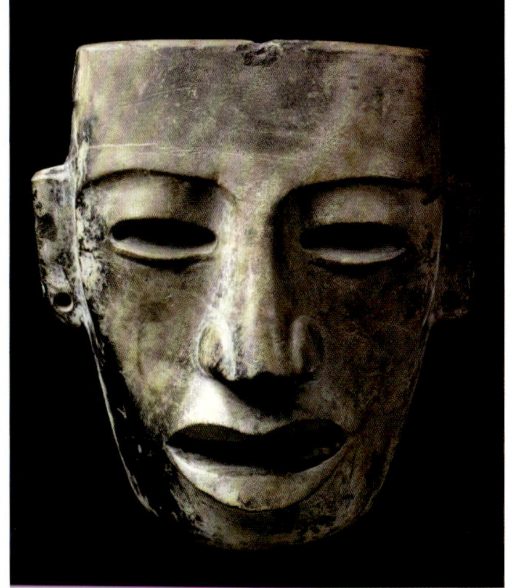

FIG. 8 Diego Rivera, *Tehuanas*, 1923, fresco murals at Secretaría de Educación Pública, Mexico City

FIG. 9 Stone mask, Teotihuacan, AD 250–650, Ethnologisches Museum, Staatliche Museen zu Berlin

evokes the kinds of masks and sculptures that he would have studied at the Museum of Archaeology (FIG. 9).

Other paintings from the period show Tamayo marrying modern, industrial subjects with European painting styles, from impressionism to futurism, works echoing the ideas of the Stridentists, who embraced and celebrated modernization. In *Factory*, Tamayo depicts an industrial landscape and foregrounds electrical wires and smoke-stacks (FIG. 10). It's hard to know if the painting's somber colors, thick smoke, and absence of people suggest a negative view of industrialization, or if they are meant to portray another side of the Mexican landscape.[32] In a work from 1925 he also portrayed an airplane in flight (FIG. 11), an extremely rare example of the subject in the history of Mexican art up to that time. Tamayo created a kind of blurred image complete with a propeller in motion to suggest the speed of flight. These works demonstrate Tamayo's interest in representing a broad vision of Mexican culture beyond indigenous and mestizo subjects.

Tamayo and his contemporaries had few opportunities to present their work to the public. During his time at ENBA, students routinely presented their work in the school's hallways and classrooms. There were no galleries or exhibition

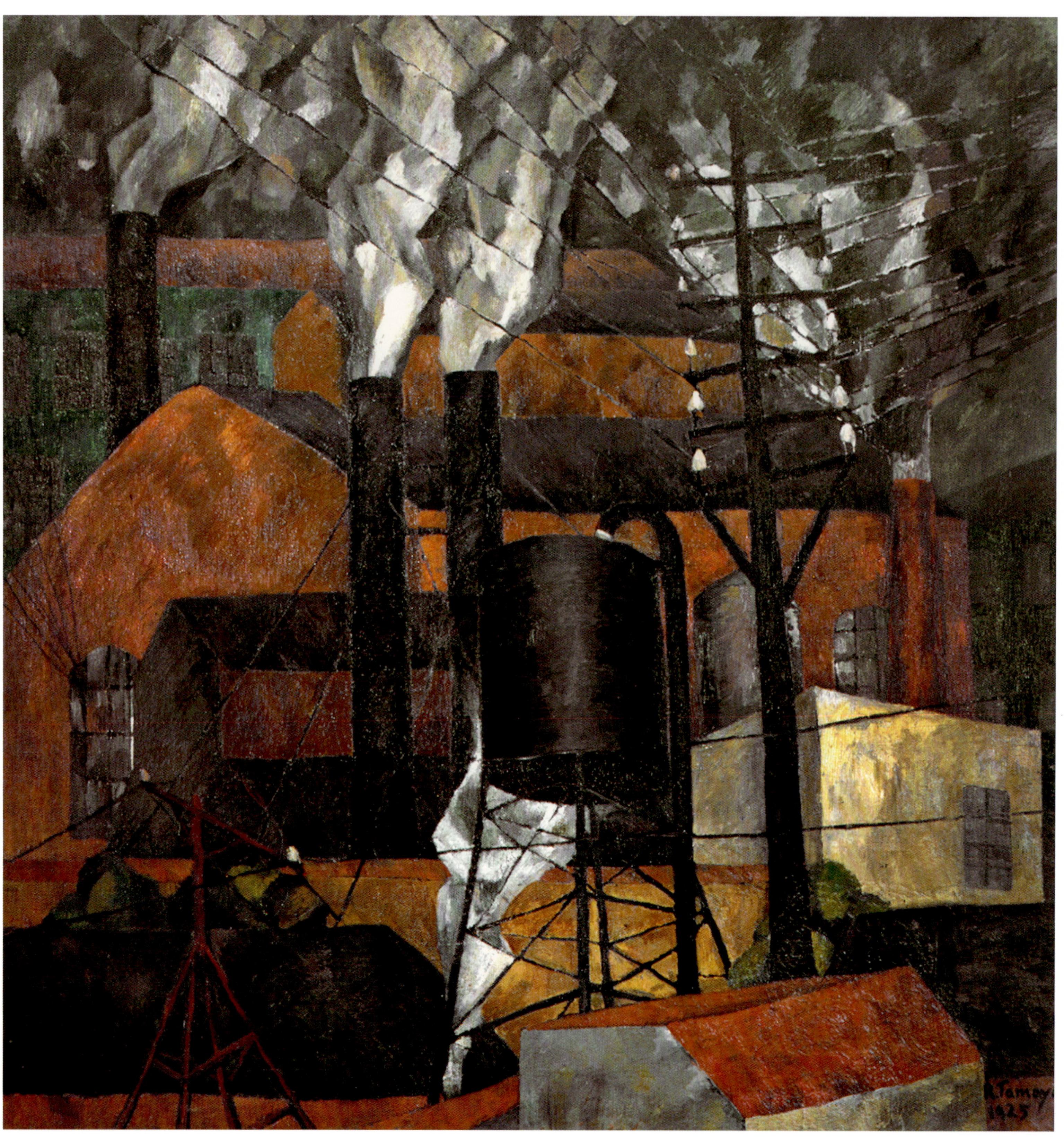

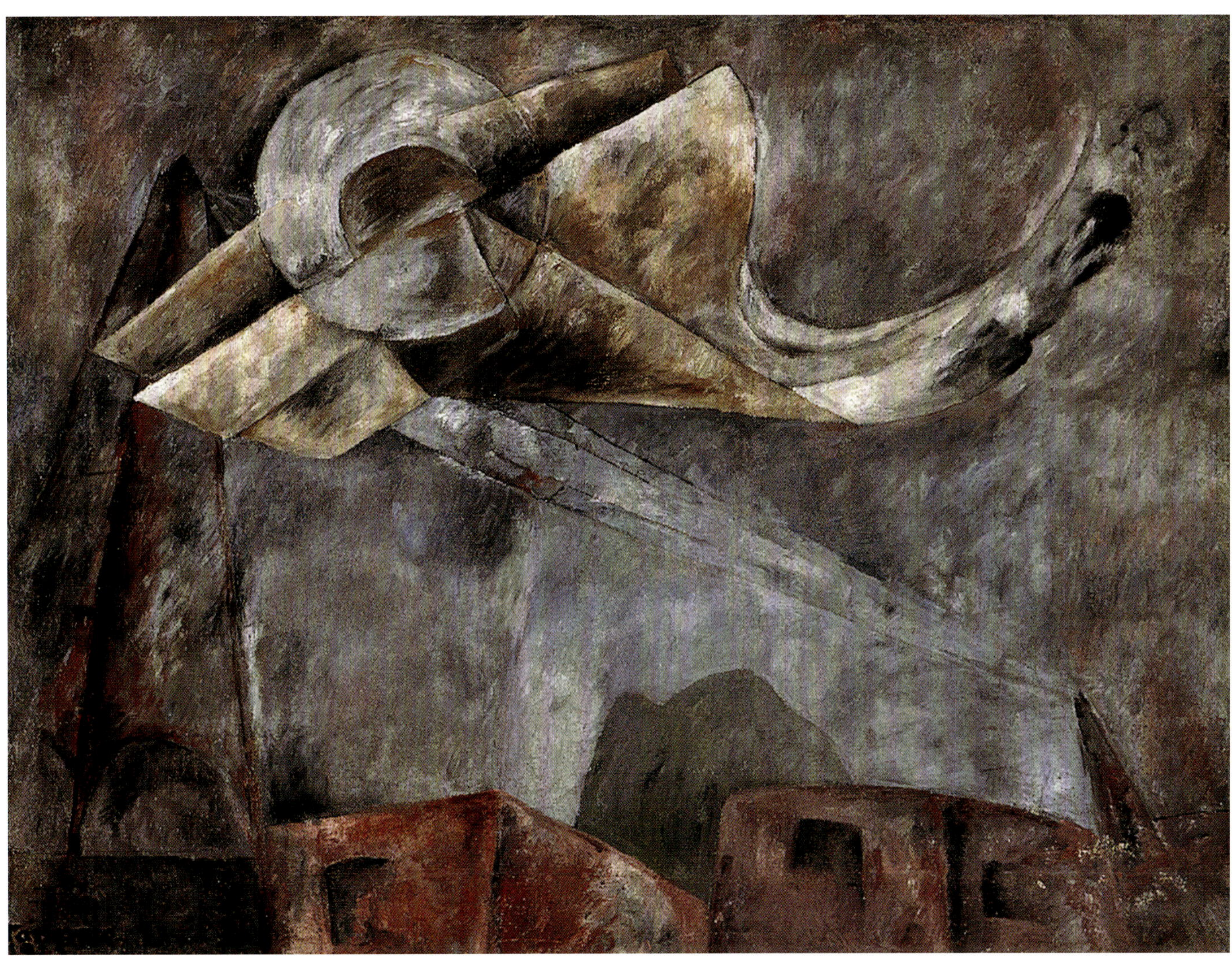

FIG. 10 Rufino Tamayo, *Factory* [*Fábrica*], 1925, oil on canvas, 39 × 39 in. Private collection

FIG. 11 Rufino Tamayo, *Airplane* [*Aeroplano*], 1925, oil on canvas, 23 ½ × 31 ½ in. Los Angeles County Museum of Art, The Bernard and Edith Lewin Collection of Mexican Art

spaces in Mexico until 1929, when artist and critic Carlos Mérida established the Galería de Arte Moderno under the auspices of the government of Mexico City.[33] Wanting to share his work with the public, Tamayo organized his first solo exhibition in 1926. He rented an empty storefront on Avenida Madero and presented twenty paintings, with subjects ranging from portraits and rural scenes to domestic still lifes and industrial subjects.

Reviews of Tamayo's show not only shed light on how critics were beginning to view his art—ideas that would endure throughout much of Tamayo's career—they also hint at emergent debates within the Mexican art scene. In favorable assessments of the exhibition, critics highlighted Tamayo's dedication to the craft of painting, as well as his "innate" creativity, which they associated with his indigeneity. Xavier Villaurrutia, who wrote the introduction to the exhibition's catalogue, also highlighted the geometric basis of Tamayo's compositions: "No anecdote, no subjects fill the paintings' imaginary emptiness. Rather, there are simple objects or groups of masses that convey geometric harmony."[34] Bernardo Ortiz de Montellano also emphasized Tamayo's indigeneity, but only after pointing out two tracks in his art: one "contemporary" and focused on modern subjects (factories, etc.), and the other more "personal," which came through in Tamayo's indigenous-themed works. Although harder to detect, Ortiz de Montellano's bifurcated argument is also racialized, as it places Tamayo's indigenist concerns in an atemporal category, separate from modern life.

Interestingly, Carlos Mérida, a Guatemalan artist based in Mexico City who also identified as indigenous, highlighted Tamayo's strong aesthetic formation: "Above all, Tamayo has a painter's disposition and a plastic sensibility…not due to prolonged mental labor, but rather due to a good education; these are the bases for Tamayo becoming a great painter, as he is hardworking, studious, investigative, attentive to the problems inherent to the plastic arts, and, above all, perfectly receptive to his own self." Mérida was taken with not just Tamayo's ability to affirm his own perspective but with his ability to express "a Mexicanism without the picturesque."[35] There is an implied comparative subtext in Mérida's response to Tamayo's art: Tamayo's Mexicanism is nonpicturesque because picturesque varieties of Mexicanism already exist. In the coming years, the critique of Mexican muralism—particularly the murals of Diego Rivera—would center on its depiction of Mexican life in picturesque terms. Although Mérida does not elaborate on this comparative context in his review, the fact that he mentions Tamayo's factory paintings and indigenous-themed works suggests that the non-picturesque qualities in his work emanate from his approach to these subjects.

The debates that were beginning to surface through and about Tamayo's art—regarding his race and the representation of Mexican culture as indigenous and/or modern—would continue to play themselves out when he arrived in New York. There Tamayo would find an eager audience interested in Mexican art. Tamayo would also seek out learning opportunities that would allow him to expand his vision of national Mexican culture.

NEW YORK, NEW YORK In September 1926, five months after he organized his first solo exhibition in Mexico City, Tamayo embarked on his first trip to New York City.[36] He yearned to be in a new environment that could stimulate his creativity. As was the case for many young Latin American artists at that time, Paris was Tamayo's real goal, but his finances made the voyage impossible.[37] Unlike Rivera, Siqueiros, and Orozco, Tamayo did not receive a scholarship, subsidy, or diplomatic post to underwrite his first trips abroad.[38] Regardless of how he arrived, New York would become instrumental to his artistic development and outlook. The cultural resources of the city exposed Tamayo for the first time to modern European art in the flesh. His interactions with New York–based artists were also key. His friendships and associations pulled him into the New York art world, helping him secure exhibiting and publishing opportunities, and exposing him to other "American" artists who were working through their own approaches to national subjects. Critically, he learned that Mexican art had an engaged audience in the United States, a factor that would keep him linked to New York for much of his career. Above all, Tamayo gained awareness of new artistic currents that would shape his artistic outlook.

Tamayo's friend, the composer Carlos Chávez first came up with the idea that they both travel to New York. Chávez had briefly visited New York between 1923 and 1924, following a lengthy and uninspiring trip to Paris. "In Europe, things are [already] done," Chávez reflected. New York, on the other hand, was especially stimulating.[39] He was taken with the modernity of electric lights, the technical advances of the music industry, and the energy of jazz. Chávez likely communicated his excitement to Tamayo, who was already open to artistic experimentation and learning. New York was increasingly becoming an attractive

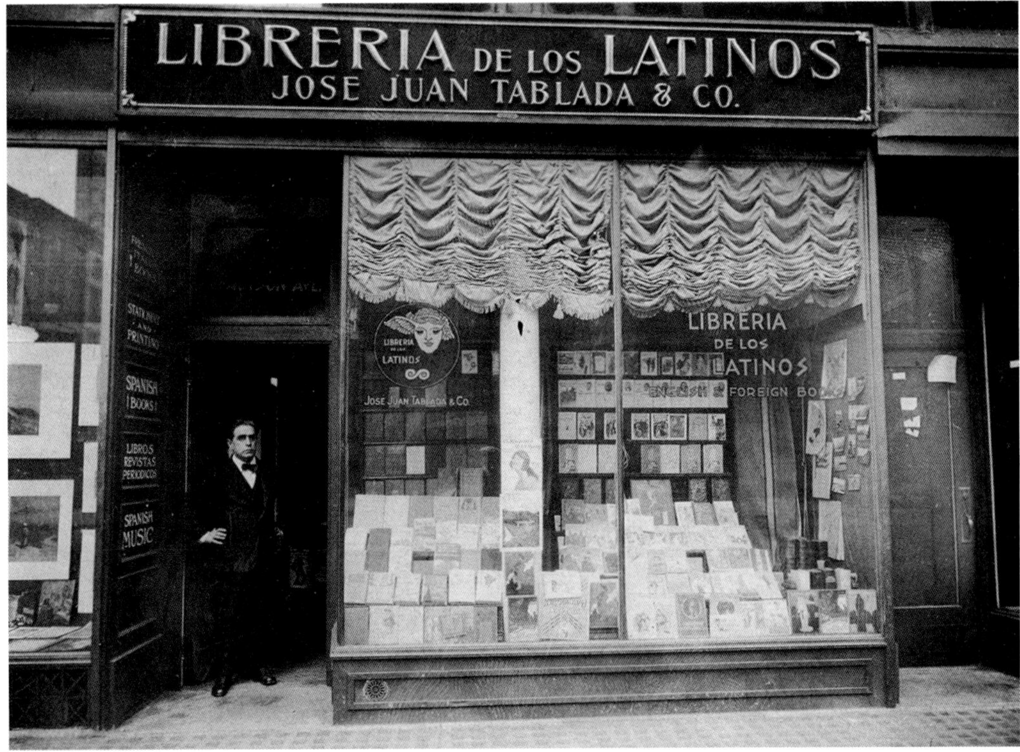

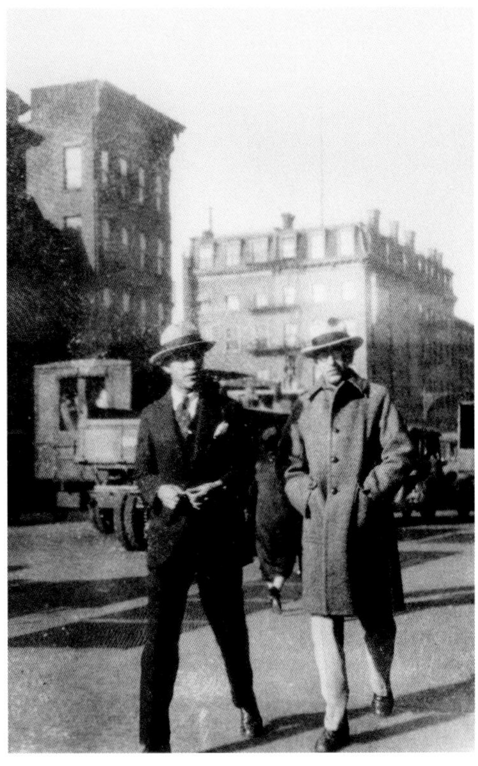

FIG. 12 Photographer unknown, *La Librería de los Latinos, José Juan Tablada & Co., New York*, n.d. Archivo Tablada, UNAM, Mexico

FIG. 13 Photographer unknown, *Tamayo and Carlos Chávez in New York*, ca. 1926. Tamayo Archive, Museo Tamayo, Mexico City

option for European artists in the first decades of the twentieth century. It also became a magnet for many Latin American artists, likely a social and cultural consequence of the expanding political reach of the United States into Latin America.[40] Some of the Mexican artists and intellectuals who made their way to New York during this time were there for political reasons, too. Several served as informal cultural ambassadors seeking to improve Mexico's public image in the United States following the turmoil of the Mexican Revolution.[41]

When they arrived in New York, Tamayo and Chávez became part of this growing Mexican presence in the city. Mexican poet, art critic, and diplomat José Juan Tablada had been living in the United States since at least 1914. In 1921 he established La Librería de los Latinos in Midtown Manhattan, which became a center for Spanish-speaking artists in New York (FIG. 12). Octavio Barreda, who worked for the Mexican consulate in New York, also welcomed many artists to his Fourteenth Street apartment home, including Luis Hidalgo, Lupe Medina, and the Guatemalans Carlos Mérida and Luis Cardoza y Aragón.[42] Miguel Covarrubias had arrived in New York from Mexico City in 1923 and by 1926 was already contributing distinctive illustrations to influential magazines like *Vanity Fair* and the *New Yorker*. He also had begun to turn his attention seriously to the booming Harlem scene in upper Manhattan.

Tamayo and Chávez rented an apartment on Fourteenth Street, which put them in the center of an important artist enclave (FIG. 13). Fourteenth Street formed the northern edge of Greenwich Village and the locus of the so-called Fourteenth Street School, a group of painters generally interested in urban realism and contemporary subjects. This neighborhood was home to Stuart Davis, Yasuo Kuniyoshi, Reginald Marsh, and Raphael and Moses Soyer, all of whom Tamayo befriended. Tamayo also met French émigré Marcel Duchamp, as well as George Biddle, who later became an important Mexican enthusiast

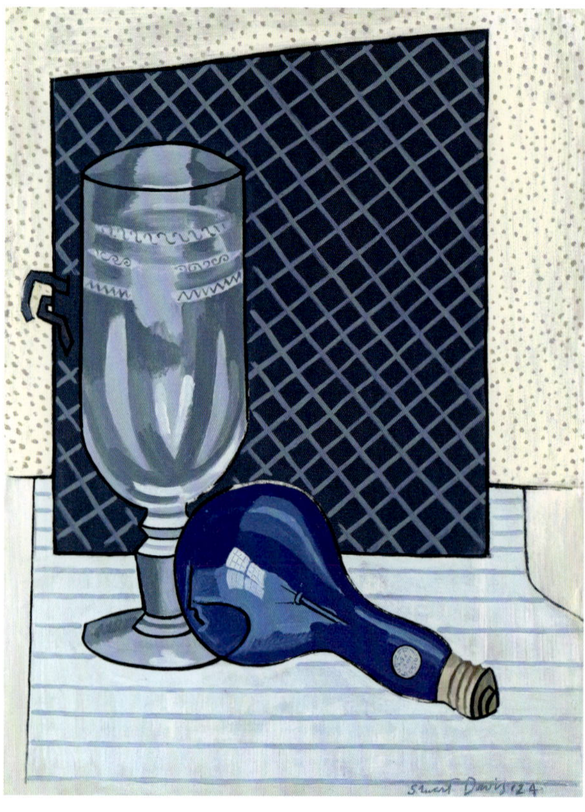

FIG. 14 Stuart Davis, *Edison Mazda*, 1924, oil on cardboard, 24 3/4 × 18 5/8 in. The Metropolitan Museum of Art, New York, Purchase, Mr. and Mrs. Clarence Y. Palitz Jr. Gift, in memory of her father, Nathan Dobson, 1982

in the United States. While Tamayo never spoke at length about his impressions of the US art he encountered, one could argue that what he absorbed from his US American peers was not technique or style, but outlook. American artists in New York were devoted to engaging their immediate world through a wide range of stylistic approaches. Tamayo witnessed Marsh's sensual and modern "New Women," Raphael Soyer's urban realism, Kuniyoshi's idiosyncratic portraits, and Davis's forward-looking approach to advertising and consumer culture. Most of these artists were committed to representing their national context in ways that engaged the latest currents in European modern art. Davis, for instance, was drawn to the cubist and collage experiments of Pablo Picasso and Georges Braque. In works like *Edison Mazda* (FIG. 14), Davis transposed these influences by placing distinctly American consumer goods at the center of his works. These connections deepened Tamayo's knowledge of contemporary art outside Mexico and broadened his awareness of what was conceptually possible under the rubric of "national" art.

Tamayo came to New York for many reasons, and seeing art up close was high on his list. He recalled: "In New York, I went berserk over painting. There I experienced the same passion that I had felt during my encounter with popular and pre-Hispanic art. I needed to analyze and investigate everything about painting, like what I had done before with pre-Hispanic art at the Museum of Anthropology."[43] Tamayo's intense exposure to painting was possible because of the city's expansive cultural resources. At the Metropolitan Museum of Art, he saw works by Golden Age Spanish masters like El Greco, Francisco de Zurbarán, and Diego Velázquez.[44] In the mid-1920s, several established galleries presented exhibitions of European art, with a particular focus on the School of Paris. Tamayo likely saw *Modern Paintings from Ingres to Picasso* at the Wildenstein Gallery, as well as *Cézanne, Matisse, Derain, Utrillo, Pascin, Marie Laurencin and Van Dongen* (1926) and *Loan Exhibition of Paintings from El Greco and Rembrandt to Cézanne and Matisse* (1927) at the Reinhardt Galleries on Fifth Avenue. In January 1927 the Valentine Gallery, which would represent Tamayo in the 1930s, presented a major Matisse survey.[45] Seeing these works, and absorbing the critical response they engendered, introduced Tamayo to the critical issues of the period and buoyed his own developing interests in the modernist appropriations of non-Western art. A review of the Matisse retrospective, for instance, highlighted how the French artist "discovered for himself the beauties of primitive art, of the Coptic textiles and negro sculpture. These, added to the subtle and powerful design of the East, formed the basis of his work for the next several years."[46] For an artist coming from Mexico, who first learned about European art through word of mouth or magazines, the experience of seeing the actual paintings must have been thrilling.

New York was not Paris, but its burgeoning cultural institutions still offered a broad sampling of international modern art. Tamayo was in New York during key moments in the histories of two important institutions, the Société Anonyme and the Museum of Living Art. In the years prior to the founding of the Museum of Modern Art in 1929, both institutions led the effort to educate the public and American artists on international avant-garde movements. These collections featured a wide swath of modern art, mostly European but some US American, including many artists and artworks now considered canonical. The art they collected, displayed, and interpreted was undoubtedly important and influential for young artists, including Tamayo. Nevertheless, it was the way these institutions framed their respective programs that likely informed Tamayo's developing perspectives on contemporary practice in the mid- to late 1920s.

Tamayo was in New York when the Société Anonyme presented the *International Exhibition of Modern Art* in 1926 at the Brooklyn Museum (FIG. 15), and a smaller version of the show at the Anderson Galleries in Manhattan. Since Tamayo knew Marcel Duchamp, who cofounded the Société with artists Katherine Dreier and Man Ray in 1921, as well as some of the New York–based artists included in these shows, it is very likely that he saw either one or both exhibitions. The exhibitions were organized by Dreier and presented an extraordinary range of modern art, from German Expressionism to cubism, neoplasticism, futurism, and early surrealism. Even as the Brooklyn Museum's exhibition catalogue grouped artists by nationality, the installation itself was literally and conceptually kaleidoscopic. Works in divergent

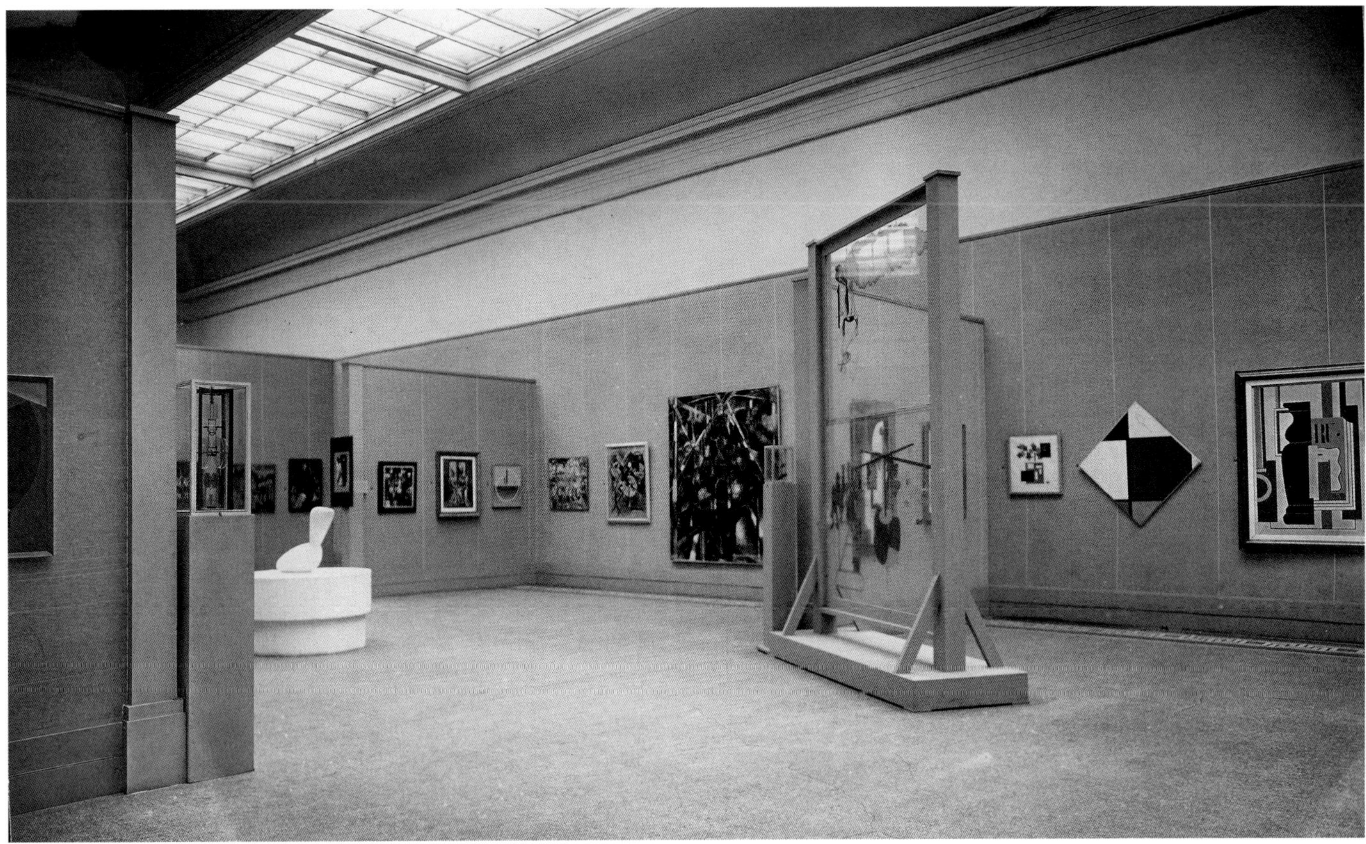

FIG. 15 Installation view of *International Exhibition of Modern Art*, Brooklyn Museum, November 1926–January 1927. Beinecke Rare Book and Manuscript Library, New Haven, Connecticut

styles and depicting a variety of subjects could be found in close proximity to one another. In the exhibition catalogue for the Anderson Galleries venue, Dreier wrote, "The dominant thought in assembling these groups...was to show how universal Modern Art has become, and that, instead of dying out, as its enemies are constantly proclaiming from the house-tops, it is growing in volume, strength and vigor as the years pass on."[47] The subtext here, and throughout Dreier's introduction, is the robust educational role the Société assumed in the face of intense public hostility toward modern art in the United States. Dreier believed that in Europe "there exists a larger appreciative audience—people who intellectually realize what the artist is striving for," whereas in America "it is not the art to which [people] respond, but the subject which it represents."[48] As a result, the exhibition was organized to benefit the development of modern art in America and to educate the public about the philosophical aims of the modern artist. This approach of displaying art outside of any national classifications must have been striking to Tamayo, who was coming from a stridently nationalist context. Tamayo later reflected, "Before going to New York, our tradition was most important. This continues to be so for me, but I acquired a sense of the universal, that art must be understandable in all the corners of the world."[49]

Albert Eugene Gallatin, who in 1927 showcased his personal collection as the Gallery of Living Art at a space on the New York University campus close to where Tamayo lived, had similar educational and artistic goals. His collection was less eclectic than the one Dreier assembled, although several artists like Braque, Picasso, Piet Mondrian, and Jean Arp were included in both collections. Gallatin was trained in the formalist tradition of Clive Bell, and tended to gravitate toward formalist abstraction.[50] He considered paintings by Picasso, Gris, Léger, and Braque to be the foundation of his collection. Even as the work of several Americans—artists like Man Ray and Charles Demuth, whom Gallatin considered "younger and more adventurous"—was presented as well, the goal of the museum was to highlight important examples of modern art in order to stimulate advanced artistic production in the United States. Gallatin hoped his gallery would be the place where "artists, students and collectors can see a representative selection of the most vital forms of contemporary art."[51] Gallatin articulated his antinationalist or internationalist stance from the very beginning. In one of his first statements about his gallery, Gallatin noted, "While we shall make every effort to encourage American art, there will be no nationalist propaganda."[52]

In viewing exhibitions like these, Tamayo absorbed the conceptual orientation of contemporary artists and their advocates in the United States, as well as the varied styles in which artists painted. Tamayo's measured comments about what he saw and liked in New York suggest that he was very much looking at artistic techniques as well as trajectories. "Picasso," Tamayo reflected, "is the most important contemporary artist, but Matisse and Braque are better painters. Of the younger [artists], Chirico interests me."[53] Matisse, Braque, and Picasso were amply represented in many of the exhibitions that Tamayo saw. Judging by his later production, Tamayo was taken with Matisse's lush color, geometric structure, and repetitive patterning. Works such as *Interior, Flowers and Parakeets* (FIG. 16), on view at the Reinhardt Galleries in 1927, brought all of these elements together in a single canvas. The painting contains elements that Tamayo would later adapt in his own practice: elaborate stage set–like interiors with layers of space that recede into the distance. Tamayo saw countless examples of modernist still lifes, including works by Picasso

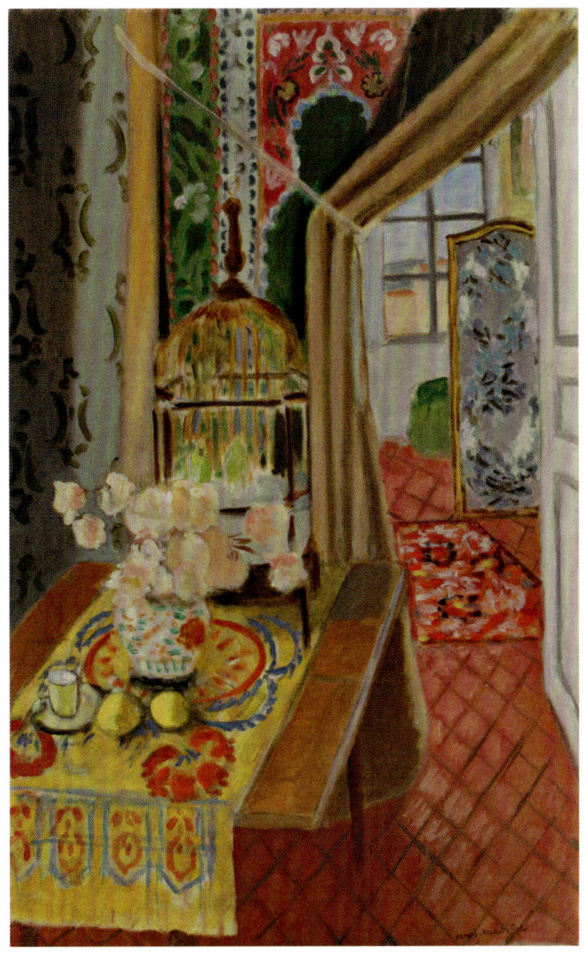

FIG. 16 Henri Matisse, *Interior, Flowers and Parakeets*, 1924, oil on canvas, 46 1/4 × 29 in. The Baltimore Museum of Art, The Cone Collection, formed by Dr. Claribel Cone and Miss Etta Cone of Baltimore, Maryland

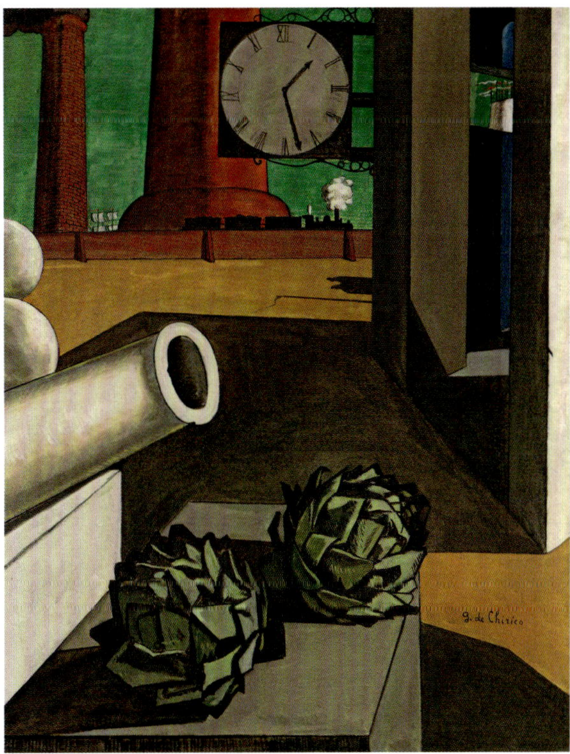

FIG. 17 Giorgio de Chirico, *The Philosopher's Conquest*, 1913/14, oil on canvas, 49 1/4 × 39 in. The Art Institute of Chicago, Joseph Winterbotham Collection

and Braque, whose textural and varied application of paint taught him how to create a collage-like aesthetic on canvas and conceive of still life as a vehicle for experimentation.

Given his accolades of de Chirico in late 1928, it is very likely that Tamayo saw the Italian artist's first solo exhibition in New York, at the Valentine Gallery, earlier in the year.[54] Several de Chirico works were also shown in the Société Anonyme exhibition at the Brooklyn Museum in 1926, where de Chirico was referred to not as a surrealist, but as the leader of the Italian Metaphysical school.[55] The Valentine show included many of de Chirico's later, less-esteemed works, as well as some of his iconic compositions, such as *The Philosopher's Conquest* (FIG. 17), which features his signature incongruous objects and temporal juxtapositions in mysterious public spaces that suggest dreams or melancholic states. Henry McBride, a major New York critic supportive of modernism, appreciated de Chirico's irreverent attitude toward the classics and his ability to "jumble the past and the present."[56] Perhaps de Chirico's engagement of antiquity from the perspective of the present appealed to Tamayo's own interest in conceiving a modern art practice that was informed by Mexico's complex pre-Hispanic, colonial, and modern history.

Tamayo came to New York to immerse himself in a new cultural environment, but also to show his own work, which he brought with him from Mexico. He reconnected with Walter Pach, a key organizer of the 1913 Armory Show, whom he had met earlier in Mexico in 1922. Upon Tamayo's arrival in the city, Pach introduced the artist to Carl Zigrosser, director of the Weyhe Gallery, who soon offered Tamayo his first solo show. Covarrubias also facilitated key introductions to important New York cultural figures, like Frank Crowninshield, editor of *Vanity Fair*, who would later write about Tamayo's art.

Tamayo also began to connect with enthusiasts of Mexican culture in the United States, including Frances Flynn Paine and Anita Brenner.[57]

Tamayo's first exhibition in New York, at the Weyhe Gallery, took place in October 1926, less than a month after he arrived. Founded in 1923, the Weyhe Gallery was a promoter of modern art and works on paper, in particular, and was just becoming associated with Mexican art in the United States.[58] From the mid-1920s through the 1930s, the gallery exhibited and sold prints by *Los tres grandes*, yet Tamayo was the first Mexican artist to have a solo show there. Tamayo exhibited several watercolors, oil paintings, and prints that he brought with him from Mexico (including the painting *The Family*; see pl. 1), as well as several prints he had made in New York at the suggestion of Zigrosser.[59] It is not clear how many works from his previous Mexico City show were also presented at the Weyhe Gallery, but his New York show leaned more heavily toward Tamayo's "personal" or indigenous track, to use one of the poles proposed by Mexican art critic Bernardo Ortiz de Montellano.[60] A review of the Weyhe exhibition published in Mexico in 1927 reproduced several watercolors populated by barefoot men and native women wearing *rebozos* (head wraps) and holding baskets.[61] This rural indigenist imagery is echoed in Tamayo's woodblock prints from the period (pls. 2–7), in which the woodgrain striations on the prints themselves are so prominent that they underscore the status of each print as an autonomous artwork. Critic Xavier Villaurrutia would later call Tamayo's prints "sculptural."[62] These prints undoubtedly relate to the printmaking revival that took off in Mexico starting in the early 1920s.[63] Tamayo, like many artists, produced affordable woodblock prints of indigenous and urban subjects that relate variously to his paintings, with their combined interest in landscape, popular art (in this case religious retablo painting), and the transposition of pre-Columbian sculptural forms onto the bodies of contemporary Mexicans. He later depicted a kind of revolutionary subject, a soldier with a large sombrero resting his rifle on the ground. The small brochure published in conjunction with the show does not necessarily discount the formal aspects of Tamayo's art, but it does begin to articulate racialized ideas about Mexican art in general and Tamayo's art in particular. The text suggests that Tamayo's art was both a vehicle for representing the "Mexican art spirit" and a product of "the vigorous art movement that has grown up in our neighboring country." The text frames his art in a non-Western context: "His art has little European influence in it and derives almost entirely from Mexican and Indian sources." Subsequent exhibitions suggest that both Tamayo and promoters were eager to cast the artist and his work outside of a European artistic frame.[64]

By 1927, Tamayo had become even more intertwined with the growing interest in, and market for, Mexican culture and art in the United States, a factor that led him to see the opportunities that existed in New York for Mexican artists. His work was featured in two shows presented at the Art Center, a conglomerate arts organization and exhibition space founded in 1920 that had strong ties to the design industry.[65] The group show, which took place in early 1928 and was organized by Frances Flynn Paine and Anita Brenner, with the financial backing of the Mexican government and American patrons like Abby Aldrich Rockefeller, sought to improve the image of Mexico in the United States and emphasize the continuity of Mexican creativity across art forms—from fine art to applied art.[66] But it was Tamayo's solo show at the Art Center in November 1927 that proved more significant for him. Crowninshield, the *Vanity Fair* editor, wrote the introduction to a small exhibition brochure, which strongly framed

Tamayo and his art in racial terms. In addition to his publishing activities, Crowninshield was an avid collector and enthusiast of African and modern art, an interest that likely informed his observations about Tamayo.[67] Recalling an early interaction with Crowninshield, Tamayo noted how he had advocated that contemporary artists look toward so-called primitive art for inspiration: "Mr. Crowninshield said very important things about the art of African peoples and the pre-Hispanic and popular art of Mexico. I would listen intently because I too believed that so-called 'high' art was moving closer and closer to popular art and the art of primitive peoples."[68]

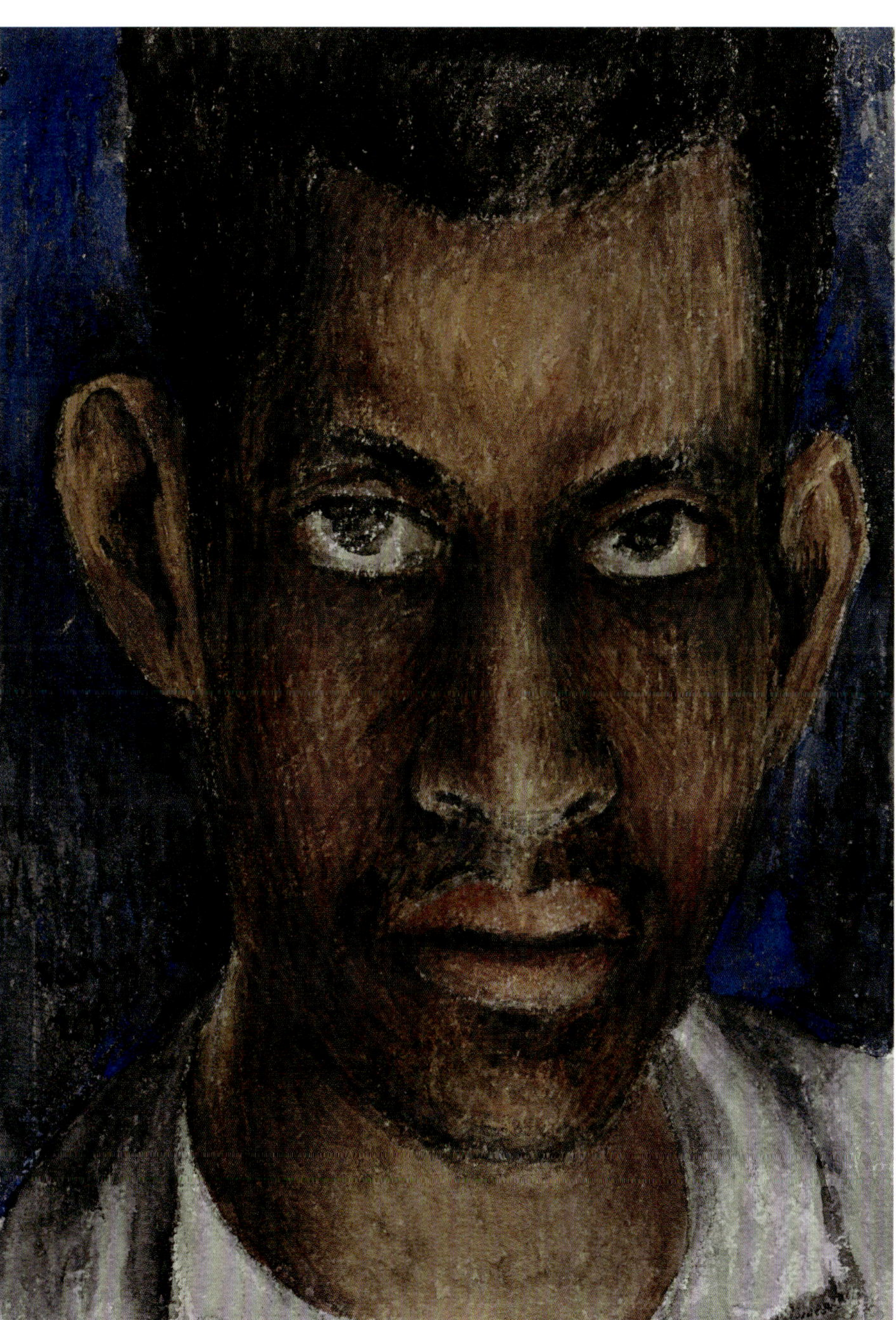

FIG. 18 Rufino Tamayo, *Self-Portrait [Autorretrato]*, 1927, watercolor and gouache over black chalk, 9 15⁄16 × 7 in. The Cleveland Museum of Art, Gift of Mrs. Malcolm L. McBride, 1957.432

Crowninshield's statement on Tamayo, however, went beyond emphasizing aesthetic primitivism; it suggested that Tamayo himself was a primitive. After noting that Mexican art is "definitely Indian in parentage" and that Tamayo's approach derives from within and "not from the teachings of any master," Crowninshield added that "the *esprit de race* in this young artist is so strong, the native solution in him so saturated, that it naturally enough tends to remove his canvases (for Anglo-Saxon eyes at least) from the realm of the unusual or familiar."[69] Here Crowninshield adapted the collegial French World War I motto *esprit de corps* into "a biologically determined spirit."[70] His text also began to promote the falsehood that Tamayo was essentially a self-taught artist creating out of a natural inner force. The reviews of Tamayo's Art Center exhibition followed Crowninshield's lead. They practically quote his statement verbatim and argue that Tamayo's work reveals "an authentic quality of race and place."[71] Tamayo's 1927 self-portrait, which graced the cover of the exhibition's invitation, shows him working to capitalize on the appeal of his "racial" authenticity (**FIG. 18**). Donning dark brown skin, a broad nose and full lips, Tamayo looks practically African, a characterization that Anna Indych-López has argued positioned him "at the interstices of Mexican *indigenismo* and modern primitivism."[72] Tamayo created this self-portrait at the same time that his friend Miguel Covarrubias attained acclaim for his *Negro Drawings*, first seen in *Vanity Fair* and later published as a book in 1927 (**FIG. 19**).[73] Tamayo did not adopt Covarrubias's caricatured approach to racial representation but may have

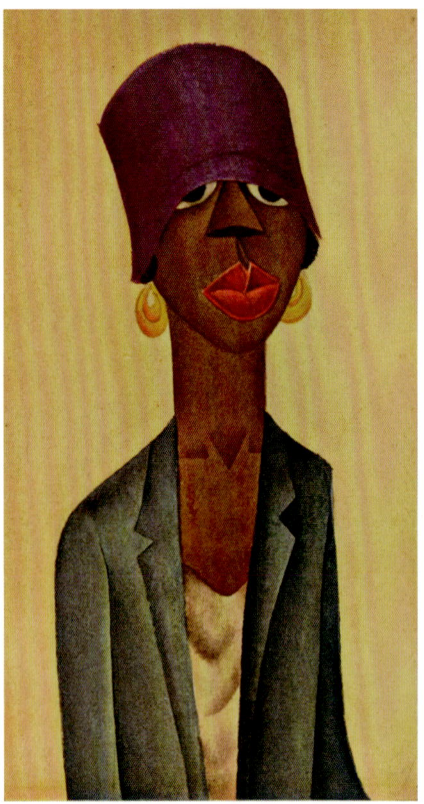

FIG. 19 Miguel Covarrubias, *Lennox Avenue Type*, ca. 1924, drawing. Collection unknown

been swayed by the vogue for African American culture to draw out his own "racial" connection to a so-called primitive culture. The perception of Tamayo as a primitive Indian would continue throughout his career, as a result of how others saw him and how he strategically presented himself.

In addition to exhibitions, Tamayo's work appeared in several issues of the *New Masses*, an important left-wing journal whose writers worked closely with artists during the 1920s and 1930s.[74] Stuart Davis and Miguel Covarrubias were on the editorial board and may have been instrumental in introducing Tamayo's work to the journal. Given the political orientation of the *New Masses*, it is unsurprising that Mexican art and subjects were covered throughout the 1920s and 1930s. Between 1926 and 1929, illustrations by artists associated with Mexico regularly appeared in its pages and on its covers. Drawings by Diego Rivera and photographs of his murals presented subjects tied to the Mexican Revolution. Three covers featured photographs by Mexican-based Italian photographer Tina Modotti, all of which depict post-revolutionary Mexican subjects, including strikes, agricultural workers, and Mexicanized emblems of communism, as in the photograph of a hammer and sickle placed atop a sombrero from the October 1928 cover (FIG. 20).

Tamayo's contributions to the *New Masses* in the 1920s encompassed indigenous and proletarian subjects that US audiences increasingly expected to see from a Mexican artist. In some ways, Tamayo's subjects echo the rural peasant archetype that traveling American artists emphasized in their representations of Mexico.[75] Similar to small vignettes by Jean Charlot that appear in several issues, Tamayo's January 1927 cover features a brown-skinned couple wearing simple muslin clothing (FIG. 21).[76] The male figure holds a long, thick, wooden rod, and the woman, who stands barefoot, wears a *rebozo*, the traditional accoutrement of the Mexican *campesina*. The image recalls the watercolors Tamayo presented at the Weyhe Gallery in 1926, and it's possible that he adapted one for this cover. In a 1929 cover illustration, Tamayo shifted to a more proletarian direction, depicting a tightly cropped view of a worker's face framed by a machete (FIG. 22). Tamayo's appearance in the *New Masses* should not be surprising. As an emerging artist, he was likely open to opportunities to share and publish his work, and may have created works in keeping with the interests of New York audiences.

Tamayo, however, did venture beyond audience expectations of what a Mexican artist could or "should" focus on. His lesser-known contributions to the *New Masses*, which include some interior illustrations, reveal an artist processing his immediate environment and even responding to the artwork of his New York peers. Tamayo was drawn above all to the modern American

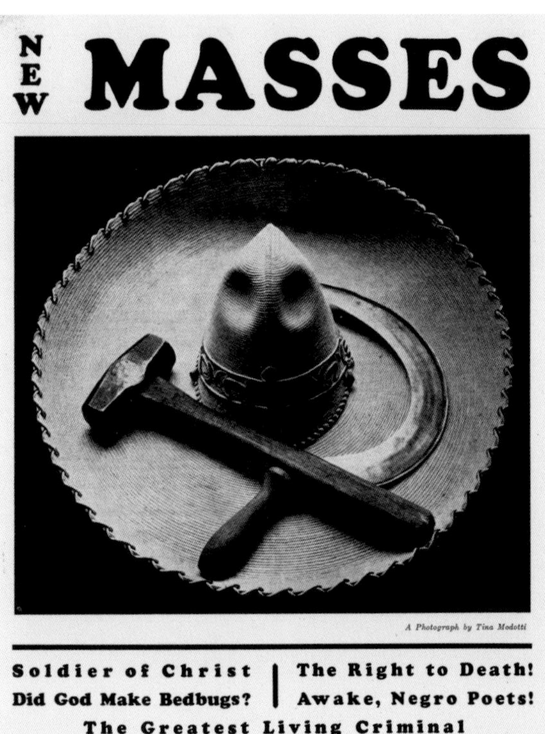

FIG. 20 Tina Modotti, cover photograph for *New Masses*, October 1928

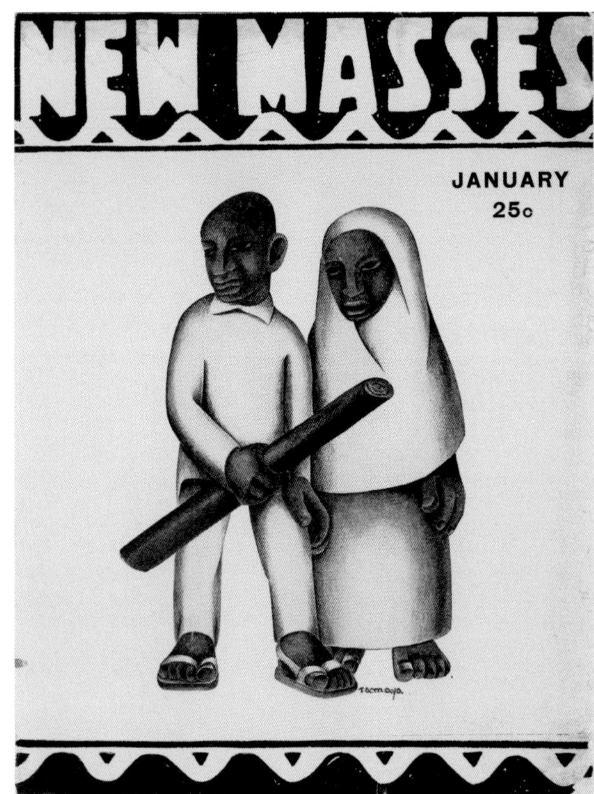

FIG. 21 Rufino Tamayo, cover illustration for *New Masses*, January 1927

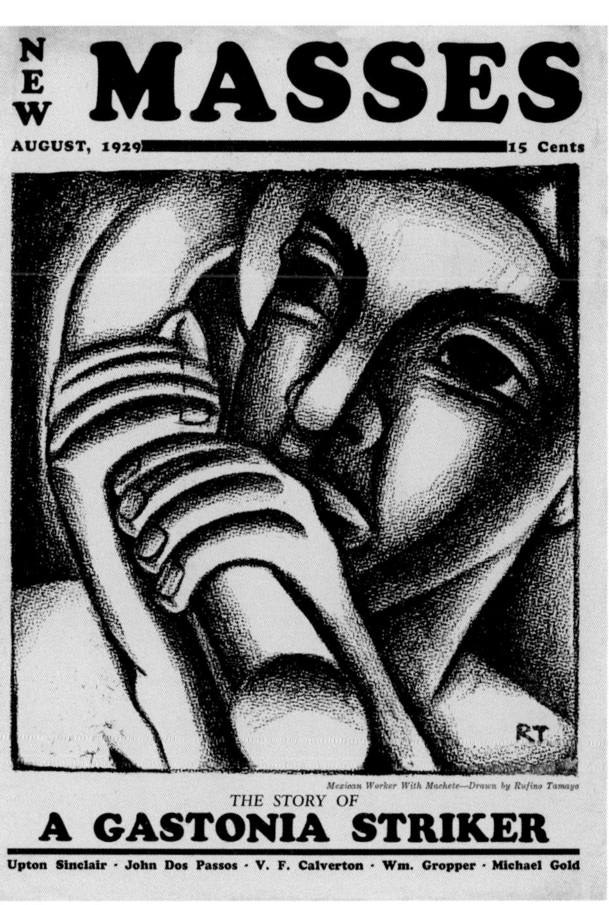

FIG. 22 Rufino Tamayo, *Mexican Worker with Machete,* cover illustration for *New Masses*, August 1929

woman and the modernity of the city. His April 1927 drawing of well-dressed women in hats, coats, and heels conversing either on a sidewalk or a subway car (FIG. 23) echoes the image of the "New Woman" that began appearing in commercial advertising and in the work of American artists like Reginald Marsh in the 1920s. Ellen Wiley Todd argues that these new icons of womanhood emerged out of the social and economic transformations of the interwar years, which brought women into the workplace and, by extension, public spaces as clerical workers and sales associates in thriving shopping districts like Fourteenth Street.[77] Tamayo's women are less prettified than Marsh's El riders (FIG. 24), who wear fur-collared coats and makeup, but the caption beneath Tamayo's image does suggest a sassy assertiveness becoming of a modern woman.[78] His July 1927 cover, alternatively, may have been inspired by a trip to Coney Island, a favorite haunt of many American artists and a subject that had appeared

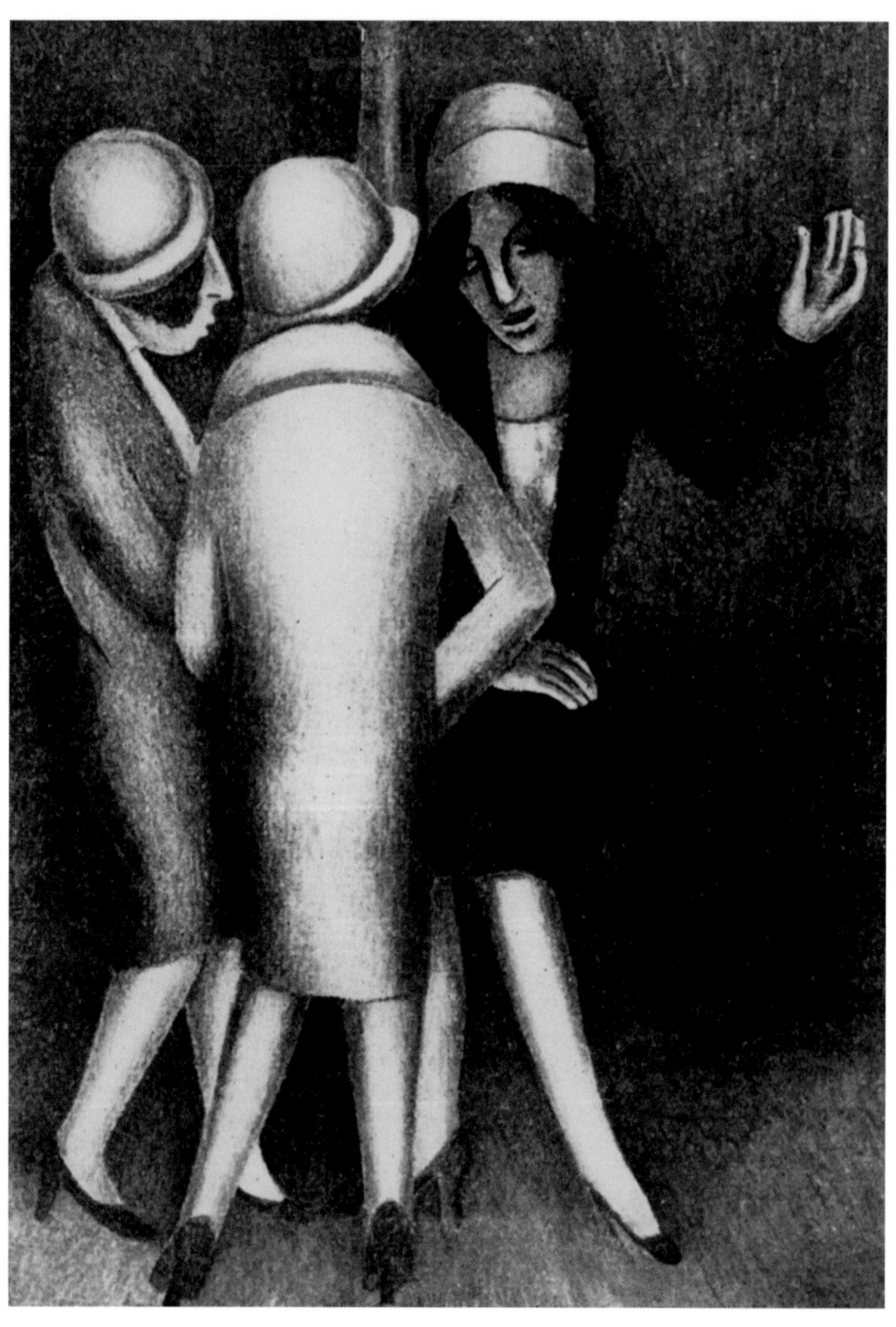

FIG. 23 Rufino Tamayo, untitled illustration for *New Masses*, April 1927

previously in the pages of the *New Masses* (**FIG. 25**). Louis Lozowick's print *Coney Island* (**FIG. 26**), which was featured in the July 1926 issue, focuses on the architecture of Coney Island and the enormous crowds that enjoyed the amusement park under electric lights.[79] Tamayo likely visited Coney Island during his first trip to New York, in 1926, and was taken with American women in swimsuits, a sight that must have been novel if not shocking for a Mexican artist coming from a more socially conservative society. His illustration, which at first appears uncharacteristic for Tamayo, actually resembles Picasso's solidly drawn and outlined figures, neoclassical compositions like *The Lovers*, which Tamayo had the occasion to see at the Reinhardt Galleries in January 1927 (**FIG. 27**).[80] This comparison reveals that Tamayo was immediately processing the European art he encountered through the prism of his actual experience.

Tamayo also contributed smaller illustrations of construction workers in the urban environment, allowing him to further develop subjects about modernization that he had initiated in Mexico. Tamayo was in New York during a skyscraper boom and was taken with this distinctive feature of the city's landscape. "¡¡¡I'm drowning in this sea of skyscrapers!!!,"[81] Tamayo wrote to a friend in 1926. His illustrations for the *New Masses*, which include a drawing of several workers digging or jackhammering and surrounded by tall buildings and a steel beam, focus less on the buildings than on the workers who erected them (**FIG. 28**). Tamayo's drawings undoubtedly relate to the presence of construction workers in New York and the editorial interest of the *New Masses* in urban laborers. They likely also express Tamayo's own impressions of a city that was dramatically more modernized than Mexico City.

Despite these positive experiences to display and share his work, New York was economically difficult. Tamayo's poor health—he suffered

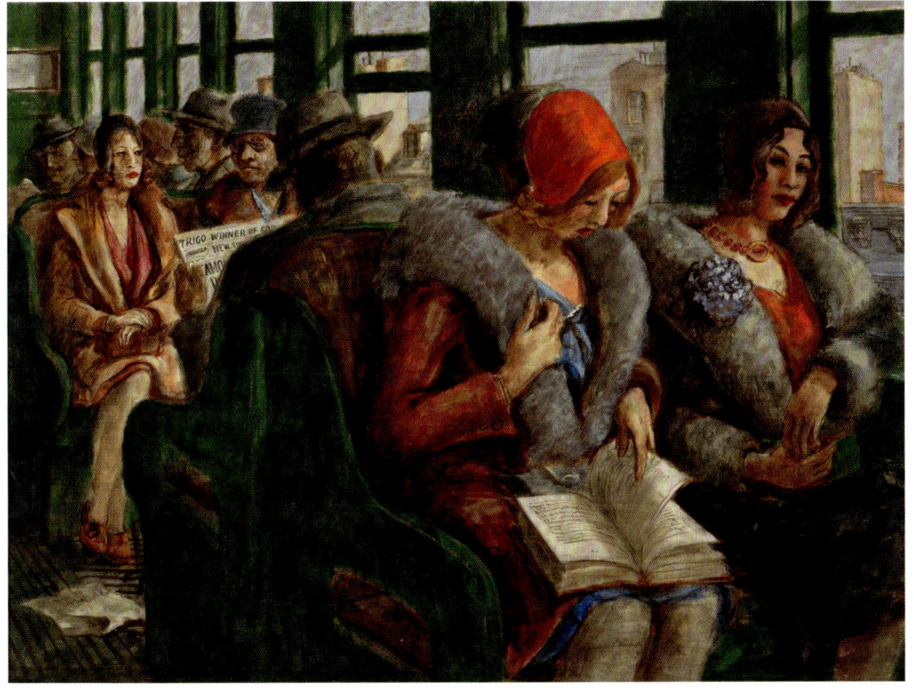

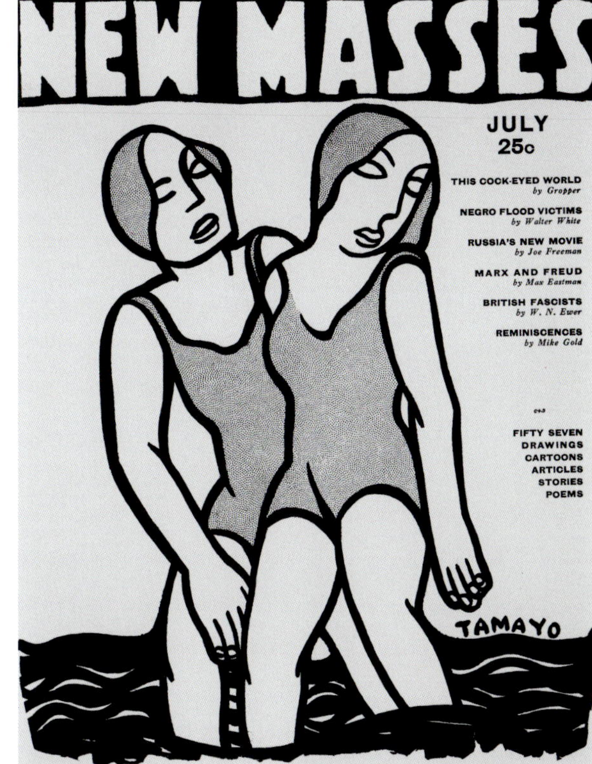

Clockwise from above:

FIG. 24 Reginald Marsh, *The El*, ca. 1928, oil on canvas, 30 × 40 3/16 in. Whitney Museum of American Art, New York, Felicia Meyer Marsh Bequest

FIG. 25 Rufino Tamayo, cover illustration for *New Masses*, July 1927

FIG. 26 Louis Lozowick, *Coney Island*, ca. 1925/printed 1972, lithograph on paper, 13 × 8 1/2 in. Smithsonian American Art Museum, Gift of Adele Lozowick, 1981.119.19

FIG. 27 Pablo Picasso, *The Lovers*, 1923, oil on linen, 51 1/4 × 38 1/4 in. The National Gallery of Art, Washington, DC, Chester Dale Collection

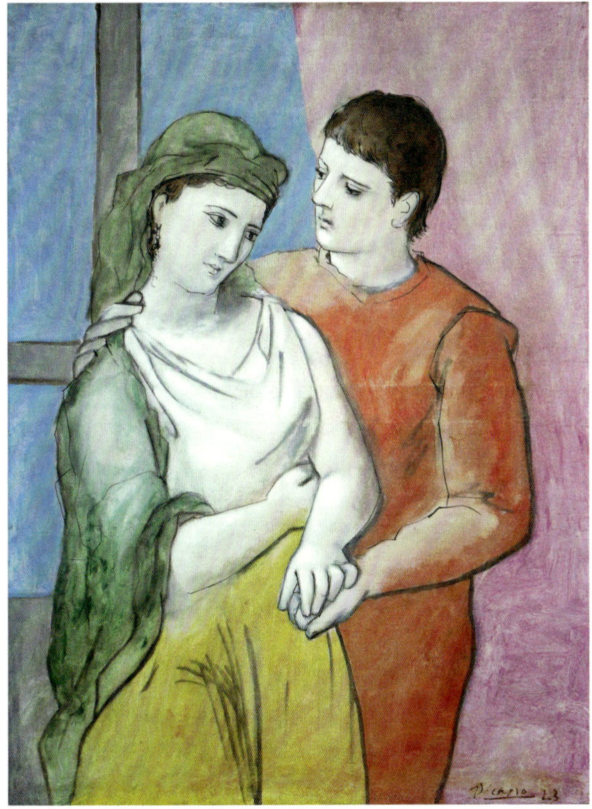

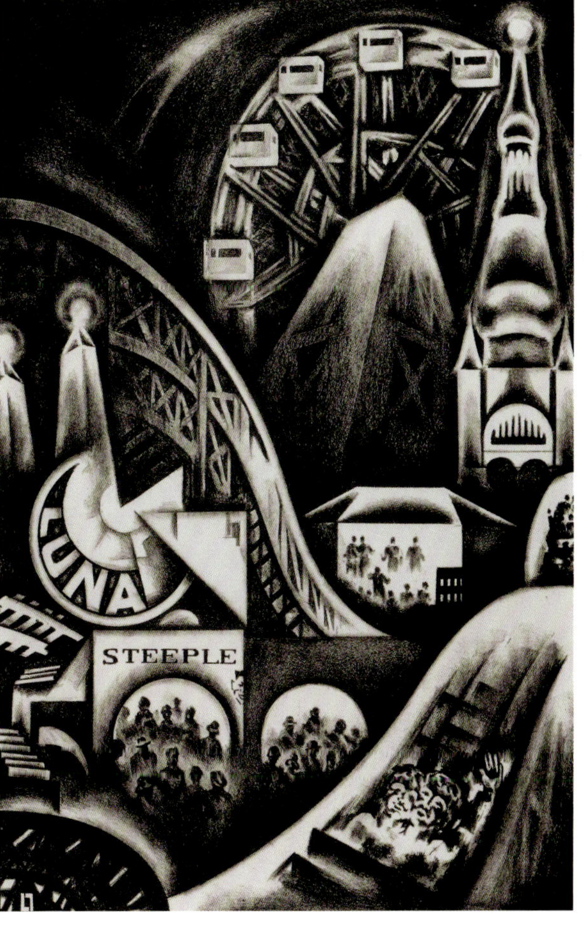

from digestive problems—and finances forced him to return to Mexico around June 1928. But he did not give up on New York. He returned again in 1930, at which point the economic realities of the Great Depression made a lengthy stay untenable.[82] He continued to produce New York–themed works, including an exuberant little watercolor and gouache titled *Coney Island* (1931; pl. 15). Tamayo's friezelike composition gathers his impressions of the iconic amusement park and its attractions: the crescent moon decorations of Luna Park, the park's billowing American flags, Ferris wheel, roller coaster rides, clowns, and scantily clad dancers on stage. Tamayo's impressions were surprisingly jubilant given that the United States was in the midst of the Great Depression.

Whether he was based in New York or Mexico City in the late 1920s to early 1930s, Tamayo's work continued to circulate in New York. He was given a two-person show with Mexican artist Joaquín Clausell at the John Levy Galleries. The pairing of Clausell, a kind of Mexican post-impressionist, with Tamayo indicates the extent to which Tamayo's art had begun to conceptually shift in new directions. In a review of the show, critic Edward Alden Jewell characterized Tamayo as both modern and Mexican and his work as revealing "the flavor of the school of Paris," intimating how Tamayo had already begun to assimilate the lessons of his New York years.[83] Jewell was generally positive about works like *Seashells* (1929; pl. 9), then titled *Arrangement with Seashells*, that juxtapose natural and man-made consumer objects—in this case, seashells, an ear of corn, a light bulb, and a pack of cigarettes—recalling the work of de Chirico and Stuart Davis. Other critics were more skeptical of Tamayo's ties to Mexican art and the School of Paris. Reviewers for *Parnassus* described him as "more of a colorist than a nationalist," and Murdock Pemberton's review for the *New Yorker* noted how "Tamayo has taken after the French and almost lost all of his heritage."[84] While these assessments are both narrow and misguided—corn, after all, is indigenous to the Americas and a staple food for ancient and contemporary Mexicans alike—they reveal Tamayo's evolving profile as an artist working outside the expected Mexican mold.

Tamayo's increasing identification as both Mexican and modern also emerged in response to his participation in the first blockbuster exhibition of the Mexican vogue period, *Mexican Arts*, which was organized by René d'Harnoncourt for the American Federation of Arts and opened at the Metropolitan Museum of Art in 1930 before traveling nationwide to seven venues. D'Harnoncourt, an Austrian count who would later become director of the Museum of Modern Art, was a self-taught Mexicanist who at the time was a buyer of Mexican crafts and antiques for Frederick Davis's Sonora News Company store in Mexico City.[85] He not only developed an expertise in Mexican popular art and antiquities, he also befriended the leading artists of the Mexican Renaissance. As installation pictures of the exhibition make evident, *Mexican Arts* leaned more heavily toward popular art and textiles than modern Mexican art. In various essays about the show, d'Harnoncourt laid out a historical narrative emphasizing how Mexico's indigenous heritage and history of racial intermixture had shaped its national culture. The exhibition, he noted, "only includes works of art characterized by the fusion of Indian and foreign elements."[86] His catalogue essay suggested a "humble" thread that united the historical eras of the exhibition, from the colonial period to the present: "The roots of the modern painter go deep into the simple life of the Mexican people, and the tradition of his work is genuinely Mexican, dating

FIG. 28 Rufino Tamayo, *Construction Workers*, illustration for *New Masses*, November 1929

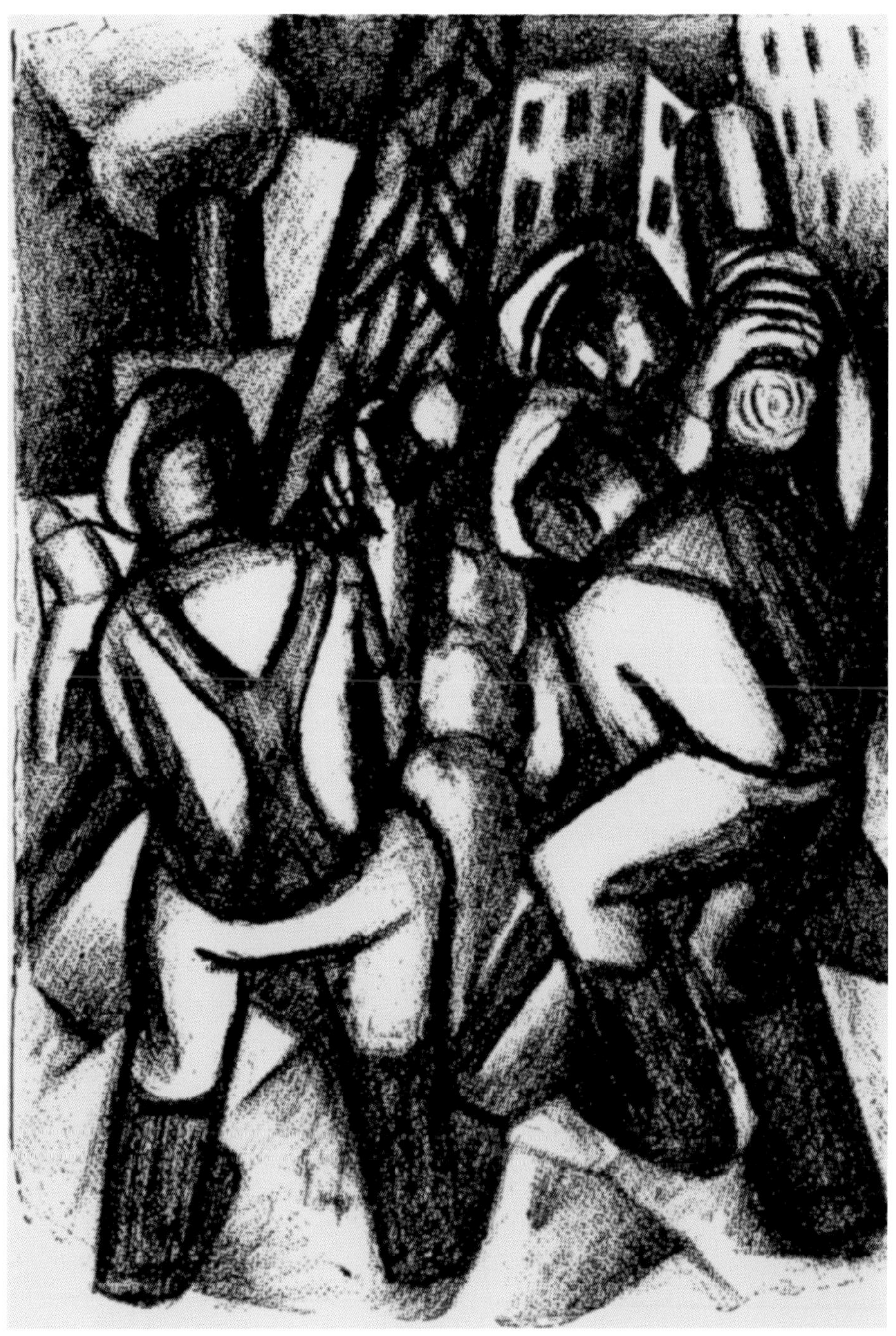

from the picture writing and frescoes of the pre-Conquest Indian, through the primitives, the *retablos*, and the native secular paintings, down to the turbulent present."[87]

D'Harnoncourt did not write extensively about the modern paintings on display, but the little he did say framed this work as an extension of the spirit of Mexican folk artisans, ideas that were perpetuated in the popular press by critics who celebrated how the decorative arts and handicrafts on display revealed Mexico's so-called primitive national culture.[88] Thus, it is hard to know why he chose to include Tamayo's *Mandolins and Pineapples* (1930; pl. 10), a work that shows the artist "Mexicanizing" the model of Matisse's domestic interiors. Similar to *Seashells*, Tamayo here depicts a crop that is associated with the Americas. *Mandolins and Pineapples* appealed to one important visitor: Duncan Phillips, a major collector of modern art of the United States and Europe. Phillips visited the *Mexican Arts* exhibition and immediately wrote to Frances Flynn Paine, expressing his excitement over the Tamayo painting and asking for it to be sent to Washington for his consideration. "I'm waiting to hear what you say about the Pineapple picture of Tamayo," he wrote. "It seemed to me about the best [picture] in the Mexican show at the Metropolitan."[89] Phillips acquired the painting, and by February 1931 it was on display at the Phillips Memorial Art Gallery.

Opened in a portion of Phillips's family home in Washington, DC, in 1921, the Phillips Memorial Art Gallery housed Duncan's collection. While the Gallery did not set out to present a comprehensive picture of modernism, it was an important venture that demonstrated the rising profile and patronage of modern art in the United States. In this way, the Phillips Memorial Art Gallery shares a similar spirit with the Société Anonyme and the Gallery of Living Art. Tamayo appears to be one of a few non-European or US artists to enter Phillips's collection at this early date, signaling that the collector appreciated Tamayo's work outside of a strictly Mexican context.[90] Phillips installed *Mandolins and Pineapples* in a gallery that united works under the rubric of "Twentieth-Century Lyricism."[91] With the exception of Tamayo, Charlot, and Russian-born artist John Graham, all of the artists represented in this space were from the United States; artists such as Marsden Hartley and Arthur Dove, whose work was emotive, expressionistic, and sometimes abstract, were also featured in the gallery. What Phillips meant by *lyricism* is not entirely evident, but his choices suggest that the category included works that were not realist or narrative. Phillips, however, did not discount Tamayo's "primitive" side: his brochure placed Tamayo, Charlot, and Graham into a "primitive imagery" subcategory, a strange categorization for Tamayo's Matisse-inspired composition. Even so, Phillips's installation offers evidence of how Tamayo was beginning, at least in part, to shed his association with "Mexican painting," then mostly defined by the narrative, socially driven work of the muralists.

Tamayo's initial trips to New York were not financially lucrative but were transformational on other fronts. He was able to absorb modern European art firsthand, an experience that allowed him to gain confidence and draw his own informed opinions about contemporary art. He entered a parallel yet distinct American art world where fellow artists were also negotiating ideas about what constitutes "national" art. He witnessed a growing interest in non-Western art and European primitivism in US artistic circles. Tamayo exhibited fairly widely in solo and group shows, including the landmark *Mexican Arts* at the Metropolitan Museum of Art, experiences that brought his work to the attention of Mexican enthusiasts in the United States. The acquisition of *Mandolins and Pineapples* by the Phillips Memorial Art Gallery placed him in an important echelon of artists that were patronized by a growing cadre of collectors who were enthusiastic about US and international modern art. Tamayo emerged from his initial New York sojourns ready to advance his art in new directions.

LEADER OF A NEW SCHOOL OF MEXICAN PAINTING In December 1928, only a few months after returning from his first trip to New York, Tamayo participated in the *Exposición de pintura actual* (Exhibition of Contemporary Painting), an important group show organized by the literary group los Contemporáneos (the Contemporaries), who sought to define "a vital current in contemporary art."[92] Critics argued that works by Tamayo and his peers Abraham Ángel, Carlos Mérida, and Manuel Rodríguez Lozano presented "new aesthetic principles" that were "universal in tone."[93] Later, in 1929, Mérida opened the Galería de Arte Moderno and gave Tamayo a one-person show, which drew enthusiastic crowds and critical attention.[94] Already critics were proclaiming Tamayo the "leader of a new Mexican school of painting," a role he would increasingly emphasize in his own statements about his art.[95] What was so new about Tamayo's post–New York production? What had New York contributed to his art and how did he marshal these resources within the Mexico City art scene to which he also belonged?

Between his return to Mexico in 1928 and the 1930s, Tamayo embarked on an experimental phase that began to solidify his own approach to art and increasingly established his reputation as an artist willing to challenge the tenets of the Mexican School. Tamayo's New York experiences were crucial to both efforts. His recently acquired firsthand knowledge of modern

European art informed his turn toward classic genres, such as still lifes and nudes, which he reformulated in a Mexican context. While he never formally adopted surrealism by name, he did use its strategies to create works that resisted legible narratives and emphasized the imaginative aspect of art making. His affiliation with the Contemporáneos, an interdisciplinary group of writers, poets, and visual artists, was crucial in this regard. The Contemporáneos questioned the use of art as a political instrument, embraced internationalism, and valued individualism as the cornerstones of national culture. They, along with Tamayo, embraced notions of tradition and universalism as a way to bring the particularities of Mexican culture into communion with international currents.[96] It was during these years that Tamayo began to formulate his alternative vision of *mexicanidad.* Tamayo was just as interested in defining Mexican culture as his contemporaries. Yet the lessons he learned in New York helped him to look at the Mexican past and present in nonlinear, allegorical terms that offered a different perspective on national culture and history.

Among the paintings that Tamayo created when he returned from New York were a series of still lifes and nudes that set out to localize classic art historical genres, especially those redefined by European modernists. *The Yellow Chair* (1929; pl. 8) is an early example of Tamayo's recasting of still life within a Mexican context. The painting depicts an atypical still-life scene. Instead of placing objects on top of a table, Tamayo placed a fruit dish holding apples, pears, and tropical mangoes atop the seat of a yellow-painted chair, the kind that was associated with rural parts of Mexico. The red-and-white fruit dish resembles the style of several varieties of terra-cotta pottery produced throughout Mexico that Tamayo would have seen at the *Exhibition of Popular Arts* in 1921. In a way, the chair and fruit dish play the same role: they both refer to popular art traditions that Tamayo associated with indigenous creativity and which he saw as essentially Mexican. Tamayo captures these objects and their unique coloring, and places them at the very center of his art making. Notably Tamayo both peppers this composition with Mexican referents and hints at the European models that drew his admiration. This might explain the cloth on top of the Mexican dish—it is as if Tamayo were adapting Paul Cézanne's central use of the tablecloth.

Yet the presence of a single domino on the right-hand corner of the chair renders this no ordinary still life. Indeed, the fruit, chair, and domino might all be found in a domestic context; however, the artist's reasons for pairing them are not easily explained. The painting distantly recalls Giorgio de Chirico's incongruent juxtapositions in enigmatic public spaces (see fig. 17). Tamayo seems more interested in uniting disparate things in still lifes that allude to Mexican daily life than in re-creating the atemporal dreamscapes of the Italian master. This is more evident in *Seashells* (pl. 9). With its mix of urban, rural, consumer, and natural objects, the painting may reference Mexico's various regions and their uneven path to modernization.[97]

Tamayo's synthesized approach to art making—referencing Mexican and European elements simultaneously—informed other genres as well. In 1931, Tamayo created several nudes, including *Woman in Grey* (**FIG. 29**) and *Nude* (pl. 11), both of which feature nonwhite models whose large physical proportions recall some varieties of pre-Columbian terra-cotta sculpture. This is especially true of *Woman in Grey*, which pictures a female figure with pointed breasts that echo Nayarit sculptures that Tamayo may have been familiar with (**FIG. 30**). Her figure dominates the composition and evokes monumentality despite

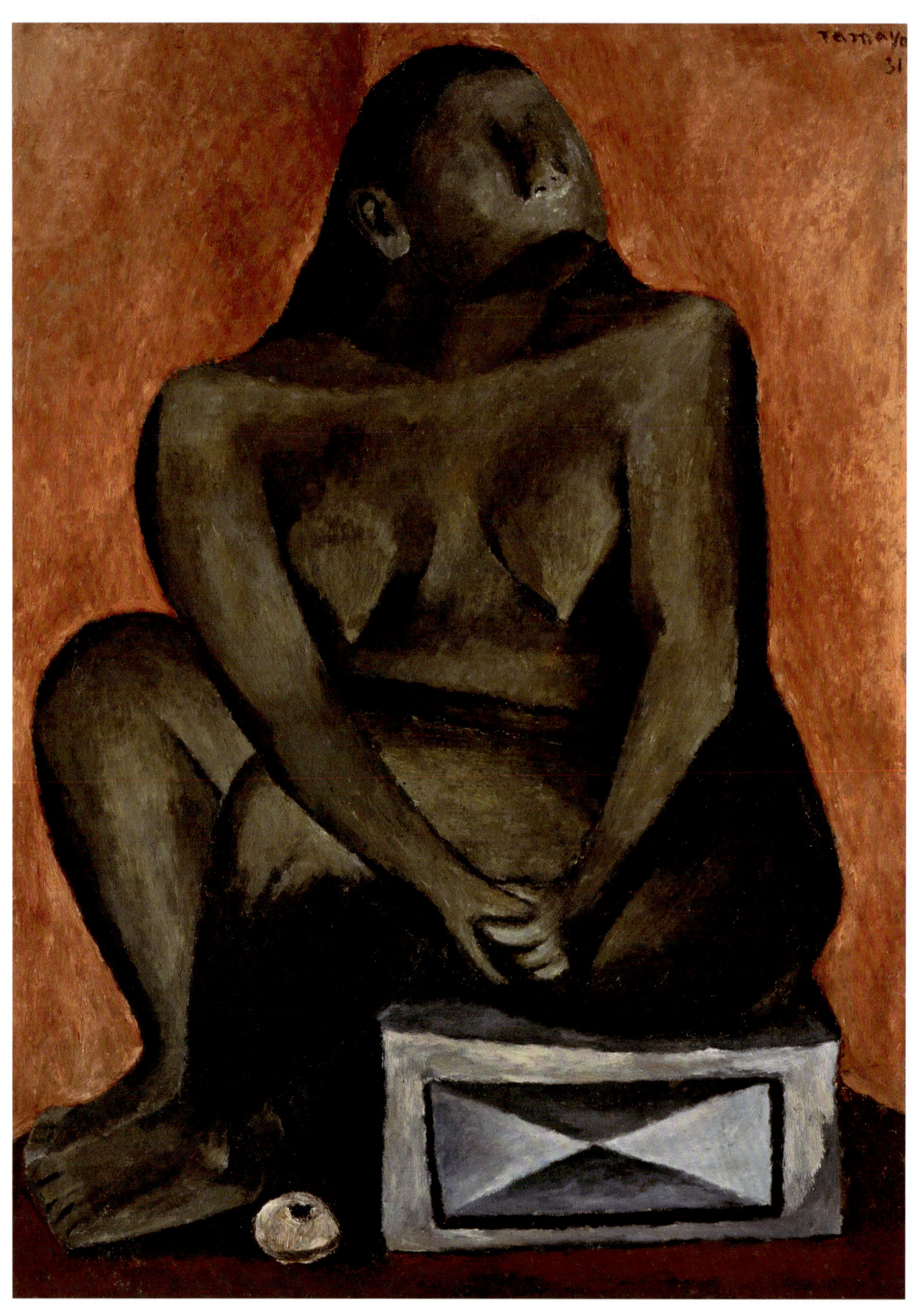
Tamayo
31

FIG. 29 Rufino Tamayo, *Woman in Grey* [*Mujer en gris*], 1931, oil on canvas, 33 3/4 × 24 13/16 in. Museo de Arte Moderno—INBA

FIG. 30 Standing female figure, Nayarit, West Mexico, 300 BC–AD 300, earthenware, 25 1/2 × 9 3/4 × 7 11/16 in. National Gallery of Victoria, Melbourne, Purchased through The Art Foundation with the assistance of Colgate-Palmolive Pty Ltd., Fellow, 1982

the modest size of the canvas. While the figure itself is gray, Tamayo reserved a terra-cotta color for the painting's background. The figure's face, which has no eyes or mouth, is undefined, much like the environment in which she sits. She rests atop a curious box with a geometric design that resembles the unexplained objects commonly seen in the paintings of de Chirico (FIG. 31).

Some scholars have related these works to the primitive nudes of Henri Rousseau and Paul Gauguin.[98] While these relationships may indeed be valid, the work of Matisse may be more relevant here, and especially his well-proportioned nudes set against "Eastern" interiors that Tamayo likely saw in New York (FIG. 32). Whereas *Woman in Grey* conjures a timeless place, *Nude* incorporates specifically Mexican referents. Tamayo, like Matisse, places his nude in a culturally specific space, evoking a rock-covered wall (known as *construcción de careadas*), a common feature in pre-Hispanic and colonial architecture.[99] A brick ledge in the foreground and bordering the figure on either side might reference a modern, industrial period, by contrast. Electrical or telephone wires, which appear in other Tamayo paintings of this period, are presented near the brick ledge and in the background along the landscape. Protected by a dog—perhaps yet another pre-Columbian reference—the sleeping nude is surrounded by a complex evocation of Mexico's past and present.[100] Here Tamayo reveals his own approach. Rather than create narratives that portray different phases of Mexican history, as was done in many mural programs, Tamayo draws on surrealist strategies to take a nonnarrative tactic. He does not depict a specific "heroic" moment in time, but rather presents various historical signifiers for viewers to decipher.

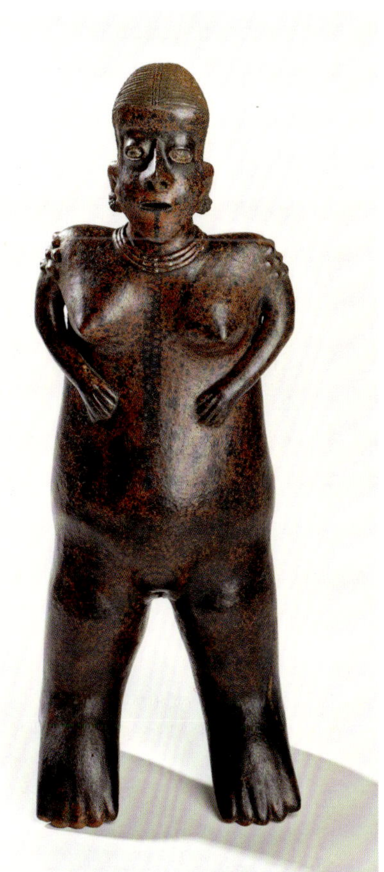

As Tamayo's work and ideas began to circulate in Mexico, he became associated with the Contemporáneos, who hailed artistic individuality and embraced aesthetic experimentation and cosmopolitanism, and who supported Tamayo's own developing ideas. The Contemporáneos disapproved of the muralists' narrative realism and their evocation of Mexican culture solely in relation to peasants, the proletariat, or the Revolution. Their vocal critique of Mexican muralism—which they believed could lead to propaganda—ensured a contentious relationship with several Mexican artists, including Diego Rivera, and to some extent Orozco. Their eponymous journal, *Contemporáneos*, gave a platform to writers, poets, critics, and artists who shared an interest in renovating, not rejecting Western culture.[101] As several scholars have noted, the Contemporáneos circle was one of the first groups to embrace surrealism in Mexico.[102] They, too, championed de Chirico, whose work was discussed and even illustrated in their journal. In

1928 the journal published "Fragmentos sobre Chirico," an article by French writer Jean Cocteau that described de Chirico's work as poetic, nonexact, and nonpicturesque, terms that some critics applied to Tamayo's art as well.[103]

During this time, Tamayo followed de Chirico's example and created works that pictured the artistic act of creation, in effect visualizing his developing philosophy about art making.[104] In works like *Academic Painting* (1935; pl. 14), for instance, Tamayo presented an artist surrounded by many sources of potential inspiration, including figures and things that could be interpreted as national and/or cosmopolitan references. A white nude resting her arm on a classicized urn, a flying victory figure holding a wreath, a flowering shrub, a hanging blue sphere, and a Mexican clown all vie for the artist's attention. Here an artist appears before a canvas portraying a nude in front of a classicized building. Tamayo depicts these representational elements amid framing devices and formal elements such as a drawn-back curtain and a decorative striped border. As viewers we are confronted with two works of art simultaneously—the painting before us and the one represented within the canvas—suggesting an infinite set of aesthetic possibilities.

As his ideas matured and homed in on reinterpreting Mexican modernity beyond the narrative approaches of the muralists, Tamayo allied himself with other Mexican artists who, like him, were pursuing more personal and imaginative paths in their expressions of modern Mexican culture. Tamayo's nonnarrative paintings had something in common with other Mexican artists that Tamayo associated with at this time, especially Manuel Álvarez Bravo and María Izquierdo, who was also affiliated with los Contemporáneos. Tamayo, Álvarez Bravo, and his wife, Lola Álvarez Bravo, had been good friends in the early 1930s,

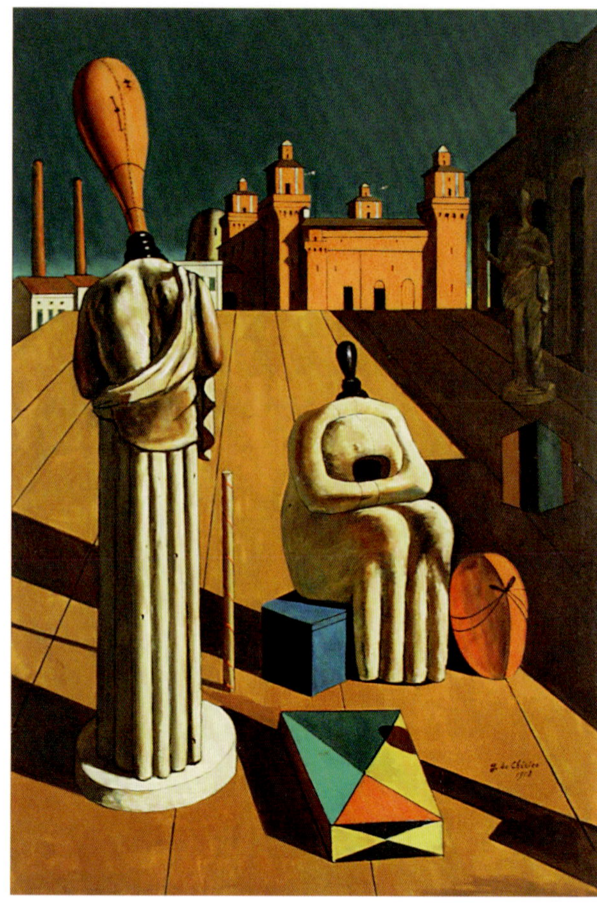

FIG. 31 Giorgio de Chirico, *The Disquieting Muses* (first painted in 1917), 1947, oil on canvas, 38 ½ × 26 ⅛ in. University of Iowa Museum of Art, Gift of Owen and Leone Elliot

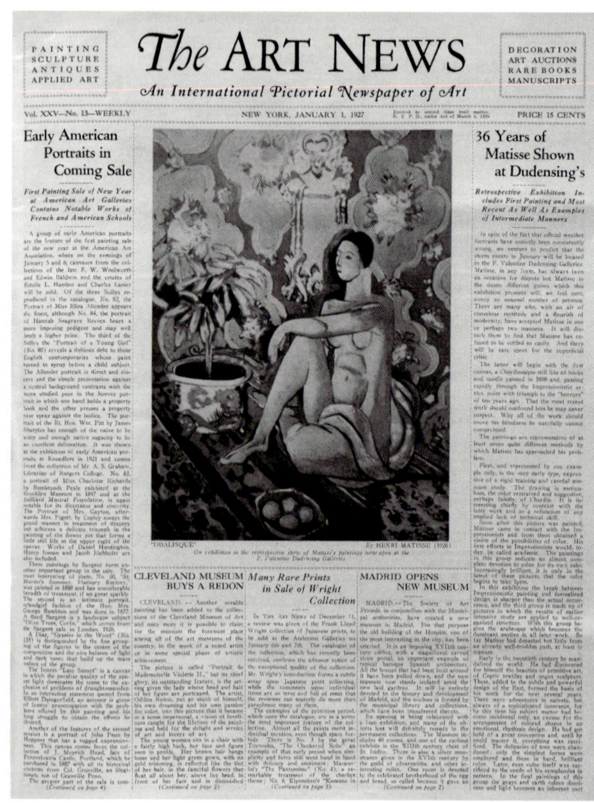

PAINTING SCULPTURE ANTIQUES APPLIED ART

The ART NEWS

An International Pictorial Newspaper of Art

DECORATION ART AUCTIONS RARE BOOKS MANUSCRIPTS

Vol. XXV—No. 13—WEEKLY — NEW YORK, JANUARY 1, 1927 — PRICE 15 CENTS

Early American Portraits in Coming Sale

First Painting Sale of New Year at American Art Galleries Contains Notable Works of French and American Schools

36 Years of Matisse Shown at Dudensing's

Retrospective Exhibition Includes First Painting and Most Recent As Well As Examples of Intermediate Manners

"ODALISQUE" — By HENRI MATISSE (1926)

On exhibition in the retrospective show of Matisse's paintings now open at the F. Valentine Dudensing Galleries

CLEVELAND MUSEUM BUYS A REDON

Many Rare Prints in Sale of Wright Collection

MADRID OPENS NEW MUSEUM

FIG. 32 Review of Henri Matisse exhibition at the Valentine Gallery in New York, *The Art News*, January 1, 1927

FIG. 33 Manuel Álvarez Bravo, *The Dog's House* [*La casa del perro*], 1932, silver gelatin print, 6 3/8 × 8 5/16 in. The J. Paul Getty Museum, Los Angeles

FIG. 34 María Izquierdo, *Amazona blanca* [*White Horsewoman*], 1932, watercolor and gouache on paper, 11 × 8 7/16 in. Blanton Museum of Art, The University of Texas at Austin, Gift of Thomas Cranfill, 1980

when Tamayo was in a relationship with Izquierdo. Together, they gravitated toward Mexican street culture, including *carpas* (tent shows) and other popular celebrations, which opened their eyes to the richness of Mexican daily life.[105] During the 1930s, Tamayo and Manuel Álvarez Bravo created works, including *Waiting Woman* (1936; pl. 22) and *The Dog's House* (FIG. 33), that drew on the quotidian and juxtaposed man-made and natural elements in enigmatic ways. Izquierdo's works, some of which depict female circus performers standing precariously on top of show animals, also appear dreamlike (or nightmarish) given their barren and nondescript environment (FIG. 34). These individual approaches to Mexican daily life stood in contrast to the collective, sociopolitical thrust of muralism.

During the 1930s, Tamayo employed surrealist strategies to reconceive historical subjects that had been treated by the muralists. *Homage to Juárez* (1932; pl. 13), for example, presents an unconventional "portrait" of Benito Juárez, Mexico's first indigenous president who led the country before and after the French occupation. The year before Tamayo painted this canvas, Rivera had just completed the central staircase mural of his Palacio Nacional cycle, which placed the likeness of Juárez at the apex of an epic and compressed view of Mexican history (FIG. 35). In the mural, Juárez is portrayed holding the Constitution of 1857 directly above a violent conquest scene, a pairing that may suggest the eventual "native" triumph over foreign invaders. Rather than recount the history of Juárez, Tamayo's painting offers a representation of his image in public space, and overlays several components: a pedestrian walking in front of the sculpture, a view of two buildings (one modern, the other neoclassical), and a mysterious figure dressed in white running in the street, perhaps chasing the descending *globo de Cantoya*, a festive aerostatic balloon used during Mexican celebrations. These elements suggest a commemorative celebration; however, their disjointedness does not clearly point to reverence for Juárez. In fact, the figure in the foreground stares away

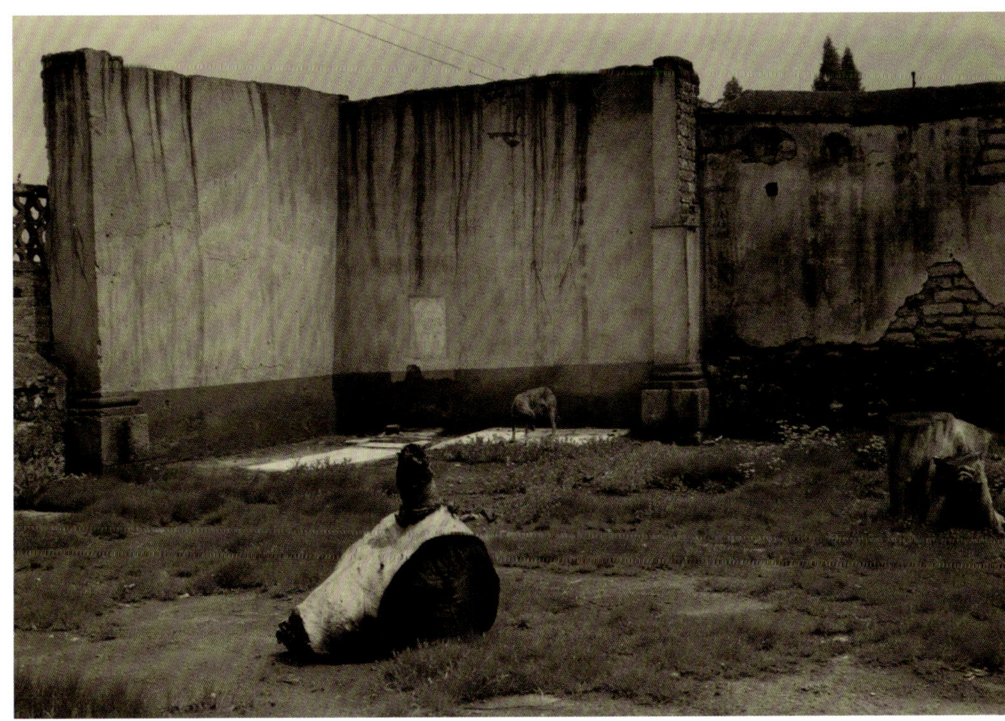

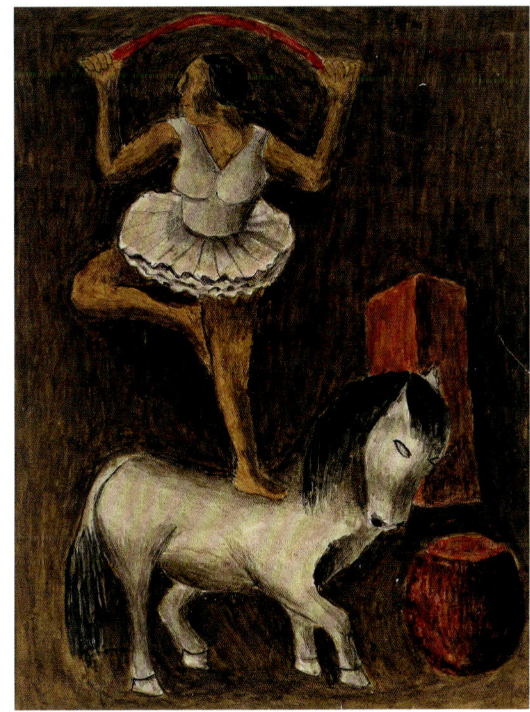

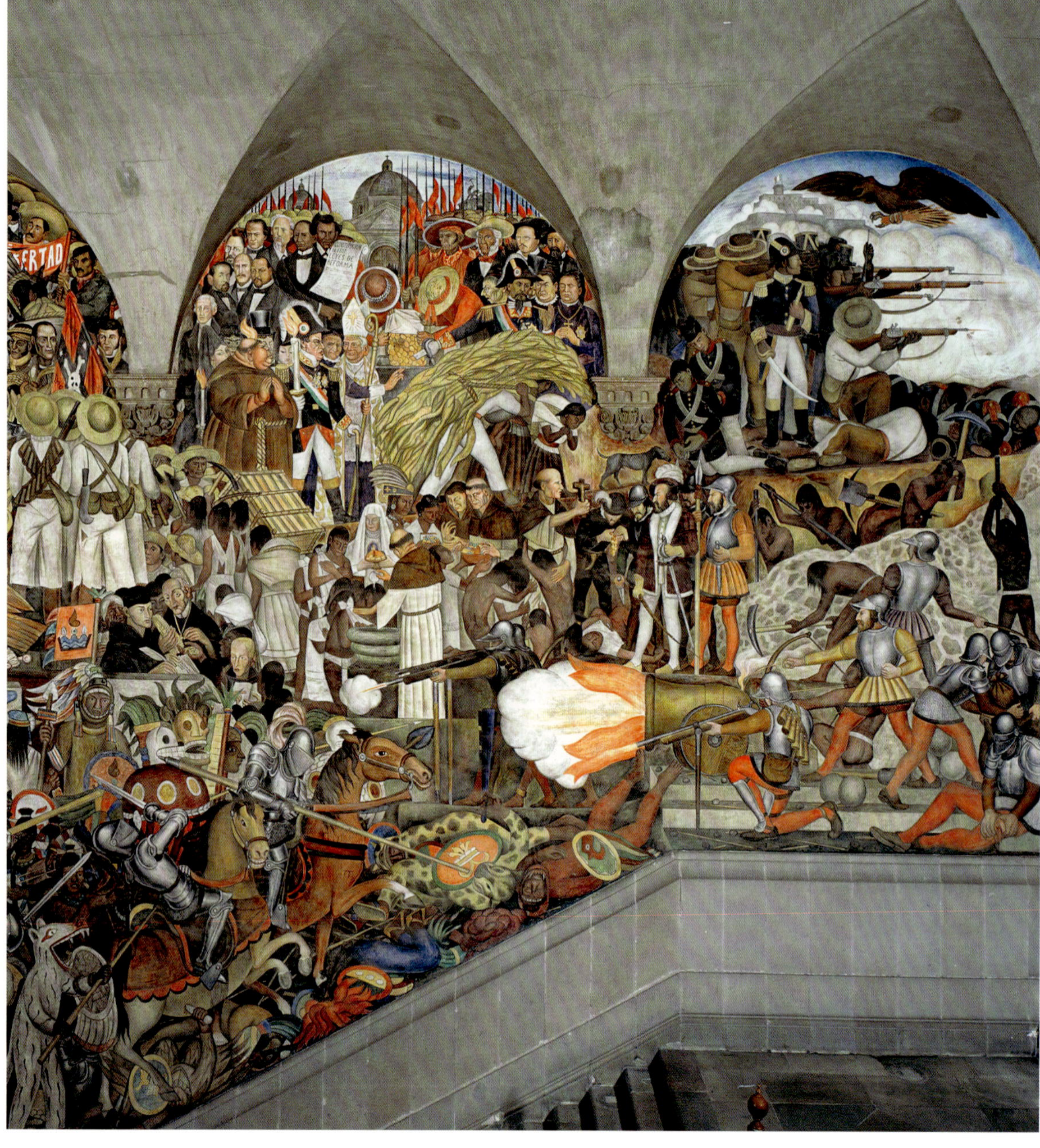

FIG. 35 Diego Rivera, fresco, 1931, central staircase, Palacio Nacional, Mexico City

FIG. 36 Rufino Tamayo, *Song and Music [El canto y la música]* (detail), 1933, Subdirección de Laboratorios y Apoyo Académico (formerly the Escuela Nacional de Música), Mexico City

from the bust, as if she were oblivious to its presence. As others have argued, Tamayo's painting does not proffer the narrative clarity or the celebratory intent of Rivera's mural.[106]

Tamayo also completed his first mural commission in the 1930s, an opportunity that allowed him to present his alternative vision of Mexican modernism in a medium inextricably tied to *Los tres grandes*. Painted on the walls surrounding a staircase at the Escuela Nacional de Música (National School of Music) in 1933, *Song and Music* (FIG. 36) portrays several hieratic allegories standing and floating in shallow space that hold instruments such as horns and mandolins, or have open mouths to evoke singing. In choosing to portray a musical subject through the visual arts, Tamayo evinced the Contemporáneos' interest in the symbolic equivalences between the different branches of art. Tamayo described these figures as Indian and scholars have equated their

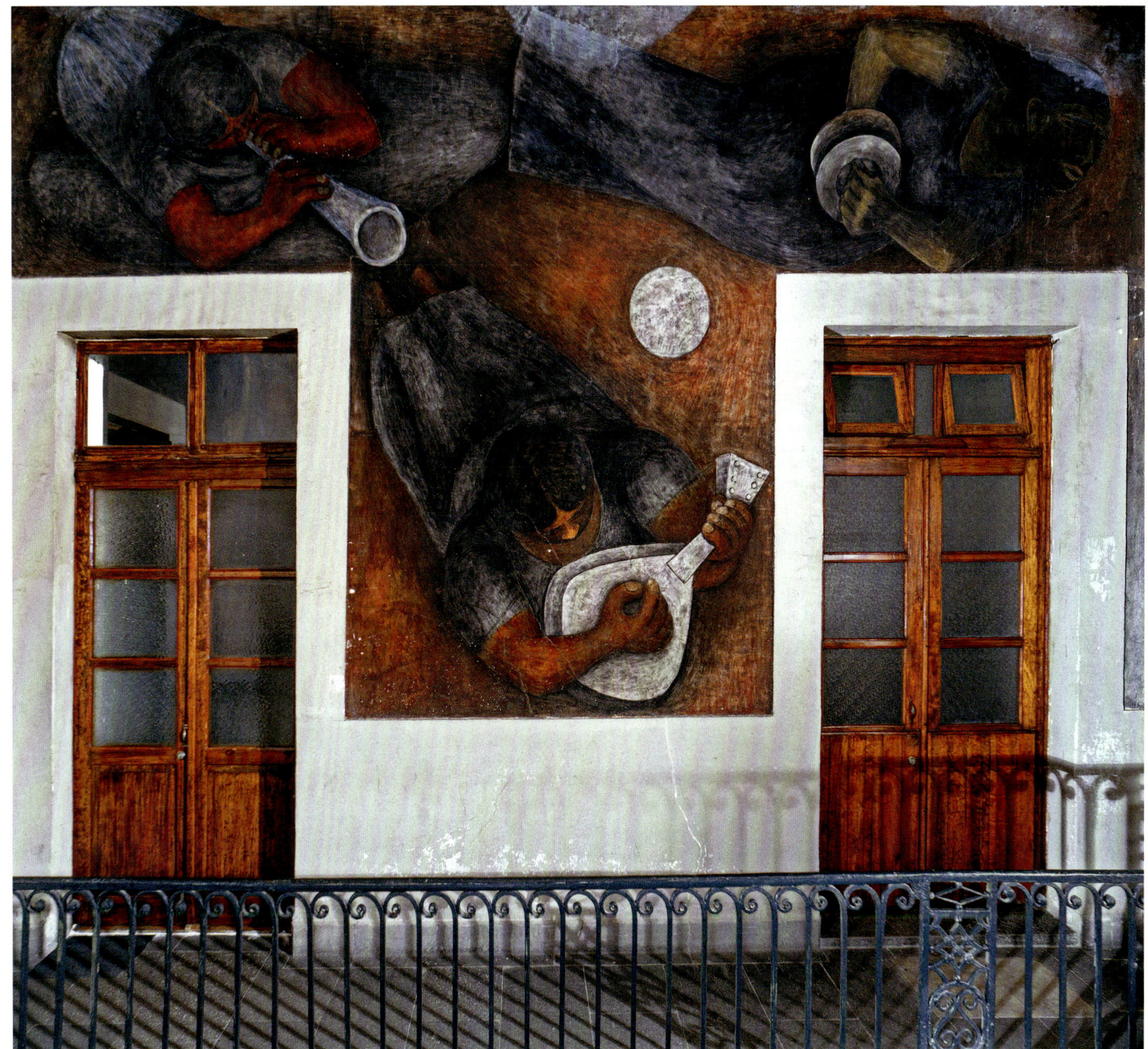

solid physiques with pre-Columbian art. They also bring to mind Tamayo's indigenous nudes of the early 1930s, as does his choice of somber and earth-toned colors. Like other muralists, Tamayo turned to allegory and sought to match his subject to the site, yet the correspondences end there. His female figures are neither sexualized nor anguished as in some murals by Rivera and Orozco, nor does *Song and Music* depict a specific moment in time or personage. Rather, Tamayo depicts allegories immersed in a creative act that unfolds under a moonlit sky in a timeless space. Here, Tamayo's celestial referent dually conjures pre-Columbian astronomy as well as iconic works by de Chirico and Joan Miró, including his *Dog Barking at the Moon* that was in the collection of the Gallery of Living Art, which pictures moons and nighttime scenes.[107]

By the early 1930s, Tamayo had arrived at a working understanding of his artistic goals, so much so that he wrote one of the lengthiest artist statements of his career: "El nacionalismo y el movimiento pictórico" (Nationalism and the Pictorial Movement). As Karen Cordero Reiman has argued, the text offers a sophisticated and atypical picture of Mexico's national artistic scene as one in which Mexican artists represent various ethnic, racial, and even transnational groups.[108] In spite of this diversity, Tamayo believed that mestizo and indigenous cultures were the basis upon which Mexico should derive its unique artistic characteristics. In contrast to "epidemic" approaches to art among the "precursors" of national painting—here Tamayo implies but does not name the Mexican muralists—Tamayo urged a turn to the rudimentary elements of art making, such as color and proportion, which he believed were unique to each racial group: "Differences in color, in the proportions of forms, and in the organization of both characterize or should characterize the plastic production of the different races."[109] As racially essentializing as this pronouncement is, Tamayo advocated for an aesthetic—not thematic—understanding of Mexico's artistic particularities. While concerned with identifying the true plastic elements that could define Mexican expression, he believed Mexican artists should not isolate themselves but instead should be receptive like antennas: "We should forget our foolish egotism that lies behind our nationalist position, to become like an antenna that receives messages from all parts, taking in whatever is beneficial to us."[110]

In Mexico, Tamayo's ideas and works placed him at the center of debates about the nature of Mexican art. The debates focused not only on whether art should be political or nationalist but also on the very nature of artistic representation. Critics like Chano Urueta crystalized Tamayo's position as a Mexican artist deeply dedicated to his artistic medium above all else: "But Tamayo is Tamayo, and he is Mexican to the same extent as any other one of our painters could be. Few have portrayed in such a capable and sensitive fashion the marvelous physical experience (or nature) of the medium [and] of knowledge conveyed by the senses."[111] Others highlighted how Tamayo redefined the subjects of Mexican art, and even found ways to make the formal aspects of his art making Mexican: "[Tamayo is] tremendously Mexican without the pretension of making art nationalist; simple to the point of boldness, not only with respect to his subjects but also in his drawing and even his use of colors."[112]

Tamayo promoted the argument that art and politics should not mix, yet this stance doesn't explain the full range of his work in the 1930s, nor his affiliation with leftist periodicals and groups in both the United States and Mexico. Whereas his ties to the *New Masses* in New York may have been superficial, that was not the case in Mexico, where Tamayo joined the Liga de Escritores y Artistas Revolucionarios, or LEAR, in 1934.[113] LEAR was founded in 1933 as a popular-front organization—Communist Party affiliation was not required for membership—that advocated for the rights of the Mexican working class and combatted fascism at home and abroad. LEAR rose during an especially challenging period in Mexican history, which saw the rise of violent right-wing groups that targeted workers. The intensity of the period was broadly felt; by the mid-1930s, most artists and intellectuals in Mexico were affiliated with LEAR.[114]

Nonetheless, it is hard to reconcile the tone of LEAR's platform, articulated in their six declarative principles, with the arguments Tamayo made about his own art. His dedication to plastic values and a Mexicanism of essence borne out of the study of Mesoamerican and popular art bear little in common with LEAR's focus on class struggle.[115] While Mexican artists had long been radicalized,

FIG. 37 Unknown artist, cover illustration for *Frente a Frente*, January 1935

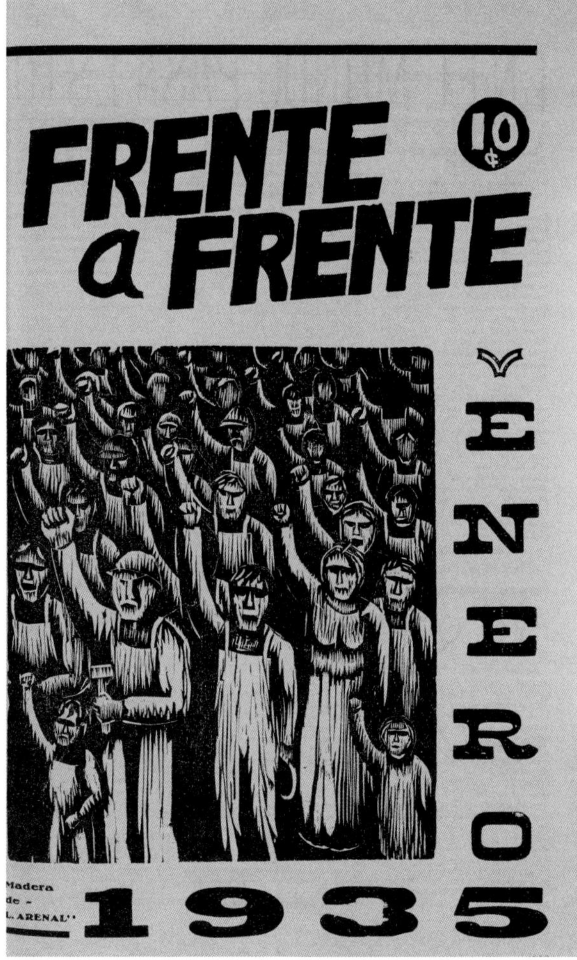

LEAR embraced a strident, class-based Marxist position.[116] LEAR condemned both exploitative capitalist enterprises and the Mexican government's false socialism. Tamayo's own statements imply similar sentiments about the shortfalls of Mexican socialism. For Tamayo, the populist rhetoric of other political groups formed by artists, namely the Technical Workers, Painters, and Sculptors Union of Mexico, to which the muralists belonged, was ineffective since "the Indians and the workers continued to be exploited as always."[117] It appears that the artist did not have the same opinion of LEAR. Photographs in Tamayo's archive suggest that he may have even participated in LEAR protests.[118] He was sympathetic to workers' rights and class dynamics in Mexican society, and he broadly interpreted LEAR's commitment to mount a "widespread intellectual campaign in favor of the great masses of workers and *campesinos*."[119]

In 1935, Tamayo created several paintings that show how he represented the pressing social concerns of Mexican society. Karen Cordero Reiman has eloquently argued that Tamayo's work during this period critically comments on the effectiveness of monumental public art.[120] Some of these works take up a traditional Mexican School subject: labor. *Factory Workers' Movement* (1935; pl. 12) depicts laborers outside a vast industrial factory. In the far background, in front of a chain-link fence, a lone figure stands on a platform, a raised arm urging a call to action. This posture points to a recurring motif in several issues of LEAR's official journal, *Frente a Frente*, including the January 1935 cover, which portrays a sea of men with raised arms (FIG. 37). In the foreground of his painting, Tamayo depicts a large group of workers, some of whom hold *huacales*, handcrafted containers used in Mexico for transporting goods.[121] One of the most compelling features of the painting is the group of workers in the darkened foreground that directly engages the viewer. This is not a sanitized picture of factory labor; the cramped workers are caught in an unwelcoming space. In fact, the foreground is so dark that viewers must strain to perceive several dark-skinned laborers that appear to blend into the environment. The painting does not distance the viewer from the immediate scene; instead the viewer is face-to-face with the harsh realities of the Mexican worker.

The works Tamayo created in Mexico between the late 1920s and the mid-1930s reveal two things. First, that his New York experiences shaped his vision of modern Mexican art. And second, that Mexican history need not be repudiated but embraced on more open-ended terms. In other words, Tamayo embraced notions of *arte puro* not as a rejection of Mexican subjects but as a reformulation of them. His involvement with LEAR, and his experience creating works in response to current events, additionally set an important precedent for Tamayo, which he would take up again when he returned to New York.

RETURN TO NEW YORK In 1936, Tamayo returned to New York for his longest and most significant tenure. He came along with several LEAR colleagues to attend the American Artists' Congress (AAC) (FIG. 38). The AAC was a popular-front organization of artists who aimed to combat worldwide fascism and national crises like the Great Depression. That a Mexican delegation was invited attests to the high regard for Mexican artists in the United States and to the perception that they had something important to contribute to debates about the relationship between art and politics. Tamayo was not a speaker at the event, but his compatriots José Clemente Orozco and David Alfaro Siqueiros both addressed the congress.[122] Orozco's remarks did not lay out a specific prescription for revolutionary art; he instead focused on practical matters related to the artist's relationship to unions, the market, and art schools. Siqueiros discussed the need to experiment with the materials, formats, and sites of revolutionary art. But the event showed Tamayo that Mexican art continued to be relevant to US artists, who were grappling with their own questions about the nature and effectiveness of politicized art, as well as the direction of modern American art. On a practical level, the AAC likely enabled Tamayo to reconnect with his earlier New York acquaintances, like Stuart Davis, who served as the national executive secretary of the AAC.[123] Tamayo and his new wife, Olga, who accompanied him on this visit, had not initially intended to stay long, but their two-week trip turned into a residence that lasted until 1949.[124]

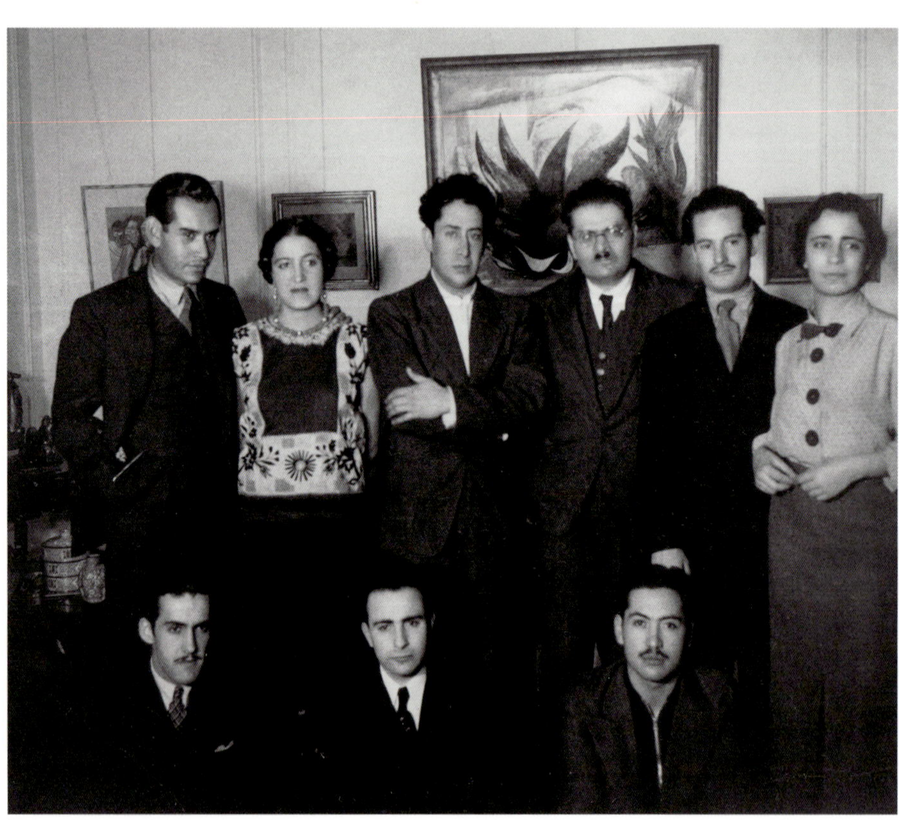

FIG. 38 Mexican delegation to the American Artists' Congress, New York, 1936. Top (left to right): Rufino Tamayo, Olga Tamayo, David Alfaro Siqueiros, José Clemente Orozco, Roberto Berdecio, and Angélica Arenal; bottom: Jesús Bracho, Luis Arenal, and Antonio Pujol. Collection of Sala de Arte Público Siqueiros, Mexico City

This lengthier residence—always peppered by Rufino and Olga's summers in Mexico—would prove decisive for Tamayo's art and reputation.[125] In New York, Tamayo once again immersed himself in a thriving cultural milieu with greater access to European and US art and a local art scene actively debating the value and nature of socially committed modern art. He also found a receptive art market and critical community that was interested in Mexican art and increasingly open to his experimental work and divergence from muralism. Tamayo's art and subjects reveal that he absorbed and responded to the cultural goings-on in the city, especially the heightened presence of the art of Pablo Picasso. He presented his work in galleries and museums in New York and other cities and became a visible actor in the US cultural scene. This thirteen-year period would have its personal and historical crises—such as World War II—that further contributed to a shift in Tamayo's style and subjects. The art he made and the debates that circulated around it garnered the attention of critics, collectors, and institutions that increasingly supported a turn away from the realist and narrative styles that had dominated the Mexican and US art scenes in the 1930s.

Tamayo returned to New York in the midst of the Great Depression and benefited, albeit temporarily, from the federal programs established to support artists, the availability of which may have contributed to his initial decision to stay. In March 1936, one month after having arrived in New York for the AAC conference, Tamayo joined the ranks of the newly established Federal Art Project (FAP), which employed artists to create artwork for public buildings. He applied to paint a WPA mural at Kings County Hospital in Brooklyn, but the work was never realized.[126] Even though foreign nationals were dismissed from the ranks of federal arts programs in 1937, during and after his time with these programs Tamayo created work directly related to his US context, which for the most part obviated direct sociopolitical critique. He returned to subjects tied to the idea of the modern metropolis that had captured his attention in the late 1920s. These works, while forming just a small portion of his creative output of the mid-1930s, reveal the extent to which Tamayo remained committed to experimentation and interested in evoking contemporary history in an open-ended way.

The New York–themed works range from modest watercolors like the street scene *Shower* (1936; pl. 17), created specifically for FAP, to larger oil paintings that represent his other experiences in the city. *Shower* depicts two women, perhaps nurses sporting capes, caught in conversation on a rainy day in New York. James Oles has argued that Tamayo's muted color palette in *Shower* not only recalls the New York canvases of Orozco, which portray alienated pedestrians walking through the concrete streets of the city, but also may convey Tamayo's impressions of the dark days of the Depression.[127] *Ships* (**FIG. 39**), portrays two fishermen, their backs to the viewer, who stare out at a large passenger vessel. It is possible that Tamayo witnessed such a scene during one of his maritime voyages between Mexico and the United States.[128] As in *Factory Workers' Movement* (pl. 12), here Tamayo positions the viewer as a worker looking out on the world. The difference between the modest fishing boat with a chain-link railing and the larger, multitiered boat that the fishermen observe suggests a distinction between the workers and the unseen passengers on the other vessel. Despite the implied class references, Tamayo approaches the scene with a sense of playfulness; he lays out two schematically composed fish in the foreground and signs his name on the lifesaver hung on the railing.

Tamayo also continued to create nonnarrative works that home in on popular culture, in a way offering his own version of American scene painting that sought to capture the daily life and culture of the United States.[129] He remained devoted to still lifes, producing some fanciful examples, like *Three Ice Creams* (1938; pl. 20), that relate to the growing popularity of ice cream in the United States during the late 1930s and early 1940s. This contemporary still life, composed of three goblets of colorful ice cream and an artfully arranged strawberry pie, might be situated in a domestic context, complete with wallpaper and blue and white tasseled curtains. *Strawberry Ice Cream* (1938; pl. 19), one of Tamayo's larger paintings of this period, juxtaposes visual elements of New York cafés where soda fountain drinks were sold. The elements incorporated here—a soda jerk, a child, a checkerboard table, ice cream, and an oval form reminiscent of the ornate mirrors used

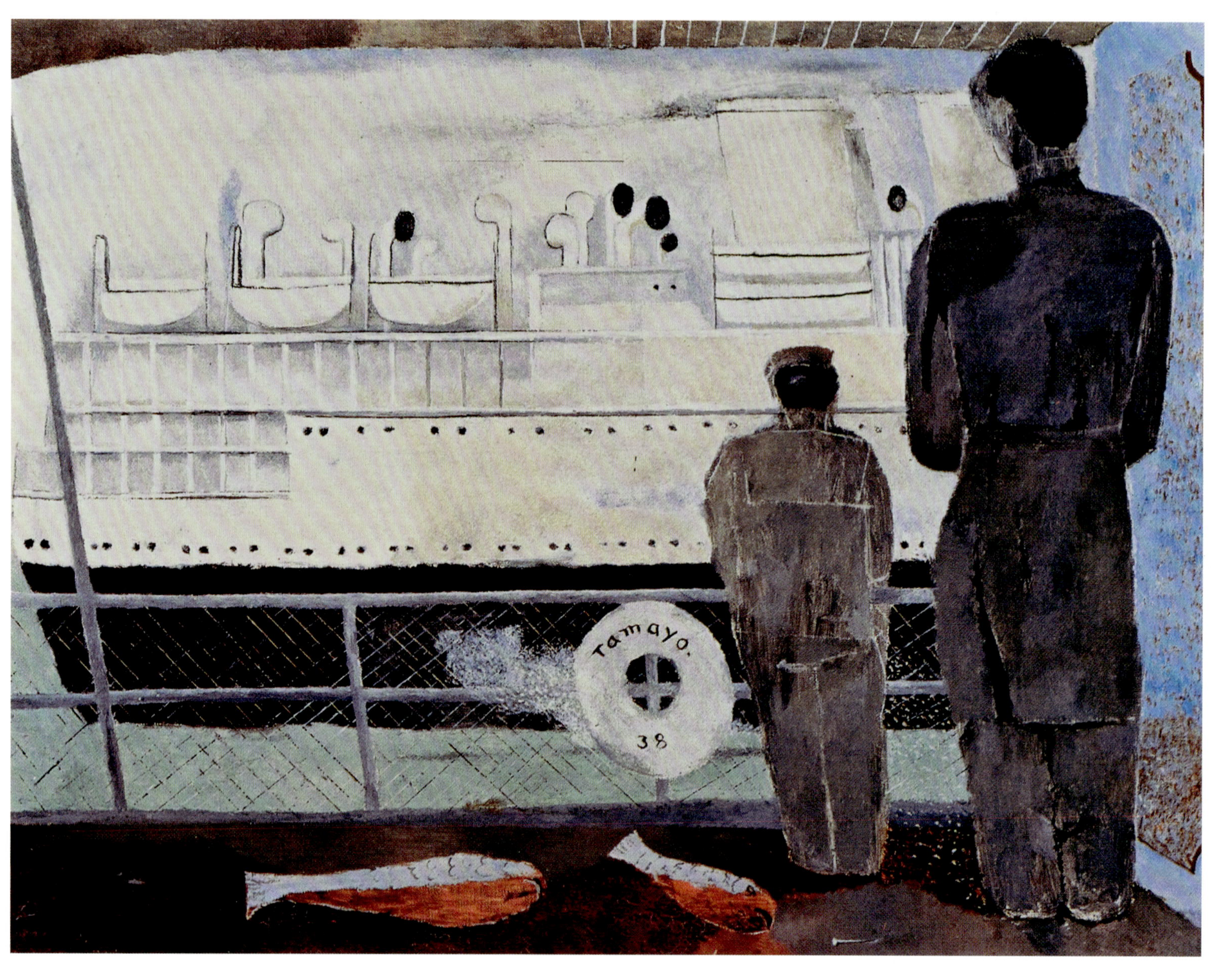
Tamayo.
38

FIG. 39 Rufino Tamayo, *Ships*, 1938, oil on canvas, 17 ¾ × 23 ⅝ in. Collection unknown

FIG. 40 William J. Glackens, *Soda Fountain*, 1935, oil on canvas, 48 × 36 in. Courtesy of the Pennsylvania Academy of the Fine Arts, Philadelphia, Joseph E. Temple Fund and Henry D. Gilpin Fund

in ice cream parlors—appear like episodic fragments, with no strong narrative thread to unite them. The two figures stare out unemotionally at the viewer, conjuring a dazed and disconnected psychological state. Tamayo shared an interest in soda fountain cafés with other New York–based artists, including Guy Pène du Bois and William Glackens.[130] Glackens's impressionistic *Soda Fountain* (FIG. 40), for example, depicts two female patrons eating at a café counter; one wipes her mouth with a napkin and stares out into space, not connecting with the other figures in the scene. While both works capture the psychological experience of modernity, Tamayo models a different approach to American scene painting, one that is less invested in realist narratives or social critique.

For *Carnival* (pl. 16), Tamayo once again turned his attention to Luna Park, an amusement park within Coney Island that was a quintessential symbol of American modernity for many early twentieth-century New York artists. The cacophonous scene features circus performers, spectators, electric lamps, and motifs drawn from the facade of the park entrance (FIG. 41). Here, too, Tamayo tackles a favorite subject of many New York–based artists, including his acquaintance Reginald Marsh. In works like *Wonderland Circus, Sideshow, Coney Island* (FIG. 42), Marsh represented Coney Island as a place of carnal freedom, interracial contact, and seedy underworlds.[131] The heightened sexuality of the women, in their form-fitting dresses, skirts, and tops, is to a lesser extent implied in Tamayo's gouache, which includes two feminized forms propped up above and behind the spectators in the midground of the painting. Dressed in white bathing suits, the figures resemble mannequins and could reference the beauty pageants held periodically at the park.[132] *Carnival* echoes Marsh's compositional density and interest in the multiracial visitors to the park, yet Tamayo balances his attention on the visitors and the physical features of the park itself. His inclusion of a billowing US flag suggests that he may have sought to depict an iconic emblem of US national culture and modernity. Rather than a satirical vision of the comingling of different social classes in US culture, Tamayo takes artistic license to imagine a fantastic scene featuring large crescent moons and enormous clowns.

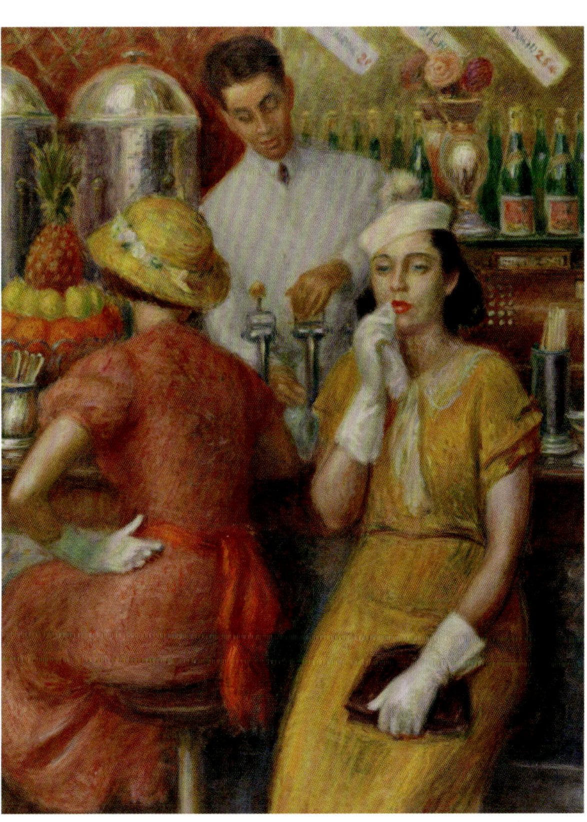

While some critics praised Tamayo's New York–themed works for their synthesis of School of Paris styles with the subjects of modern life, others had a hard time reconciling these works with his Mexican background, revealing their desire for overt "Mexican" subjects and their narrow expectations of Mexican artists. A *New York Sun* critic, for instance, commented, "Tamayo is at present a resident of New York and must be considered a welcome visitor, although for his own sake, he must not prolong

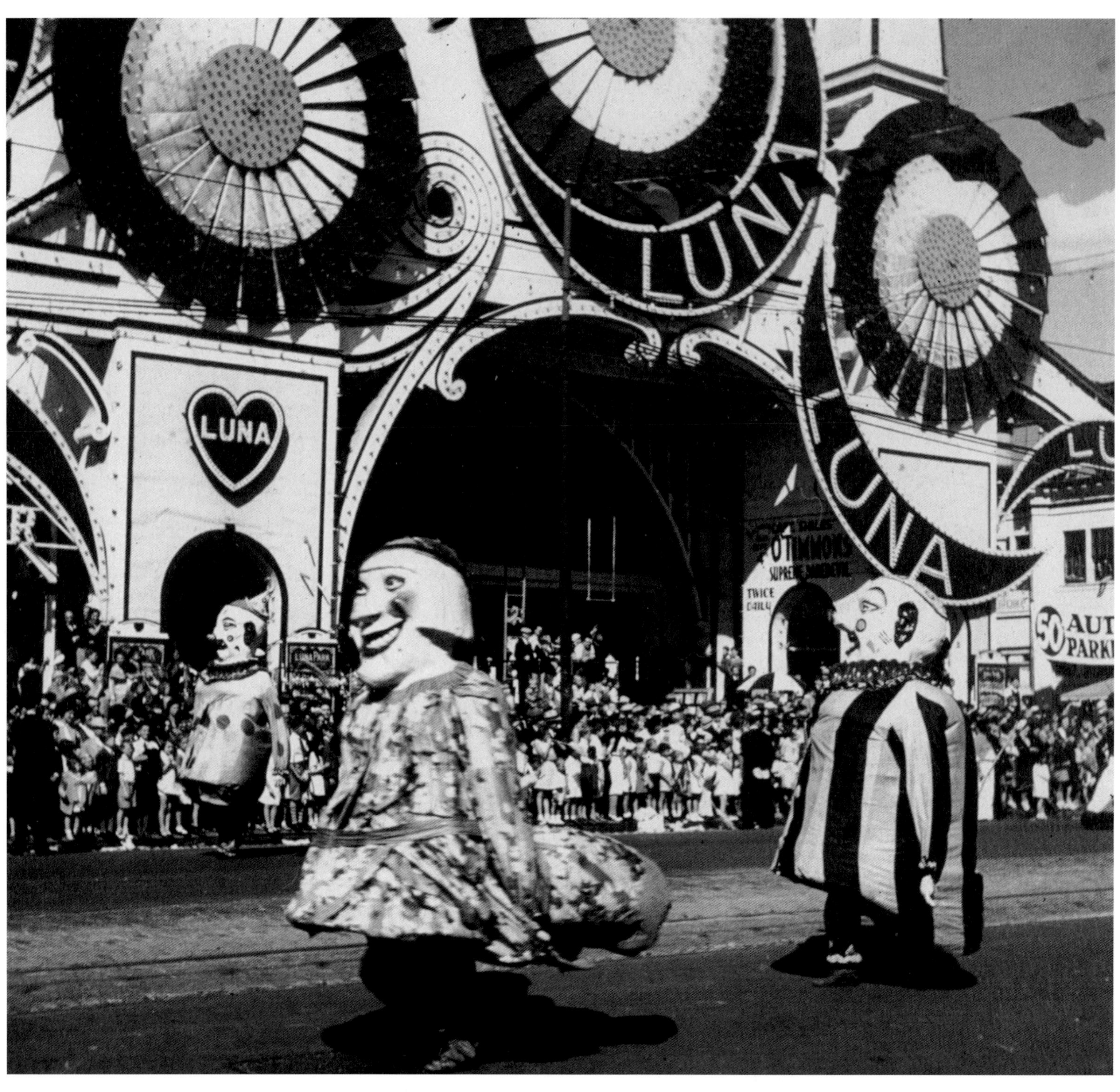
LUNA
LUNA
LUNA
TWICE

the visit."[133] Another found Tamayo's strawberries, watermelons, and ice cream "not so tempting."[134]

Although some critics did not appreciate them, Tamayo's New York–themed works offer insight into what he made of his time in the city. *New York Seen from the Terrace* (1937; pl. 18), his most iconic canvas from this period, encapsulates his approach to the city as a place where he could display and expand his own ideas about art making. Edward Sullivan identifies the male figure on the right as Tamayo holding a monocular and taking in a focused view of the skyline. In the middle ground, Tamayo depicts his wife, Olga, soaking in a panoramic view.[135] The painting registers Tamayo's continued fascination with the modernity of this American city, conveyed by the presence of skyscrapers and an American flag.[136]

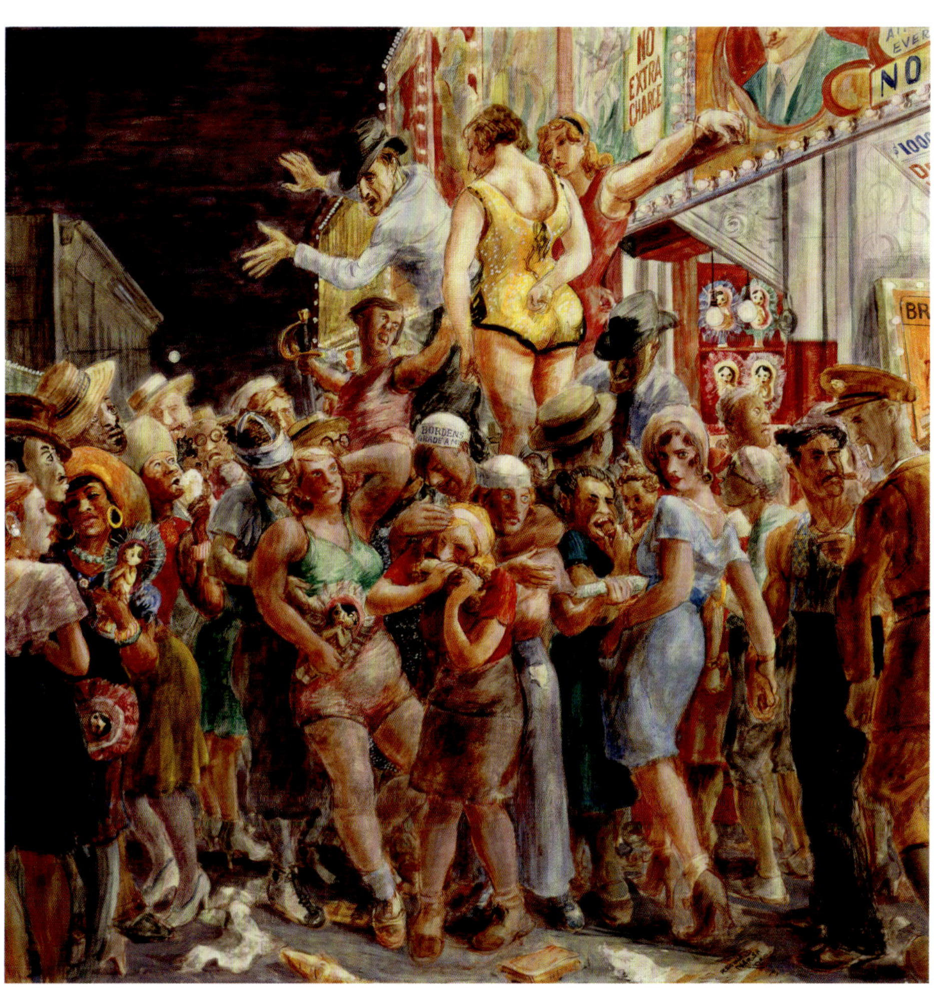

FIG. 41 Parade outside Luna Park on Coney Island, New York, n.d.

FIG. 42 Reginald Marsh, *Wonderland Circus, Sideshow, Coney Island*, 1930, tempera on canvas stretched on Masonite, 48 ¾ × 48 in. Collection of The John and Mable Ringling Museum of Art, the State Art Museum of Florida, Florida State University, Museum Purchase, 1976

The tall, gray monoliths suggest the exterior metal cladding of then-recently built skyscrapers like the Empire State Building (1931) or the Chrysler Building (1930), but do not depict these or other known buildings. Other structures are playfully rendered with red stripes or graphic patterns. Tamayo peppers the composition with white, de Chiricoesque spheres spread on the terrace floor, adding a playful element that reifies the painting's status as an artistic representation. This imagined urban vista is juxtaposed with a still-life arrangement: two large watermelon slices resting on a table. Like the artist and his wife, the watermelons can stand as a Mexican referent; the fruit has been associated with Mexican still-life painting since at least the nineteenth century. Tamayo, in effect, stages an encounter between Mexican and cosmopolitan culture. Here the fruit and the buildings are equivalent: both are sources of artistic inspiration that the artist arranges at will. Much like *Academic Painting* (pl. 14), *New York Seen from the Terrace* is a painting about the act of artistic creation. He absorbs his world, but does not faithfully represent it.

New York Seen from the Terrace powerfully demonstrates the extent to which Tamayo's vision of the city differed from that of his Mexican peers. Diego Rivera represented the New York skyline in *Frozen Assets* (FIG. 43), likely the most controversial portable mural presented at his MoMA retrospective in the early 1930s.[137] Here Rivera presents a cross section of downtown New York City life. In between horizontal registers that capture views of impressive skyscrapers, which may represent the economic power of capitalism, and bank vaults that store financial assets, Rivera depicts hordes of working class New Yorkers waiting for a subway and countless homeless people asleep in a wharf. Tamayo's ample terrace could of course allude to middle- and upper-class life, but his vision of the city is devoted to formal experimentation rather than biting social critique. Tamayo's playful skyscraper view is also a far cry from Orozco's dark, alienated depictions of New York, which he created during his residence in the city between 1927 and 1934. In 1930, on the heels of the stock market crash of 1929, Orozco created his own skyscraper painting, *The Dead* (FIG. 44), an allegorical urban landscape of fallen and crumbling buildings that suggests the end of prosperity.[138] The three paintings lay out distinct perspectives on New York—two deeply critical and the other a personal and artistic vision that celebrated US modernity.

The style and subject of *New York Seen from the Terrace* also suggest that Tamayo was somewhat more aligned with his New York, rather than his Mexican, peers.[139] His brief affiliation with the Federal Art Project led to his participation in several federal exhibitions, including *New Horizons in American Art* at the Museum of Modern Art in 1936, where he undoubtedly saw several of Berenice Abbott's *Changing New York* photographs (FIG. 45). Like Tamayo, Abbott captured elevated views of New York that revealed the city's ambitious and historically diverse architecture. She includes both skyscrapers and shorter (and older) brick and stone buildings to convey how the city had physically—and by extension socially—changed. Tamayo's canvas is less historically minded, even though he, too, includes a red building with a top-story arcade that was common in late nineteenth-century buildings like the Puck and De Vinne Press Buildings near Greenwich Village.[140] Tamayo was also likely familiar with the shaped canvases of Charles Green Shaw that rendered the tall architecture of the city into colorful rectangular forms that to some extent resemble some of Tamayo's abstracted and minimally embellished skyscrapers were it not for Shaw's crisply painted and unmodulated geometric style (FIG. 46).[141]

Although it's difficult to read strident political critique in Tamayo's New York–themed work, the artist was still interested in capturing the American scene in open-ended ways that echoed his approach to Mexican subjects earlier in the 1930s. Interestingly, references to Harlem and African Americans in New York do not figure strongly in Tamayo's work, a surprising fact given his personal friendship with Covarrubias. Through Covarrubias and African American artists' own travels to Mexico, Tamayo met several Harlem Renaissance artists, including Aaron Douglas, Langston Hughes, and James Van Der Zee. Rufino and Olga were even photographed by Carl Van Vechten, the well-known artist, writer, and Harlem patron. Tamayo likely heard Aaron Douglas's address at the AAC, which criticized the superficial and caricatured treatment of African American subjects in American art and culture.[142] One Tamayo painting that represents a dark-skinned family of three may represent a black family, although its ambiguities raise more questions than answers (1936; pl. 21). Even though Tamayo's approach to skin color was never literal, depicting dark-complexioned people in a painting presented in New York could signify African Americans—even if critics never caught on to this possible allusion. Since Tamayo was known to depict himself and other Mexicans with dark brown skin and was probably cognizant of the existence of Afro-Mexicans, it is impossible to read his dark-complexioned figures definitively as either Mexican or African American.[143] The drawn-back curtains that frame the family grouping recall the conventions of studio photography, a popular art form that had long inspired Tamayo and which was also embraced by the African American community in New York at that time. The humble nature of the figures' attire and environment, however, diverges from the expressly middle-class studio portraits of James

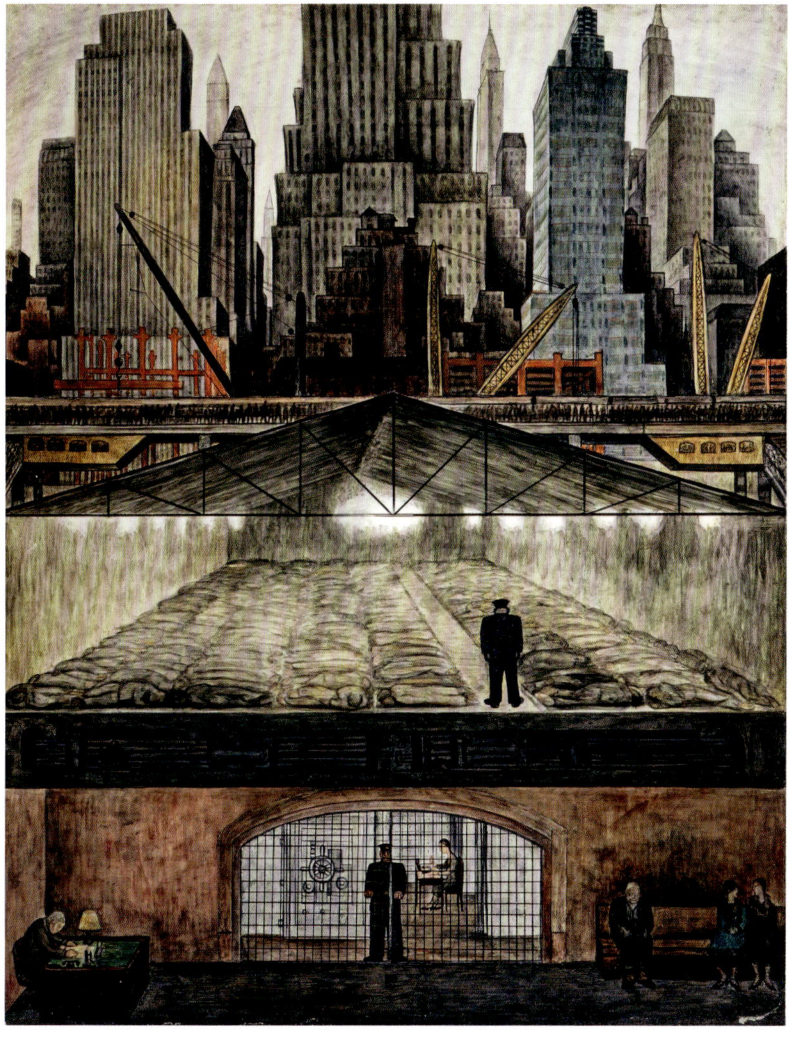

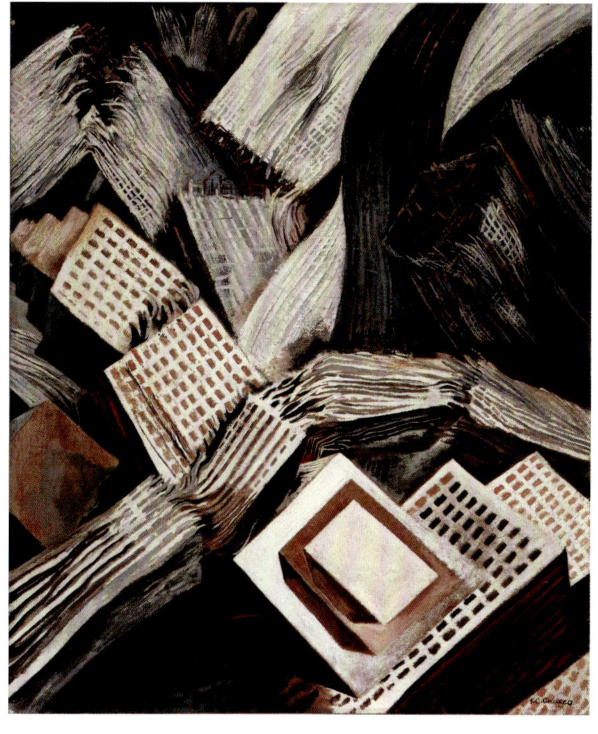

FIG. 43
Diego Rivera, *Frozen Assets*, 1931, fresco on reinforced cement in a galvanized-steel framework, 94 1/8 × 74 3/16 in. Museo Dolores Olmedo, Xochimilco, Mexico

FIG. 44
José Clemente Orozco, *The Dead*, 1930, oil on canvas, 26 7/8 × 22 1/4 in. Colleción Museo de Arte Carrillo Gil–INBA, Mexico City

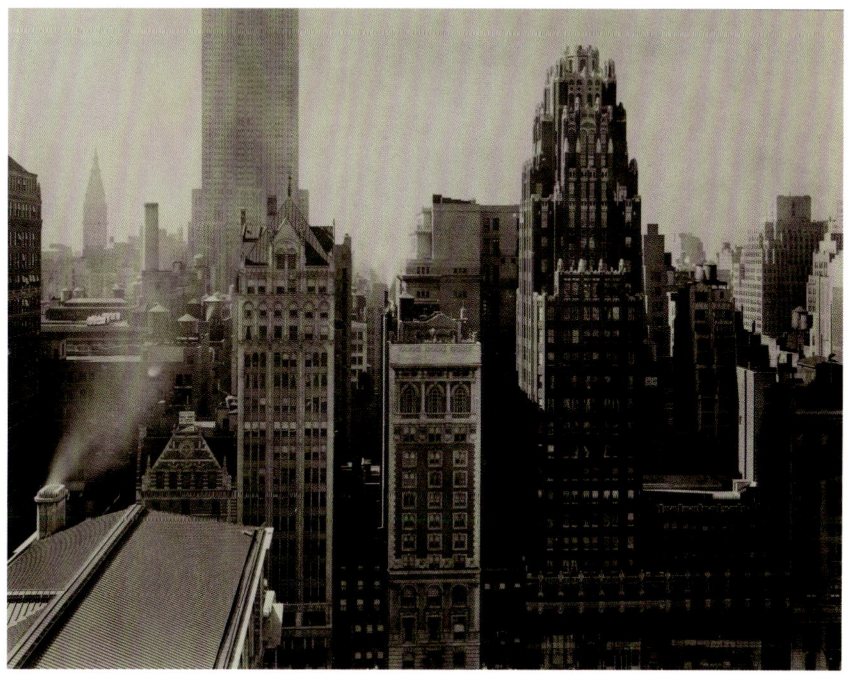

FIG. 45
Berenice Abbott, *40th Street between Fifth and Sixth Avenues, Manhattan*, September 8, 1938, 8 × 10 in. Museum of the City of New York

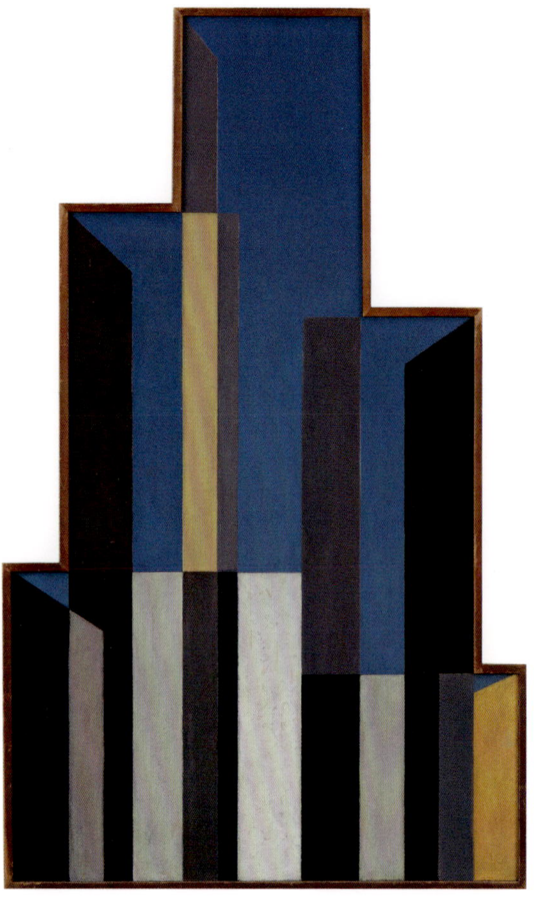

FIG. 46 Charles Green Shaw, *Polygon*, 1937, oil on wood panel, 36 ¼ × 22 ¼ in. Weatherspoon Art Museum, The University of North Carolina at Greensboro, Gift of Mr. and Mrs. Herbert S. Falk Sr., 1973

Van Der Zee and the more informal photographs available for purchase in places like Coney Island that tended to represent a single sitter.[144] *The Family* may relate to Tamayo's exposure to African Americans, even if the painting's ambiguous elements—the circular toy hanging in the sky, a bird perched on the roof of a building in the background, and the expressionless faces of the three figures—make it hard to place culturally or geographically.

While painting his New York–themed works, Tamayo continued to delve into Mexican subjects, using his signature nonnarrative approach that differed from the politicized and working-class subjects of the muralists. *The Pretty Girl* (1937; pl. 23), which was inspired by a studio photograph of a young Olga Tamayo and her sister (FIG. 47), pictures a young girl with a blank stare standing amid incongruous objects and elements: a classicized column and railing, a water jug, spools of thread on the ground, a flying bird, and a small Mexican flag waving on a flagpole. While some of these elements may relate to childhood, their placement together in a barren and unspecified environment renders them enigmatic. The figure's formal attire, nonetheless, suggests a middle-class subject, quite distinct from Rivera's portraits of poor children where they stand barefoot on the street and stare uncomfortably at the viewer.

Tamayo's distinct approach to Mexican subjects is exemplified by his *Tehuana* series, which depicts a revered female icon of Mexican culture (pls. 24–26). Tehuanas, native women from the Tehuantepec region who headed matrilineal societies, became potent national symbols in Mexican art starting in the early twentieth century. Later prominent Mexican women, including Frida Kahlo, Rose Covarrubias, and Olga Tamayo, adopted their dress as a means to express their class, gendered, and/or nationalistic allegiances. Tamayo's Tehuanas, while they do retain references to their distinctive ensembles and braided hair, are also fields on which the artist plays with color, composition, and even the application of paint on its support. *Women of Tehuantepec* (1939; pl. 26), the most ambitious and stately of the three canvases, suggests a fruit market, but the force of the painting rests on its vibrant color and composition. It is arranged like a stage set, with layers of rectangular forms that recede into the shallow distance. Tamayo's paint spills outside of the outlines of the objects they describe. Another painting, *Woman* (1938; pl. 25), achieves a similar effect. Within an architectural space featuring pink columns and a green sky, three figures balancing fruit baskets on their heads parade through a street. The skirt of the most visible figure on the left is so abstractly painted that it gives the impression of unfinished canvas dripping with paint. Mystery suffuses *Two Women*

(1939; pl. 24), where the figures walk through a dark and moody landscape with gray mountains and a large diagonal earth-toned wall. Gone are the symbolist resonances of Saturnino Herrán's 1914 *Tehuana* (see fig. 2) or Rivera's ethnographic and exotic realism (see fig. 8). Instead, geometry, mood, and textured paint dominate.

Tamayo was productive in New York in the 1930s and 1940s in part because he found both work and gallery representation that afforded him a level of financial security. Perhaps his greatest anchor was his teaching position at the Dalton School, an elite college preparatory school located on the Upper East Side of Manhattan. He obtained this job in 1938 as a result of his Latin American network.[145] Later, in the 1940s, Tamayo also ran a painting workshop at the Brooklyn Museum Art School. For a brief period in 1937, he joined the Julien Levy Gallery, a highly respected venue for surrealist art in New York in the 1930s. One of his longest commercial affiliations was with the Valentine Gallery, a prestigious gallery that represented both US and European artists. Between 1939 and 1947, he had six solo shows at the Valentine Gallery, almost one per year. After the Valentine Gallery closed in the late 1940s, Tamayo briefly joined Pierre Matisse, before moving to the celebrated Knoedler Gallery, which would represent him through the early 1960s. Despite the mixed accounts of his commercial success during his years at Valentine, Tamayo's gallery representation provided a steady and visible venue for his art in the city.[146]

The criticism generated by Tamayo's exhibitions helps illuminate not only perceptions of his art but also the shifting opinions about Mexican art during this period. Critics either routinely called out Tamayo for separating art from politics, or reveled in the formal qualities of his art. Henry McBride, an important New York critic who would write repeatedly about Tamayo's art, highlighted how Tamayo relied "completely upon painting as a means of expression," and that he was "unaware of politics and propaganda."[147] As if speaking directly about *Women of Tehuantepec*, another critic appreciated Tamayo's architectural design: "The Tamayo canvases then, are compositions chiefly notable for their superb design and thrilling use of color. They are rather architectural in construction, planes and volumes being manipulated with careful regard for their relationships to each other. The result is an almost monumental dignity."[148] Emily Genauer reflected on Tamayo's connections to the School of Paris. She described *The Family* as "a big group recalling the sound architectural principles of Cézanne, but much more fantastically imaginative in detail and general effect."[149] These kinds of responses cemented Tamayo's reputation as an artist working in a very different way than his

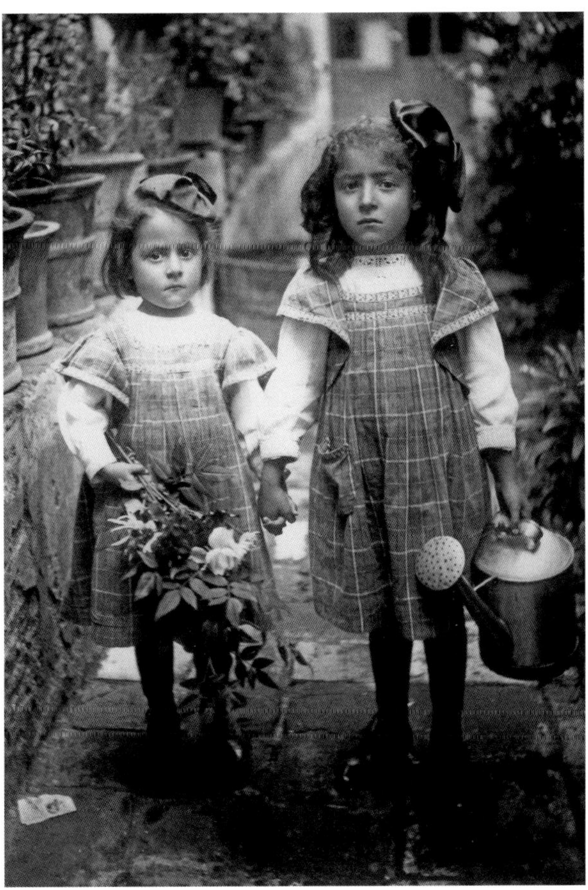

FIG. 47 Childhood picture of Olga Rivas (right) with her sister, Déborha, date unknown. Tamayo Archive, Museo Tamayo, Mexico City

most prominent Mexican contemporaries—*Los tres grandes*.

Framing Tamayo's art as surrealist was also a common feature of critical reviews. This association stemmed, in part, from Tamayo's own reliance on enigmatic juxtapositions and his association with the Julien Levy Gallery and other promoters of surrealism in the United States, like Howard Putzel.[150] Surrealism gave critics another framework to distinguish Tamayo from his Mexican contemporaries. Eleanor Jewett's review describes Tamayo as "one of the few Mexicans who is heading more toward surrealism than propaganda."[151] The surrealist claim, however, had another side as well, since it allowed critics to cast Tamayo the person as a racial primitive. Writing in 1937, for instance, Howard Devree saw "both abstract and surrealist tendencies" in Tamayo's work, yet still claimed that these approaches had not "overwhelmed the primitive in him."[152] Howard Parker found a way to tie Tamayo's surrealism to his Mexican or indigenous background: "Many of Tamayo's paintings can be called surrealistic, which is to say symbolistic: but the inclusion of a degree of mysticism… never interferes with the visual esthetic concept. He is a mystic because that is in his nature—even, perhaps, his blood."[153] As Michael Leja has discussed, the modernist primitivism of nonwhite artists like Tamayo was generally attributed to their innate "race"—implied in Parker's allusion to blood—and not the artist's own aesthetic choices or intellectual interests.[154] This association drew the attention of New York–based artists, like the burgeoning abstract expressionists, who valued so-called primitive art as an inspirational source for contemporary art.

Already in the late 1930s, US-based critics compared Tamayo to his Mexican peers in ways that favored Tamayo over his muralist contemporaries. J.S., likely Joseph Solman, editor of the leftist journal *Art Front*, for example, called for a revaluation of the Mexican Renaissance, noting that Rivera's work now looks "inflated" and Siqueiros's work is "sheer bombast." Tamayo, alternatively, "has patiently furrowed an art, fragile, tenebrous, which soars above the work of most of his compatriots.… Tamayo is the most lyrical voice to come out of that country."[155] Even as the critic references Mexican peasants, he tends to speak of Tamayo's motifs—architecture, machines, landscapes, silent ruins—rather than the politics of his art.

As large exhibitions of Mexican art continued to be organized during this period—encouraged by the cultural dimensions of Franklin D. Roosevelt's Good Neighbor Policy that worked to strengthen US political influence in Latin America during World War II—critics began to view Mexican muralism as a movement of the past, and Tamayo's art as part of the future. Nowhere is this more visible than in Henry McBride's review of MoMA's 1940 blockbuster exhibition, *Twenty Centuries of Mexican Art*.[156] The enormous show encompassed the full range of Mexican visual expression—pre-Columbian art, colonial paintings and architectural models, Mexican popular art, and contemporary art, including portable frescoes by Rivera and Orozco. McBride was clear in his dislike of what he called "the loud and too-much inflated and too-little ballasted political murals.… There are signs that they are begin[ning] to wear thin." He goes on to launch a full-throated critique of Rivera, Orozco, and Siqueiros, before ending with an enthusiastic endorsement of Tamayo. "[Among] these living Mexicans it is Tamayo who carries aesthetics the furthest. He may be as political as the rest of them for all that I know, but when he paints he is not a politician but an artist. His 'Pretty Girl' is a delightful picture."[157] By the time the Philadelphia Museum organizes its survey of contemporary

Mexican art in 1943, curator Henry Clifford places Mexican artists into two generations, the first comprising the muralists, and the second comprising easel painters, including Tamayo. The shift argued in these interpretations—away from sociopolitical realism toward something else—becomes even more dramatic when Tamayo reaches a turning point in his art that places him in the orbit of a burgeoning generation of US artists that were also eager to reorient the direction of contemporary art in the United States.

TAMAYO, PICASSO, AND MIDCENTURY AMERICAN ART In 1939 the New York art world witnessed two seismic events that drew the attention of many artists, including Tamayo: the presentation of Pablo Picasso's *Guernica* (FIG. 48) at Tamayo's very own Valentine Gallery, and the Picasso retrospective at MoMA.[158] "This [*Guernica*'s showing] is the most sensational event in a season," wrote art critic Henry McBride, "that has not been too prodigal with excitements, and to see it is an obligatory experience."[159] The showing of *Guernica* and its related preparatory drawings along with the MoMA retrospective offered an unprecedented and thorough presentation of the famed artist's career. A dramatic "before and after" change takes place in Tamayo's art after his encounter with Pablo Picasso in the late 1930s. Tamayo's ensuing work marks a pivotal aesthetic and conceptual turn in his art, which leads to more visibility and acclaim.

Tamayo learned about Picasso by studying his art and by absorbing the pointed responses it engendered.[160] Robert Goldwater anointed Picasso a "master who represents his age in many of its finest and most disquieting aspects," and wondered if it was possible that any other artist could pick up from where Picasso left off.[161] Other critics shifted in a different direction, addressing how Picasso navigated the relationship between art and politics. Henry McBride balanced a keen attention to *Guernica*'s subject with his thoughts about what it meant for the debate about the relationship between art, politics, and propaganda:

> *Death and destruction are furiously indicated and the gestures of victims have largeness and ferocity unequaled in art since medieval times. This sounds like propaganda and in fact the picture was intended to be as such, but it ended in being something vastly more important—a work of art. Picasso is an ardent communist and in painting "Guernica" he was attacking Franco with might and main, but the futility of propaganda in the hands of an artist is once more illustrated, for always in the case of the good artist the genius of the painter takes charge of the situation and the politician in him disappears in the effort to turn out a good picture. . . .*[162]

Picasso's success at combating so-called artistic propaganda with a superbly aestheticized variety of representational art must have felt reassuring to Tamayo, who had long led the charge against the legible and narrative tendencies of Mexican muralism. *Guernica*, of course, had tragic, narrative passages that conveyed the story of the senseless bombing—a mother holding a dead child, flames emanating from the roof of a building, a victim sprawled on the ground—yet these elements were interspersed with symbolic motifs, especially Picasso's emotive horse, which elevated representation beyond the specificities of a single moment in history. Critic Elizabeth McCausland put it this way: "[Picasso] turned his gaze outward, away from the depths of subjective experience, to the tragedies of social experience."[163] Tamayo likely absorbed how critics acknowledged Picasso's efforts to both address and transcend his native Spanish history. Reencountering this Picasso—and not the 1920s Picasso of Tamayo's youth—must have led Tamayo

FIG. 48 Pablo Picasso, *Guernica*, 1937, oil on canvas, 137 3/8 × 305 1/2 in. Museo Nacional Centro de Arte Reina Sofía, Madrid

FIG. 49 Rufino Tamayo, *Woman with Pineapple* [*Mujer con piña*], 1941, oil on canvas, 40 × 30 in. The Museum of Modern Art, New York, Gift of friends of the artist

to ponder Picasso's new current strategies. The example of Picasso as a wartime artist deeply engaged in the human crises of his day also pushed Tamayo, and other New York–based artists as well, to further embrace their identity as modern artists responding to their times.

But first, Tamayo had to process the formal lessons of Picasso's art. Starting in 1939, Tamayo began another phase of intense experimentation largely in response to Picasso. Tamayo's style underwent a more radical transformation, not only after seeing *Guernica*, but by encountering several important Picasso "Negroid period" paintings, including *Les Demoiselles d'Avignon* (1907), which was part of MoMA's permanent collection and presented in the 1939 retrospective. In many ways, these works helped him to rediscover the formal aspects of pre-Columbian and Mexican popular art. As we have seen, since the beginning of his career, Tamayo based many of his painted faces on the example of pre-Columbian masks and sculptures. Works like *Woman with Fruit Basket* (1926; see fig. 7) and *Women of Tehuantepec* (1939) demonstrate how Tamayo's earlier works capture frozen facial expressions drawn from pre-Hispanic sources. In both of these paintings, the color of the face and the body are seamless. Picasso's reliance on African masks, known for their varying textures and shifting planes of perspective, drew Tamayo's attention. This is clearly seen in one of Tamayo's odes to Picasso: *Woman with Pineapple* (**FIG. 49**). Here, the face of the female figure, with her long chin, protruding lips, and colorful and segmented face, resembles not a pre-Columbian source, but the example of Fang masks that had so informed Picasso's early cubist period.[164] Tamayo extends this kind of representation to the figure's seated and partially nude body. Her torso is not one color, but a combination of gray, greenish yellow, and red, a color that matches her skirt. In this canvas, Tamayo also adopts a cubist sense of space; the figure's body comprises volumetric rounded shapes, like her breasts, as well as flattened areas (her skirt, the background). Other canvases, including *Woman with a Bird Cage* (1941; pl. 28), follow this pattern

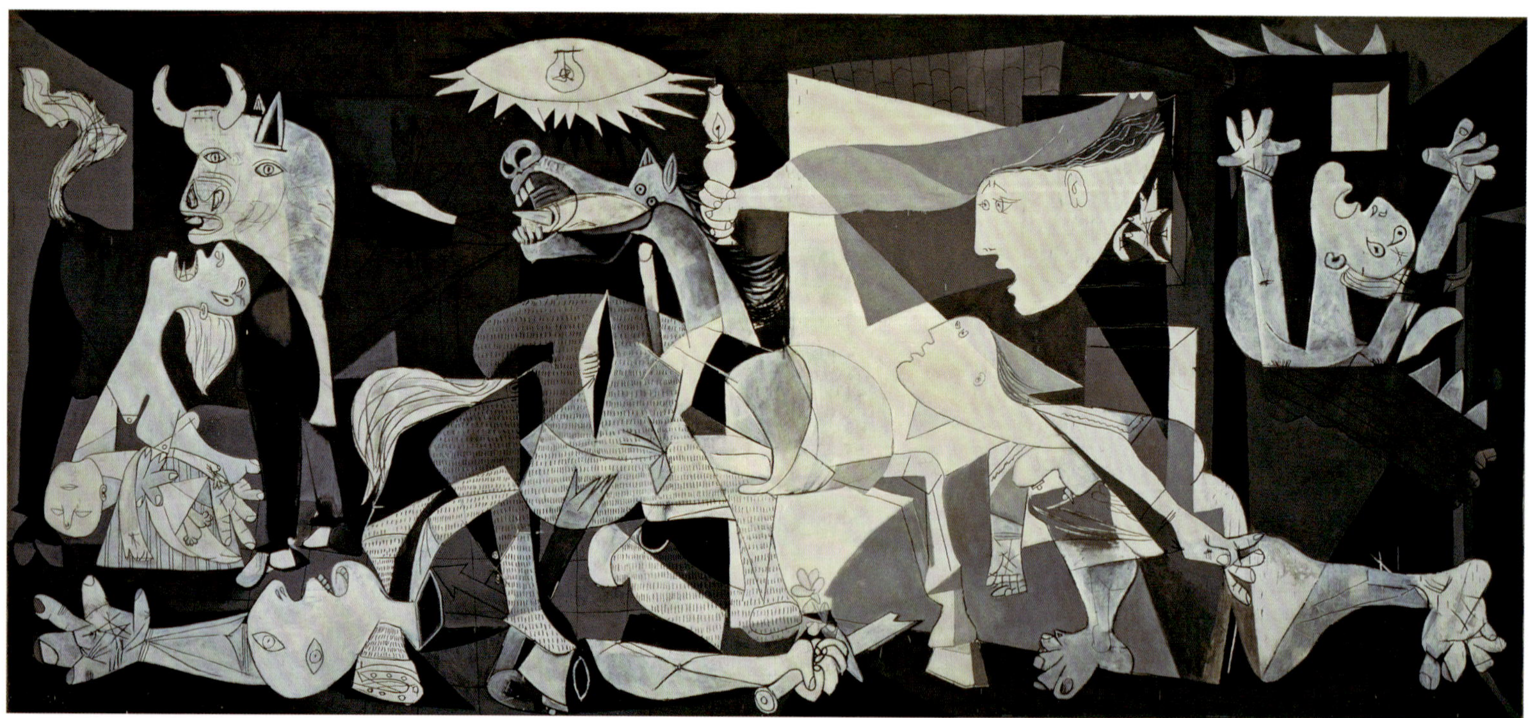

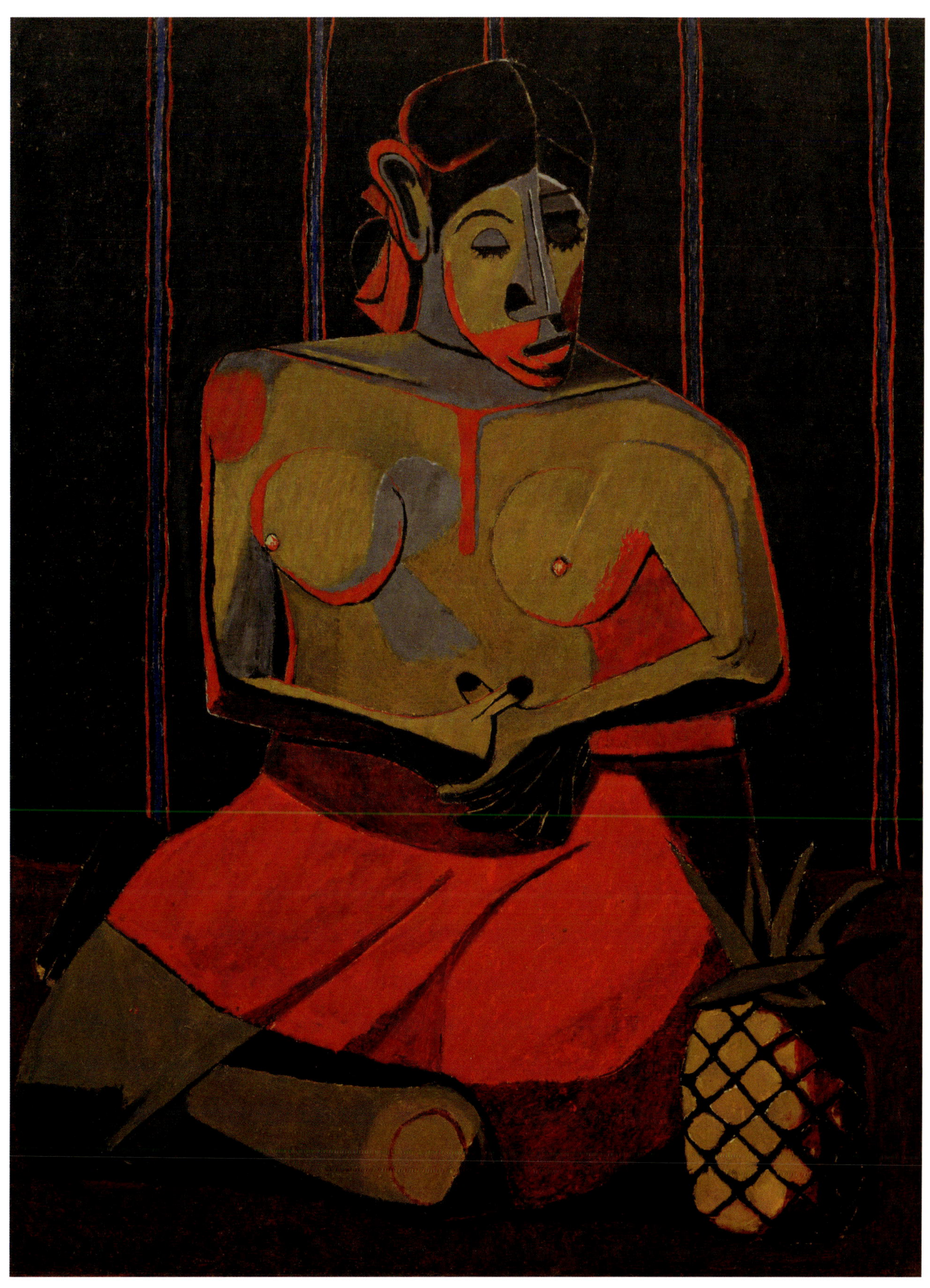

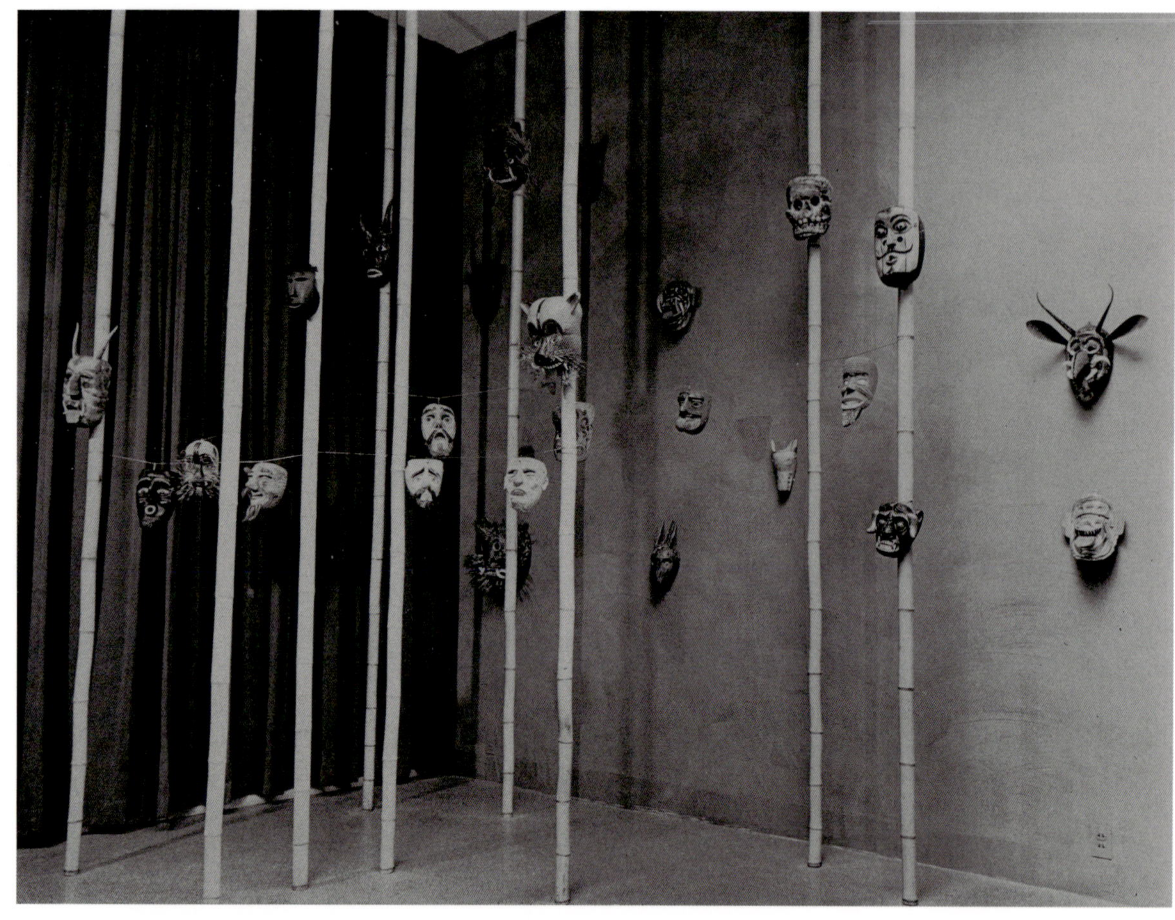

FIG. 50 Installation view of ritual masks in the exhibition *Twenty Centuries of Mexican Art*, 1940, at the Museum of Modern Art, New York. Photographic Archive, The Museum of Modern Art Archives, New York

FIG. 51 Rufino Tamayo, *Nature and the Artist: The Work of Art and the Observer*, 1943, fresco remounted on muslin, 54 3/4 × 126 1/2 in. Smith College Museum of Art, Northampton, Massachusetts, Commissioned in honor of Mrs. Dwight W. Morrow (Elizabeth Cutter, Class of 1896)

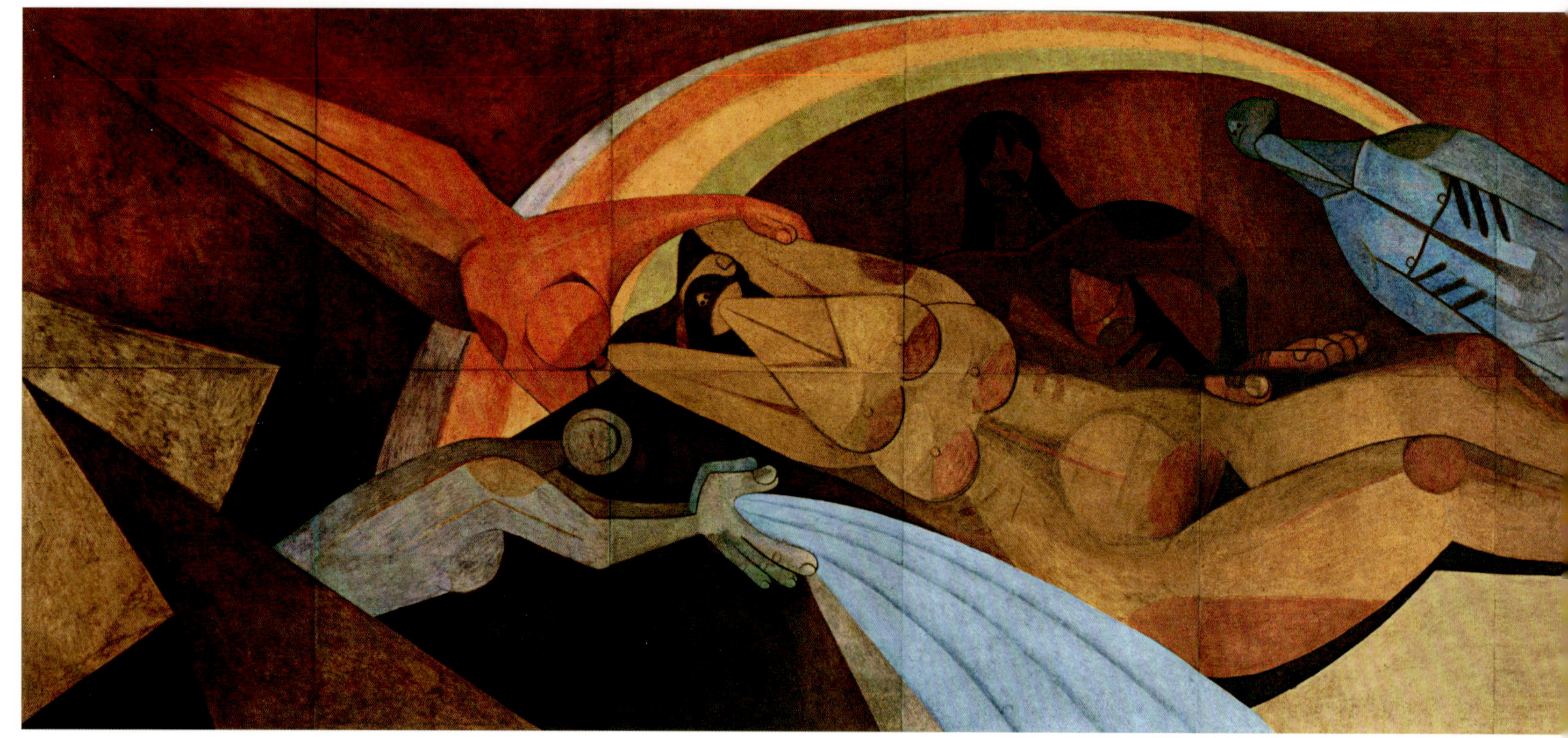

to an even greater extent. In this painting, created the same year as *Woman with Pineapple*, the breasts are depicted from two different perspectives simultaneously, which is a classic cubist (and Cézannesque) technique.

Picasso was the primary though not the sole influence on Tamayo's renewed interest in masks. After the 1939 Picasso retrospective, MoMA presented two important shows that prominently featured masks and could have reinforced Tamayo's changing interest in them as a formal device: *Twenty Centuries of Mexican Art* (1940) and *Indian Art of the United States* (1941). In both shows, masks were creatively installed to highlight their status as discrete objects. Tamayo, of course, was very familiar with the Mexican masks on view in *Twenty Centuries of Mexican Art*, since his work was also featured in the exhibition. In one display, colorful "ritual dance masks" were installed at various levels on vertical bamboo poles, possibly suggesting people of different heights in a crowd or festival celebration (FIG. 50). The installation in *Indian Art of the United States* adopted an even more dramatic style, with masks hung directly on the wall and lit from the bottom up in a darkened room. It is difficult to know which specific masks Tamayo quoted after 1939. In *Woman with a Bird Cage*, for instance, Tamayo appears to blend the toothy grin of masks from the Jalisco and the segmented color fields of masks from Mexico City.[165] It is clear that in the immediate years following these exhibitions and the Picasso retrospective, Tamayo's painted faces become complex fields of abstract design that often pack an emotional punch.

Even though *Guernica* is a large oil painting, its scale is mural sized, and in the 1930s it was referred to as such. Tamayo was drawn to its ambitious scale, and when he successfully secured his first fresco mural commission in the United States, he adopted elements and strategies drawn from *Guernica* and other Picasso paintings. In

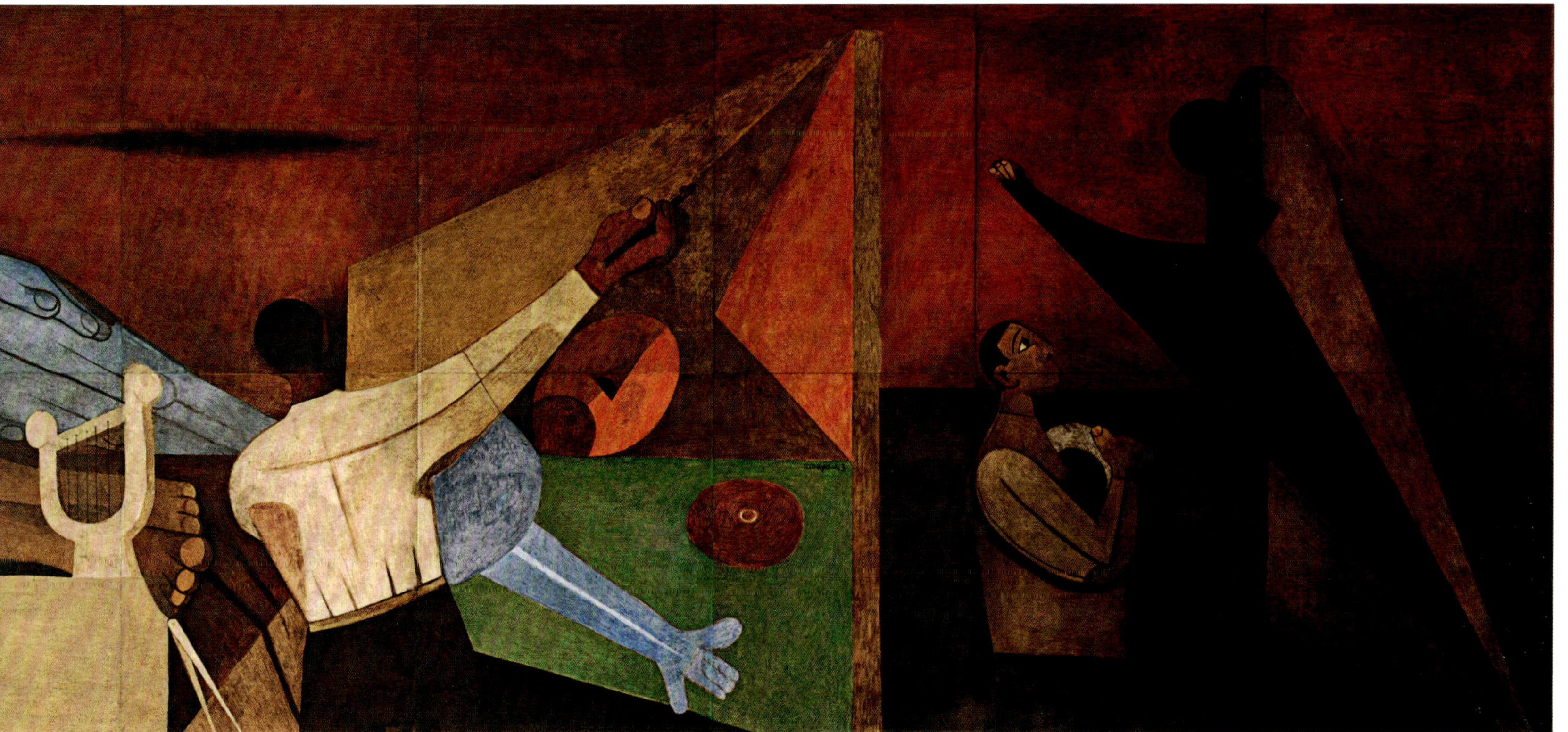

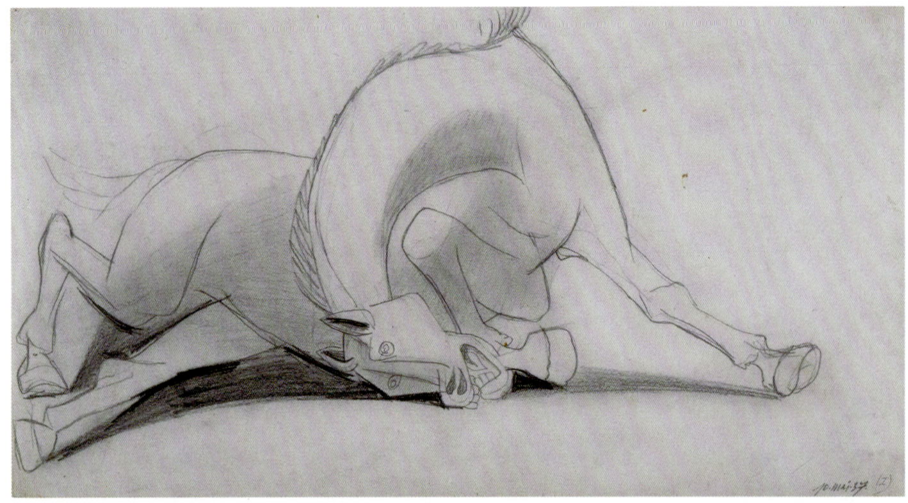

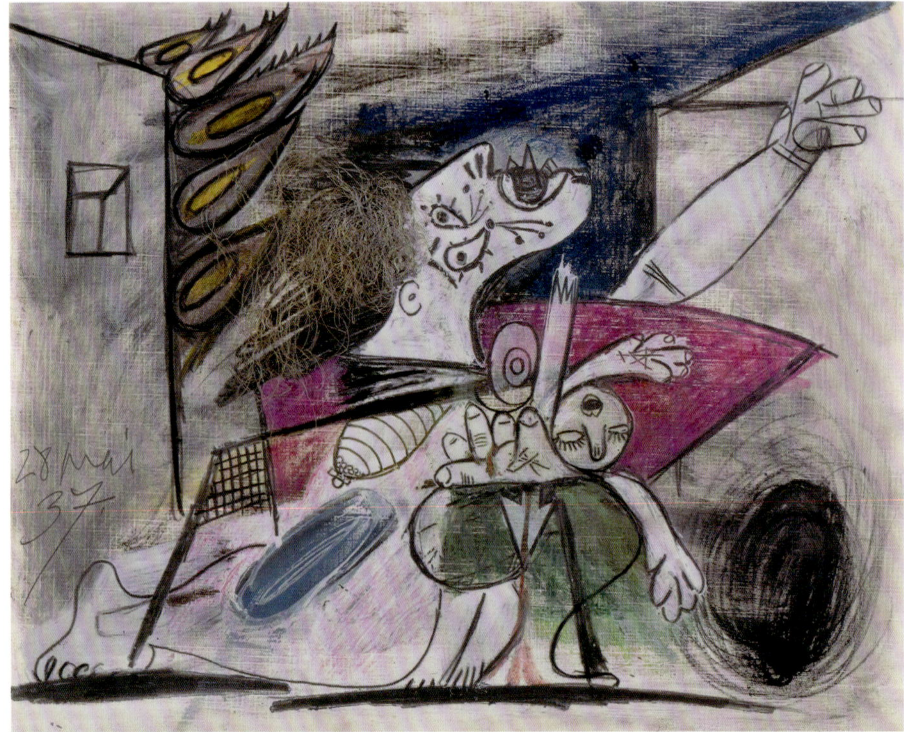

1943, Tamayo painted *Nature and the Artist: The Work of Art and the Observer* (FIG. 51) at the Art Library at Smith College in Northampton, Massachusetts.[166] In this mural Tamayo returns to a recurring motif in his oeuvre: the artist in the act of artistic creation. The main part of the mural portrays an artist painting and surrounded by allegories of nature and the elements (earth, water, air) that inspire him; the second part presents the spectator absorbing the resulting work of art. Even as this mural is to a large extent geometrically composed and does not resemble the style or the iconographic denseness of *Guernica*, its visual anchor is a large reclining female figure representing nature that brings to mind the centrality of the horse in Picasso's composition. Tamayo's approach to the human figure continued to shift as well. Heads are represented by simple round shapes, and the bodies appear unclothed and with emphasized rib cages that resemble the papier-mâché *calaveras* (skeletons) used in Mexican festivals.

But it was Picasso's animal imagery that would powerfully redirect Tamayo's art and style in the early 1940s. Starting with *Animals* (1941; pl. 32), Tamayo assimilates Picasso's animal imagery so intensely that it spurs several dramatic changes in his own art. From the beginning of Tamayo's career, he was consistently committed to engaging the modern experience. After witnessing *Guernica*, he comes to understand that Picasso's animals were powerful allegories that conveyed contemporary human suffering. In the years that followed, Tamayo would portray many distressed and aggressive animals, echoing Picasso's work yet transforming his example by the infusion of intense color and strategic use of space to suggest either barren landscapes, as in *Animals*, or confined environments that visualize tension. *Dog Barking at the Moon* (1942; pl. 33), another early animal painting, places a howling dog in between an angular wall on the right and a distant mountain on the left. In both works, Tamayo models the dogs' physiques on pre-Columbian and Mexican popular art sources; he portrays them with exposed rib cages and attenuated vocal cords to convey starvation and heightened emotion.[167] Tamayo's more pared-down approach could also have been informed by Picasso's sparer preparatory sketches for *Guernica*, also on display at the Valentine Gallery

FIG. 52 Pablo Picasso, *Study for the Horse [I]*; sketch for "Guernica," May 10, 1937, Paris; graphite on paper, 8 5/16 × 17 7/8 in. Museo Nacional Centro de Arte Reina Sofía, Madrid

FIG. 53 Pablo Picasso, *Mother with Dead Child [IV]*; sketch for "Guernica," May 28, 1937, Paris; pencil, colored crayons, gouache, and hair, 9 1/4 × 11 1/2 in. Museo Nacional Centro de Arte Reina Sofía, Madrid

and MoMA, which isolated elements of the large painting (FIG. 52). This link between Picasso and Tamayo was so strong during those years that one critic identified Tamayo as "the one artist to portray the Mexican *Guernica*."[168]

But it is not always clear that Tamayo set out to portray "Mexican" subjects. As James Oles has powerfully demonstrated, Tamayo created his animal paintings and fiery cataclysms of the 1940s when he was living in the United States, a country at war. In 1943, Tamayo's work appeared in the Pierre Matisse exhibition *War and the Artist*, which appropriately framed Tamayo's work within its contemporaneous historical context.[169] Because Tamayo feared being drafted, the entry of the United States into World War II was a period of great personal anxiety for the artist.[170] He created his paintings during this time of personal crisis and as a witness to the spread of fascism, the violence of war, and genocide. In his later years, Tamayo reflected how deeply he was shaken by events like the Holocaust.[171] Works like *Fire* (1946, pl. 36), which depicts figures running from a burning building, suggest the violent events of war. The painting amplifies an element in *Guernica*, and the subject of one of Picasso's preparatory drawings that were included in both the Valentine Gallery and MoMA exhibitions (FIG. 53). Tamayo portrays an unclothed man and woman with flailing arms, perhaps representing universal human beings in a state of vulnerability. The majority of Tamayo's war-period paintings are less direct; they do not so much depict specific events as allegorize war's violence and anxieties.[172]

Lion and Horse (1942; pl. 31) stages these tensions as an encounter between predator and prey. The lion, whose red eyes and teeth leap off the canvas, circles the horse, who raises his front legs in response. The subject of a lion attacking a horse is, of course, amply represented in art history, most famously by English artist George Stubbs in the late eighteenth century. Tamayo's warring animals, who stand near a fallen column and beneath an unnatural chemical-green cloud, nevertheless embody aggression and the environmental aftermath of warfare.

One of Tamayo's most ambitiously scaled animal paintings, *Girl Attacked by a Strange Bird* (1947; pl. 35), directs animal aggression at a human being. The painting portrays a solitary child with raised arms running from a large bird, perhaps an eagle. The bird's sharp, open beak aims toward the girl's narrow and vulnerable neck. A flowering cactus is the only other element in the dry, barren landscape. Given the popular associations between birds and airplanes, it is easy to understand why during wartime birds were associated with airborne warfare.[173] During World War II, when planes became weaponized instruments of war, soldiers were known to paint them with aggressive animal imagery.[174] Mexican flight crews deployed in the Philippines, for example, came to be known as the Águilas Aztecas (the Aztec Eagles).[175] Tamayo's aggressive bird could conjure planes as instruments of war and allegories of fear.

The war period was also personally challenging and Tamayo learned to use his newly acquired pictorial strategies to explore private angst as well. During the late 1930s and early 1940s, Olga lost two pregnancies and also suffered from psychological problems that ultimately led to her hospitalization.[176] *The Doctor* (1939; pl. 29) may be related to these very intimate crises. The painting portrays a doctor, perhaps making a house call, as implied by the elaborate wrought iron bed in the background. The figure holds a lit cigarette, as if to suggest a pause in a conversation. This is not a mimetic representation of a human face, nor the depiction of a simple domestic residence. *The Doctor* suggests an intense experience or conversation that may sadly relate to Olga's delicate health.[177] In fact, Tamayo's *Animals*, which has largely been understood as an evocation of the uncertainties of war, was painted when Olga was hospitalized in New York and was prone to violent behavior. Tamayo's friend Luchita Hurtado, who housed Tamayo when Olga was hospitalized, argued the barking, angry dogs evoked Olga's temporary aggressive state.[178]

Tamayo created other paintings—many of which include or imply the presence of his wife—that could be viewed through an autobiographical lens. *The Lovers* (1943; pl. 30), presumably a double portrait of Tamayo and Olga, can also be interpreted in personal terms. The woman's head and the caged bird overlap, suggesting her emotional and mental inaccessibility. A letter from Tamayo to his friend, the writer Carlos Pellicer conveys Tamayo's concerns with potentially "[losing] Olga forever."[179] The abstract red form between the couple—whose color is reinforced in their arms and hands—conveys their strong emotional bond in spite of the troubled times. One contemporary critic perceived the emotional intensity of this canvas: "*Lovers* is the most remarkable [of Tamayo's current show]. The figures have a psychological tenseness of relationship borne out in an enveloping red cape and by a shadow thrown in the manner of Chirico on the lichen-green background."[180]

Despite these personal and historical associations, critics especially highlighted the "primitiveness" that this new direction revealed. Henry McBride, for example, praised Tamayo for being aware of "contemporary aesthetics" and for tapping into feelings that "spring unmistakably from a Maya past that is so remote that it is practically beyond the reach of history."[181] One of the most vivid accounts of this tendency is Jean Charlot's review for the *Magazine of Art*. His comments are so potent that they must be quoted at length:

> *The picturesque allusions in modern guise that his northern public had come to expect, the toy shapes, the candy hues, fall short of this new urge whose far-flung motors feed on more disquieting strains. Distortions of the human figure are no longer meant for purposes of wit—as plastic puns. They are bona-fide distortions of passion. While Greco's mark holiness, Tamayo's liberties with man's frame suggest a ripper's surgery, or the craft of the Mexican village witch baking bits of hair and nail filings from the intended victim inside a clay doll, with deadly purpose. In these later pictures, certain dogs or dragons open jaws as barbed with teeth and as ravenous as the vampire-headed beings that sit Buddahwise* [sic] *(but with none of Buddah's* [sic] *static acceptancy) on the Zapotecan funeral urns dug up in the painter's native Oaxaca.*[182]

Charlot spared no words to primitivize Tamayo's new approach; in fact his review does not relate the change in his art to the war years.[183] Another critic followed suit and described Tamayo's *Dog Barking at the Moon* as a "red monster against a furious blue sky recognizable as a member of that breed which Tamayo's pre-Columbian ancestors once fattened as a table delicacy."[184] Tamayo had hit his stride and the critical response framed it as a result of his implied or direct access to primitive culture.

This positive reception was soon reflected in his mounting patronage, institutional support, and social prestige. In 1942 alone, Tamayo's paintings enter the collections of three major museums. MoMA acquired *Animals* in 1942 and presented the painting in several permanent collection displays between 1943 and 1944.[185] When the Art Institute of Chicago acquired *Woman with a Bird Cage*, Tamayo became the second Mexican artist to enter the prestigious Joseph Winterbotham Collection, which was originally established to build the museum's collection of European art.[186]

Duncan Phillips acquired *Carnival* (1941; pl. 27), the second Tamayo painting (after *Mandolins and Pineapples*) in his collection. Tamayo's success reached beyond New York and the East Coast. The San Francisco Museum of Art acquired *Lovers* in 1945. The Arts Club of Chicago, a leading supporter of modernist art in the Midwest, also presented a solo exhibition of Tamayo's art in 1945. In the mid-1940s, H. W. Janson, at the time a young professor and curator at Washington University in St. Louis, built an impressive collection of modernist art from the United States and Europe. He acquired *Lion and Horse*, making Tamayo the only Mexican and Latin American artist in the collection.[187] Robert Goldwater, the rising art historian specializing in non-Western art and modernist primitivism, wrote an impressive Tamayo monograph in 1947, where he described the artist as a "Mexican but not a Mexicanist."[188] A new generation of US private collectors, including Lee Ault, Roy Neuberger, and Joseph Pulitzer, purchased Tamayo paintings, and often shared their private collections in public exhibitions at galleries and museums including MoMA and the Whitney Museum of American Art.[189] News of Tamayo's art appeared in popular magazines like *Look* magazine and the society pages, and his photographic likeness was captured by prominent fashion photographers like Irving Penn and John Rawlings (**FIG. 54**). Penn's portrait of Tamayo for *Vogue* was part of a series depicting major personalities that transformed New York into a leading cultural hub in the postwar era.[190]

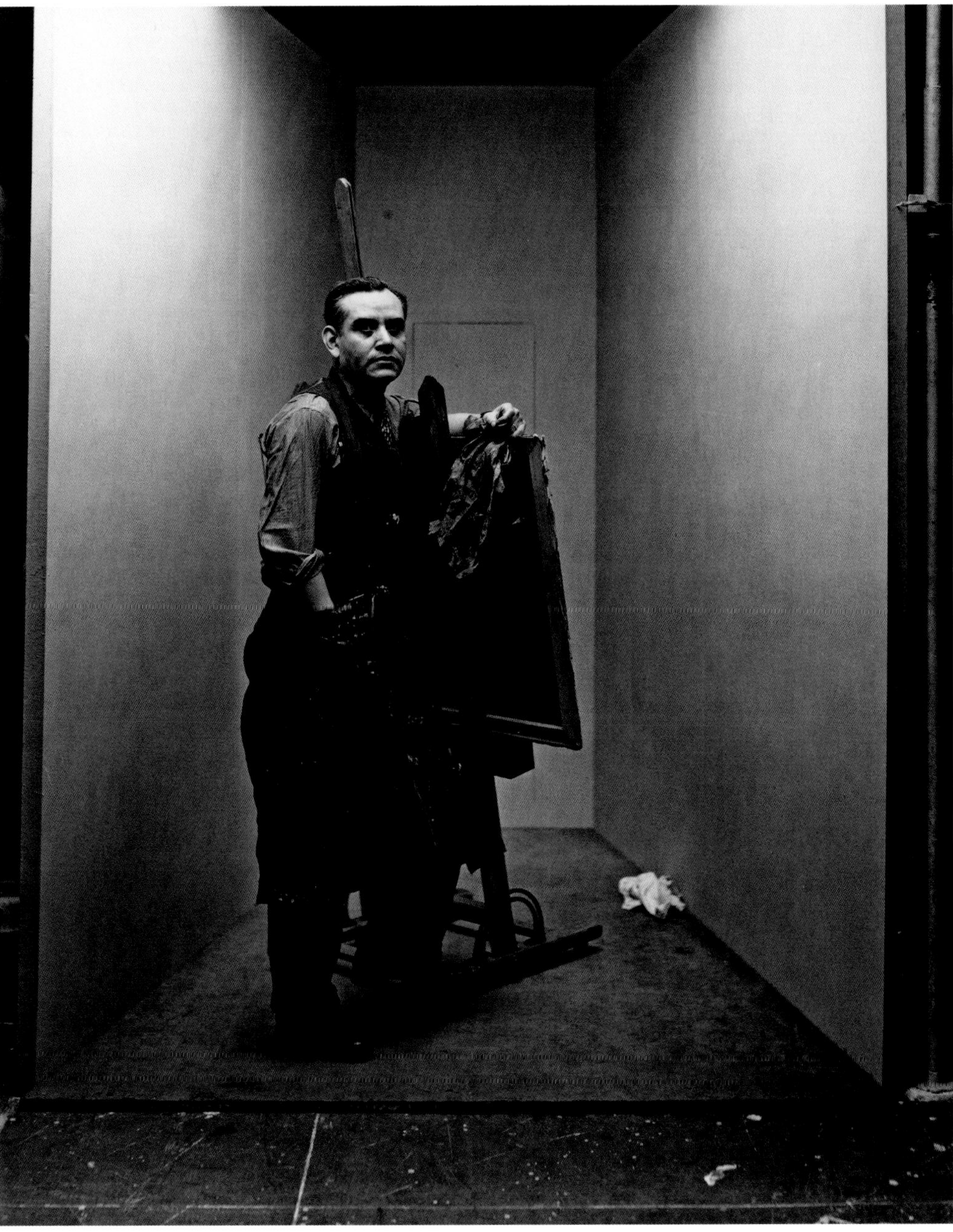

FIG. 54 Irving Penn, *Rufino Tamayo* (2 of 2), New York, 1947

It's not only that Tamayo and his art were gaining prestige; it's the network in which he and his art circulated that is noteworthy. The institutions and collectors who supported his art were deeply committed not to social-realist art, but to modern European masters. When Lee Ault presented his modernist collection at the Valentine Gallery, which included three Tamayo paintings, only five of the sixty-eight works on view were by non-European artists. Ault later wrote the catalogue introduction for Tamayo's 1947 solo exhibition at the Cincinnati Art Museum that distinguished Tamayo's art from the picturesque tendencies in Mexican art, and instead underscored Tamayo's aesthetic relationship to Matisse, Braque, and Picasso.[191] Even as Tamayo's Mexican background was not denied, many Tamayo supporters highlighted his relationship to the

School of Paris. For the Art Institute of Chicago, Tamayo's new works revealed his indebtedness to Picasso, Braque, and pre-Columbian sources—such as Aztec masks and Mexican tezontle stones—which museum staff associated with his forms and colors.[192]

The 1940s were a period of triumph and acclaim for Tamayo in the United States and Mexico. Between 1946 and 1948, he had two important solo exhibitions in Mexico City that reinserted him into debates over national art in Mexico, which were to some extent covered in the US press.[193] The heated back-and-forth between Tamayo, Siqueiros, and Orozco provided Tamayo with the opportunity to express his own perspectives on modern art. In an interview with Mexican journalist Antonio Rodríguez, Tamayo emphasized his brand of "realism" and his on-going commitment to exploring the modern age:

> *My painting is perfectly realist... and happily is not descriptive and will never be because I believe the artist is a creator.... My painting is also very human because it is attentive to our lives, except that it does not present itself to the spectator already digested by way of a subject. Instead it is intimately kept, giving the spectator the opportunity to make their own interpretation.*[194]

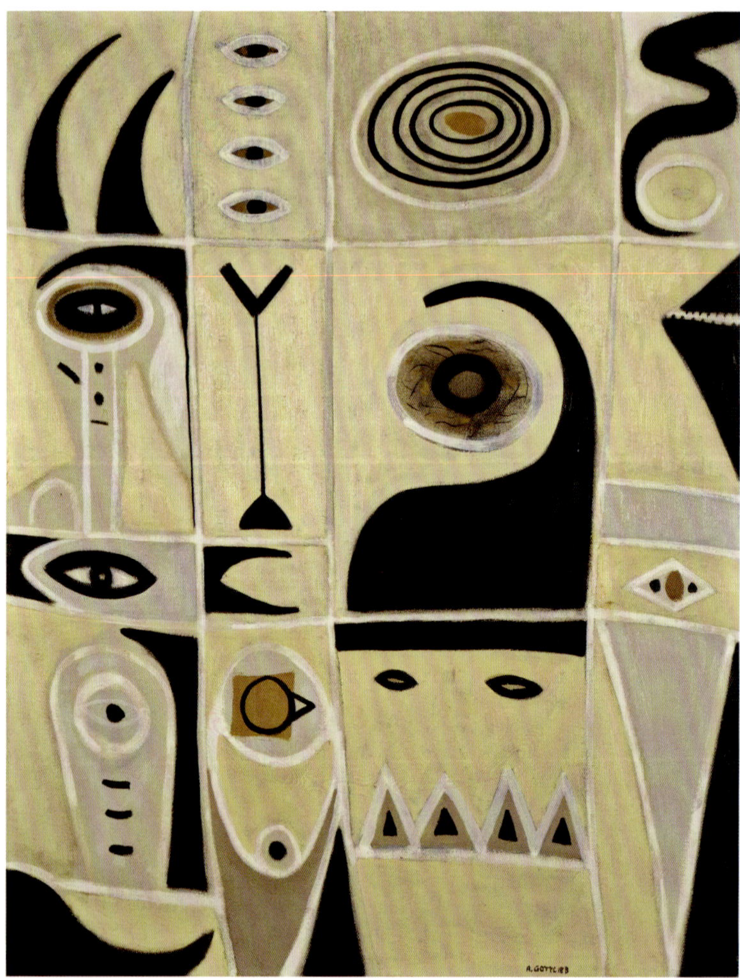

FIG. 55 Adolph Gottlieb, *Evil Omen*, 1946, oil on canvas, 38 × 30 in. Collection Neuberger Museum of Art, Purchase College, State University of New York, Gift of Roy R. Neuberger

As his art began to routinely circulate in museums and galleries in New York and beyond, it introduced and elicited ideas about pressing issues in the field of modern art. While Tamayo's art was often discussed within the context of "Mexican art," the questions it raised—about the nature of art and representation, the depiction of national culture, social realism, and propaganda—had a wider resonance, as demonstrated by his patronage, which often placed him in a more international context.

Tamayo's interests especially overlapped with the rising generation of abstract expressionists, who were also grappling with the place of the artist in an uncertain postwar reality and who sought to advance new directions in US art. The abstract expressionists were never a defined group, but were instead a set of artists who knew one another, shared common interests, and were beginning to establish themselves in the art market. Tamayo had little direct contact with Jackson Pollock, Adolph Gottlieb, and Mark Rothko, the three artists he was most often paired with in exhibitions and publications, but he shared their admiration for European modernism, deep interest in indigenous art and culture, and commitment to representing the modern experience in intensely personal and nonnarrative terms. Tamayo's ability to balance "American" and universal interests in his work also overlapped with the aims of his New York peers. Tamayo and the new wave of abstract expressionists developed simultaneously in New York, and their art came to define key elements of postwar art in the United States.

Artist Barnett Newman was one of the first to relate Tamayo with the abstract expressionists. In 1945, when he was more active as a critic and curator, Newman wrote an article highlighting the similarities between Tamayo and Gottlieb. Newman's opening paragraph framed key aspects of their art and the major stakes revealed by their pairing:

> *[A]n analysis of their working aesthetics should give us a clue to the attitude that ought to motivate our American artists and those art laymen who are concerned with the establishment of an "American" tradition. Tamayo and Gottlieb are alike in that, working in the free atmosphere of the art tradition of the School of Paris, they have their roots deep in the great art traditions of our American aborigines. This artistic synthesis has permitted them to produce works that are making a powerful imprint on the art of our times, both in America and in Europe. Only by this kind of contribution is there any hope for the possible development of a truly American art, whereas the attempts of our nationalist politics and artists, in both South and North America, have failed and must continue to do so.*[195]

Newman paired Tamayo and Gottlieb for three interrelated reasons: first, because they shared similar "working aesthetics," by which Newman meant their shared interests in indigenous art of the Americas; second, because their art united formal elements of Native American art within the rubric of Parisian modernism; and third, to highlight how their successful union of these traditions exemplified the future of American art.

Indeed, Newman was correct in his analysis of the two artists' shared interest in the indigenous art of the Americas and their opposition to the dominant artistic frameworks of their national milieus. Before Newman wrote this article, he had expressed his desire to advance a new phase of American art, and looked to the ancient arts of the Americas, and implicitly to the example of Latin American artists, as a key element in actualizing this goal.[196] Like other US thinkers before him, Newman strategically defined Native American art in hemispheric terms, including North, South, and Central America, thereby opening up the possibility of equating Tamayo and Gottlieb as "American" artists. Beginning with his *Pictographs* series in the early 1940s, Gottlieb was turning his attention to the art of the Northwest Coast Indians.[197] His interests informed works like *Evil Omen* (**FIG. 55**), in which he incorporated Tlingit textile motifs, such as schematic eyes and teeth, into gridded compositions. Whereas Gottlieb did not necessarily frame his work in nationalistic terms—although his sources of inspiration cast his art as "American"—he began the series at a time when he and his close friend Mark Rothko were exploring alternatives to the provincialism of American art.[198]

Newman advocated for American art yet still questioned the role of nationalism in art. In the article on Tamayo and Gottlieb, he condemns American scene painters and social realists, as well as the "leaders of Mexican nationalist art" who "show a lack of understanding of what art is about—of its nature."[199] Newman sought to bring US art in line with the example of the School of Paris, which was dedicated to "exploring the visual world in search of truth."[200] While he does not use the word *universal*, the word *truth* implies a similar sentiment. He goes on to write, "Only chauvinist arrogance can lead us to believe that we in the *great* Americas can afford to disregard this international standard and substitute the narrow one of our immediate environment."[201]

Newman's assertions echo Tamayo's first definitive artist statement, written in 1933, in which he presciently argued for openness to universal (i.e., European) art: "It is essential that we break down the wall of our nationalism...and that we bring together the lessons of the world, to utilize and to later surpass. France currently offers an excellent example of this way of working."[202] It is understandable, then, that Newman would turn to Tamayo's example in his argument on behalf of a more globally engaged American art.

Tamayo's disdain for overtly nationalist subjects continued to manifest itself in the context of projects allied with the abstract expressionists. Gallerist and surrealist-promoter Howard Putzel included Tamayo in his 1945 exhibition *A Problem for Critics*, the first exhibition to unite the core group of artists that would become known as the abstract expressionists. Like Newman, Putzel aimed to identify the start of "real American painting," which for Putzel rested in part from its moving away from direct resemblances.[203] Several Tamayo paintings appear in the *Tiger's Eye*, an interdisciplinary avant-garde publication that featured the work of several abstract expressionists and European artists.[204] The editors, Ruth Stephan and John Stephan, invited Tamayo to write a statement for the inaugural issue. His poetic contribution, which prefaced several illustrations of his and Rothko's work, highlighted the difference between "miles of painted canvases, that try to tell us the ultimate world of the philosophical, social or political order" and "fragments in which preoccupation is noted by the equilibrium of plastic elements, and that constitutes true painting." Here Tamayo characterizes true painting not by its depiction of "social or political order," but by the balance of its plastic elements.

Newman's strategic Tamayo/Gottlieb alliance for the benefit of US art does not discount the context that bound Tamayo to the abstract expressionists. Tamayo and his New York peers developed their ideas in the same milieu, absorbing the same stimuli. They attended the same exhibitions and were often drawn to the same artists, a fact made evident by comparing their work. Following MoMA's Picasso retrospective, in 1939, Pollock created several animal paintings, including *The She-Wolf* (**FIG. 56**), that center on a single animal and expand on Picasso's spontaneous painting style in *Guernica*.[205] Betraying his interest in archaic myths, Pollock's title references Romulus and Remus, the mythical founders of Rome who were suckled by a wolf. Pollock activates his canvas with linear forms that both outline the wolf's body and animate the space around it. Tamayo's animal paintings demonstrate his attraction to Picasso's iconography, which he treated in a sparer, more boldly colored style. Tamayo's *Mad Dog* (1943; pl. 34) similarly depicts a nursing dog with extended teats, yet this canine is set in a Mexican environment suggested by a nopal cactus, a plant associated with the Mexica pictograph that still appears on the Mexican flag. Color, rather than line, drives the painting's intensity. The desperate, rabid dog, its rib cage visible, licks the ground, showing signs of a depraved appetite. Its tongue matches the color of the red-hot sky. While both artists resort to figuration, this comparison reveals the extent to which each artist responded differently to Picasso's example. Pollock drew upon some aspects of the Spanish master's process that relied on a looser and cruder brushstroke. Tamayo focused on Picasso's allegorical turn and intense visualized emotion. Pollock eventually moved on to "veil the image"; Tamayo never abandoned it.[206]

Tamayo and the abstract expressionists all lived through World War II and created works that addressed the existential crisis unleashed by the war and its aftermath, which they were able to understand through the power of myth. In a

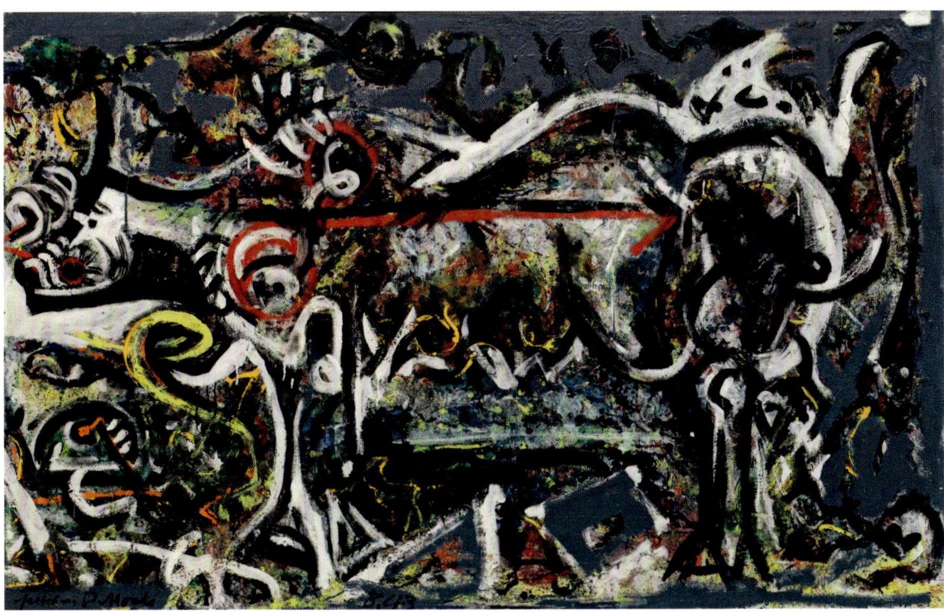

FIG. 56 Jackson Pollock, *The She-Wolf*, 1943, oil, gouache, and plaster on canvas, 41 ⅞ × 67 in. The Museum of Modern Art, New York, Purchase

1943 statement, Gottlieb and Rothko expressed their perspective:

> *If we profess a kinship to the art of primitive men, it is because the feelings expressed have a particular pertinence today. In times of violence, personal predilections of niceties of color and form seem irrelevant. All primitive expression reveals the awareness of powerful forces, the immediate presence of terror and fear, a recognition and acceptance of the brutality of the natural world as well as the eternal security of life.*[207]

While Tamayo did not explicitly reference myth in the early 1940s or adopt the language of Modern Man discourse so popular with the early abstract expressionists, his art did have mythic implications.[208] Tamayo's reliance on ancient visual sources as the basis for his contemporary-minded paintings paralleled the principles of Modern Man discourse, which conceptually linked the existential crisis of the postwar era to the tragic myths of non-Western cultures. While less explored in the literature, there are also relationships between Tamayo's subjects and indigenous belief systems. Tamayo's interest in eclipses, for example, considered an evil omen in some Mesoamerican cultures, informed paintings that suggest the destruction of war like *Cataclysm* (1946; pl. 37). Here an eclipse is implied by a darkened orb in the sky that bears a white edge, evoking the moment when the moon blocks the sun. Beneath this solar phenomenon, figures run in response to the bright rays that pierce the atmosphere. The explosiveness of the rays emanating from above and from the smoky clouds suggests the aftereffects of a bomb or explosion. The eclipse imaged here is both real (pictured) and allegorical. Octavio Paz, one of Mexico's premier midcentury writers and perhaps Tamayo's best interlocutor since the 1950s, later described the mythical dimensions of Tamayo's art this way:

> *The painter opens doors to the old sacred universe of myths and images that reveal the double condition of man: his atrocious reality and simultaneously, his no less atrocious irreality.... Tamayo is not an intellectual, nor an archaeologist. This modern man is also very old. And the force that guides his hand is not different from the one that moved his Zapotec ancestors.*[209]

Paz's description—which reveals his own reliance on Modern Man discourse—conjures similar temporal shifts to those present in the statement by Gottlieb and Rothko, and the connective place of myth between past and present.

Tamayo and Pollock in particular also responded to the showing of Joan Miró's *Constellations*, which were presented at Pierre Matisse in 1945 when Tamayo was still affiliated with the gallery. Miró initiated the series at the outbreak of World War II, in 1939, and it subsequently came to be interpreted as his spiritual and artistic response to the war.[210] Many of Miró's paintings from the series feature fields covered with moonlike and abstract shapes that are often connected to one another with lines to suggest constellations. Some of the works, like *Woman in the Night*, include figures

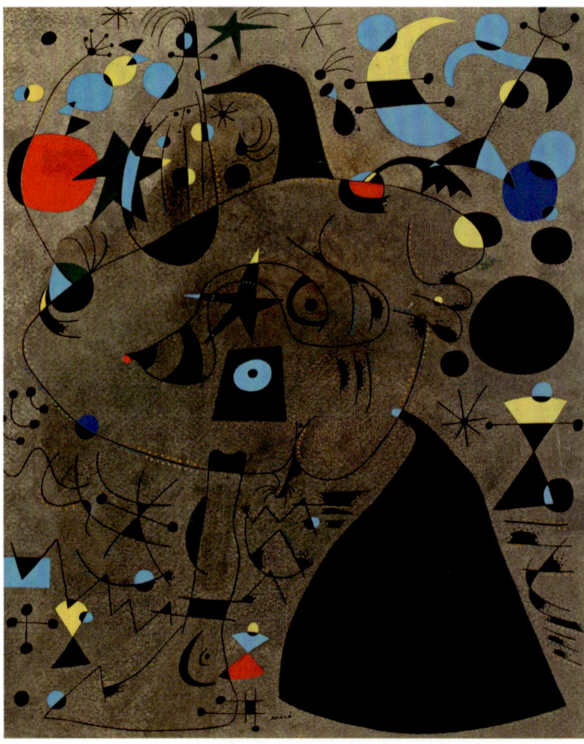

FIG. 57 Joan Miró, *Woman in the Night*, from the *Constellations* series, Varengeville, France, April 27, 1940, gouache and oil wash on paper, 18 ¼ × 15 in. Collection Martin Z. Margulies

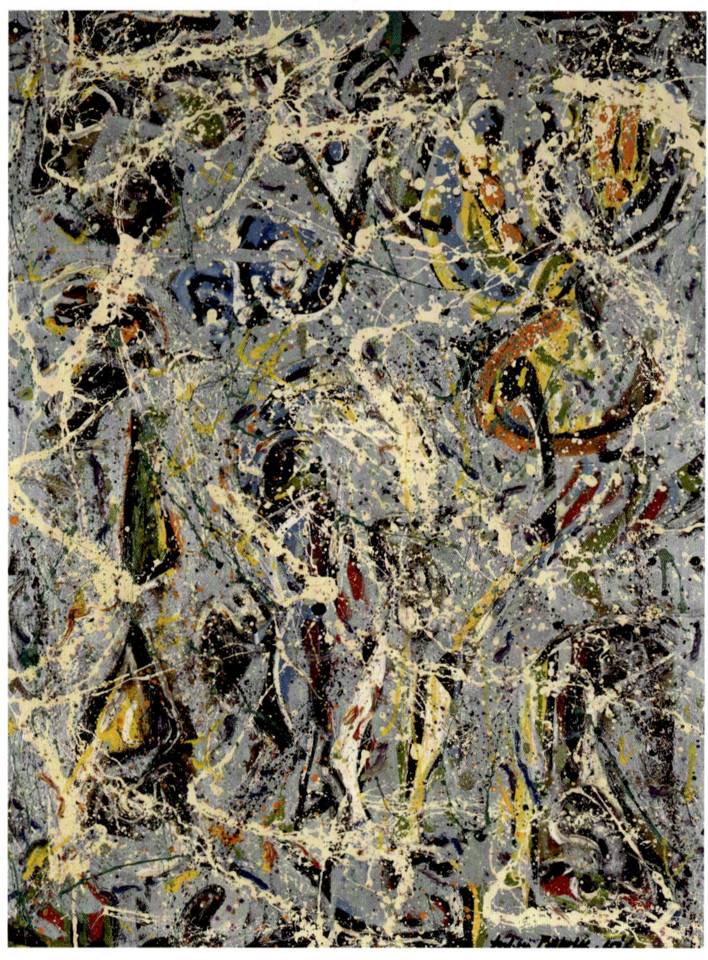

FIG. 58 Jackson Pollock, *Galaxy*, 1947, oil, aluminum paint, and gravel on canvas, 43 ½ × 34 in. Joslyn Art Museum, Omaha, Nebraska, Gift of Miss Peggy Guggenheim

that respond to a celestial scene (FIG. 57). Tamayo had long depicted moons in his painting, but after seeing Miró's *Constellations*, the sky acquired new meaning for him. His celestial paintings take on many guises, from works that evoke postwar anxiety to others that suggest peace. In *Total Eclipse* (ca. 1946; pl. 39), Tamayo depicts two figures responding to a solar eclipse. The figures' gesturing arms suggest surprise or alarm and bring to mind Tamayo's childhood memories of the fearful response triggered by the appearance of Halley's Comet in 1910.[211] Other works visualize instead humankind's eternal spiritual striving (pls. 38, 40–42). *The Full Moon*, also known as *Rooftops* (1945), pictures a quiet and sparkling night sky seen above the roofs of several buildings. The scene, which looks like a view seen from a window, implies a viewing subject contemplating the sky. *Heavenly Bodies* (1946) pictures that subject as an abstracted figure on the right whose body blends in with the landscape and who stares out at a flickering display of stars or a constellation. Other paintings, like *Man Searching the Heavens* (1949), appear to veer off toward science fiction, as they visualize a diaphanous link between a person and circular object or disk in the sky like the kind that were increasingly sighted in the United States and around the world during those years.[212] Whether real or imagined, Tamayo's figures echo those in Miró's *Constellations*.

Tamayo shared these cosmic interests with Pollock, who around the same time initiated his own body of celestial-themed paintings inspired in part by Miró's example and popular science.[213] In works like *Galaxy* (FIG. 58), Pollock created a layered painted surface, again animated by linear forms, with no clear representational image. Pollock was taken with the ways in which Miró scattered pictorial references all over his composition. As in Tamayo's *Heavenly Bodies*, white streaks of paint suggest the movement of stars or comets. Yet, without a horizon line or human markers, Pollock's work does not so much represent space as evoke its mystery and unknowability.[214] In very different styles, Pollock and Tamayo visualized the desire for hope and renewal that follows the end of a crisis.

Tamayo and the early abstract expressionists had much in common, yet their interests, approaches, and goals were not exactly parallel. Tamayo embraced surrealist strategies, but not the notions of the unconscious that were so important to Pollock, Gottlieb, and others. Pre-Columbian art was essential to Tamayo's art, and while he often argued for his ancestral connection to this art, he did not characterize this bond in atavistic terms—though critics did. Tamayo simplified his forms, practicing a kind of abstract-figuration, but rejected complete abstraction, a position that ultimately led to his dismissal by Clement Greenberg, the leading art critic of the postwar period. In a now well-known review, Greenberg criticized Tamayo for not "dissolving his emotion into the abstract elements of style."[215] For him, Tamayo's paintings were unsuccessful because the artist's emotion was illustrated and not expressed. Greenberg's view of midcentury modern art was narrow, but it did have increasing currency in the United States. In his dedication to the figure, Tamayo shared more with a maturing Picasso than his New York peers, a difference that would ultimately obscure Tamayo's place in future narratives of US midcentury art, as Greenberg's perspective began to hold greater and greater sway. Tamayo and the abstract expressionists, nonetheless, would continue to be linked, especially as the Cold War intensified. By 1953, when Tamayo unveiled *Man*, his large-scale portable mural commissioned by the Dallas Museum of Art, which adapts the theme of his aspirational painting *Women Reaching for the Moon* (1946; pl. 41), newspaper coverage either describes him as apolitical or "an outspoken anti-Communist."[216]

While Tamayo continued to spend time in New York and to show work with the abstract expressionists in several Whitney Annuals, he gradually shifted his professional attention elsewhere.[217] Between 1948 and 1949, Tamayo began his slow departure from New York and by 1949 had made Paris his primary home, and from there he launched an even broader international career. He participated in European exhibitions of Mexican art and, most importantly, in the 1950 Venice Biennale, which brought him great acclaim. In Europe, and especially Paris, Tamayo found a critical establishment more willing to embrace his brand of abstract figuration and interested in capitalizing on his ties to the School of Paris. The Parisian intelligentsia, now witnessing the rise of New York as the center of the art world, sought ways to reposition themselves in relation to contemporary art. Tamayo offered them an opportunity to prove their continued relevance in the field.[218]

By the early 1950s, Tamayo's international acclaim occasioned his second, and final, return to Mexico "after [a] 15-year exile," as *Life* magazine announced.[219] At a time when the Mexican state was resituating itself in a Cold War world, and wanted to project a more cosmopolitan and politically neutral face vis-à-vis the artistic strongholds of Paris, New York, and Russia, Tamayo's abstract figuration found a welcome platform.[220] He became a "symbolic rebel" for a younger generation of Mexican artists in the 1950s who championed the human figure in art and rejected both social realism and pure abstraction.[221] By then, he had begun to reconceive of the mural as a field upon which to represent epic Mexican and human history. In the tradition of Picasso's *Guernica* and the abstract expressionists' large-scale canvases, he created portable murals

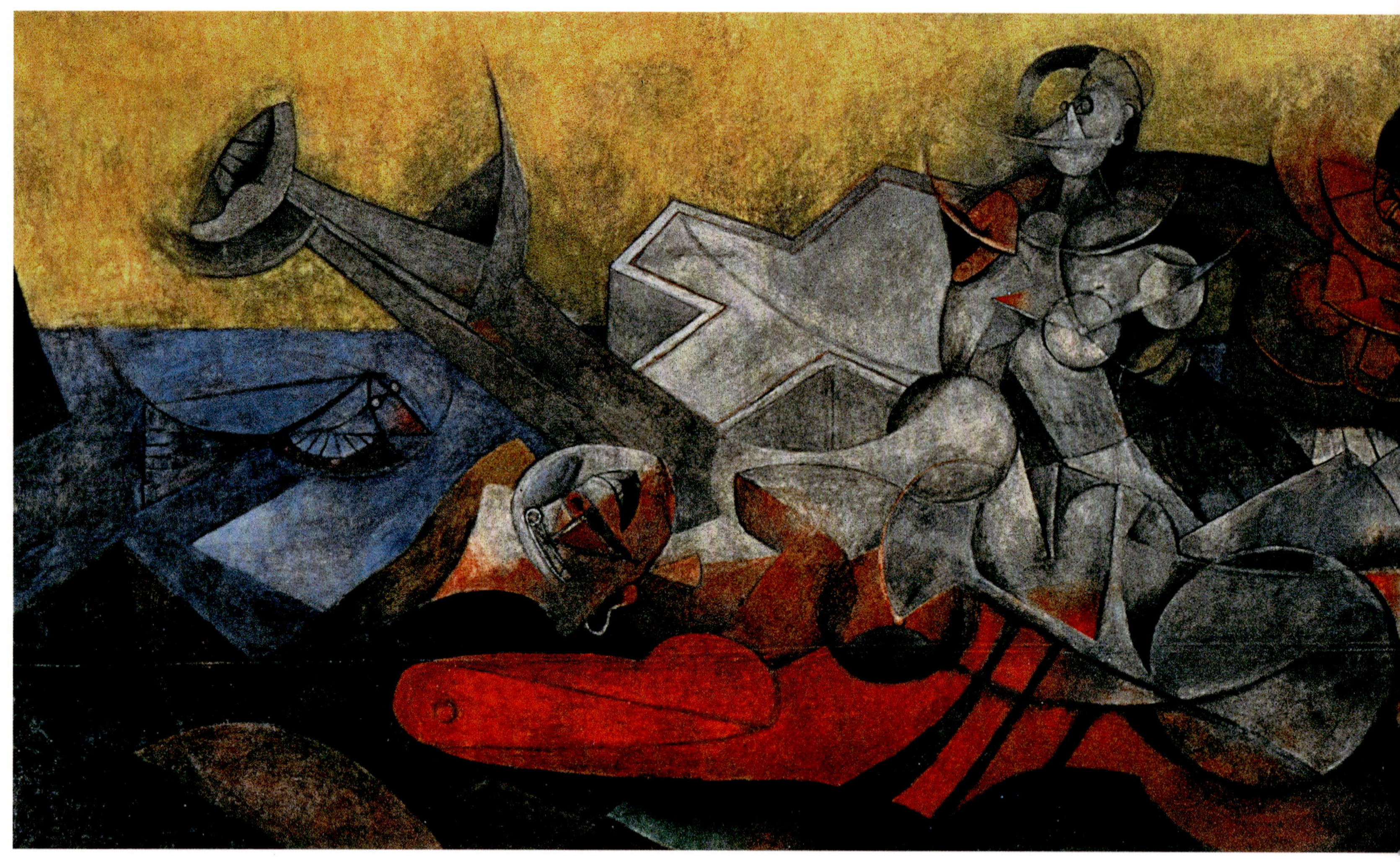

FIG. 59 Rufino Tamayo, *America* [*América*], 1955, Vinylite and sand on canvas, 158 ¼ × 560 ¼ in. Private collection

that were no longer reliant on architecture as a defining (or confining) element. His prestigious commissions for the Palacio de Bellas Artes (the Palace of Fine Arts) cemented his cultural prestige and official patronage in Mexico. His murals reimagined key themes of Mexican muralism—*mestizaje*, Mexican history—into nonnarrative, humanist, and allegorical terms.

Despite his embrace of universalism, Tamayo never entirely abandoned Mexican subjects, a factor that was more and more at odds with the tendencies of the US art world. MoMA, which at one point in the 1940s had entertained presenting a Tamayo solo exhibition, abandoned the idea.[222] In prominent exhibitions like *Abstract Painting and Sculpture in America* (1951) and the *Americans* series during its 1950s iterations, MoMA shifted away from the indigenous / Pan-American / School of Paris lens of Newman's early essays toward a conception of the art of the United States as existing outside the bounds of European and Latin American art.[223] The burgeoning international profile of US art during this era no longer required a legitimizing link to a Mexican or European art history. Tamayo, on the other hand, appeared tied to an earlier Pan-American frame of reference. After he tied for first prize in the 1953 São Paulo Biennial, Olga Tamayo wrote to the Knoedler Gallery urging them to encourage the US press to emphasize that Tamayo was the first "American from America" to win such an international honor.[224]

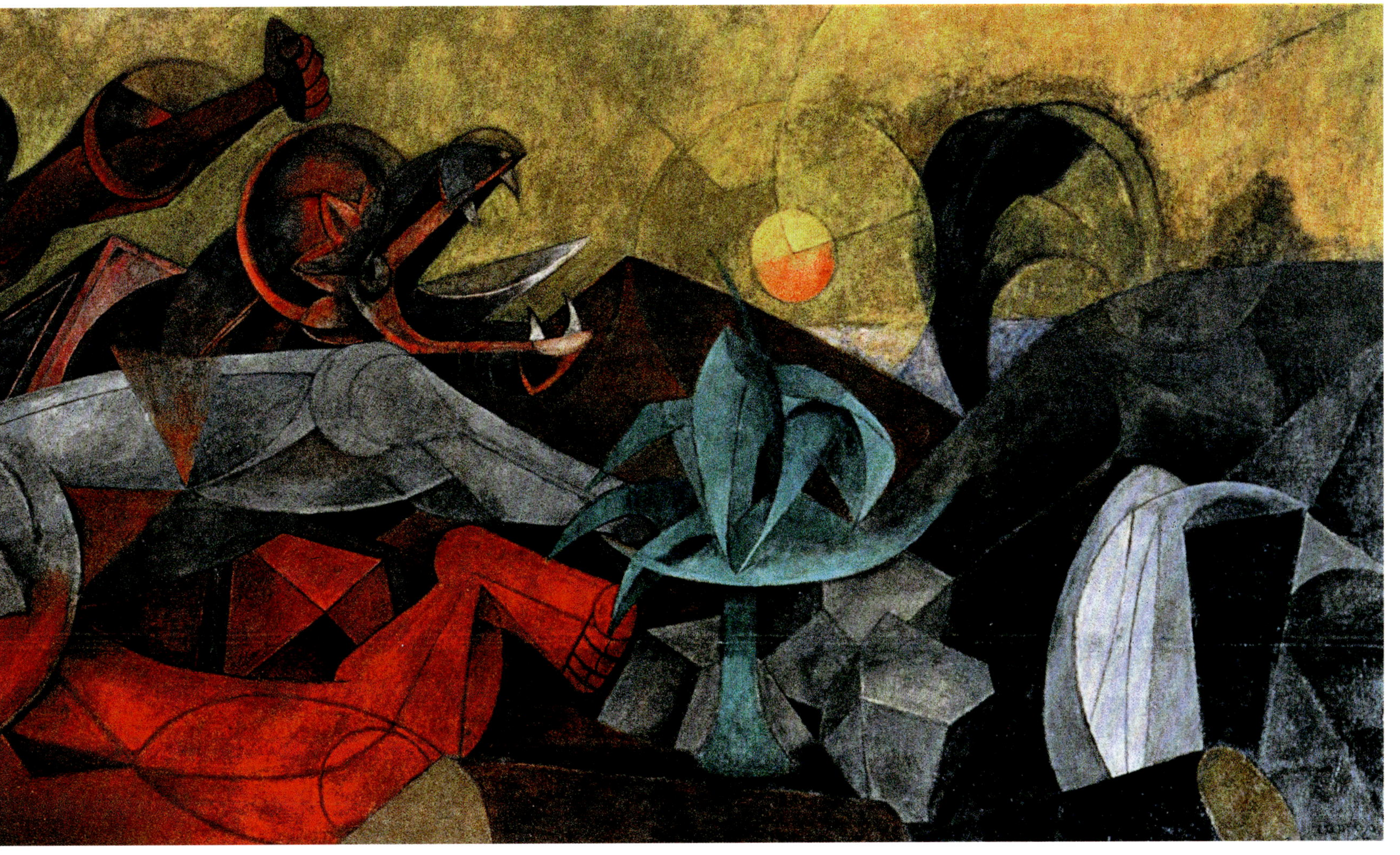

By 1955, Tamayo had completed his *America* mural (FIG. 59) for the Bank of the Southwest, based in Houston, Texas, a kind of geographic gateway linking the United States and Latin America. Tamayo's enormous mural (measuring 13 by 46 feet) presents an allegory of American origins as rooted in the region's colonial history and dual Native American and European heritage. Tamayo described the mural along these lines:

> *The figure in the lower part of the composition represents America. It is surrounded by the sea to emphasize its geographical situation. Because of its great proportions, this figure conveys the idea of abundance, the main characteristic of our continent. Abundance is shown too, by the fish, a symbol of wealth of the sea; by a plant, symbol of the richness of our land; an oil geyser and a water spring, symbols of underground resources. In the upper part of the mural are two embracing figures, signifying the melting of America's two basic races, whose cultural contributions enrich her spiritually. The figure at the left, in white, is the white race, and next to it is the cross, symbol of Occidental culture. The figure at the right, in brown, is the Indian race. Its cultural contribution is represented by the plumed serpent, or Quetzalcoatl, symbol of pre-Columbian culture.*[225]

His red-and-white recumbent America recalls the centrality of Picasso's horse in *Guernica*, yet rather than evoke the tragedies of war, the mural allegorizes the distant past. The central allegory's open mouth and outstretched arm can suggest the shock of birth or the violence of conquest. Here Tamayo's conception of American hemispheric history tilts more toward a Mexican view of *mestizaje*, rather than the US experience of European settlers, Native American reservations, African slavery, imperial incursions, and waves of immigration. To a certain extent he does attempt to conjure the specificities of US history. Near the red foot of America, Tamayo depicts a green plant, with splaying leaves evocative of corn, an essential crop for both the United States and Mexico. As a possible reference to a Texan industry, he includes an oil geyser emanating from the land. Even his use of the term *melting* to describe the coming together of European and indigenous populations brings to mind notions of the US "melting pot," still a common descriptor of American society in the 1950s. Tamayo would continue to find an audience and patrons in New York after his departure, yet his exhibitions isolated, rather than integrated him into the US cultural context that nurtured him during his formative years. Later in life, Tamayo himself would indirectly distance his approach to art making from that of the abstract expressionists. Tamayo was not short on praise for artists like Jackson Pollock, but he was also dismissive when he considered their contributions as technical and their art requiring critical interpretation to be understood.[226] Tamayo's commitment to the figure was key to his definition of humanism and his desire to communicate with his audience.

Rufino Tamayo came of age during an era of profound cultural change in his native Mexico. He absorbed the period's reassessment of indigenous cultures, and interpreted pre-Columbian and Mexican popular art in aesthetic terms. Seeking new horizons, he ventured to New York, placing himself at the center of a transformative period in the art of the United States. "I was made in New York," Tamayo said later in his life, acknowledging the city's role in his development as an artist.[227] It was there that he encountered other artists who were on a similar path to define themselves and the art of their country. The city's stimulating museums and galleries opened his eyes to a breadth of aesthetic options that allowed him to reconceive the goals of modern Mexican art. Tamayo benefited from the platform and patronage afforded to Mexican artists in the United States, which drew a spotlight to his brand of modernist, but not social-realist Mexican art. The combination of encountering Picasso and witnessing the global crises of the war period profoundly shaped his art. These productive years raised his artistic profile in the United States, helping to stir dialogue that resonated with US artists who shared his desire to emotively visualize the angst of the postwar era. Tamayo's New York story is a complex one that reveals how his immersion in the US art world shaped his art and how in turn his presence had ripple effects in the broader art world, especially at the end of his New York tenure. The rising abstract expressionists may not have emulated Tamayo's style, but as they were beginning to assert a new direction in contemporary art, they (and their supporters) drew resolve from his prominent example as an American artist driven by aesthetic and not overt sociopolitical concerns.[228] Influence, in other words, comes in many forms. The Mexican impact on the art of the United States did not end with the muralists. Tamayo absorbed the New York artistic scene, was transformed by it, and also helped redefine notions of the national across the Americas at a crucial time in history.

NOTES

1. A 1947 note in Tamayo's curatorial file at MoMA that transcribes a telephone conversation notes: "Tamayo does not ever intend to become an American citizen." Rufino Tamayo Curatorial File (General), Museum of Modern Art, New York, Department of Painting and Sculpture.

2. For more on this phenomenon, see Helen Delpar, *The Enormous Vogue of Things Mexican: Cultural Relations between the United States and Mexico, 1920–1935* (Tuscaloosa: University of Alabama Press, 1992); and James Oles, ed., *South of the Border: Mexico in the American Imagination, 1914–1947* (Washington, DC: Smithsonian Institution Press, 1993).

3. Jaime Torres Bodet to Bernardo Ortiz de Montellano, April 1928, cited in Jaime Torres Bodet, *Sedienta soledad: treinta y seis cartas a Bernardo Ortiz de Montellano*, ed. Lourdes Franco Bagnouls (Mexico City: Universidad Nacional Autónoma de México, 2003), 37.

4. This idea especially comes to the fore when Tamayo returns triumphantly to Mexico City between 1946 and 1948 and presents two important exhibitions of his work. Critics highlight how his work is not known owing to his long residence in New York; other critics label him an outsider, and deride him for adopting the concerns and style of US art. See Antonio Rodríguez, "La pintura Mexicana está en decadencia, dice Tamayo: Diego Rivera, José Clemente Orozco y David Alfaro Siqueiros, en declive," *El Nacional* (Mexico City), September 22, 1947, 1; "Raíz en la esencia mexicana," *Tiempo* (Mexico City), October 3, 1947, 34; Miguel Ángel Mendoza, "Artes plásticas," *Revista de América* (Mexico City), October 4, 1947, 38; and Antonio Rodríguez, "La pintura de Tamayo es la negación de la pintura mexicana: dice Juan O'Gorman," *El Nacional* (Mexico City), July 2, 1948, 3.

5. "Tamayo; He Fuses Power of Primitive Art with Sophistication of Modern Painting, Combines Strength and Tenderness," source unknown; likely *Look*, 1943, Rufino Tamayo vertical file, Ryerson Library, Art Institute of Chicago.

6. See Jürgen Harten, *Siqueiros/Pollock, Pollock/Siqueiros* (Düsseldorf: DuMont, 1995); and Elizabeth A. T. Smith, Colette Dartnall, and William Rubin, *Matta in America: Paintings and Drawings of the 1940s* (Chicago: Museum of Contemporary Art, 2001).

7. See Edward J. Sullivan, "Tamayo, el mundillo artístico neoyorquino y el mural del Smith College," in *Rufino Tamayo: pinturas* (Madrid: Centro Nacional de Exposiciones, 1988), 14–29; and Rita Eder, "Tamayo en Nueva York," in *Rufino Tamayo: 70 años de creación* (Mexico City: INBA/Museo Tamayo Arte Contemporáneo, 1987), 55–65.

8. For example, Mary Coffey, in her study of Tamayo's murals in the United States and Mexico, established conceptual links between Tamayo's large-scale portable murals—executed after his New York period—and the expansive canvases of the abstract expressionists. James Oles powerfully revealed the strong World War II subtext of Tamayo's 1940s paintings. And Anna Indych-López turned a critical eye to Tamayo's career maneuverings in 1940s New York. Key essays by these three scholars can be found in Diana C. du Pont, ed., *Tamayo: A Modern Icon Reinterpreted* (Santa Barbara, CA: Santa Barbara Museum of Art, 2007).

9. American artist George Biddle urged President Franklin D. Roosevelt to start the New Deal arts program based on the example of Mexican muralism. See Bruce I. Bustard, *A New*

Deal for the Arts (Washington, DC: National Archives and Records Administration in association with the University of Washington Press, 1997).

10. See Alejandro Anreus, Diana L. Linden, and Jonathan Weinberg, eds., *The Social and the Real: Political Art of the 1930s in the Western Hemisphere* (University Park: Pennsylvania State University Press, 2006); and Anthony W. Lee, *Painting on the Left: Diego Rivera, Radical Politics, and San Francisco's Public Murals* (Berkeley: University of California Press, 1999).

11. See Lizzetta LeFalle-Collins and Shifra M. Goldman, *In the Spirit of Resistance: African-American Modernists and the Mexican Muralist School* (New York: American Federation of Arts, 1996); and Alison Cameron, "Buenos Vecinos: African-American Printmaking and the Taller de Gráfica Popular," *Print Quarterly* 16, no. 4 (December 1999): 353–67.

12. Herbert J. Spinden, a major scholar of Native American art in the United States, put it this way: "Mexico and Peru are acquiring new social personalities through coalescence of the traditions and capabilities of the Indian and the Spaniard. In a similar way our own aborigines must supply an ingredient to the national character of the United States. We may safely trust these first Americans with a mandate of beauty. In a world which grows mechanical they seem able to keep contact with the great illusions." See Herbert J. Spinden, "Fine Art and the First Americans," in *Introduction to American Indian Art*, vol. 2, ed. Frederick Webb Hodge, Herbert J. Spinden, and Oliver La Farge (New York: Exposition of Indian Tribal Arts, 1931), 8.

13. Grace L. McCann Morley, "The Mexican Renaissance," in *Art of Our Time* (San Francisco: San Francisco Museum of Art, 1945), 27.

14. See Francis V. O'Connor, "The Influence of Diego Rivera on the Art of the United States during the 1930s and After," in *Diego Rivera: A Retrospective*, ed. Cynthia Newman Helms (New York: W. W. Norton, 1986), 157–83; Mary K. Coffey, Sharon Lorenzo, Lisa Mintz Messinger, and Stephen Polcari, *Men of Fire: José Clemente Orozco and Jackson Pollock* (Hanover, NH: Hood Museum of Art, Dartmouth College, 2012); and Ellen G. Landau, *Mexico and American Modernism* (New Haven: Yale University Press, 2013); see especially note 9.

15. Rufino Tamayo, "El nacionalismo y el movimiento pictórico," *Crisol: Revista de Crítica* 9, no. 53 (May 1, 1933): 275–81.

16. Bambi (Ana Cecilia Treviño de Gironella), "Yo no soy el cuarto grande," *Excélsior* (Mexico City), September 9, 1953, cited in Mary K. Coffey, *How a Revolutionary Art Became Official Culture: Murals, Museums, and the Mexican State* (Durham, NC: Duke University Press, 2012), 63n130.

17. For more on official *indigenismo*, see David A. Brading, "Manuel Gamio and Official Indigenismo in Mexico," *Bulletin of Latin American Research* 7, no. 1 (1988): 75–89; and Rick A. Lopéz, *Crafting Mexico: Intellectuals, Artisans, and the State after the Revolution* (Durham, NC: Duke University Press, 2010).

18. David Alfaro Siqueiros and other signatories, "Manifesto of the Technical Workers, Painters, and Sculptors Union of Mexico," in Mari Carmen Ramírez and Héctor Olea, *Inverted Utopias: Avant-Garde Art in Latin America* (New Haven: Yale University Press, 2004), 461; emphasis in the original. See also David Alfaro Siqueiros et al., "Manifiesto del Sindicato de Obreros Técnicos, Pintores y Escultores," 1923 (Mexico City: Sala de Arte Público Siqueiros).

19. For more on the Stridentists, see Tatiana Flores, *Mexico's Revolutionary Avant-Gardes: From Estridentismo to ¡30-30!* (New Haven: Yale University Press, 2013); and James Oles, "Industrial Landscapes in Modern Mexican Art," special issue, *Journal of Decorative and Propaganda Arts* 26 (2010): 128–59.

20. Cristina Pacheco, *La luz de México: entrevistas con pintores y fotógrafos*, 2d ed. (Mexico City: Fondo de Cultura Económica, 1995), 577.

21. Ibid., 576.

22. Ibid., 577.

23. Diego Rivera, "La exposición de la Escuela Nacional de Bellas Artes," *Azulejos* 1, no. 3 (October 1921): 22.

24. For more on the exhibition and its relationship to *indigenismo*, see Rick A. López, "The Noche Mexicana and the Exhibition of Popular Arts: Two Ways of Exalting Indianness," in *The Eagle and the Virgin: Nation and Cultural Revolution in Mexico, 1920–1940*, ed. Mary Kay Vaughan and Stephen E. Lewis (Durham, NC: Duke University Press, 2006), 23–42.

25. For more on the Best Maugard method, see Karen Cordero Reiman, "The Best Maugard Drawing Method: A Common Ground for Modern Mexicanist Aesthetics," special issue, *Journal of Decorative and Propaganda Arts* 26 (2010): 44–79.

26. Karen Cordero Reiman, Arely Ramírez Moyao, and Adriana Domínguez Velasco, *Construyendo Tamayo, 1922–1937* (Mexico City: Fundación Olga y Rufino Tamayo, AC, 2013), 29–37.

27. Ingrid Suckaer, *Rufino Tamayo: aproximaciones* (Mexico City: Editorial Praxis, 2000), 72.

28. Emily Genauer, *Rufino Tamayo* (New York: Harry N. Abrams, 1974), 30–31.

29. Tamayo began collecting Mesoamerican art in the 1950s and amassed a significant collection. He later gifted his collection to the state of Oaxaca. In 1974 the Museo de Arte Prehispánico de México Rufino Tamayo opened its doors.

30. See Rivera's murals in the Courtyard of Fiestas at the Secretaría de Educación Pública. These are reproduced in Desmond Rochfort, *Mexican Muralists: Orozco, Rivera, and Siqueiros* (London: Laurence King, 1993), 62–65.

31. A bilingual checklist prepared by either Tamayo or the Weyhe Gallery in New York in the 1920s identifies this painting as *India frutera*. See John Ittmann curatorial files for *Mexico and Modern Printmaking: A Revolution in the Graphic Arts, 1920 to 1950*, Philadelphia Museum of Art.

32. Both Tatiana Flores and James Oles interpret Tamayo's industrial images in critical terms, highlighting the dark tonality of his paintings and the consistent absence of people. See Flores, *Mexico's Revolutionary Avant-Gardes*, 215–16; and Oles, "Industrial Landscapes in Modern Mexican Art," 128.

33. For more on the goals of this space, see Carlos Mérida, "La nueva galería de arte moderno/The New Modern Art Gallery," *Mexican Folkways* 4, no. 4 (October–December 1929): 184–91.

34. As translated and quoted in Adriana Domínguez Velasco, "Fragment of a Path: The Early Years: 1920–1929," in *Construyendo Tamayo*, 83. The original quote comes from Xavier Villaurrutia, "Los nuevos pintores: un sensual," reproduced in *Los Empeños*, no. 1

(April–June 1981), cited in Judith Alanís and Sofía Urrutia, *Rufino Tamayo: una cronología, 1899–1987* (Mexico City: Museo Rufino Tamayo, INBA/SEP, 1987), 14n4.

35. Carlos Mérida, "La obra de Tamayo," *Suplemento dominical de El Demócrata*, April 18, 1926, 11.

36. Tamayo arrived with Carlos Chávez on SS *Monterey* on September 10, 1926. See "List or Manifest of Alien Passengers for the United States Immigration Officer at Port of Arrival," SS *Monterey*, List 8, September 10, 1926, in *New York, Passenger Lists, 1820–1957*, ancestry.com, accessed September 8, 2016.

37. "Paris es mi *goal*, llegará el día en que iré al único lugar de la tierra donde esteré feliz, aun en la miseria. En el fondo no soy más que un místico y sólo busco la isla tranquila donde dar rienda suelta a mi inteligencia." See Rufino Tamayo to José Gorostiza, March 1, 1927, in José Gorostiza, *Epistolario (1918–1940)*, ed. Guillermo Sheridan (Mexico City: Consejo Nacional para la Cultura y las Artes, 1995), 122–23.

38. Orozco received a subsidy to establish himself in New York in 1927. See Renato González Mello and Diane Miliotes, eds., *José Clemente Orozco in the United States, 1927–1934* (Hanover, NH: Hood Museum of Art, Dartmouth College, 2002), 54.

39. Roberto García Morillo, *Carlos Chávez: vida y obra* (Mexico City: Fondo de Cultura Económica, 1960), 26.

40. See Katherine E. Manthorne, "Art School as Contact Zone: Latin American Artists and Their Teachers," in *Nexus New York: Latin/American Artists in the Modern Metropolis*, ed. Deborah Cullen (New York: El Museo del Barrio in association with Yale University Press, 2009). For artists from the Spanish-speaking Caribbean (Cuba, the Dominican Republic, and Puerto Rico), US political interventions established links between the United States and their home countries.

41. See Courtney Gilbert, "The (New) World in the Time of the Surrealists: European Surrealists and Their Mexican Contemporaries" (PhD diss., University of Chicago, 2001), 78–170.

42. Adriana Williams, *Covarrubias*, ed. Doris Ober (Austin: University of Texas Press, 1994), 18.

43. Suckaer, *Rufino Tamayo: aproximaciones*, 100–101.

44. Ibid., 98.

45. "36 Years of Matisse Shown at Dudensing's," *Art News* 25, no. 13 (January 1, 1927): 1.

46. Ibid.

47. See *International Exhibition of Modern Art Assembled by the Société Anonyme* (New York: Anderson Galleries, 1927), 2. The catalogue for the Brooklyn Museum show was written by Katherine S. Dreier and Constantin Aladjalov. See *International Exhibition of Modern Art* (New York: Brooklyn Museum and Société Anonyme, 1926), 2.

48. Dreier and Aladjalov, *International Exhibition of Modern Art*, n.p.

49. Delmari Romero Keith, *Historia y testimonios: Galería de Arte Mexicano* (Mexico City: Ediciones Galería de Arte Mexicano, 1985), 28.

50. For more on Gallatin's collection and museum, see Gail Stavitsky, "A. E. Gallatin's Gallery and Museum of Living Art (1927–1943)," *American Art* 7, no. 2 (Spring 1993): 46–63.

51. "Modern Art for New York University," *Art News* 26, no. 5 (November 5, 1927): 1. For a general introduction to the Gallatin collection, see Albert Gallatin, "The Plan of the Museum of Living Art," in *A. E. Gallatin Collection: "Museum of Living Art"* (Philadelphia: Philadelphia Museum of Art, 1954), 5.

52. "Modern Art for New York University," 1.

53. "Rufino Tamayo, pintor mexicano, nos habla de su arte," *El Universal*, December 7, 1928.

54. The de Chirico exhibition at the Valentine Gallery was on view from January 23 to February 11, 1928, when Tamayo was still in New York.

55. See Dreier and Aladjalov, *International Exhibition of Modern Art*, 61.

56. Henry McBride, quoted in Jennifer Landes, "Giorgio de Chirico and the American Critics, 1920–1940," in *Giorgio de Chirico and America*, ed. Emily Braun (New York: Hunter College, 1996), 35.

57. Gilbert, "The (New) World," 102.

58. Innis Howe Shoemaker, "Crossing Borders: The Weyhe Gallery and the Vogue for Mexican Art in the United States, 1926–40," in *Mexico and Modern Printmaking: A Revolution in the Graphic Arts, 1920 to 1950*, ed. John Ittmann (Philadelphia: Philadelphia Museum of Art, 2006).

59. John Ittmann, "Rufino Tamayo," in *Mexico and Modern Printmaking*, 104.

60. Less prominent were works that represented a modern or industrial Mexico, as had appeared in Tamayo's Mexican solo exhibition. A checklist from research files at the Philadelphia Museum of Art lists only one work, *Chimneys*, that possibly depicts an industrial subject.

61. Gabriel Fernández Ledesma, "El pintor Rufino Tamayo," *Forma* 1, no. 5 (1927): 2–3.

62. Xavier Villaurrutia, "Rufino Tamayo (1948)," in *Rufino Tamayo: antología critica*, Grandes Maestros Mexicanos 13 (Mexico City: Editorial Terra Nova, SA, 1987). This essay was first published in *México en el Arte*, no. 2 (August 1948).

63. For more on Mexico's print revival, see Flores, *Mexico's Revolutionary Avant-Gardes*, 167–76.

64. For a fuller consideration of how Tamayo strategically positioned himself within the overlapping discourses of Mexican *indigenismo* and modernist primitivism, see Anna Indych-López, "'None of Those Little Donkeys for Me': Tamayo, Cultural Prestige, and Perceptions of Modern Mexican Art in the United States," in *Tamayo: A Modern Icon Reinterpreted*.

65. "The Art Center is a federation of seven art-producing societies. It fosters all forms of art, especially those related to industry. Exhibitions in the Art Center galleries are free to the public." From the cover of *Art Center Bulletin* 9, no. 7 (April 1931).

66. Gilbert, "The (New) World," 103.

67. Crowninshield's collection of African art was presented at the Brooklyn Museum, and Suckaer claims that he was also an early patron of MoMA. Suckaer, *Rufino Tamayo: Aproximaciones*, 102.

68. Ibid., 100.

69. Frank Crowninshield, *Rufino Tamayo* (New York: The Art Center, 1927), n.p.

70. Indych-López, "'None of Those Little Donkeys for Me,'" 347.

71. See "Work of a Brilliant Young Mexican Artist Shown at Art Center," *Brooklyn Eagle*, November 20, 1927; and "The Native Expression," *Vogue*, likely 1927 or 1928.

72. Indych-López, "'None of Those Little Donkeys for Me,'" 347.

73. See Miguel Covarrubias, *Negro Drawings* (New York: Knopf, 1927). For a good discussion of the New York reception of Covarrubias's caricatures in the 1920s, see Phoebe Wolfskill "Caricature and the New Negro in the Work of Archibald Motley Jr. and Palmer Hayden," *Art Bulletin* 91, no. 3 (September 2009): 343–65. *Negro Drawings* showcases a range of Covarrubias's approaches to black subjects, from highly caricatured, almost minstrel-like figures to representations with exaggerated facial features underneath the guise of modern, sophisticated fashion.

74. Virginia Hagelstein Marquardt, "'New Masses' and John Reed Club Artists, 1926–1936: Evolution of Ideology, Subject Matter, and Style," *Journal of Decorative and Propaganda Arts* 12 (Spring 1989): 64; see also Helen Langa, "'At Least Half the Pages Will Consist of Pictures': 'New Masses' and Politicized Visual Art," *American Periodicals* 21, no. 1 (2011): 24–49.

75. James Oles describes these in Oles, *South of the Border*, 57.

76. Such illustrations by Charlot are included in the November 1926 and March 1927 issues of the *New Masses*.

77. Ellen Wiley Todd, *The "New Woman" Revised: Painting and Gender Politics on Fourteenth Street* (Berkeley: University of California Press, 1993), xxvi.

78. The caption reads: "So he says to me, he says, 'whadda you think this is a rest cure?' he says. Can you beat that? The nerve of 'im!" See *New Masses* 2, no. 6 (April 1927): 10.

79. There are two known works by Tamayo that depict Coney Island, though these were produced later—in 1931 and 1936. Boardman Robinson's August 1926 *New Masses* cover, which depicts two women wrestling on the beach, also resembles Tamayo's cover.

80. This painting was on display in *Loan Exhibition of Paintings from El Greco and Rembrandt to Cézanne and Matisse*, Reinhardt Galleries, New York, from January 15 to January 29 (inclusive), 1927.

81. Carlos Chávez, Ciro Méndez, Bernardo Ortiz de Montellano, Rufino Tamayo, and unknown to Carlos Pellicer, October 9, 1926, Sección VI, Archivo Carlos Pellicer Cámara, Instituto de Investigaciones Bibliográficas, Biblioteca Nacional, Universidad Nacional Autónoma de México.

82. There is a dispute in the literature as to when and how many times Tamayo returned to New York in the years after his first trip. Based on a ship manifest, we know that he returned to the city in September 1930. He was also present in the spring of 1931, when he participated in an exhibition at the John Levy Galleries.

83. Edward Alden Jewell, "More Mexican Canvases," *New York Times*, April 28, 1931, 31.

84. Audrey McMahon and Virginia Nirdlinger, "A Perspective View of the New York Season (1930–1931)," *Parnassus* 3, no. 5 (May 1931): 43; and Murdock Pemberton, "The Art Galleries," *New Yorker*, May 9, 1931, 40.

85. The *Mexican Arts* exhibition had its roots in the diplomatic efforts of former US ambassador to Mexico Dwight Morrow. He conceived the idea, and the Carnegie Corporation funded the very successful traveling show. For more on this exhibition, see Gilbert, "The (New) World," 104–10. James Oles, "For Business or Pleasure: Exhibiting Mexican Folk Art, 1820–1930," in *Casa Mañana: The Morrow Collection of Mexican Popular Arts*, ed. Susan Danly (Albuquerque: University of New Mexico Press, 2002), 27.

86. René d'Harnoncourt, "The Loan Exhibition of Mexican Arts," *Metropolitan Museum of Art Bulletin* 25, no. 10 (October 1930): 211.

87. René d'Harnoncourt, "Fine Arts," in *Mexican Arts* (Portland, ME: Southworth Press, 1930), 42–43.

88. See Anna Indych-López, "Mexican Curios," in *Muralism without Walls: Rivera, Orozco, and Siqueiros in the United States, 1927–1940* (Pittsburgh, PA: University of Pittsburgh Press, 2009), 75–128.

89. Duncan Phillips to Frances F. Paine, October 31, 1930, curatorial file, Phillips Collection, Washington, DC.

90. Although an extensive catalogue of the Phillips Collection does exist, it does not document all of the works in the collection. We do know that around this time Duncan Phillips acquired works by Jean Charlot and expressed admiration for Diego Rivera.

91. See "Second Exhibitions, February to June 1931," curatorial file, Phillips Collection, Washington, DC.

92. Exhibition brochure for *Exposición de pintura actual organizada por la revista Contemporáneos*, December 7–15, 1928, Pasaje América, Mexico City.

93. Gabriel García Maroto, quoted and translated in Adriana Zavala, *Becoming Modern, Becoming Tradition: Women, Gender, and Representation in Mexican Art* (University Park: Pennsylvania State University Press, 2010), 208n14.

94. "Una exposición de pintura moderna," *Revista de Revistas*, October 27, 1929, 17.

95. Jorge Montaño, "Rufino Tamayo: Leader of a New Mexican School of Painting," *Mexican Life* 5, no. 11 (November 1929): 23–27.

96. For more on Tamayo's relationship to los Contemporáneos, see Robin Greeley, "Nietzsche contra Marx in Mexico: The Contemporáneos, Muralism, and Debates over 'Revolutionary' Art in 1930s Mexico," in *Mexican Muralism: A Critical History*, ed. Alejandro Anreus, Leonard Folgarait, and Robin Adèle Greeley (Berkeley: University of California Press, 2012), 148–73; Mark A. Castro, "Tales of the City: The Contemporáneos and Modern Mexican Art," in *Paint the Revolution: Mexican Modernism, 1910–1950*, ed. Matthew Affron, Mark A. Castro, Dafne Cruz Porchini, and Renato González Mello (New Haven: Yale University Press, 2016), 311–19; and Érika Madrigal, "Tamayo y los Contemporáneos: el discurso de lo clásico y lo universal," *Anales del Instituto de Investigaciones Estéticas* 30, no. 92 (2008): 155–89.

97. Karen Cordero Reiman, "Appropriation, Invention, and Irony: Tamayo's Early Period, 1920–1937," in *Tamayo: A Modern Icon Reinterpreted*, 176–77.

98. Diana C. du Pont, "'Realistic, Never Descriptive': Tamayo and the Art of Abstract Figuration," in *Tamayo: A Modern Icon Reinterpreted*, 82–86.

99. I am grateful to Dr. Ray Hernández for helping me identify this type of Mexican wall construction. E-mail communication with the author, December 27, 2016.

100. Dogs were considered protective creatures in Mesoamerican belief systems.

101. Madrigal, "Tamayo y los Contemporáneos," 168.

102. See Courtney Gilbert, "Negotiating Surrealism: Carlos Mérida, Mexican Art and the Avant-Garde," special issue, *Journal of Surrealism and the Americas* 3, no. 1–2 (2009): 30–50; and Zavala, *Becoming Modern, Becoming Tradition*, 203–38. Both scholars affirm that surrealism in Mexico does not begin with André Breton's visit to Mexico in 1938. With respect to

Tamayo and the Contemporáneos, the metaphysical painting of Giorgio de Chirico—who at this point had not yet been fully adopted by the surrealists—is more relevant to the ideas explored here.

103. J[ean] Cocteau, "Fragmentos sobre Chirico," *Contemporáneos* 1, no. 3 (August 1928): 261–64.

104. For more examples of these works, see Braun, *Giorgio de Chirico and America*.

105. Cristina Pacheco, "40 años de fotografía," *Siempre*, May 16, 1979, reproduced in "Entrevistas con Lola Álvarez Bravo," in *Lola Álvarez Bravo: fotografías selectas 1934–1985* (Mexico City: Centro Cultural/Arte Contemporáneo, 1992).

106. Cordero Reiman et al., *Construyendo Tamayo, 1922–1937*, 72.

107. My interpretation draws on the work of several scholars, including: Ramon Favela, "Los murales de Rufino Tamayo en los Estados Unidos," in *Rufino Tamayo: 70 años de creación*; Mary K. Coffey "'I'm Not the Fourth Great One': Tamayo and Mexican Muralism," in *Tamayo: A Modern Icon Reinterpreted*, 248–67; and Robin Greeley, "Nietzsche contra Marx in Mexico."

108. Tamayo acknowledged that Mexicans are diverse and comprised of criollos, mestizos, and Indians, as well as foreign artists who reside in Mexico and participate in the national artistic scene. See Cordero Reiman et al., *Construyendo Tamayo, 1922–1937*, 23–25.

109. Tamayo, "El nacionalismo y el movimiento pictórico," 279.

110. Ibid., 281.

111. "Pero Tamayo es Tamayo, y mexicano en la medida en que cualquier otro pintor nuestro pueda serlo. Pocos son los que hayan interpretado de manera tan hábil y sensible la maravillosa experiencia física del medio [y] el conocimiento inmediato por los sentidos." Chano Urueta, "La pintura de Rufino Tamayo," *Todo*, November 1935.

112. "Es tremendamente mexicano sin pretensión de hacer arte nacionalista; sencillo hasta la temeridad, no solo en los temas sino que en el dibujo y hasta en los colores." From "Rufino Tamayo," *Universidad: Mensual de Cultura Popular* 4, no. 22 (November 1937): 48.

113. Tamayo was good friends with one of LEAR's founders and one of its most representative artists, Leopoldo Méndez. See Suckaer, *Rufino Tamayo: aproximaciones*, 55.

114. Francisco Reyes Palma, "Radicalismo artístico en el México de los años 30: una respuesta colectiva a la crisis," *Artes Plásticas: Revista de la Escuela Nacional de Artes Plásticas UNAM* 2, no. 7 (December 1988/89): 5–16.

115. For a great discussion of LEAR, see Deborah Caplow, *Leopoldo Méndez: Revolutionary Art and the Mexican Print* (Austin: University of Texas Press, 2007), 93–122.

116. Ibid., 95.

117. Suckaer, *Rufino Tamayo: Aproximaciones*, 119.

118. These photographs show protestors holding letter signs that spell LEAR, and other signage that makes reference to the president. It's not clear if Tamayo was present and/or the photographer. Photographs are deposited in the Centro de Documentación del Museo Tamayo Arte Contemporáneo, Mexico City.

119. Caplow, *Leopoldo Méndez*, 94. In fact, Ana Torres considers some of Tamayo's works from his LEAR period to be a form of social realism. See Ana Torres, *Identidades pictóricas y culturales de Rufino Tamayo: ¿Un pintor de ruptura?* (Mexico City: Universidad Iberoamericana, 2011), 128.

120. Cordero Reiman interprets the ambiguous spatial arrangement of *Factory Workers' Movement* as creating a painting within a painting that juxtaposes an ordered view of a factory in the background (as if it were a mural) and a large group of factory workers in the foreground. She notes: "These images avoid a literal reading and thus critique the rhetorical and dogmatic approach—characteristic of post-Revolutionary art that acquired increasing prominence in the early 1930s." While I do not disagree with her interpretation, the painting can be read more directly and still support her argument. See Cordero Reiman, "Appropriation, Invention, and Irony: Tamayo's Early Period, 1920–1937," 182.

121. Ibid.

122. Orozco discussed possible relationships between artists and trade unions, and Siqueiros focused on the need to revolutionize what he called the forms of art, an idea he took up with the Experimental Workshop he founded in New York shortly thereafter. Orozco's and Siqueiros's remarks are published in Matthew Baigell and Julia Williams, eds., *Artists against War and Fascism: Papers of the First American Artists' Congress* (New Brunswick, NJ: Rutgers University Press, 1986). For more on Siqueiros, see Laurance P. Hurlburt, "The Siqueiros Experimental Workshop: New York, 1936," *Art Journal* 35, no. 3 (Spring 1976): 237–46. Anna Indych-López substantively discusses Orozco's and Siqueiros's presentations at the AAC; see "Mexican Muralism in the United States in the Early 1930s: The Social, the Real and the Modern," in *Paint the Revolution*, 339–47.

123. After this trip he also renewed his ties to the *New Masses*; between 1936 and 1937, Tamayo appeared twice in the journal. A small, antifascist decoration featuring a swastika appears in the December 1936 issue, and his painting *Ritmo obrero* (1935) is illustrated in the February 1937 issue.

124. There are many conflicting accounts of when Tamayo stayed in New York. What is clear is that he came to the city in 1936 for the American Artists' Congress. Some accounts mention a subsequent return to Mexico and highlight 1938 as the date he definitively settled in New York for an extended period. Later in his life Tamayo also pointed to 1935 as the year of his return, but this has not been substantiated. He initially secured a diplomatic post that facilitated his stay in the United States. In the ensuing years Tamayo pursued other professional opportunities including teaching, which allowed him to make a livelihood in New York.

125. Tamayo stayed in New York roughly through 1949; thereafter he began to reside more in France and Mexico.

126. See Ann Prentice Wagner, *1934: A New Deal for Artists* (Washington, DC: Smithsonian American Art Museum, 2009). For more on Tamayo's participation in the FAP, see James Lynch Jr., "Tamayo Revisited," introduction to *Rufino Tamayo: Fifty Years of His Painting* (Washington, DC: Phillips Collection, 1978), 16. Ramon Favela says that Tamayo's plans for the Kings County Hospital mural were rejected. Without more definitive archival evidence, it's not clear why it was rejected, or if it was canceled because Tamayo was not a US citizen, as James Oles asserts. See Favela, "Los murales de Rufino Tamayo en los Estados Unidos," 72; and James Oles, "Rufino Tamayo," in *Blanton Museum of Art: Latin American Collection*, ed. Gabriel Pérez-Barreiro (Austin: Blanton Museum of Art, The University of Texas at Austin, 2006), 396.

127. In addition to this watercolor, a handful of Tamayo's FAP works were later deposited in collections, including the Brooklyn Museum, New York's Museum of Modern Art (*Waiting Woman*, which is included in the present exhibition), and the San Francisco Museum of Modern Art.

128. On at least two occasions, Tamayo traveled by boat to New York, sailing from Mexico, to Havana, and finally to New York.

129. While American scene painting as a category is very much associated with social realism and American regionalism, the term was never clearly defined. For instance, Stuart Davis, who was not a social realist, also categorized his work as American scene painting. See Barbara Haskell, "Quotidian Truth: Stuart Davis's Idiosyncratic Modernism," in *Stuart Davis: In Full Swing* (Munich: Prestel in association with National Gallery of Art, Washington, and the Whitney Museum of Art, 2016), 1–21.

130. See, for example, Guy Pène du Bois's *At the Soda Fountain* (1930), a painting in the collection of the Boca Raton Museum of Art in Florida.

131. For more on this image and the intense focus on Coney Island by many artists in the United States, see Robin Jaffee Frank, "'The Nickel Empire': 1930–1939," in *Coney Island: Visions of an American Dreamland, 1861–2008* (New Haven: Yale University Press, 2015), 94.

132. A picture of one of these pageants appears in Frank, "'The Nickel Empire': 1930–1939," 99.

133. Henry McBride, "Attractions in the Galleries," *New York Sun*, February 4, 1939, n.p.

134. "Tamayo, Rufino," *Cue*, February 11, 1939.

135. According to Mary-Anne Martin, who discussed this painting with Tamayo in the 1970s, Tamayo painted the canvas to appease his wife, who complained of the less than ideal view from their modest New York apartment. Author's conversation with Mary-Anne Martin, May 10, 2016.

136. He conveys his fascination with the modernity of New York in other paintings from the period, like *Aviation* (1938; whereabouts unknown). Here, Tamayo depicts the tops of several tall buildings, surrounded by electrical wires and three swirling airplanes. This painting is illustrated in *Tamayo: A Modern Icon Reinterpreted*, 155. During later visits to New York City in the 1950s and 1960s, Tamayo took many photographs of the skyline and downtown street life, often seen from high above, resembling his iconic 1937 canvas. See Pablo Ortiz Monasterio, *Tamayo: Photographer in New York* (Barcelona: RM Verlag, 2015).

137. Anna Indych-López, "Frozen Assets," in *Diego Rivera: Murals for the Museum of Modern Art* (New York: Museum of Modern Art, 2011), 116–19.

138. For more on Orozco's New York paintings, see Alejandro Anreus, "Easel Paintings, Drawings, and Lithographs, 1928–32," in *Orozco in Gringoland: The Years in New York* (Albuquerque: University of New Mexico Press, 2001), 47–90.

139. Skyscrapers have been a popular subject for New York artists since the late nineteenth century. I focus here on two contemporaneous examples that Tamayo likely saw in the mid-1930s.

140. I want to thank New York University professor Mosette Broderick for helping me identify the type of building suggested by Tamayo's red structure. E-mail communication with the author, August 10, 2016.

141. Tamayo's dealer Julien Levy and his soon-to-be dealer Valentine Dudensing were enthusiastic supporters of Shaw's work. Shaw also exhibited his *Plastic Polygons*, including the one illustrated here, at an exhibition of the American Abstract Artists at the Squibb Galleries in New York in 1937.

142. Luis Cardoza y Aragón affirms that Tamayo socialized in Harlem and knew Aaron Douglas and likely James Van Der Zee. I am grateful to Alejandro Anreus for sharing his unpublished interview with Aragón, conducted in Coyocán, Mexico, on June 23, 1987. Van Vechten mentions the sitting with Rufino and Olga Tamayo in a letter to Gertrude Stein. See *The Letters of Gertrude Stein and Carl Van Vechten, 1913–1946*, ed. Edward Burns (New York: Columbia University Press, 1986), 800–801. For Aaron Douglas's address at the AAC, see "The Negro in American Culture," in *Artists against War and Fascism*, 78–84.

143. Anna Indych-López was the first to point out the possible relationship between Tamayo's dark-skinned figures and Afro-Mexicans or African Americans; see "'None of Those Little Donkeys for Me,'" 347. Tamayo was from the state of Oaxaca, home to a significant Afro-Mexican population. While Mexico's "third root"—as the country's African heritage is commonly known—was not actively discussed until the 1990s, there is evidence of an awareness of Afro-Mexicans during the post-revolutionary period. In 1928, for instance, the bilingual journal *Mexican Folkways* published Dr. Ramon Pardo's article "Poetry of the Negroes of Oaxaca." See *Mexican Folkways* 4, no. 1 (January–March 1928): 28–30. For more on Afro-Mexicans, see Tony Gleaton, *Africa's Legacy in Mexico* (Washington, DC: Smithsonian Institution Traveling Exhibition Service, 1993); and Krithika Varagur, "Mexico Finally Recognized Its Black Citizens, But That's Just the Beginning," January 27, 2016; http://www.huffingtonpost.com/entry/mexico-finally-recognized-its-black-citizens-but-thats-just-the-beginning_us_568d2d9ce4b0c8beacf50f6b; accessed on December 27, 2016.

144. I am grateful to photography historian Emilie Boone for discussing Tamayo's painting in relation to photographs of African Americans in the 1930s. E-mail communication with the author, February 20, 2016. The cap worn by the child in the painting resembles one worn by a clown in Manuel Álvarez Bravo's photograph *El payasito*, which is reproduced in John Stringer, *The First America: Selections from the Nancy Sayles Day Collection of Latin American Art* (Providence: Museum of Art, Rhode Island School of Design, 1987), 56.

145. Carlos Dávila, a diplomat and former interim president of Chile, recommended Tamayo for the job. Dávila was on the board of Dalton, and his daughters attended the school. See Genauer, *Rufino Tamayo*, 42.

146. Indych-López, "'None of Those Little Donkeys for Me,'" 347.

147. McBride, "Attractions in the Galleries."

148. Emily Genauer, "Tamayo at the Valentine," *New York World Telegram*, February 4, 1939.

149. Emily Genauer, "Mexican Painting Exhibition Opens," *New York World Telegram*, February 12, 1938.

150. Howard Putzel, a surrealist enthusiast, presented Tamayo's work at the Paul Elder Gallery in San Francisco in 1935. For more on the show, see Ada Hanifin, "Tamayo Exhibit Is Interesting; Is an Individualist," *San Francisco Examiner*, February 3, 1935.

151. Eleanor Jewett, *Chicago Daily Tribune*, December 11, 1938, F5.

152. Howard Devree, "A Reviewer's Notebook: Brief Comment on Newly Opened Shows—Water-colors in the Ascendancy," *New York Times*, January 17, 1937, 162.

153. Howard Parker, "Rufino Tamayo," *Mexican Folkways* 7, no. 2 (1932): 75–81.

154. See Michael Leja, "The Mythmakers and the Primitive: Gottlieb, Newman, Rothko, and Still," in *Reframing Abstract Expressionism: Subjectivity and Painting in the 1940s* (New Haven: Yale University Press, 1993), 100–103. Leja's discussion is indebted to the arguments and scholarship of Lowery Stokes Sims.

155. J.S., "Tamayo," *Art Front* 3, no. 1 (February 1937): 17.

156. Cosponsored by the Mexican government, the MoMA exhibition was perhaps the most notable manifestation of a broader curatorial project at a number of US museums to promote President Franklin D. Roosevelt's Good Neighbor Policy, which advocated pan-American unity. Museums supported the policy through collaboration with Latin American institutions and the promotion of Latin American art.

157. Henry McBride, "Viva Mexico," *New York Sun*, May 18, 1940, 9.

158. For more on the presentation of *Guernica* in New York, see Herschel B. Chipp, *Picasso's Guernica: History, Transformations, Meanings* (Berkeley: University of California Press, 1988).

159. Henry McBride, "Picasso's *Guernica*," in *The Flow of Art: Essays and Criticisms*, ed. Daniel Catton Rich (New Haven: Yale University Press, 1975), 367. The article was originally published in the *New York Sun* in 1939.

160. Chipp, *Picasso's Guernica*, 161.

161. Robert J. Goldwater, "Picasso: Forty Years of His Art," *Art in America* 28, no. 1 (January 1940): 43–44.

162. McBride, "Picasso's *Guernica*," 368.

163. As quoted in Michael FitzGerald, "Reports from the Home Fronts: Some Skirmishes over Picasso's Reputation," in *Picasso and the War Years, 1937–1945*, ed. Steven A. Nash with Robert Rosenblum (San Francisco: Fine Arts Museums of San Francisco, 1998).

164. Eder, "Tamayo en Nueva York," 59.

165. Mexican masks were discussed in several publications. Tamayo may have been familiar with Roberto Montenegro, Xavier Villaurrutia, and Ramón Mena's book, *Máscaras Mexicanas* (Mexico City: Talleres Gráficos de la Nación, 1926). Montenegro organized the popular arts section of *Twenty Centuries of Mexican Art* at MoMA, and there is likely a strong correspondence between the masks reproduced in his earlier book and the ones on display in the exhibition. MoMA installation shots are not detailed enough to clearly gauge which types of masks were on display. Several articles about Mexican masks were published in *Mexican Folkways* 5, no. 3 (July–September 1929).

166. For more on this mural, see Linda Muehlig, *Nature and the Artist: The Work of Art and the Observer* (Northampton, MA: Smith College Museum of Art, 1993).

167. Tamayo would have been very familiar with pre-Columbian animal sculptures from his days at the Archaeology/Anthropology Museum in Mexico City and from several exhibitions in New York, including *Twenty Centuries of Mexican Art* at MoMA. In 1939 the journal *Mexican Art and Life*, which was edited by Tamayo's friend José Juan Tablada, published an article with an illustration of a dog with an upturned face that closely resembles the figure in *Dog Barking at the Moon*. See José Juan Tablada, "Animal Expressions in Aztec Art," *Mexican Art and Life*, no. 6 (April 1939): n.p.

168. Rosamund Frost, "Tamayo: Ancient & Modern Savagery," *Art News* 42, no. 13 (November 15–30, 1943): 10.

169. *War and the Artist* (New York: Pierre Matisse Gallery, 1943).

170. "Tengo que permanecer aquí a toda costa. Esta circunstancia, como Ud. sabe, me pone en el inminente peligro de ser llamado al servicio militar." Rufino Tamayo to Carlos Pellicer, November 22, 1942, Sección VI, Archivo Carlos Pellicer Cámara, Instituto de Investigaciones Bibliográficas, Biblioteca Nacional, Universidad Nacional Autónoma de México.

171. Conversation with Juan Carlos Pereda, Mexico City, March 18, 2016.

172. James Oles, "The Howl and the Flame: Tamayo's Wartime Allegories," in *Tamayo: A Modern Icon Reinterpreted*, 294.

173. For more on this, see Oles, "The Howl and the Flame," 302.

174. A photograph of the Flying Tigers of General Chennault is included in Stephen Polcari, "Adolph Gottlieb's Allegorical Epic of World War II," *Art Journal* 47 (Fall 1988): 204.

175. Dan Hagedorn, *Conquistadors of the Sky: A History of Aviation in Latin America* (Washington, DC: Smithsonian National Air and Space Museum, 2008), 3.

176. Luchita Hurtado, oral history interview by Amy Winter and Paul Karlstrom, 1994 May 1–1995 Apr. 13, Archives of American Art, Smithsonian Institution.

177. The fact that the Tamayos could not have children was a source of great emotional distress for the couple. The painting *The Doctor* may relate to this history. Suckaer, *Rufino Tamayo: aproximaciones*, 177.

178. Luchita Hurtado recalled when Tamayo painted *Animales* in her apartment: "[Tamayo] painted [the painting of] those dogs in the Museum of Modern Art…those wild dogs. When Olga, at one point was very ill because she went out of her head.…And she was sent to Bloomingdales, which is a mental institution north of New York. And Rufino came and lived with us and would go and visit Olga. And I'd say, 'How did it go?' And [he'd say that] she would throw things at him. She was really violent.…At that point, he painted those dogs." Hurtado, interview.

179. The letter asked Pellicer to extend Tamayo's official appointment as a representative of the Mexican government in the United States on account of Olga's condition and Tamayo's desire not to be drafted. See note 170, above.

180. Frost, "Tamayo: Ancient & Modern Savagery," 10.

181. Henry McBride, "A Modern Mayan," *New York Sun*, February 12, 1942.

182. Jean Charlot, "Rufino Tamayo," *Magazine of Art* 38, no. 4 (April 1945): 139–40.

183. Mexican critics based in Mexico also did not necessarily make the war-period connection. Andres Duarte wrote, "It is not exaggerated to say [Tamayo's painting] has left viewers in a sort of exalted, emotionally shaken psychological state. Any sensible man feels like this after being in contact with the heart of Mexico." See "Un pintor Mexicano en Nueva York," *Romance* (May 1, 1940).

184. Frost, "Tamayo: Ancient & Modern Savagery," 10.

185. Tamayo's *Animals* was presented in MoMA's 1943 survey exhibition of its Latin American collection; its inclusion in the other exhibitions between 1943 and 1944 needs to be confirmed. Tamayo was represented in these shows, but possibly with other works.

186. Lyn Delliquadri, "A Living Tradition: The Winterbothams and Their Legacy," *Art Institute of Chicago Museum Studies* 20, no. 2 (1994): 107.

187. Sabine Eckmann, with contributions by Bradley Fratello, George V. Speer, and H. W. Janson, *H. W. Janson and the Legacy of Modern Art at Washington University in St. Louis* (St. Louis, MO: Washington University Gallery of Art, 2002).

188. Robert J. Goldwater, *Rufino Tamayo* (New York: Quadrangle Press, 1947), 7.

189. For a contemporaneous list of Tamayo private collectors—including the ones mentioned here—see the credits in the "Table of Illustrations" in Goldwater, *Rufino Tamayo*, 126–31. For more on Roy Neuberger and the presentation of his collection in galleries and museums, including New York's MoMA and the Whitney Museum, see Tracy Fitzpatrick, introduction to *When Modern was Contemporary: The Roy R. Neuberger Collection* (Purchase, NY: Neuberger Museum of Art of Purchase College, SUNY, and American Federation of Arts, 2014), 16–55.

190. For example, Paz Dávila's society page goings-on covers Tamayo's opening at the Valentine Gallery in 1946; the author mentions all the well-known people that attended the event. See "Everybody's World," *Park East* (March 1946): 12. For more on Penn's personality portraits of New York cultural figures, see Maria Morris Hambourg, "Existential Portraits, 1947–48," in *Irving Penn Centennial*, ed. Maria Morris Hambourg and Jeff L. Rosenheim (New York: Metropolitan Museum of Art, 2017), 70–75.

191. See the catalogue *Modern Paintings: The Lee Ault Collection* (New York: Valentine Gallery, 1944); and Lee Ault, *Rufino Tamayo* (Cincinnati, OH: Cincinnati Modern Art Society and Cincinnati Art Museum, 1947).

192. Dorothy Odenheimer, "Woman with Bird Cage by Tamayo," *Bulletin of the Art Institute of Chicago* 37, no. 3 (March 1943): 34–35.

193. Articles published in the United States that reference debates in Mexico include: "Rufino Tamayo Here, Comments on His Art," *St. Louis Post-Dispatch*, November 12, 1948, 3D.

194. Tamayo, quoted in Antonio Rodríguez, "Orozco no cambia, no investiga, siempre se repite: Tamayo está listo para defenderse; la controversia sigue su marcha," *El nacional: órgano oficial del gobierno de México* (Mexico City), September 26, 1947. Translation by E. Carmen Ramos.

195. Barnett Newman, "The Painting of Tamayo and Gottlieb (1945)," in *Barnett Newman, Selected Writings and Interviews*, ed. John P. O'Neill (New York: Knopf, 1990), 71–72.

196. See Barnett Newman, "Pre-Columbian Stone Sculpture (Wakefield Gallery)," and "Pre-Columbian Stone Sculpture (Revista Belga)," in *Barnett Newman: Selected Writings and Interviews*, 61–65.

197. W. Jackson Rushing, *Native American Art and the New York Avant-Garde: A History of Cultural Primitivism* (Austin: University of Texas Press, 1995), 161–68.

198. Harry Cooper, "Starting with Oedipus: Originality and Influence in Gottlieb's Pictographs," in *Adolph Gottlieb: Pictographs 1941–1951* (New York: PaceWildenstein, 2004), 9.

199. Newman, "The Painting of Tamayo and Gottlieb (1945)," 72.

200. Ibid., 73.

201. Ibid., 72.

202. Tamayo, "El nacionalismo y el movimiento pictórico," 280.

203. Howard Putzel, *A Problem for Critics* invitation (1945), n.p., Adolph Gottlieb papers, 1929–1967, Archives of American Art, Smithsonian Institution. For more on Putzel and this exhibition, see Leja, *Reframing Abstract Expressionism*, 24–27.

204. Ann Eden Gibson, *Issues in Abstract Expressionism: The Artist-Run Periodicals* (Ann Arbor, MI: UMI Research Press, 1990), 2.

205. Michael C. FitzGerald, "'This Is 1950. This Is When It's Going to Happen,'" in *Picasso and American Art* (New York: Whitney Museum of American Art in association with Yale University Press, 2006), 191.

206. "Veil the image" refers to the idea that Pollock began his classic drip painting with representational imagery, which he then obscured with layers of paint. For a greater discussion of Pollock and Picasso, see FitzGerald, "'This Is 1950. This Is When It's Going to Happen,'" 168–237.

207. Adolph Gottlieb and Mark Rothko, "The Portrait of the Modern Artist (1943)," in *Primitivism and Twentieth-Century Art: A Documentary History*, ed. Jack Flam and Miriam Deutch (Berkeley: University of California Press, 2003), 274.

208. Modern Man discourse explores the relationship between so-called primitive man and modern man, a concept that circulated in popular anthropology journals and books around World War II. Leja, "The Mythmakers and the Primitive," 47–120.

209. Octavio Paz, "Tamayo en la pintura mexicana (1951)," *Panorama* 1, no. 1 (1952): 55–56.

210. For more on Miró's *Constellations*, see Lilian Tone, "The Journey of Miró's Constellations," *MoMA*, no. 15 (Autumn 1993): 1–6; and "Joan Miró: The Beautiful Bird Revealing the Unknown to a Pair of Lovers," in *MoMA Highlights: 350 Works from the Museum of Modern Art, New York*, 2d. ed., ed. Harriet Schoenholz Bee and Cassandra Heliczer (New York: Museum of Modern Art, 2004), 186.

211. Bambi (Ana Cecilia Treviño de Gironella), "Rufino Tamayo relata los pecados de su infancia," *Excélsior*, May 9, 1972, cited in Norma Ávila Jiménez, *El arte cósmico de Tamayo* (Mexico City: Praxis/Universidad Nacional Autónoma de México, 2010).

212. Tamayo was interested in popular science in the 1940s and after. Reports of flying saucer sightings were beginning in those years, in newspapers across the United States. One such article, which Tamayo may have read: Murray Schumach, "'Disks' Soar Over New York, Now Seen Aloft in All Colors," *New York Times*, July 8, 1947, 1.

213. Kirsten A. Hoving, "Jackson Pollock's 'Galaxy': Outer Space and Artist's Space in Pollock's Cosmic Paintings," *American Art* 16, no. 1 (Spring 2002): 82.

214. Ibid., 85.

215. Clement Greenberg, "Art," *The Nation*, March 8, 1947, 284.

216. See "Noted Painter to Do Mural for Museum," *Dallas Morning News*, January 19, 1952, n.p.; and Frank Gagnard, "Tamayo Painting Previewed," *Dallas Morning News*, August 21, 1953, part I, 15.

217. The Whitney Museum presented Tamayo's work in their Annual exhibitions, but did not acquire his work for the permanent collection. In a 1950 letter to Olga Tamayo from Harry Brooks of the Knoedler Gallery, Mr. Brooks stated that he was unsuccessful at selling Tamayo's work to the Whitney because the museum did not "[classify him] as a United States painter." See Harry A. Brooks to Olga Tamayo, October 7, 1950, Knoedler Gallery Archives, Getty Research Institute, Los Angeles, 1950, box 883.

218. Gilbert, "The (New) World," 314–34.

219. "Tamayo: After 15-Year Exile, Mexican Painter Wins Fame at Home," *Life*, March 16, 1953, 98–105.

220. For an excellent examination of this dynamic, see Mary K. Coffey, "A Palace for the People," in *How a Revolutionary Art Became Official Culture*, 25–77.

221. For more on this younger generation, see Shifra M. Goldman, *Contemporary Mexican Painting in a Time of Change* (Albuquerque: University of New Mexico Press, 1995), 16–20.

222. René d'Harnoncourt papers, Museum of Modern Art, New York, Series IV Directors Correspondence 1949–1968, folder 8, correspondence with William A. M. Burden, 1965–66.

223. For more on these exhibitions, see Martica Sawin, epilogue to *Surrealism in Exile and the Beginning of the New York School* (Cambridge, MA: MIT Press, 1995), 410–25; and Lynn Zelevansky, "Dorothy Miller's 'Americans,' 1942–1963," in *The Museum of Modern Art at Mid-Century: At Home and Abroad*, ed. Barbara Ross Geiger and Lucy O'Brien (New York: Harry N. Abrams, 1994), 57–97.

224. Olga Tamayo to Lelia Wittler of the Knoedler Gallery, January 4, 1954, Knoedler Gallery Archives, Getty Research Institute, Los Angeles, 1954, box 932.

225. Tamayo's description of the mural appears on page 11 of a "Welcome Book" brochure issued by the Bank of the Southwest upon its opening. A copy of the brochure can be found in Rufino Tamayo vertical file in the library of the San Francisco Museum of Modern Art.

226. Genauer, *Rufino Tamayo,* 58.

227. Pacheco, *La luz de México*, 583.

228. Mary Coffey also cites Tamayo in her recent essay on the relationship between Latin American and US American modernisms. See "US American Art in the Americas," in *A Companion to American Art*, ed. John Davis, Jennifer A. Greenhill, and Jason D. LaFountain (West Sussex: Wiley-Blackwell, 2015), 281–98.

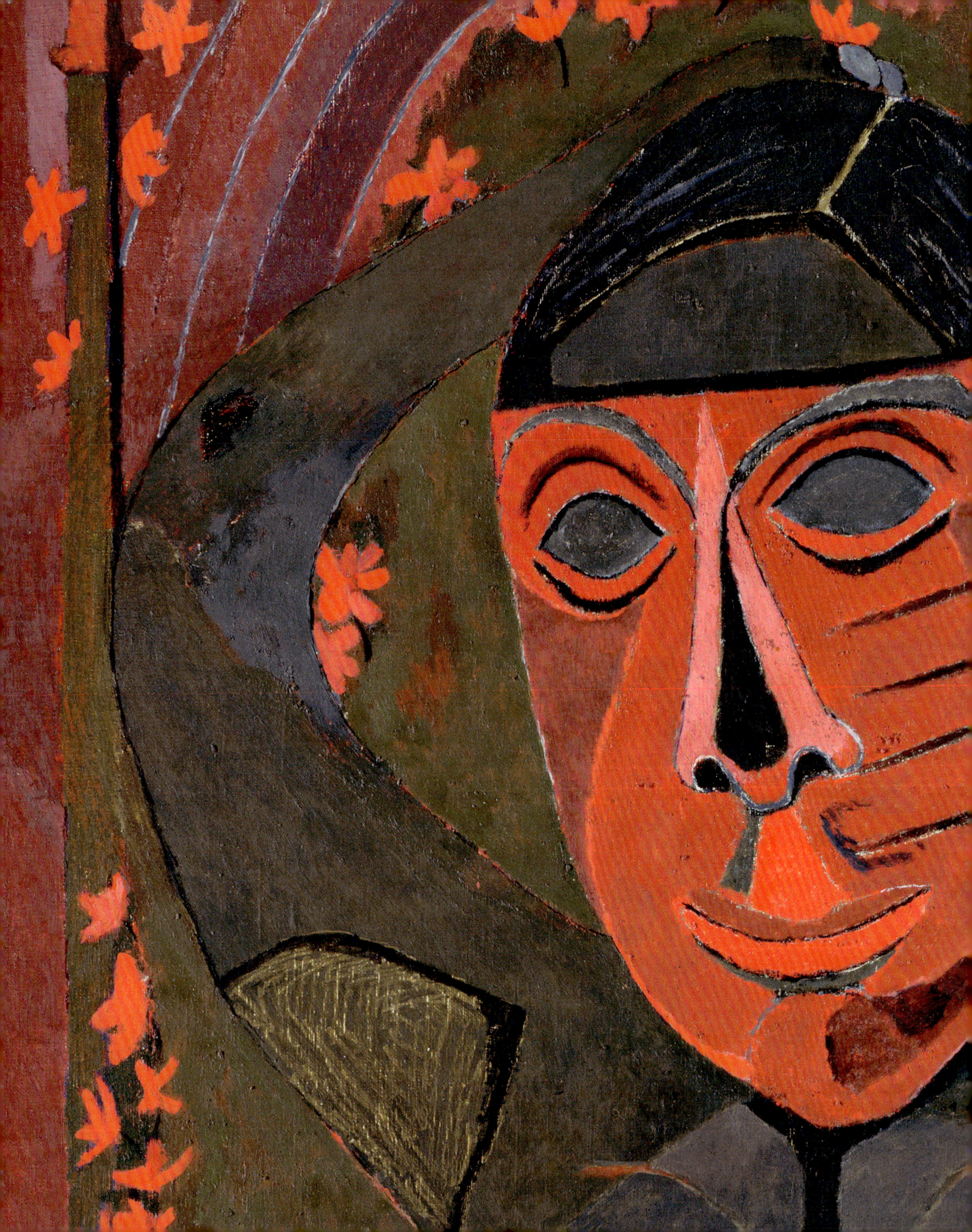

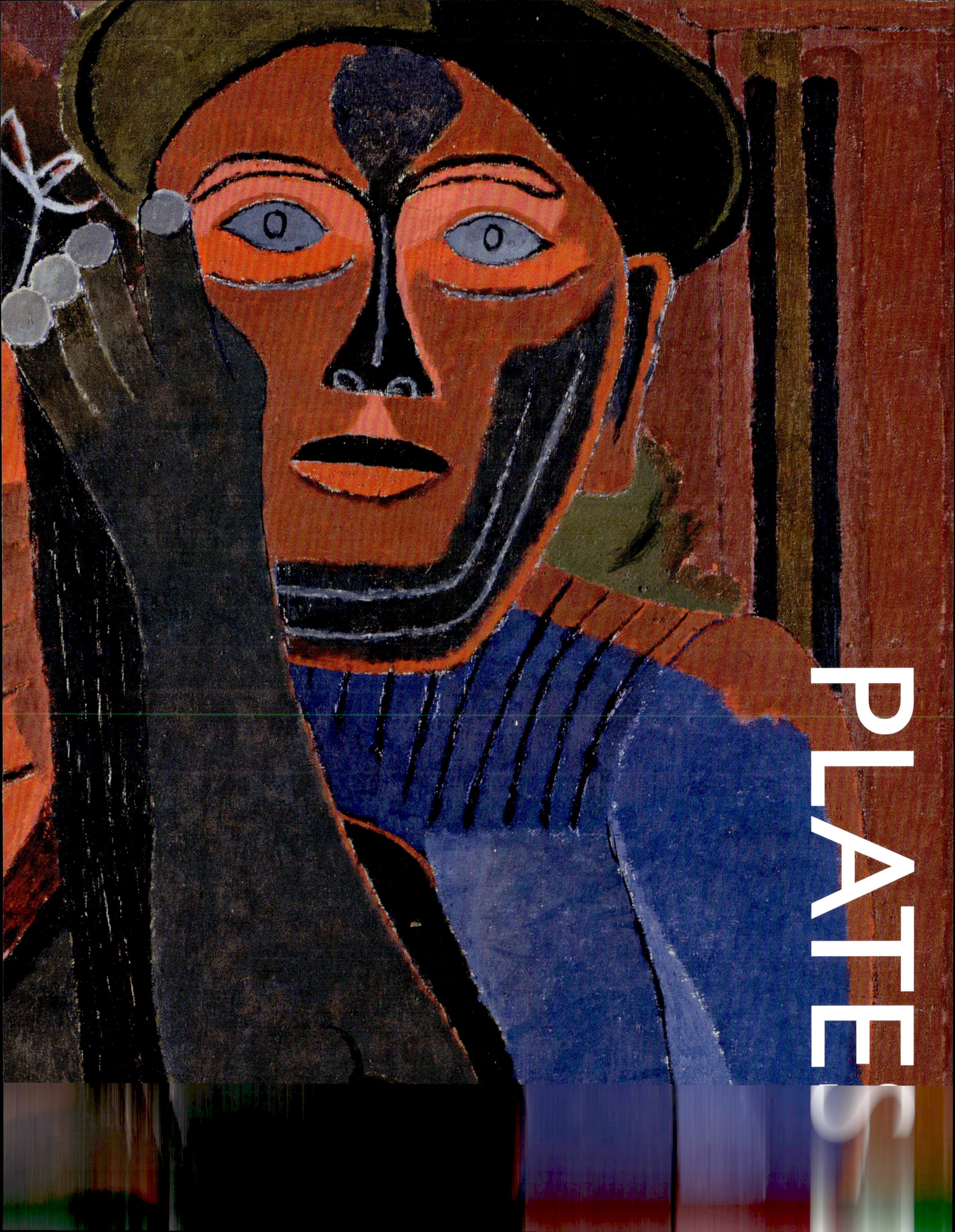

PLATES

Preceding pages:
Carnival [*Carnaval*], 1941;
detail. See p. 115.

All plates represent works in the exhibition *Tamayo: The New York Years.*
Spanish titles are given in brackets [/].

1

THE FAMILY
[LA FAMILIA]

1925
oil on canvas
28 ¾ × 33 in.

William and Christopher Brumder Collection

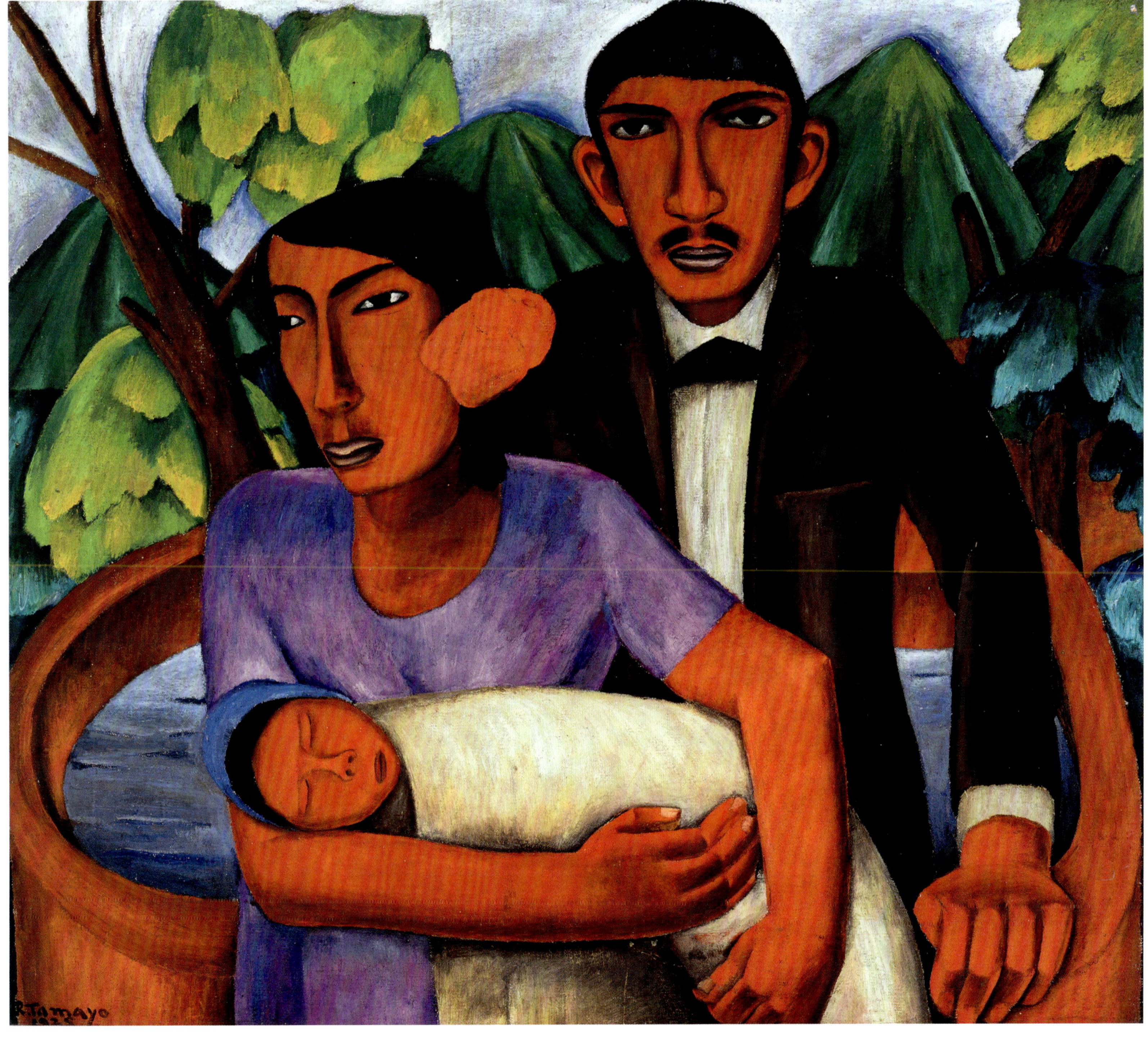

2

MAN AND WOMAN
[HOMBRE Y MUJER]

1926
woodcut
sheet: 12 1/8 × 12 in.
image: 9 7/8 × 9 7/8 in.

Smithsonian American Art Museum,
Museum purchase, 1976.27

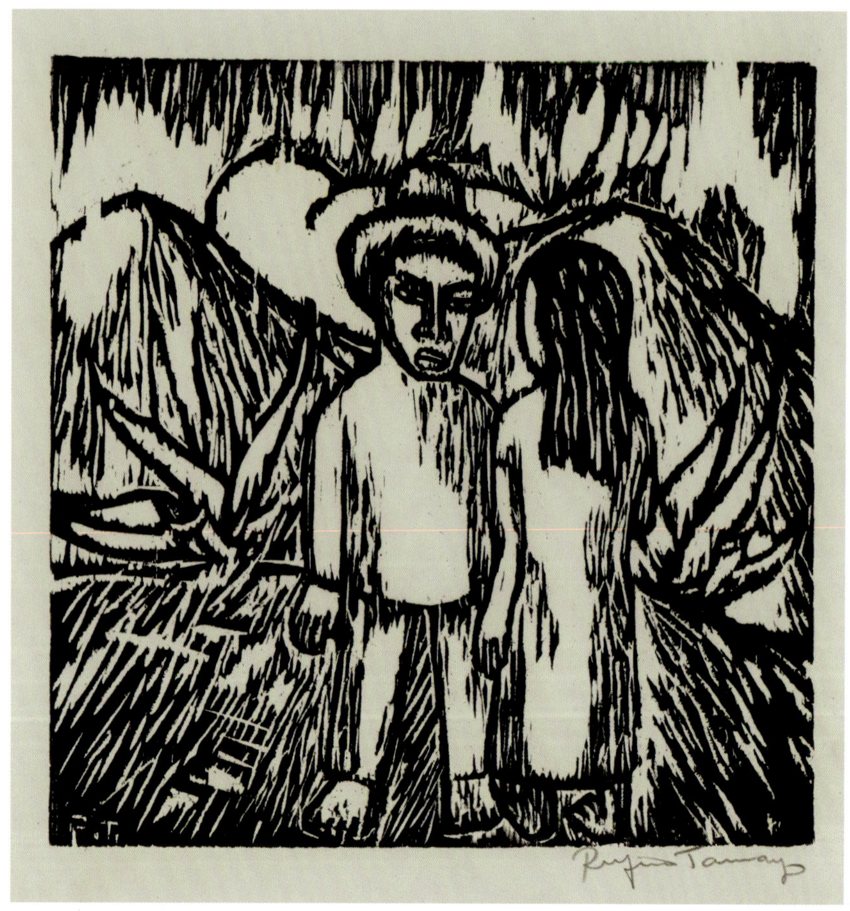

3

THE WOODCUTTER
[LEÑADOR]

ca. 1926–30
woodcut
sheet: 15 15⁄16 × 12 13⁄16 in.
image: 10 1⁄16 × 9 13⁄16 in.

The Metropolitan Museum of Art, New York, Gift of Carl Zigrosser, 1930

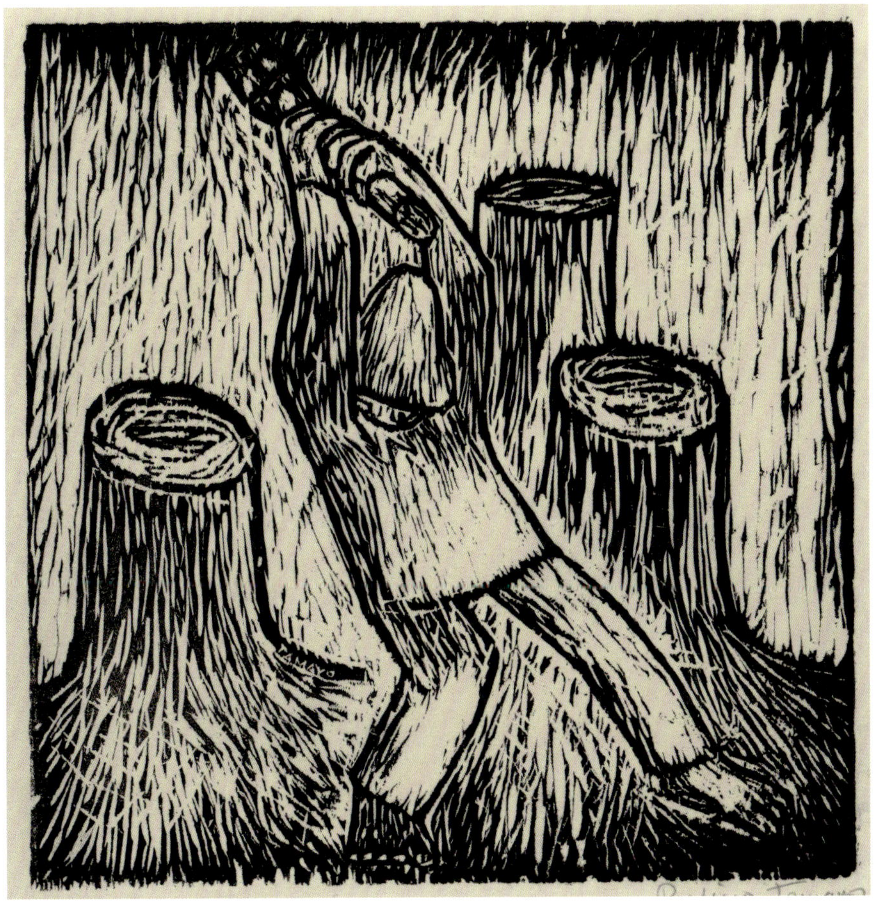

4

VIRGIN OF GUADALUPE
[LA VIRGEN DE GUADALUPE]

1926–27
woodcut
sheet: 9 ½ × 12 ⅛ in.
image: 7 ¼ × 9 ⁹⁄₁₆ in.

Museum of Fine Arts, Boston, Eleanor A. Sayre Fund

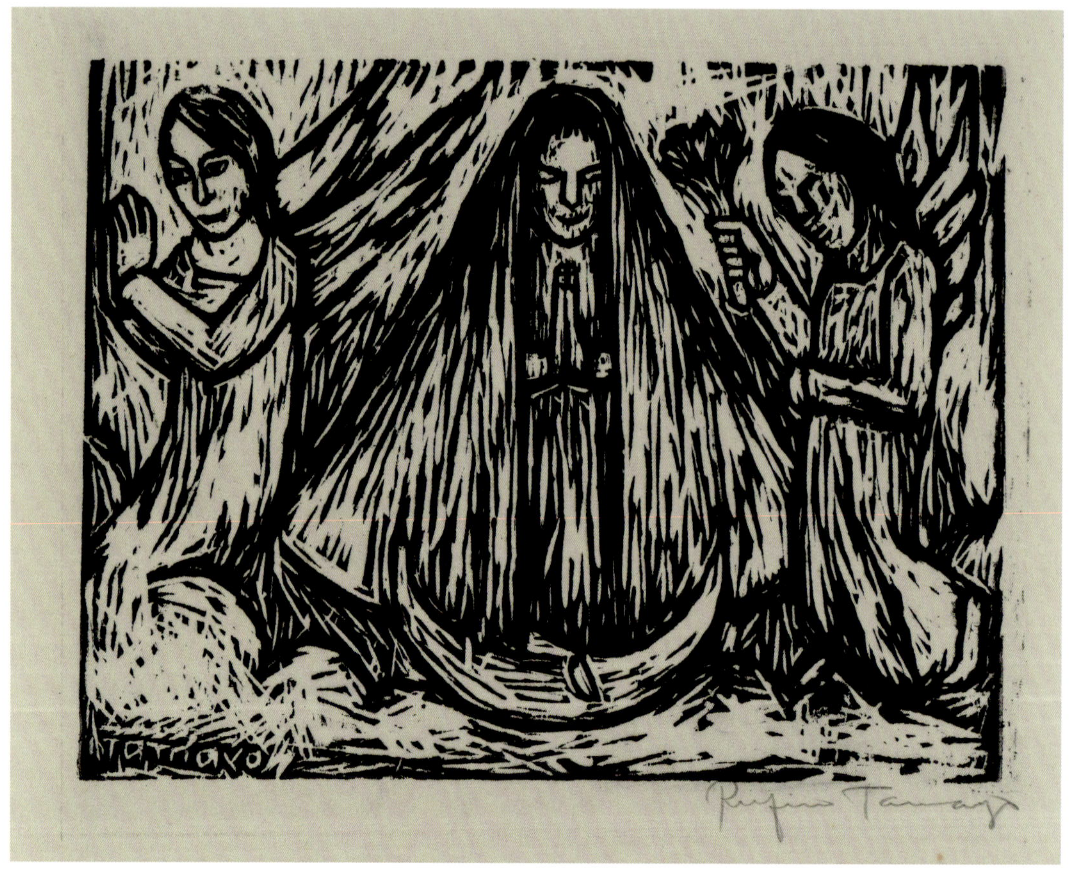

5

MAN WITH MAGUEY
[HOMBRE CON MAGUEY]

1931
linoleum cut
sheet: 9 × 6 ½ in.
image: 8 ¼ × 4 ⅞ in.

Smithsonian American Art Museum,
Museum purchase, 1980.4.2

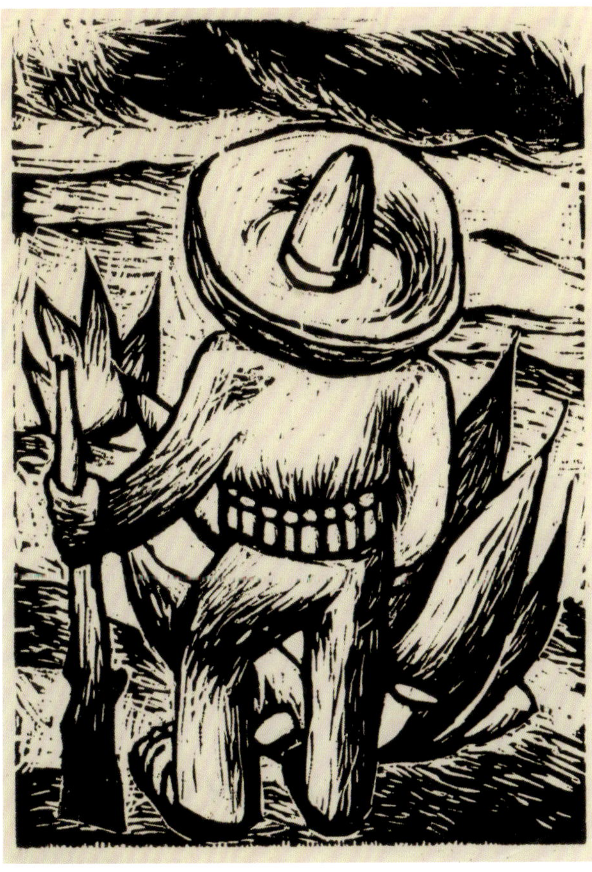

6

HEAD II (GRIEF)
[CABEZA II (PESAR)]

ca. 1926–28
woodcut
sheet: 16 × 12 15/16 in.
image: 10 × 9 7/8 in.

Museum of Fine Arts, Boston,
Gift of W. G. Russell Allen

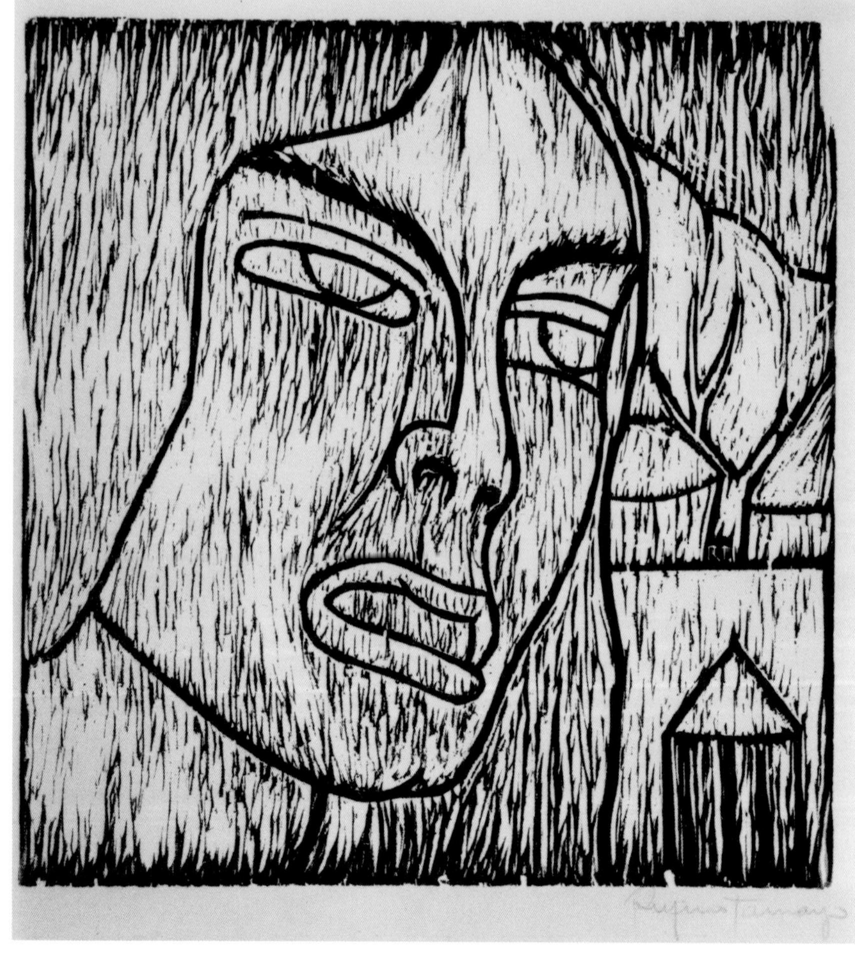

7

TWO MERMAIDS, ONE PLAYING A GUITAR
[DOS SIRENAS, UNA TOCANDO UNA GUITARRA]

ca. 1926–30
woodcut on Japan paper
sheet: 9 ¼ × 12 in.
image: 6 ⅛ × 8 ¼ in.

The Metropolitan Museum of Art, New York, Gift of Jean Charlot, 1931

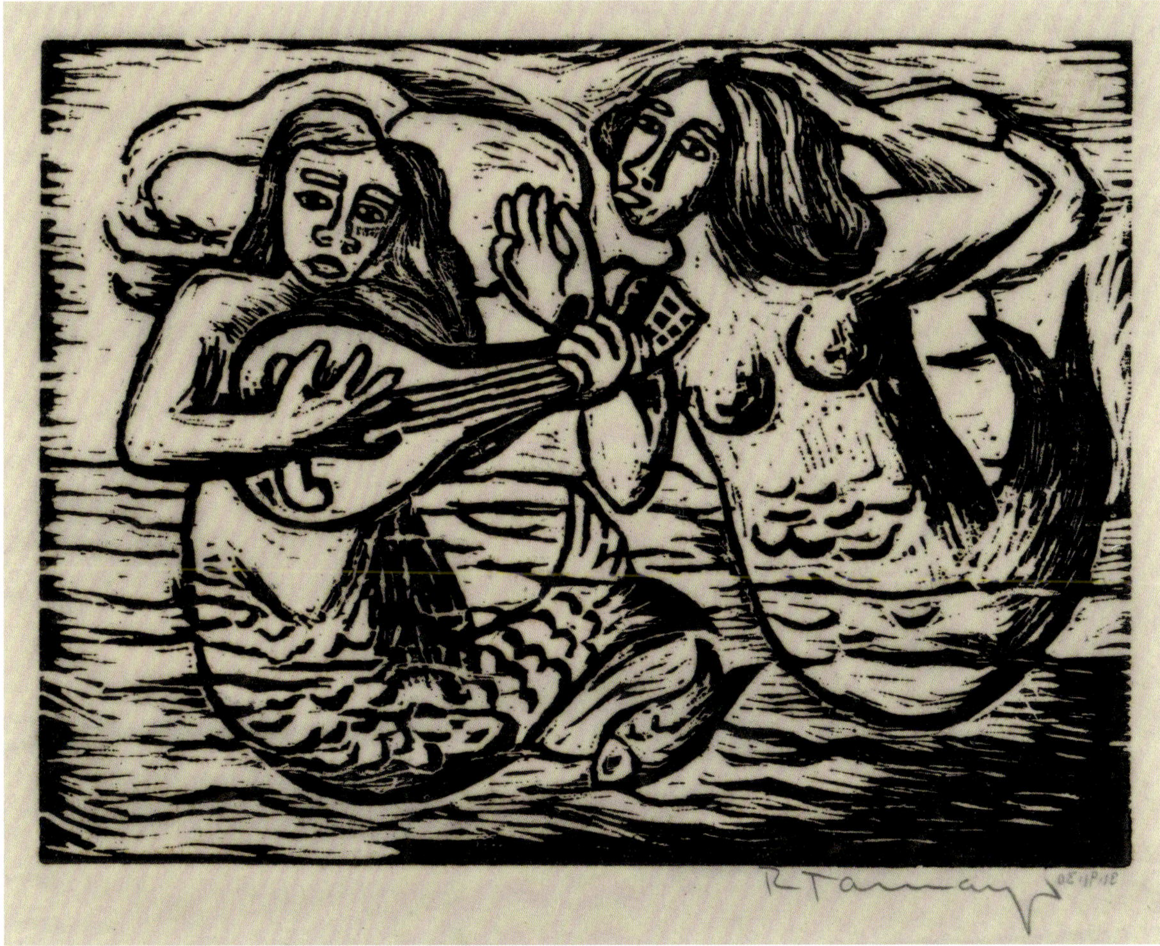

8

THE YELLOW CHAIR
[SILLA AMARILLA]

1929
oil on canvas
29 7⁄8 × 25 1⁄8 in.

Private collection, Courtesy of
Galería Ramis Barquet, New York

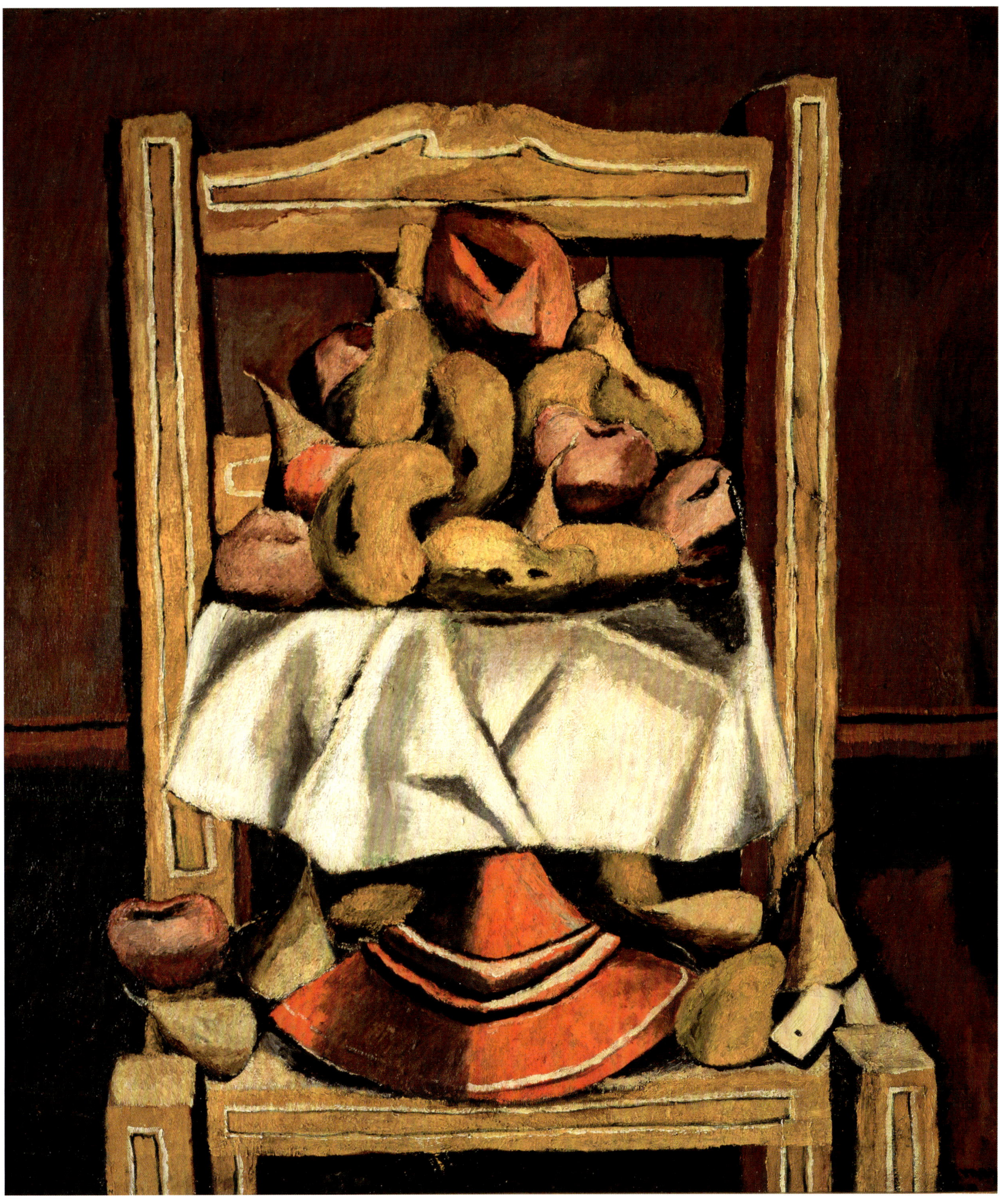

9

SEASHELLS
[LOS CARACOLES]

1929
oil on canvas
23 1/4 × 24 13/16 in.

Private collection

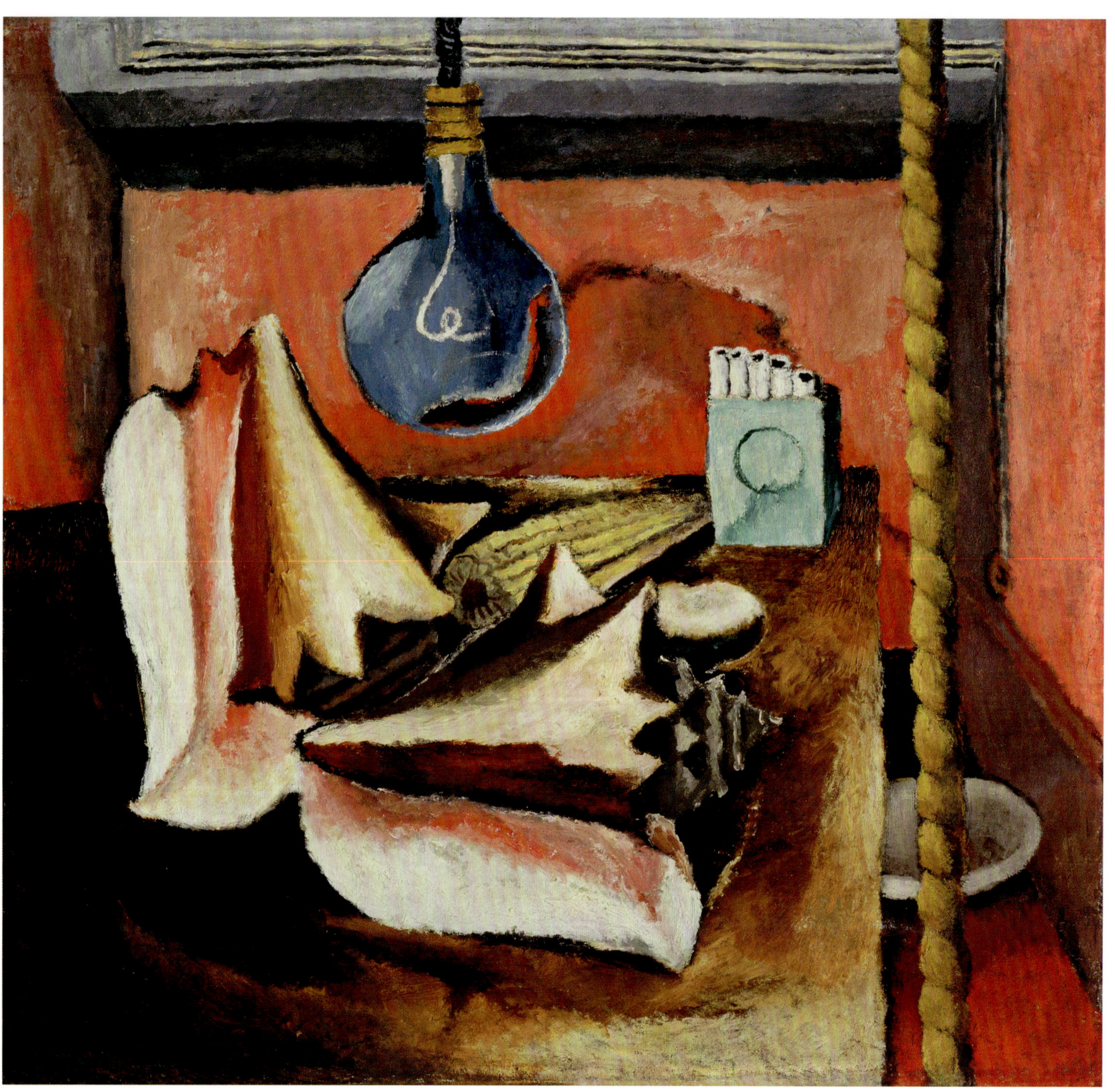

10

MANDOLINS AND PINEAPPLES
[MANDOLINAS Y PIÑAS]

1930
oil on canvas
19 ¾ × 27 ½ in.

The Phillips Collection,
Washington, DC, Acquired 1930

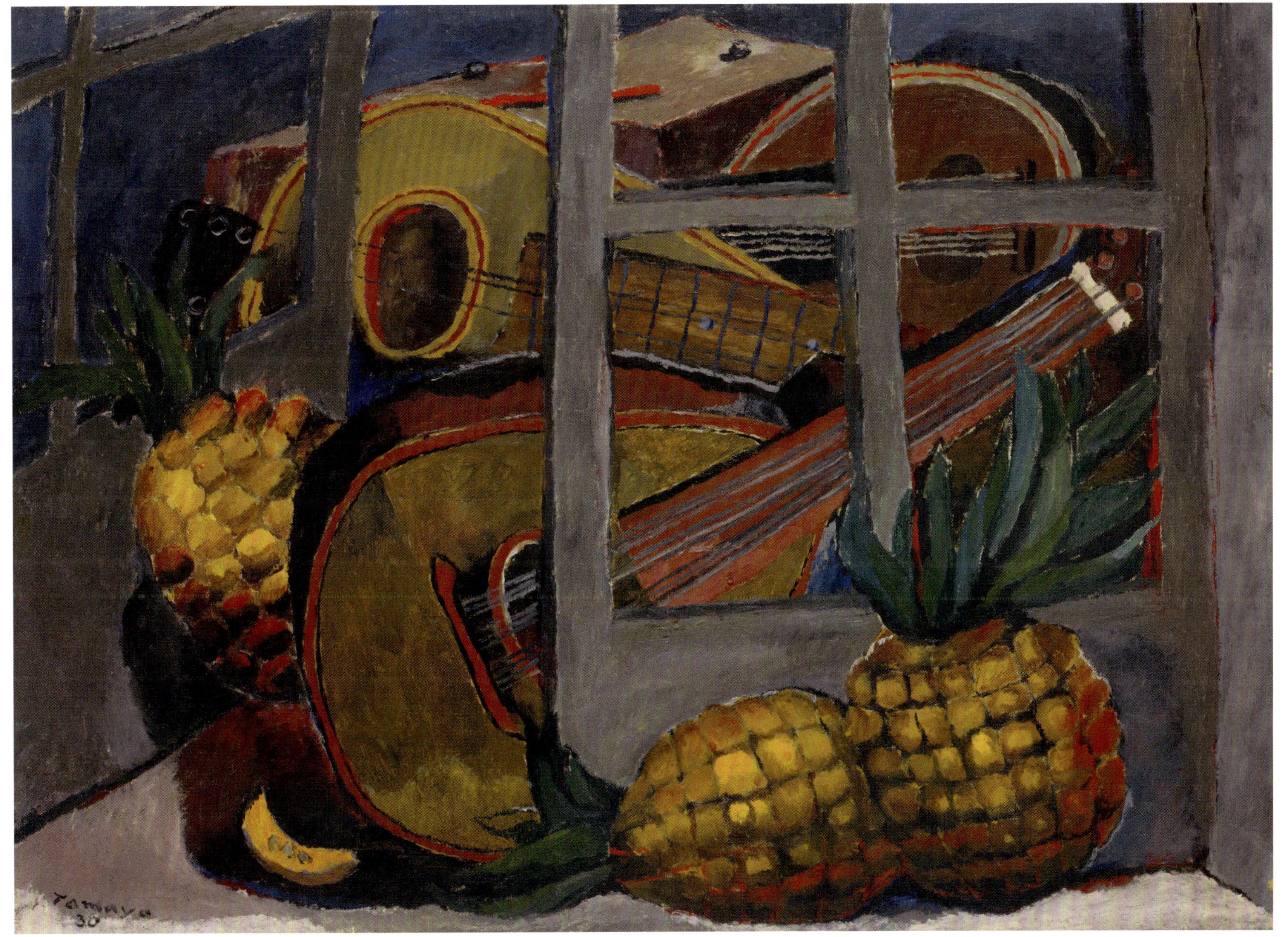

11

NUDE
[DESNUDO]

1931
oil on canvas
37 ¼ × 56 ¾ in.

Dallas Museum of Art,
Dallas Art Association Purchase

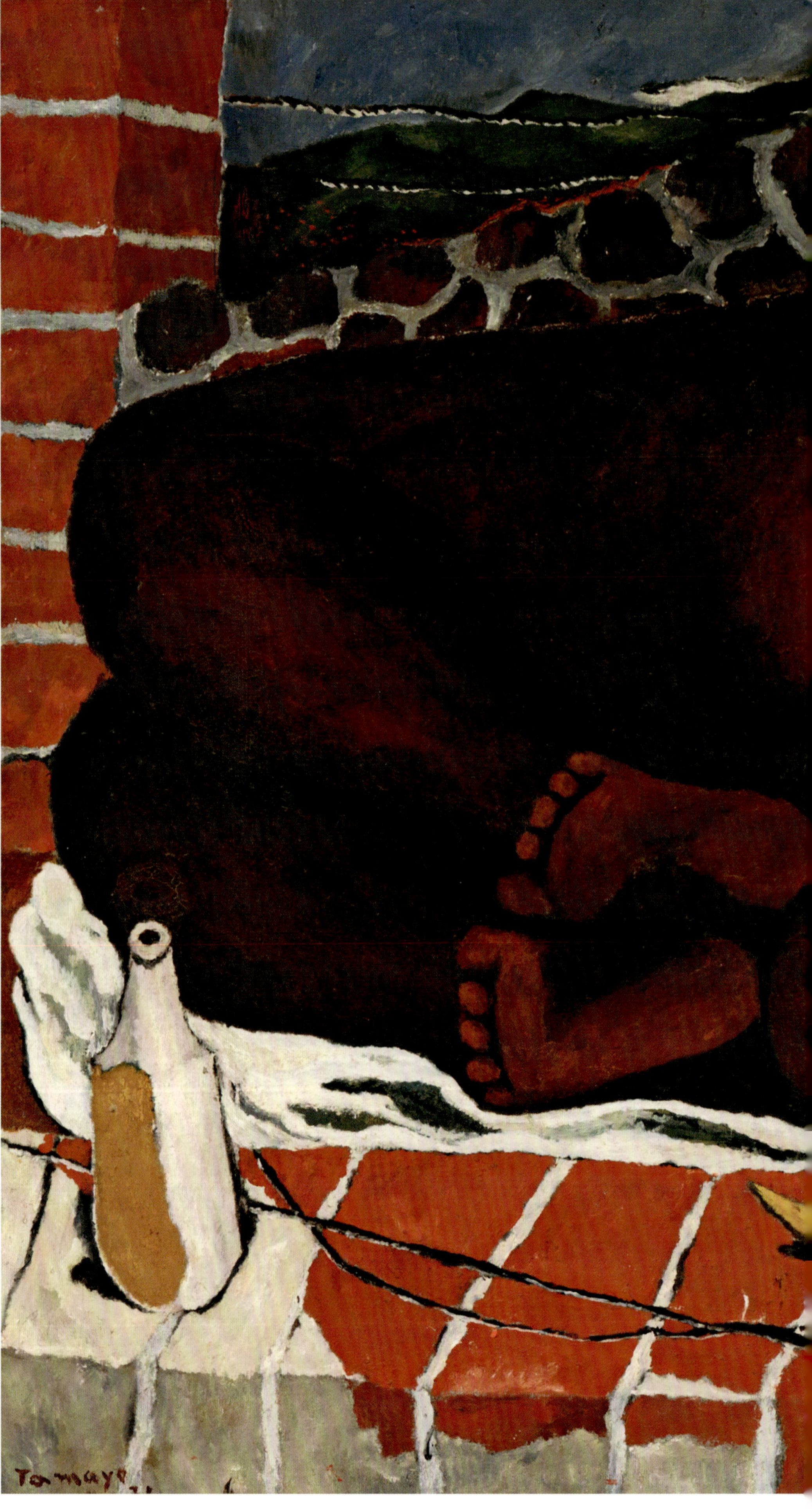

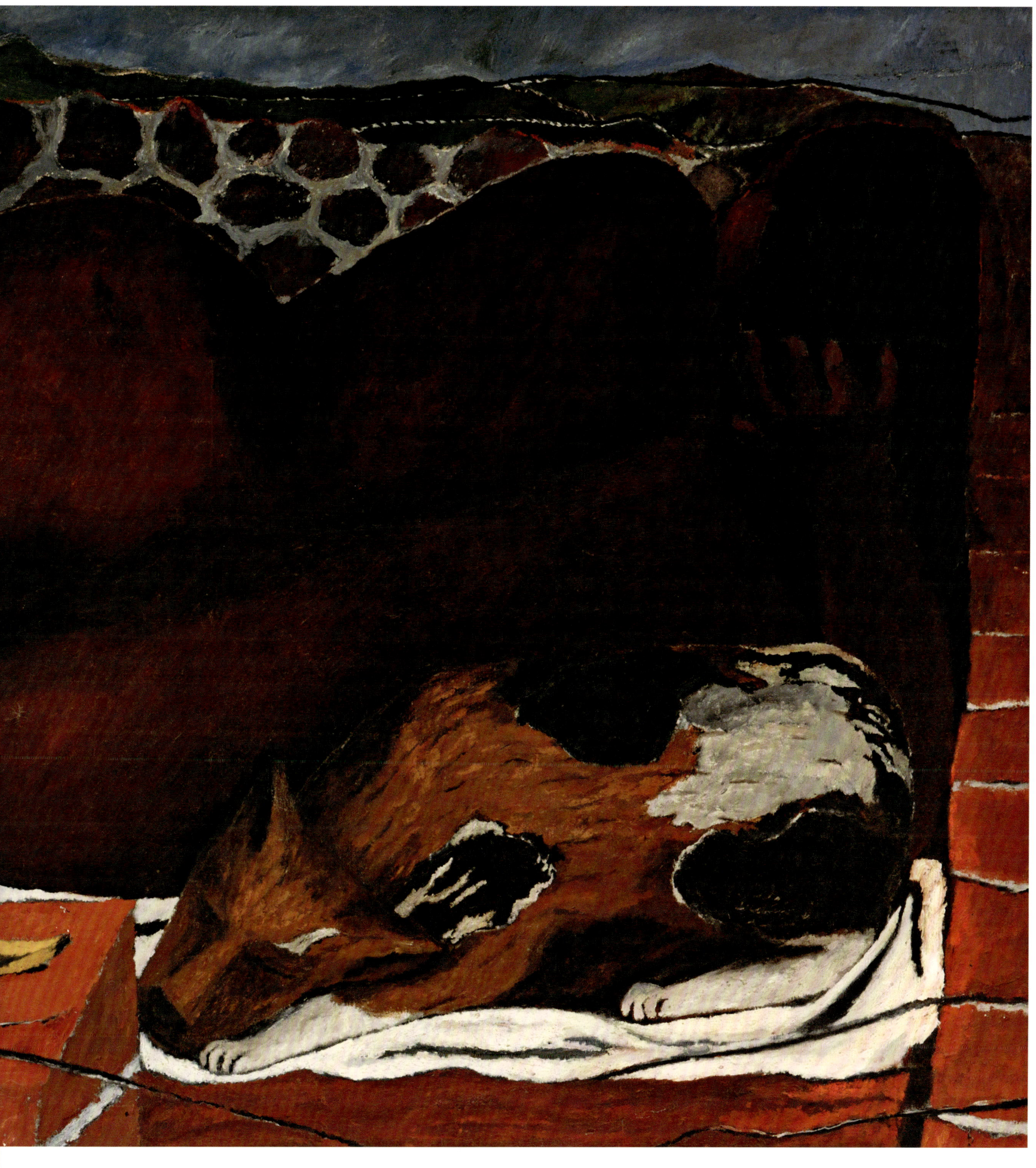

12

FACTORY WORKERS' MOVEMENT
[MOVIMIENTO FABRIL]

1935
oil on canvas
22 1/4 × 26 3/8 in.

Collection of Brian and Florence Mahony

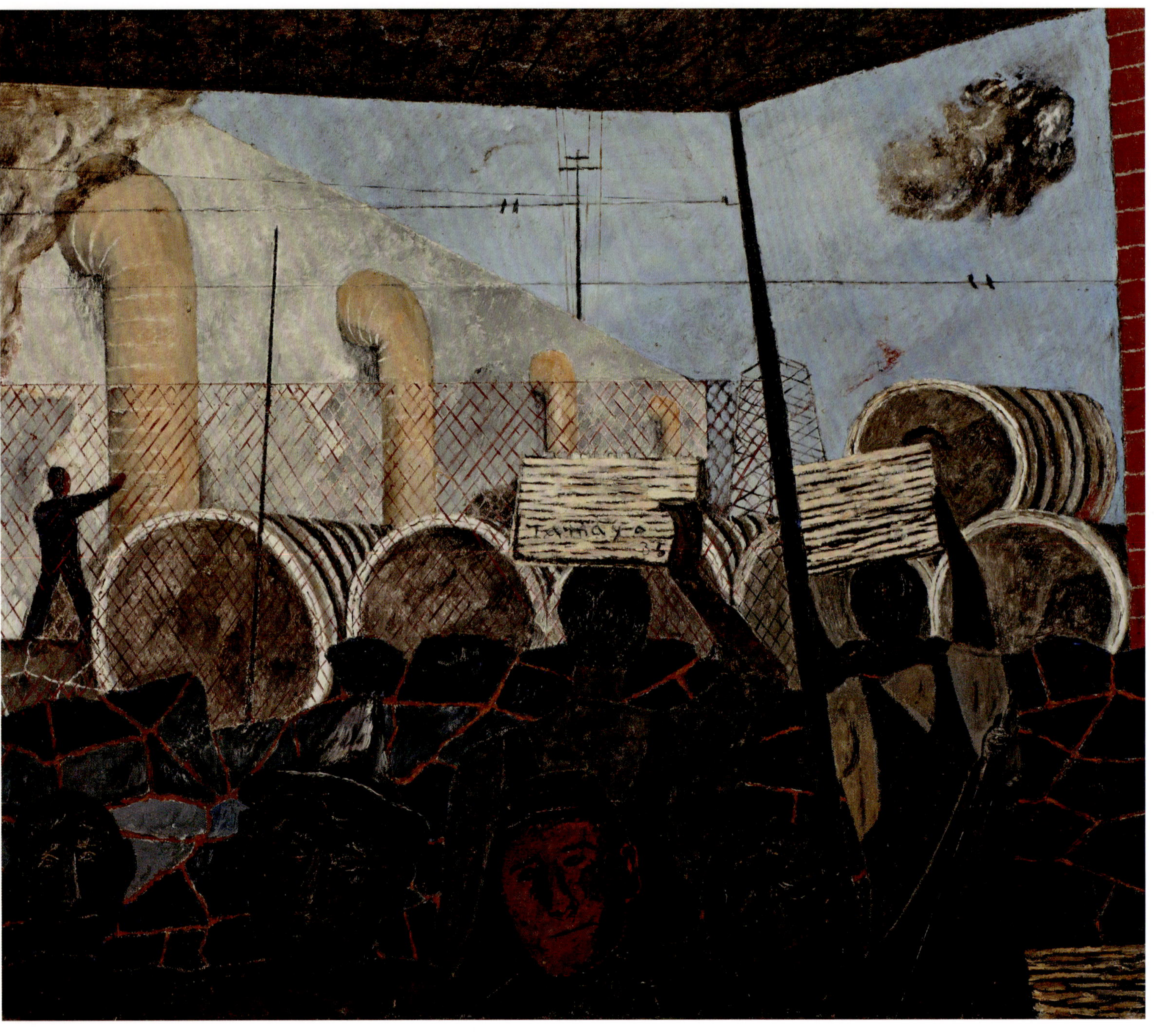

13

HOMAGE TO JUÁREZ
[HOMENAJE A JUÁREZ]

1932
oil on canvas
23 5/8 × 29 1/8 in.

Museo de Arte Moderno—INBA

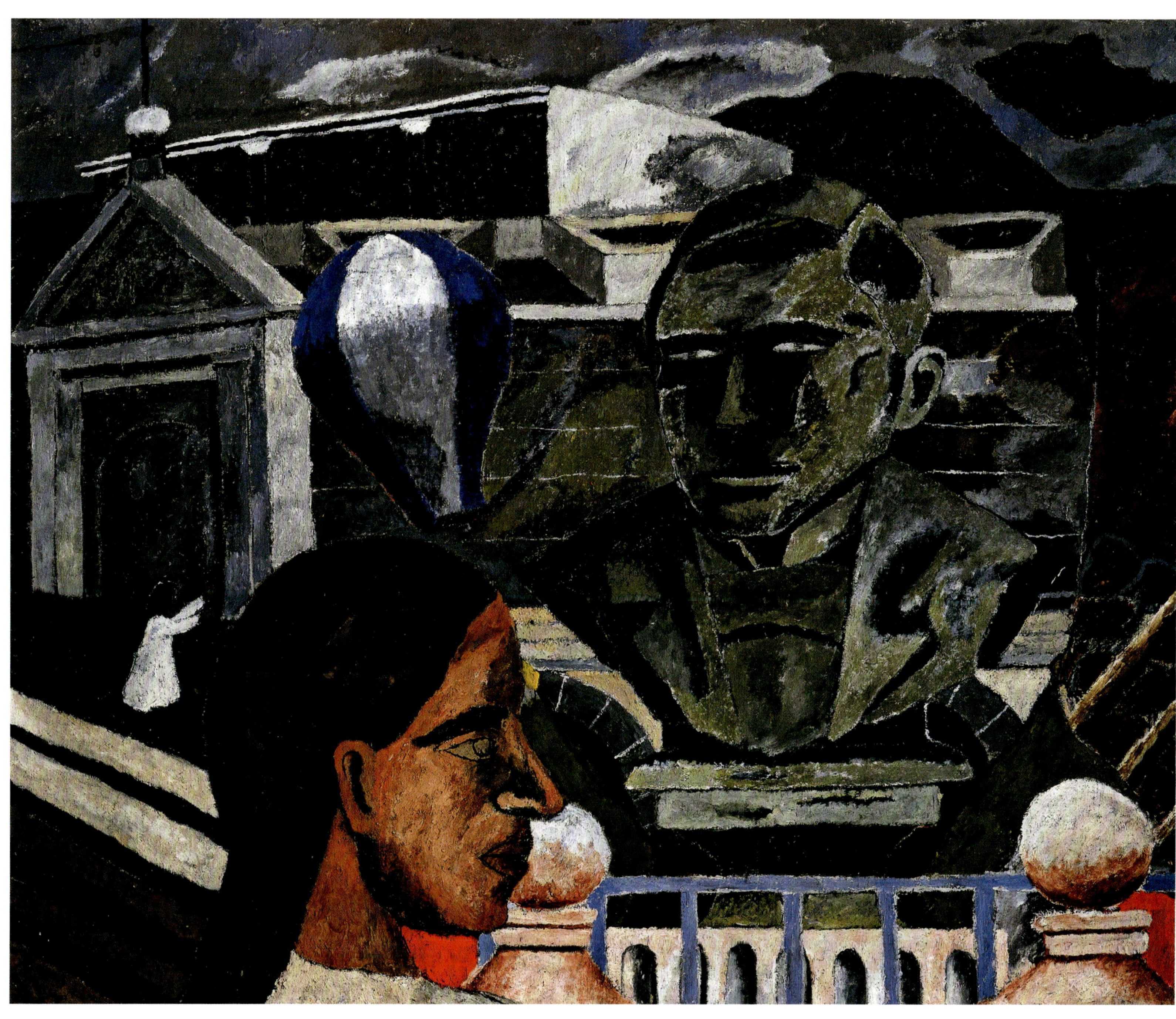

14

ACADEMIC PAINTING
[PINTURA ACADÉMICA]

1935
oil on canvas
25 ¾ × 21 ⅞ in.

Hirshhorn Museum and Sculpture Garden, Smithsonian Institution, Washington, DC, Gift of Joseph H. Hirshhorn, 1966

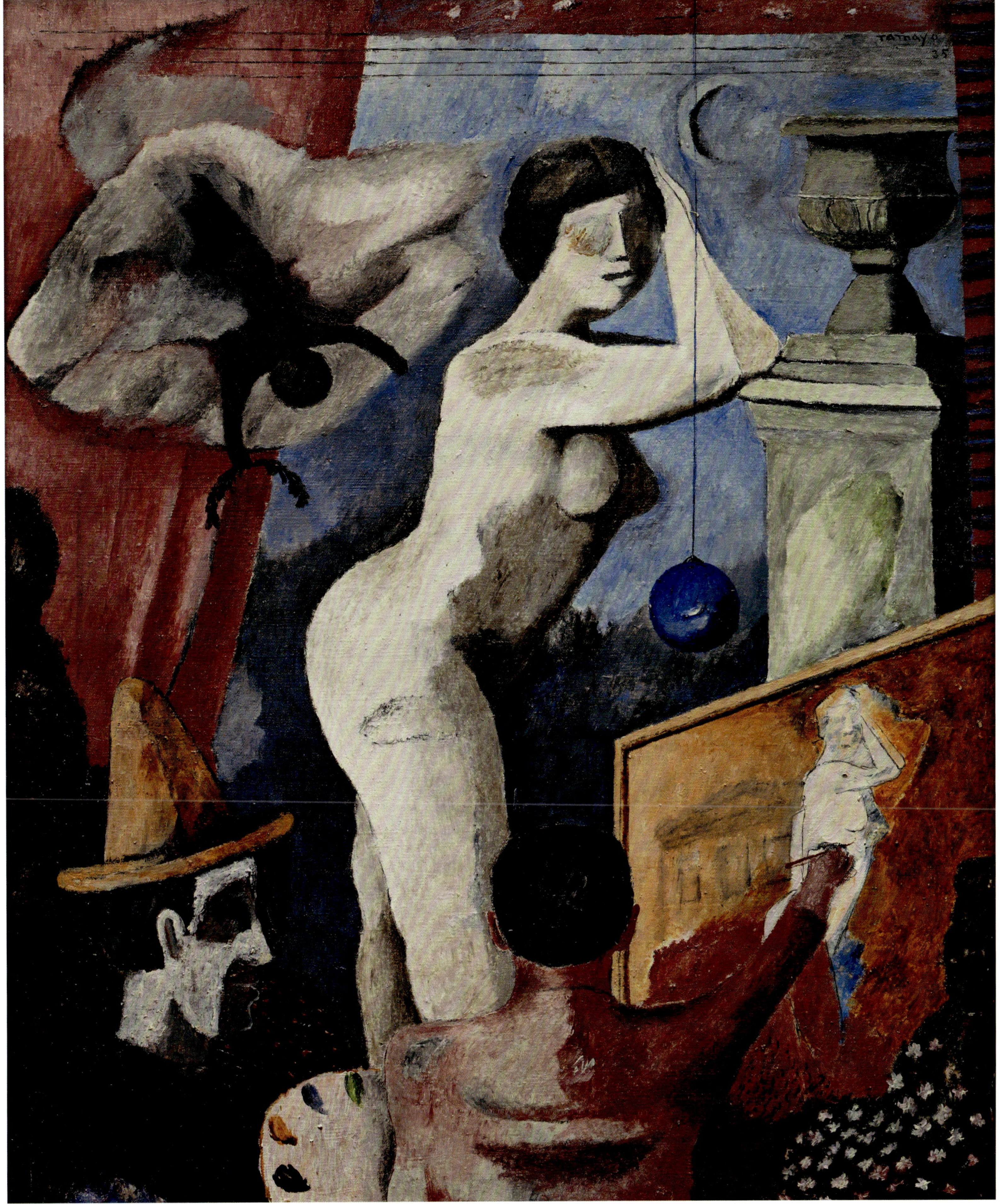

15

CONEY ISLAND

1931
gouache and watercolor
6 ½ × 20 in.

Collection of Gianfranco Arnoldi

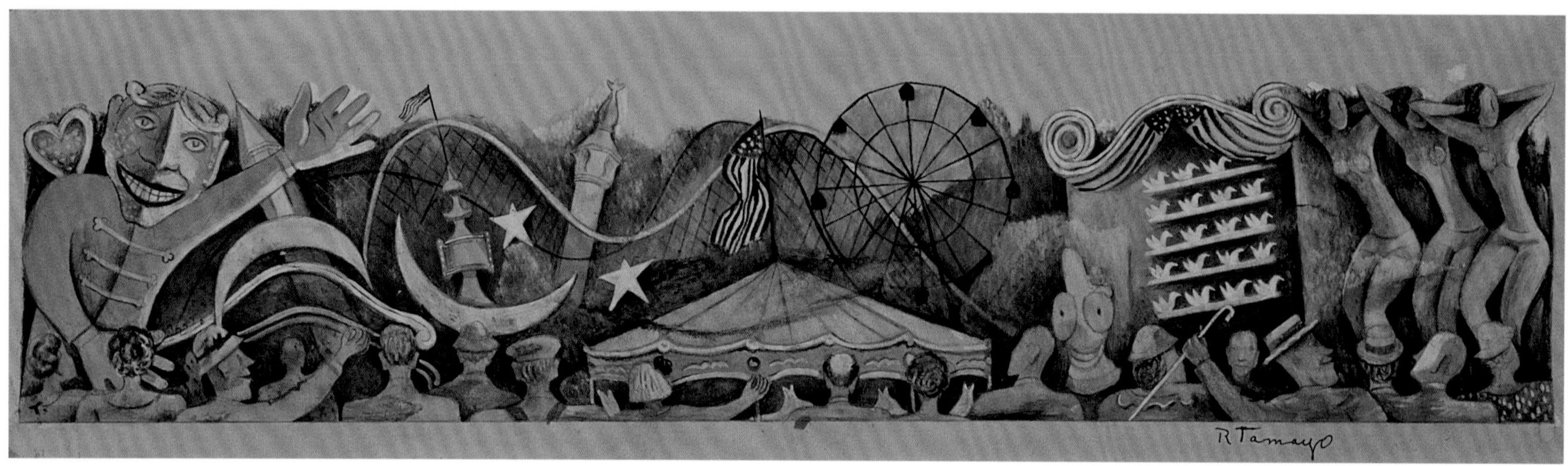

16

CARNIVAL
[CARNAVAL]

1936
gouache on paper
15 × 22 in.

Smithsonian American Art Museum, Museum purchase through the Luisita L. and Franz H. Denghausen Endowment, 2017.22

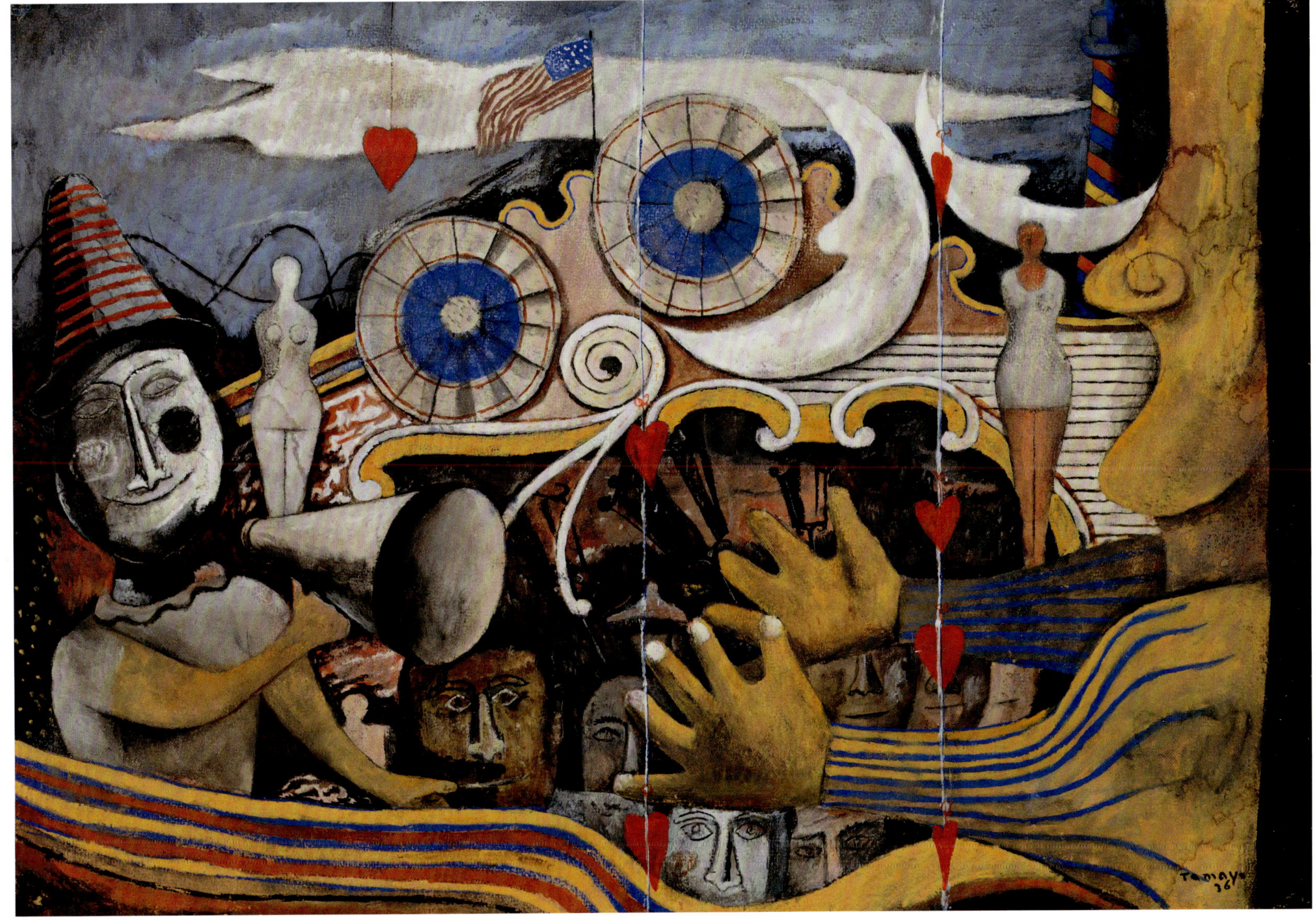

17

SHOWER
[AGUACERO]

1936
watercolor and pastel
on paper
12 3/8 × 8 11/16 in.

Blanton Museum of Art,
The University of Texas at Austin,
Deposit from the Work Projects
Administration, United States
Government, 1943

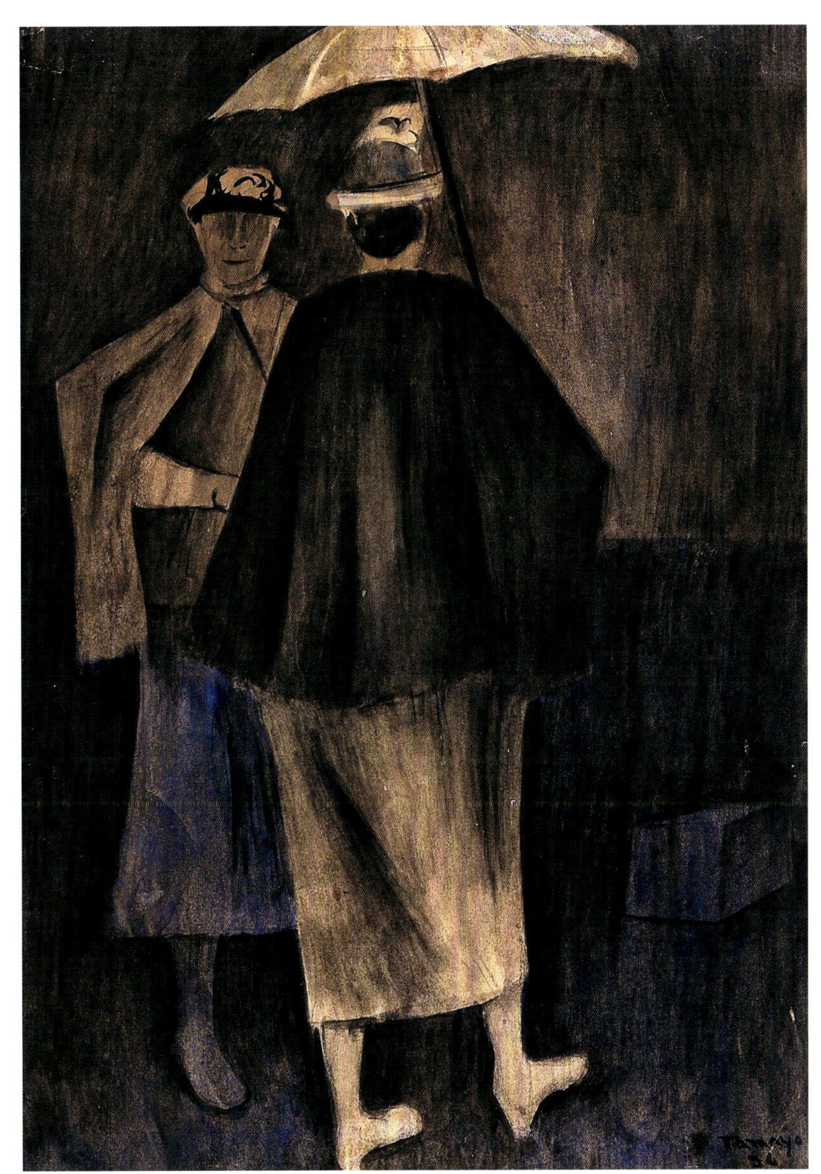

18

NEW YORK SEEN FROM THE TERRACE
[NUEVA YORK DESDE LA TERRAZA]

1937
oil on canvas
20 3⁄8 × 34 3⁄8 in.

FEMSA Collection

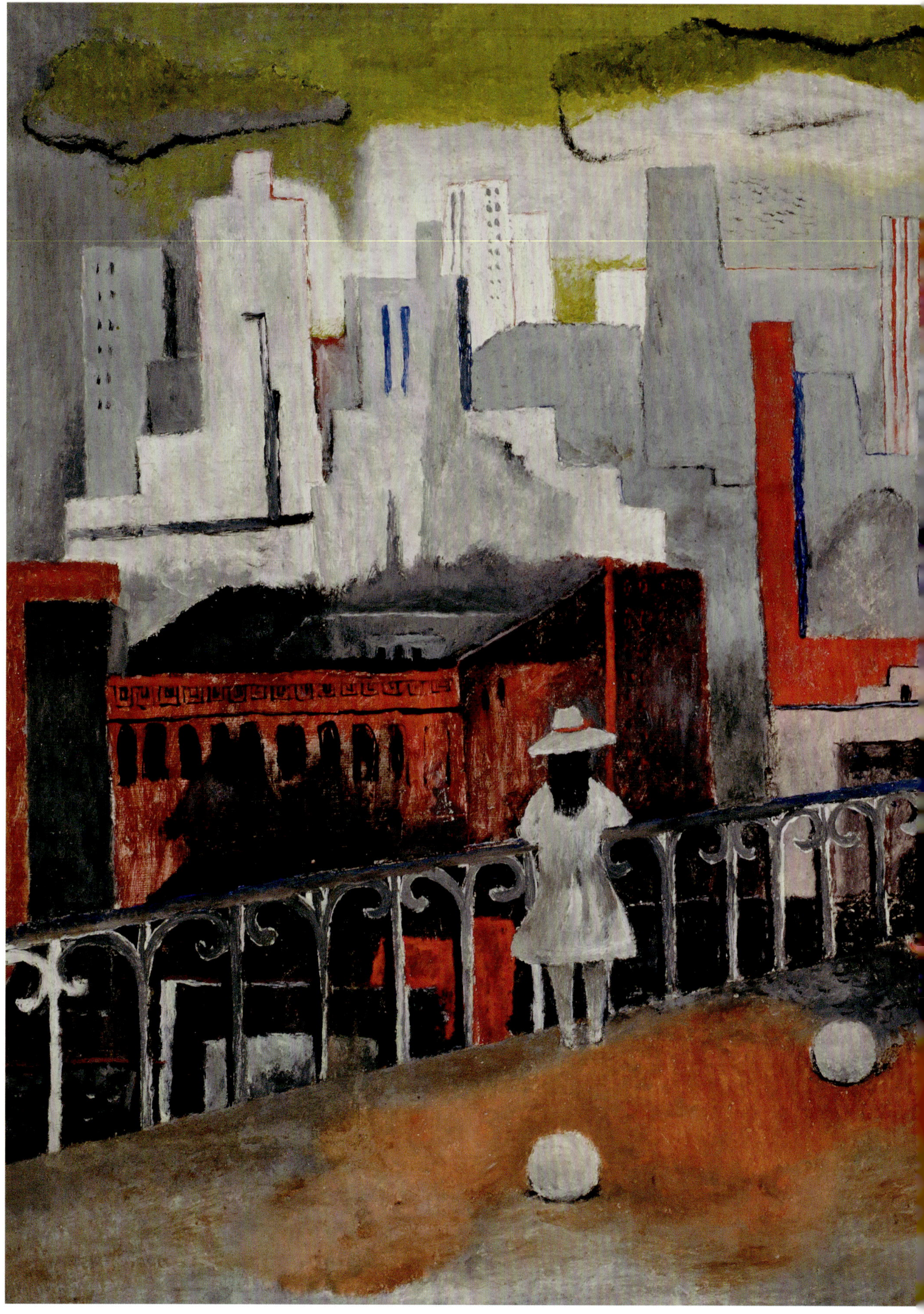

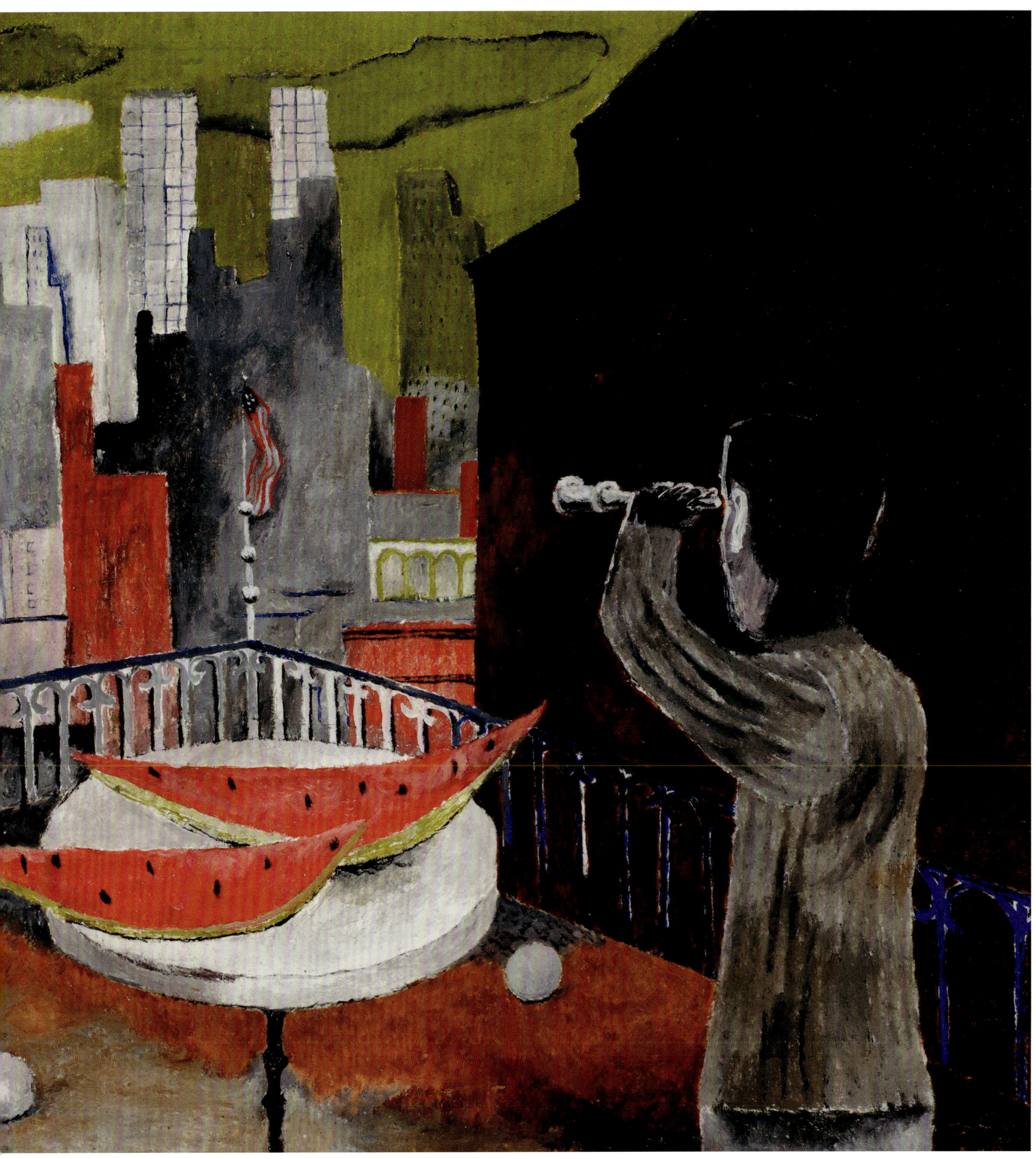

19

STRAWBERRY ICE CREAM
[HELADO DE FRESA]

1938
oil on canvas
17 ½ × 24 in.

Collection of John Fox and Sandy Allen

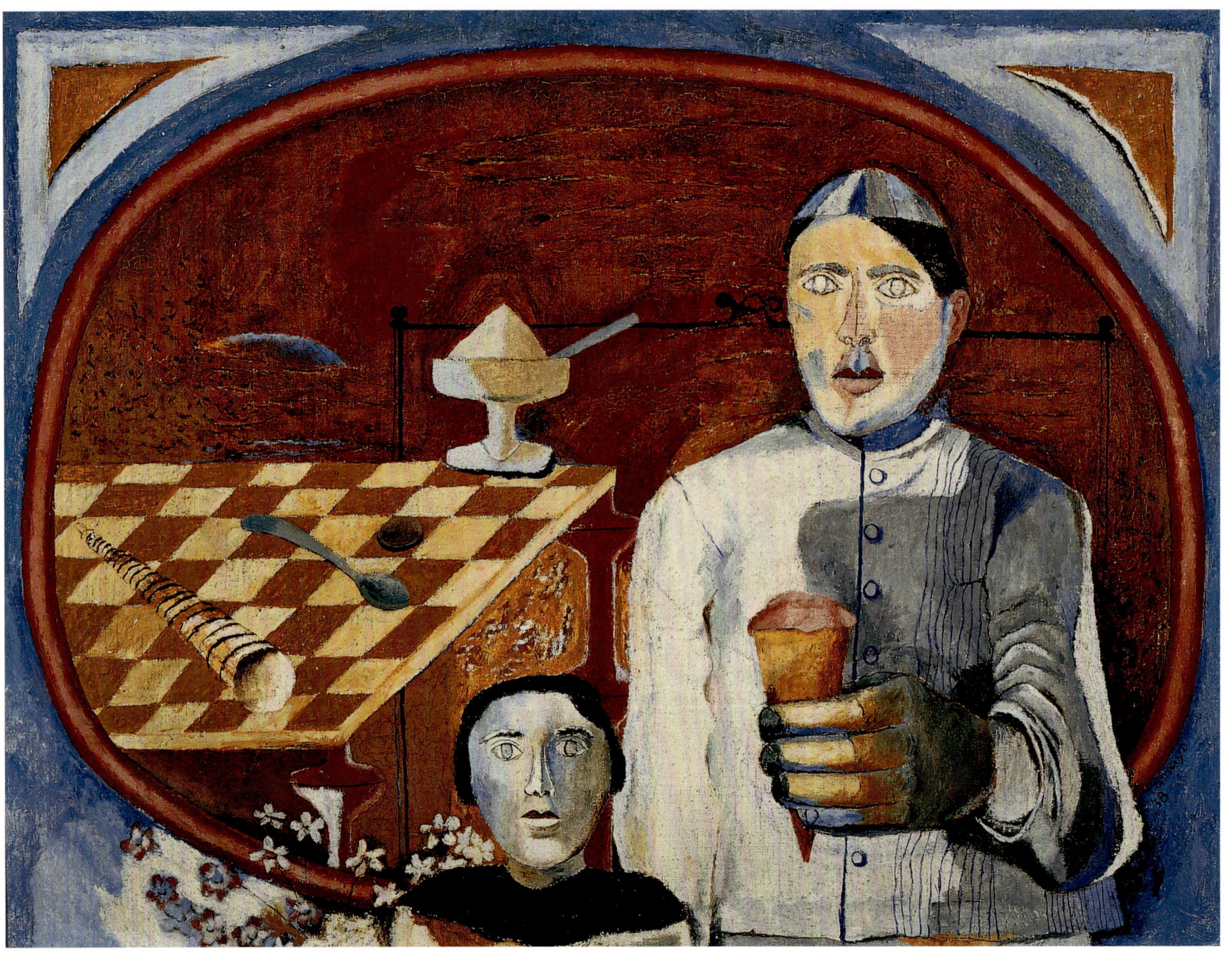

20

THREE ICE CREAMS
[TRES HELADOS]

1938
oil on canvas
17 7/8 × 23 3/4 in.

Collection of Mrs. J. Todd Figi

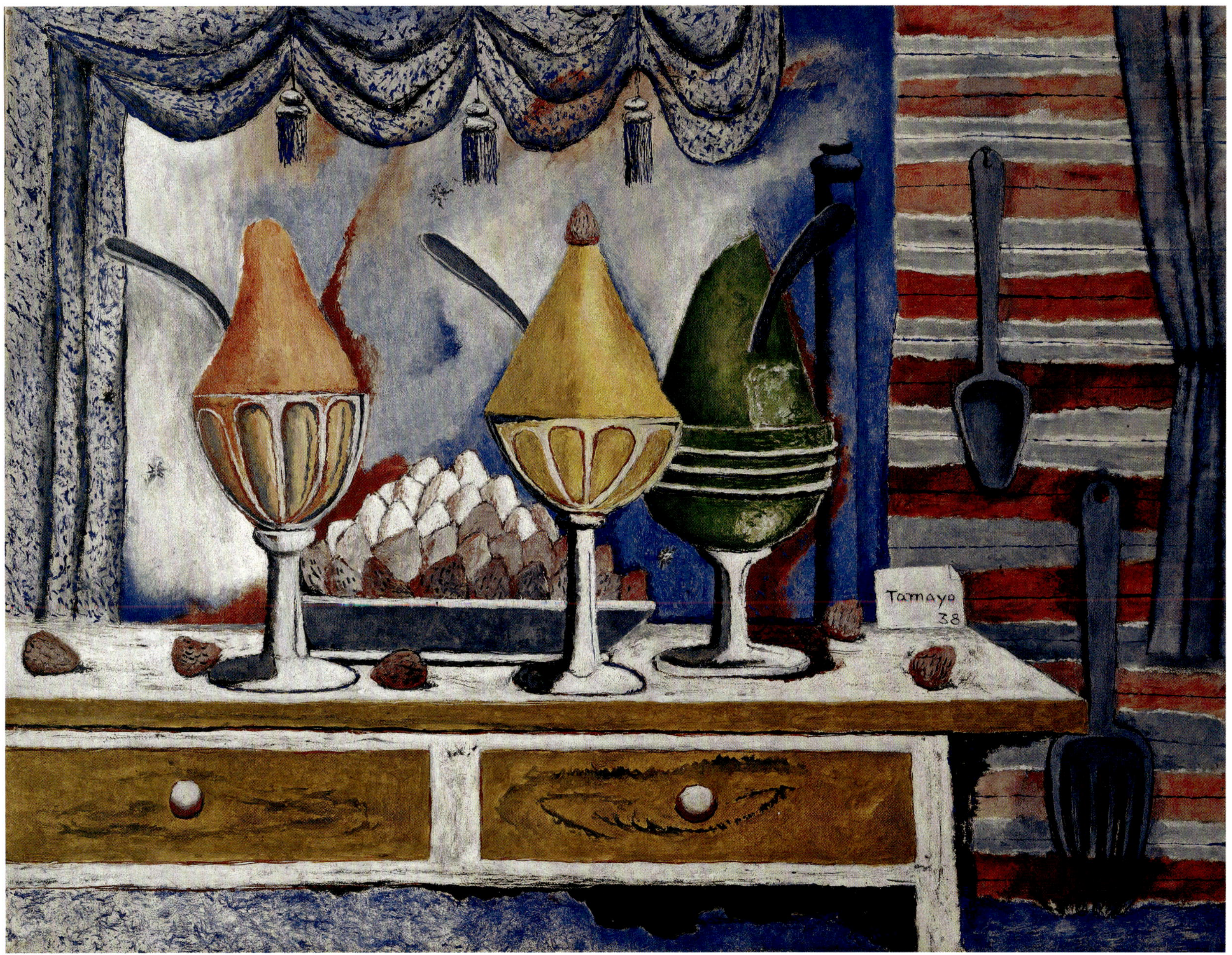

21

THE FAMILY
[LA FAMILIA]

1936
oil on canvas
31 7/8 × 47 5/8 in.

The Minneapolis Institute of Art,
Gift of Noma and William Copley

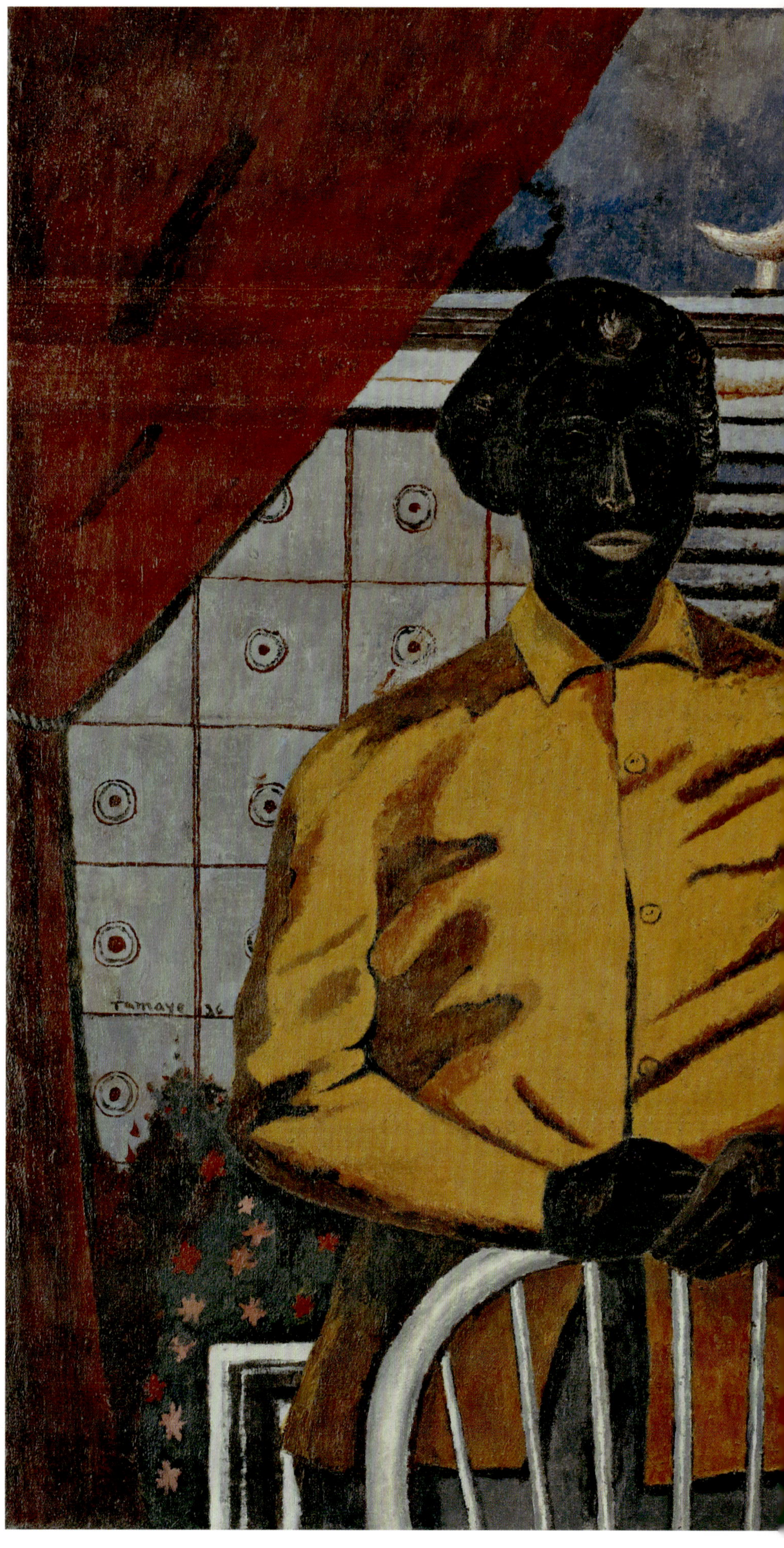

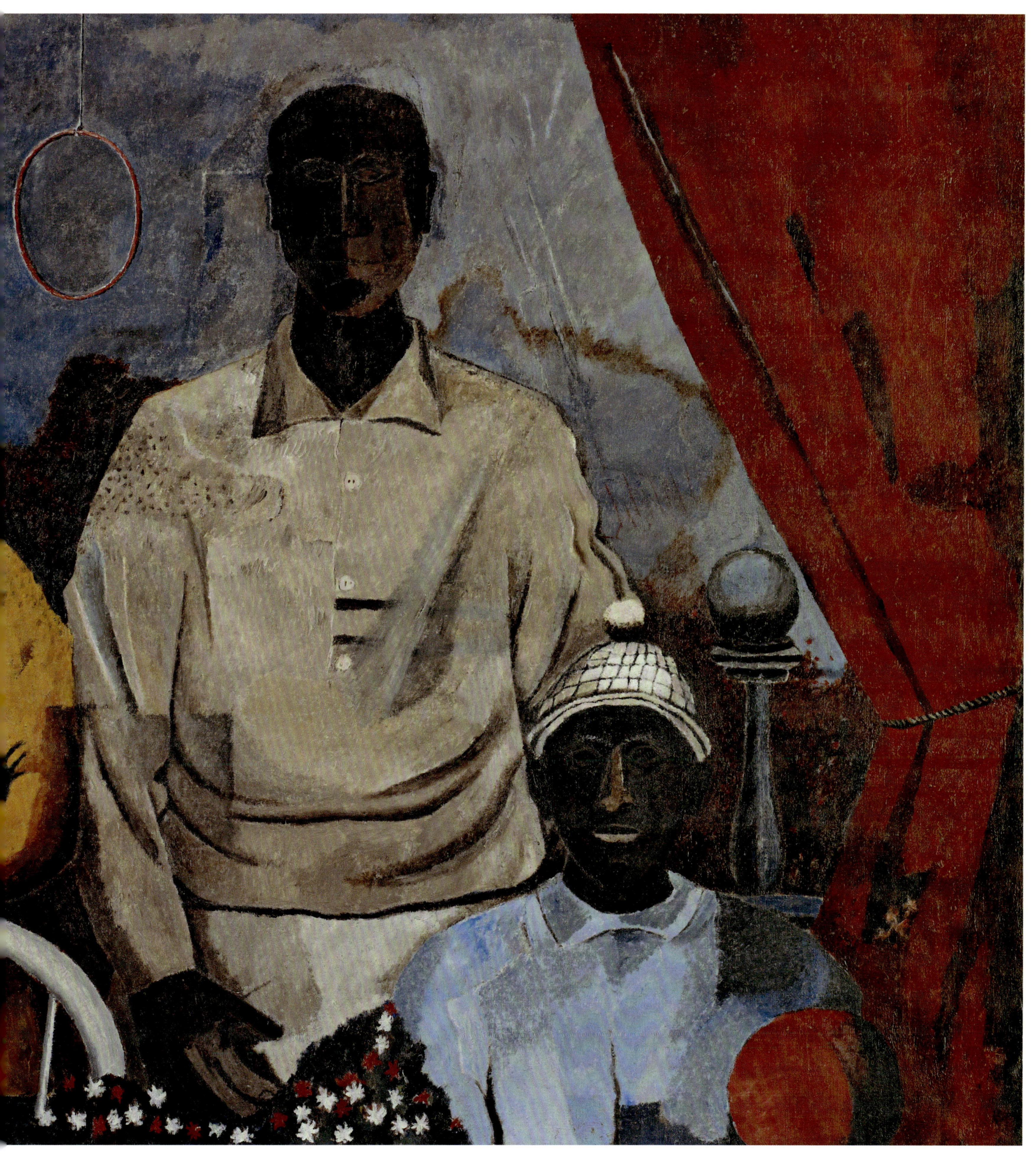

22

WAITING WOMAN
[MUJER ESPERANDO]

1936
watercolor on paper
15 × 20 ¾ in.

The Museum of Modern Art, New York, Extended loan from the United States WPA Art Program; Fine Arts Collection, Public Buildings Service, General Services Administration

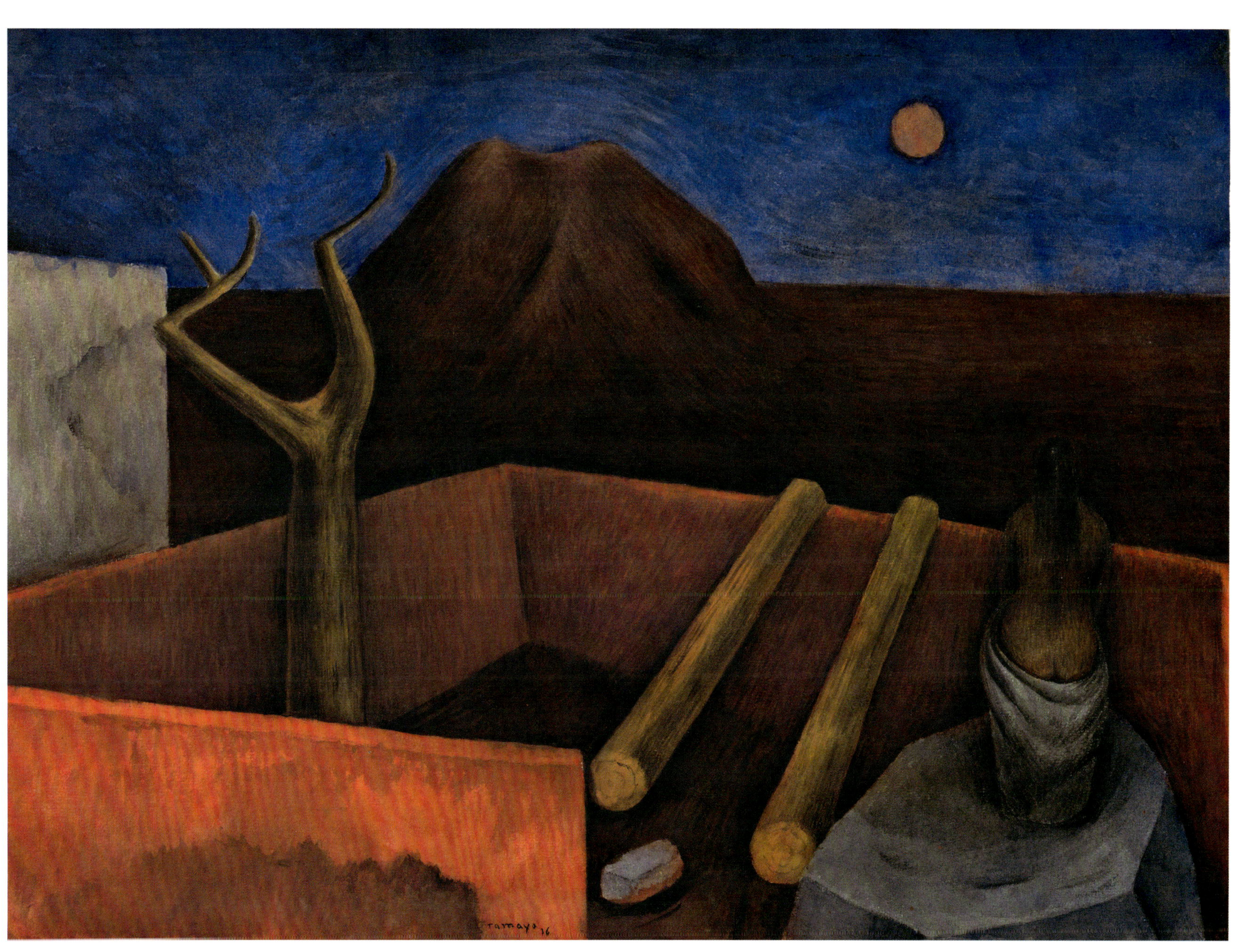
Tamayo 36

23

THE PRETTY GIRL
[NIÑA BONITA]

1937
oil on canvas
48 1/8 × 36 1/8 in.

Private collection

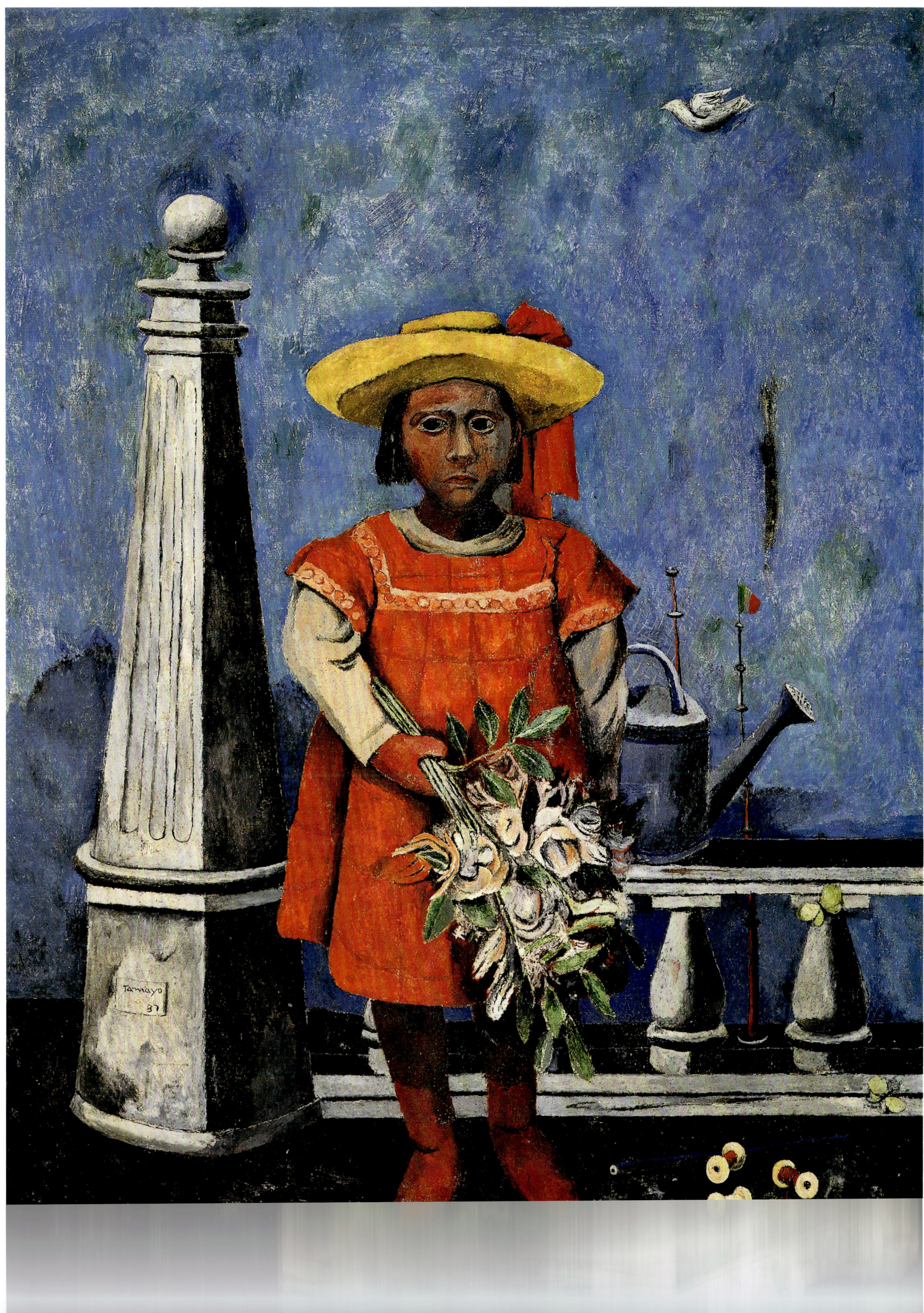
Tamayo
37

24

TWO WOMEN
[DOS MUJERES]

1939
gouache on canvas
14 5⁄16 × 24 3⁄8 in.

Museum of Art, Rhode Island School of Design, Providence, Mary B. Jackson Fund

25

WOMAN
[MUJER]

1938
oil on canvas
35 5⁄8 × 27 5⁄8 in.

The Museum of Modern Art, New York, Estate of John Hay Whitney

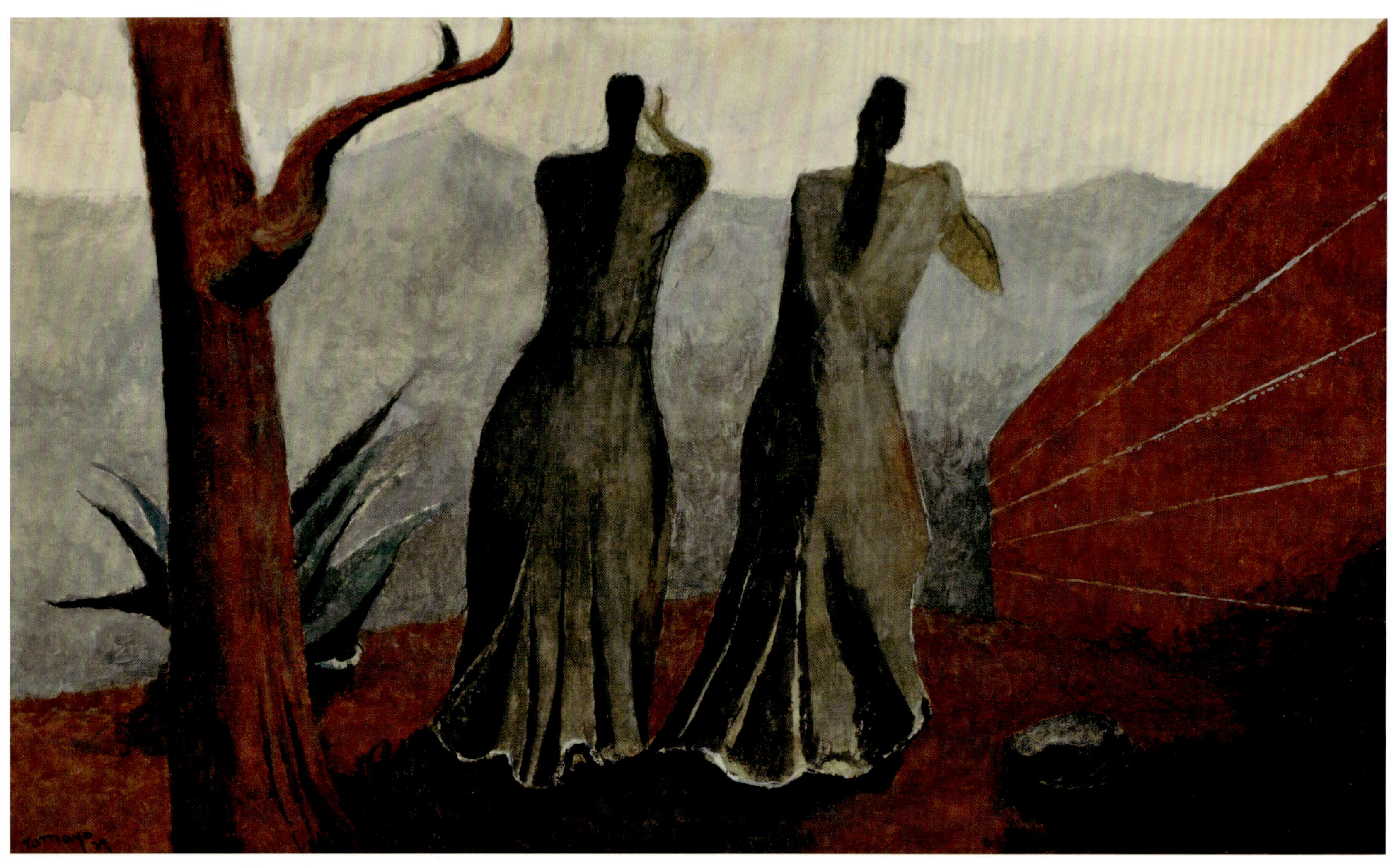

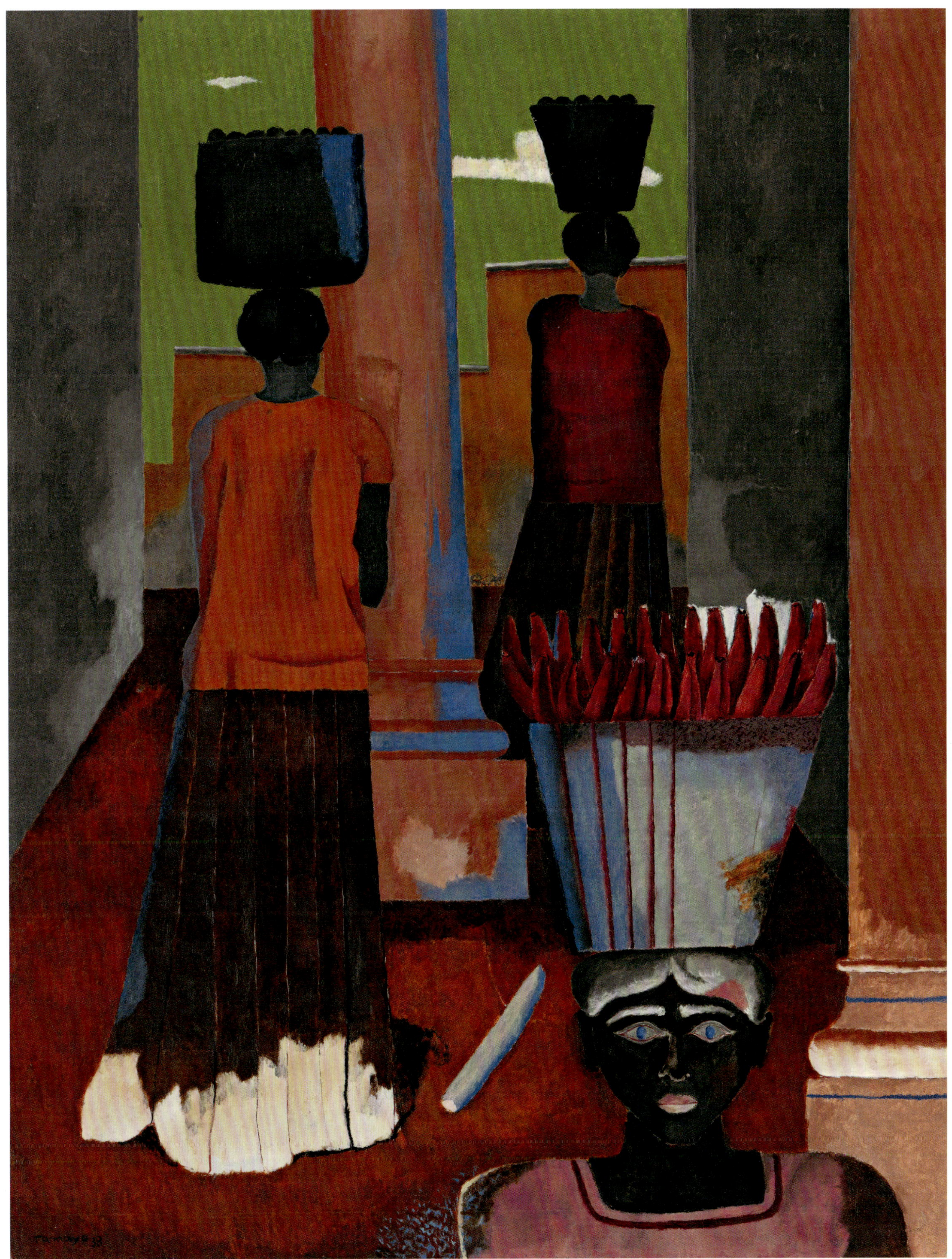

26

WOMEN OF TEHUANTEPEC
[MUJERES DE TEHUANTEPEC]

1939
oil on canvas
33 7/8 × 57 1/8 in.

Albright-Knox Art Gallery, Buffalo, New York, Room of Contemporary Art Fund, 1941

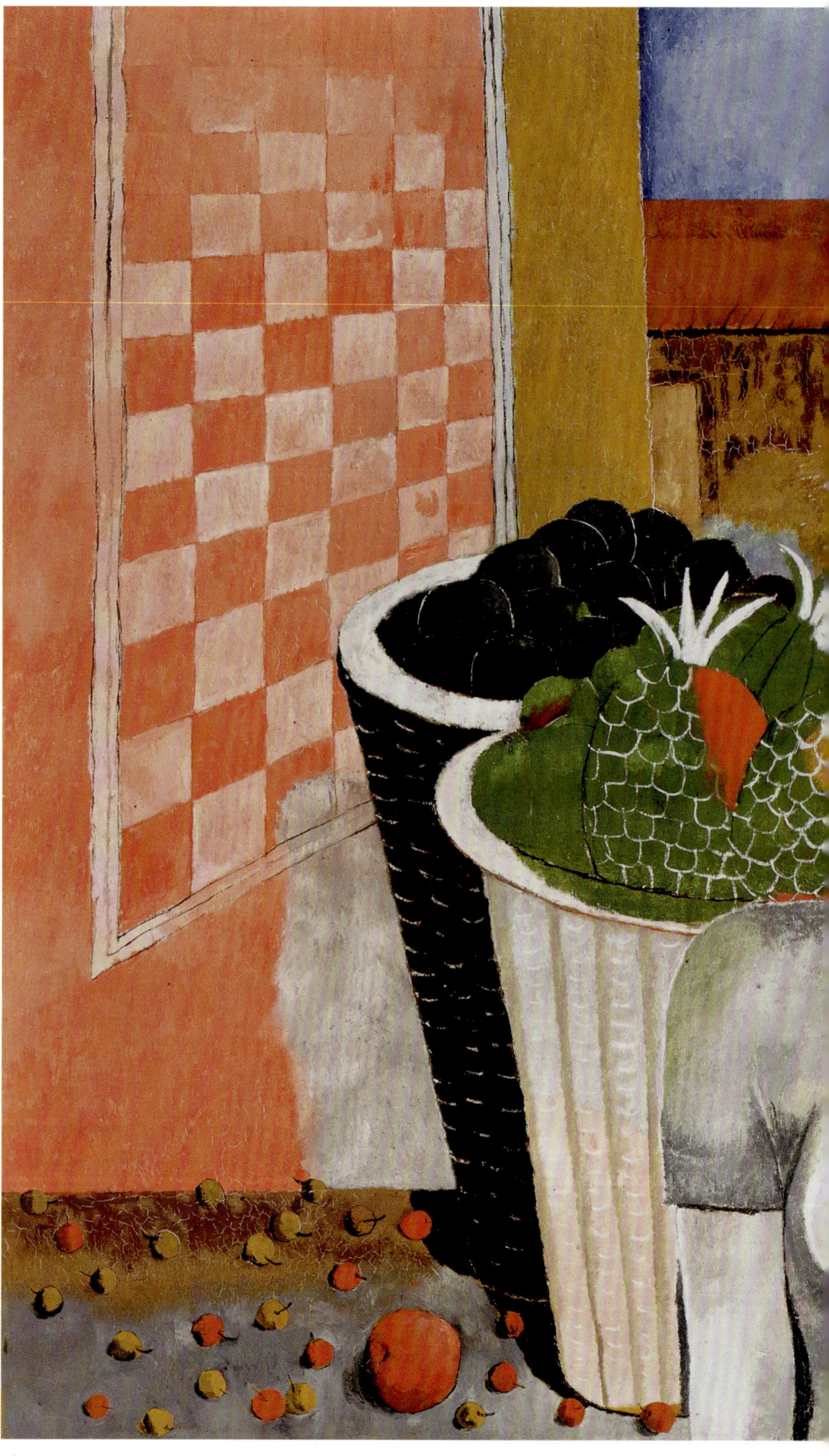

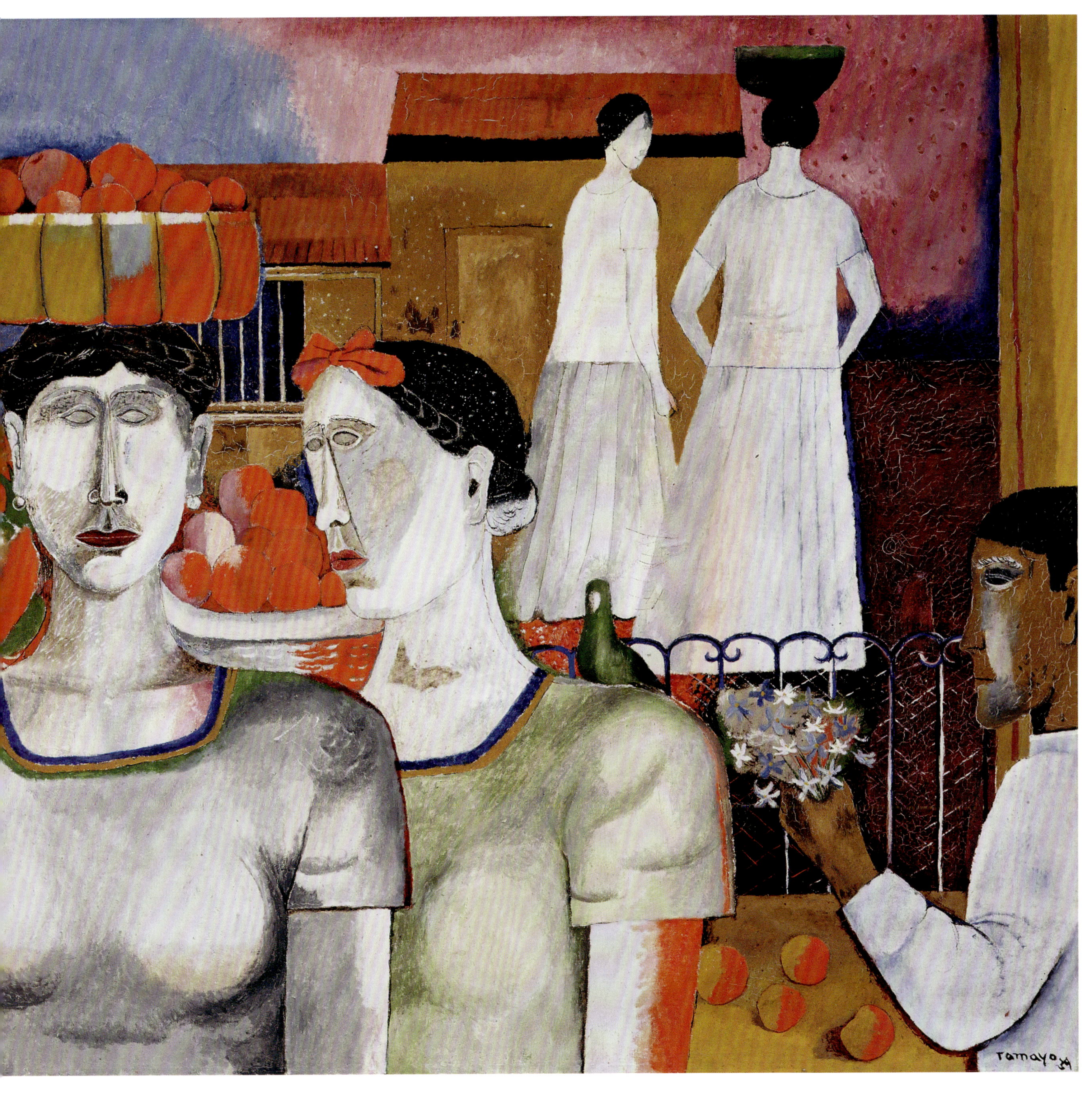
tamayo

27

CARNIVAL
[CARNAVAL]

1941
oil on canvas
44 1/8 × 33 1/4 in.
The Phillips Collection,
Washington, DC, Acquired 1942

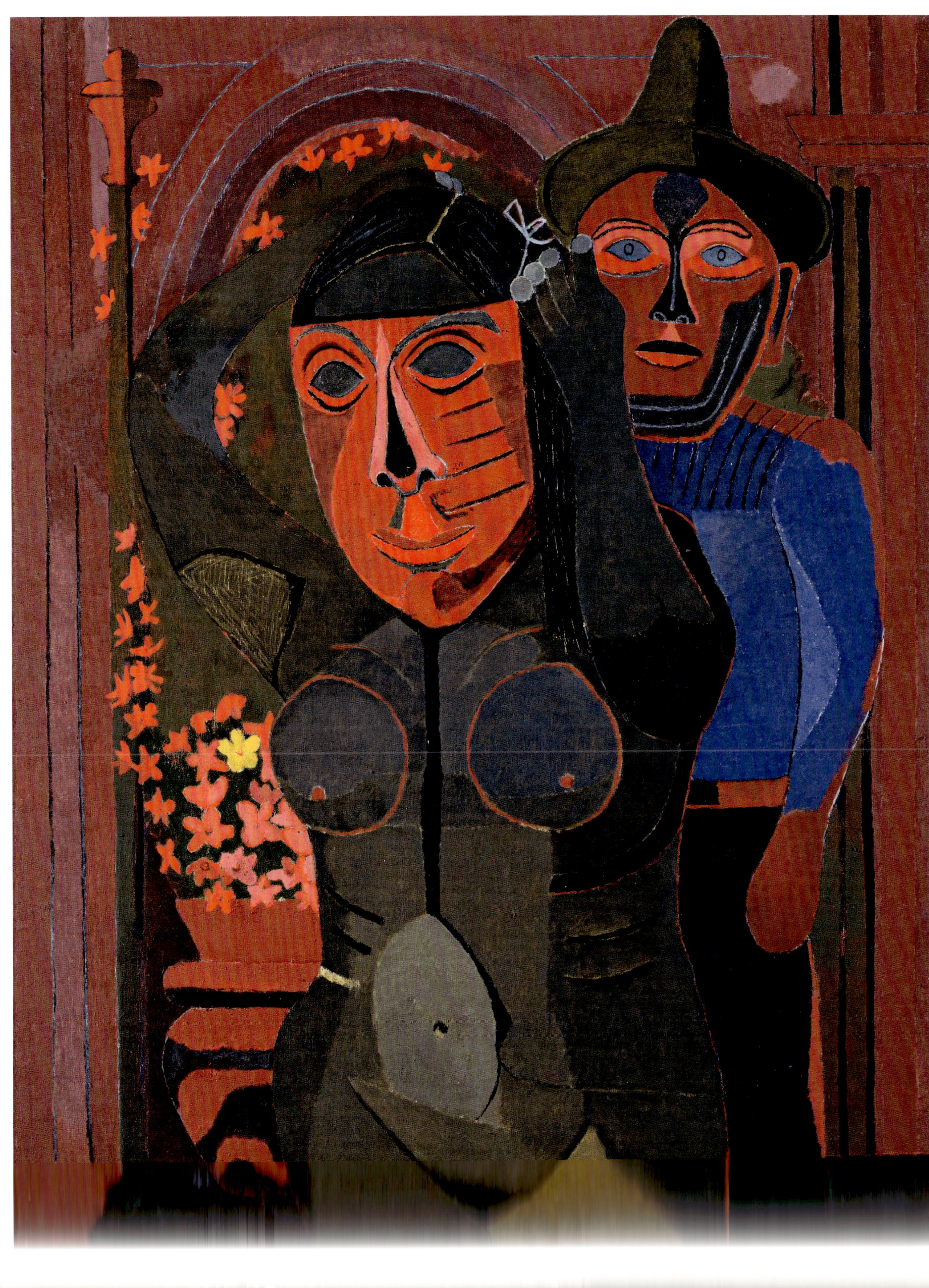

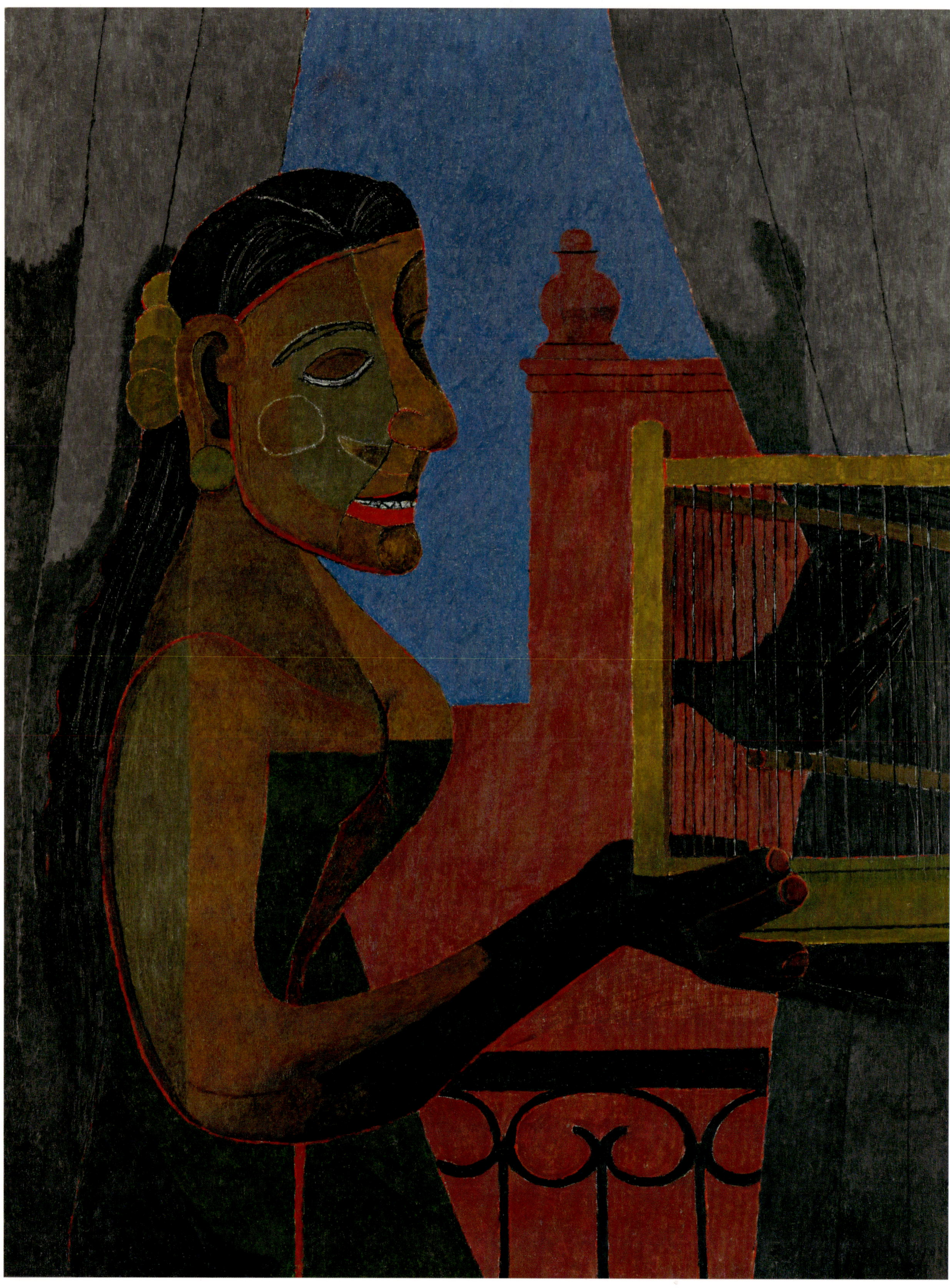

28

WOMAN WITH A BIRD CAGE
[MUJER CON UNA JAULA]

1941
oil on canvas
43 ¼ × 33 in.

The Art Institute of Chicago, Gift of Joseph Winterbotham Collection

29

THE DOCTOR
[EL MÉDICO]

1939
oil on canvas
22 ¾ × 17 in.

Collection of Stanley and Pearl Goodman, a promised gift to the NSU Art Museum, Fort Lauderdale, FL

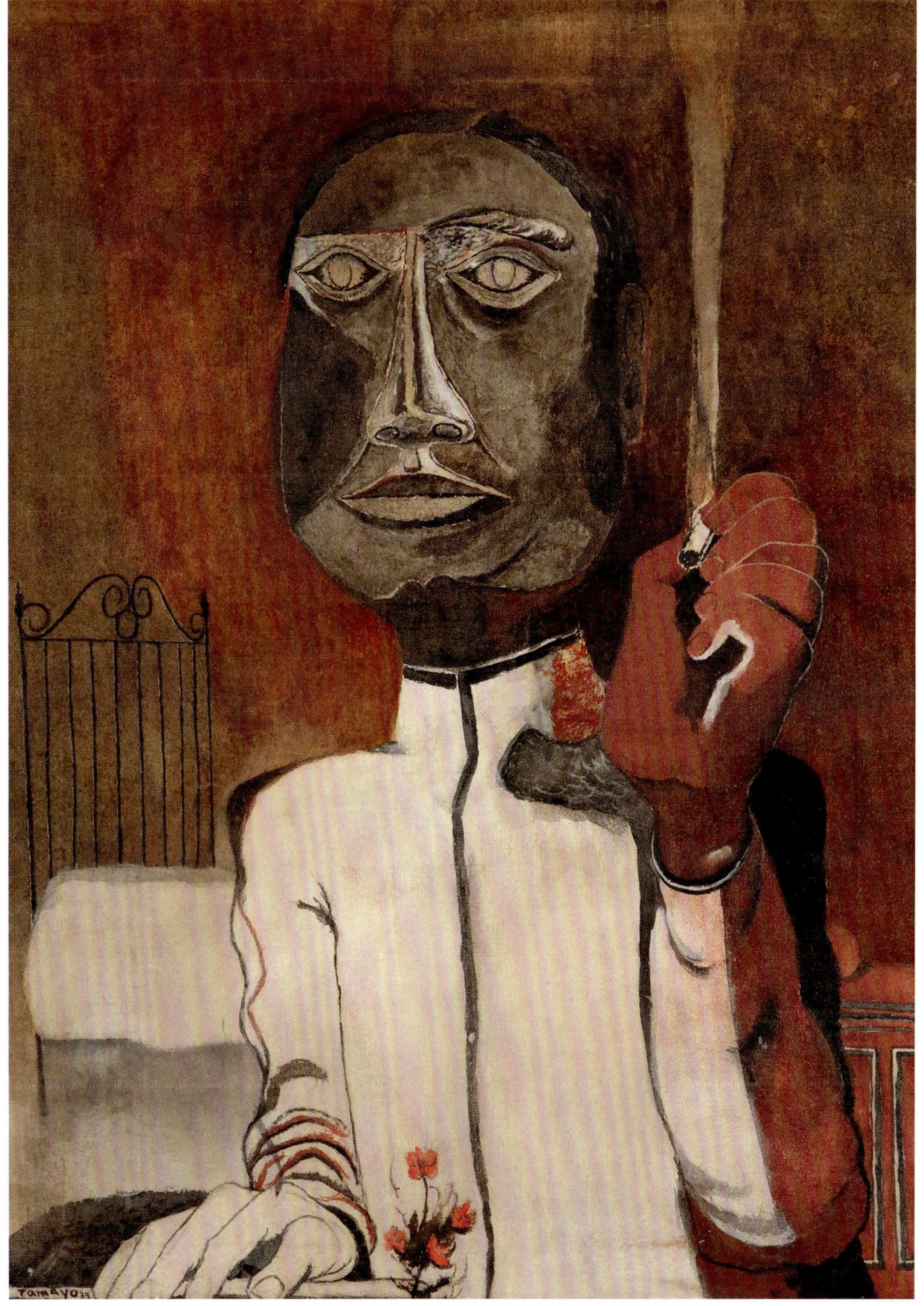

30

THE LOVERS
[AMANTES]

1943
oil on canvas
34 ¼ × 44 ¼ in.

San Francisco Museum of Modern Art, Purchase with the aid of funds from W. W. Crocker

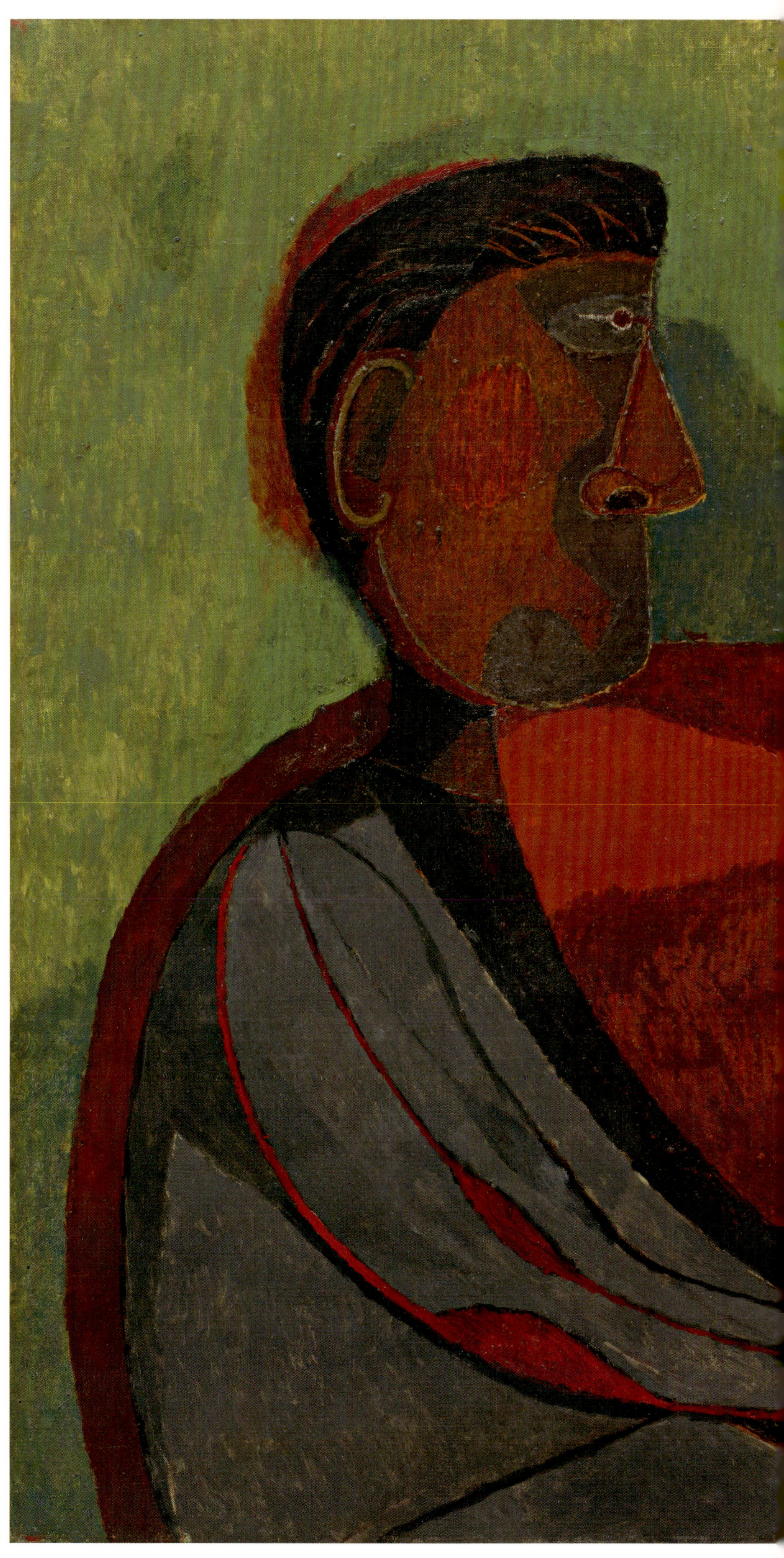

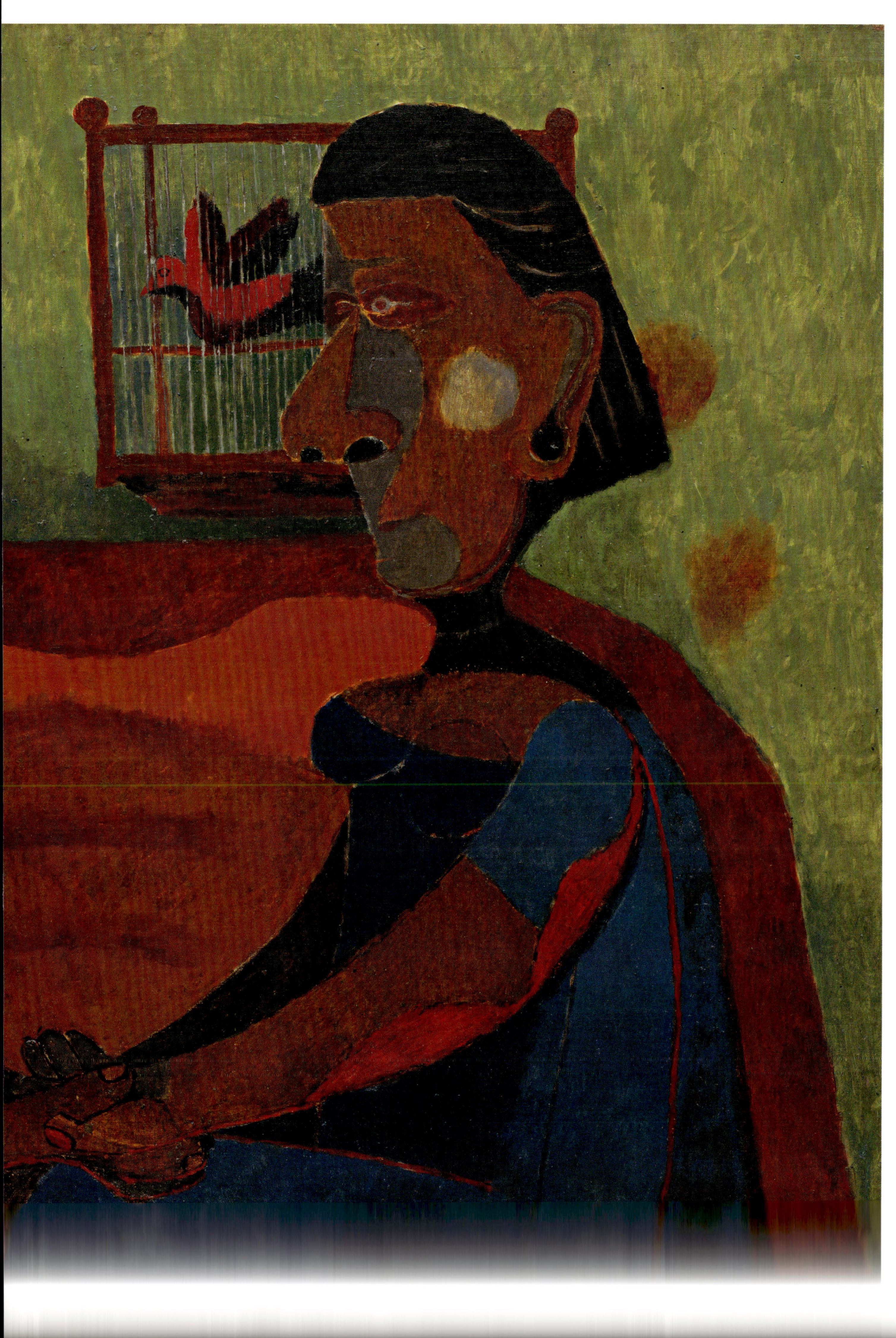

31

LION AND HORSE
[LEÓN Y CABALLO]

1942
oil on canvas
36 1/4 × 46 1/2 in.

Mildred Lane Kemper Art Museum, Washington University in St. Louis, University purchase, Kende Sale Fund, 1946

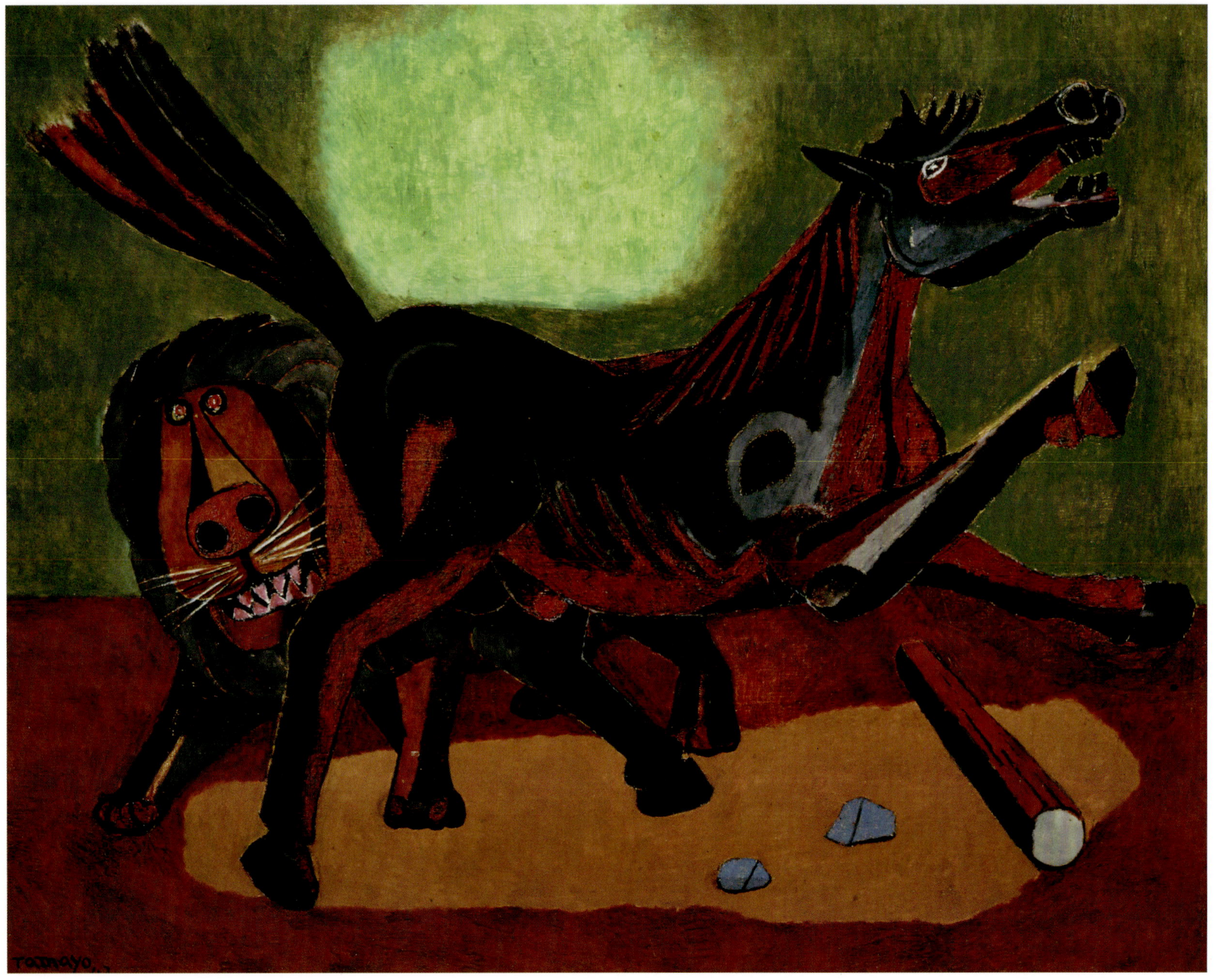

32

ANIMALS
[ANIMALES]

1941
oil on canvas
30 1/8 × 40 in.

The Museum of Modern Art,
New York, Inter-American Fund

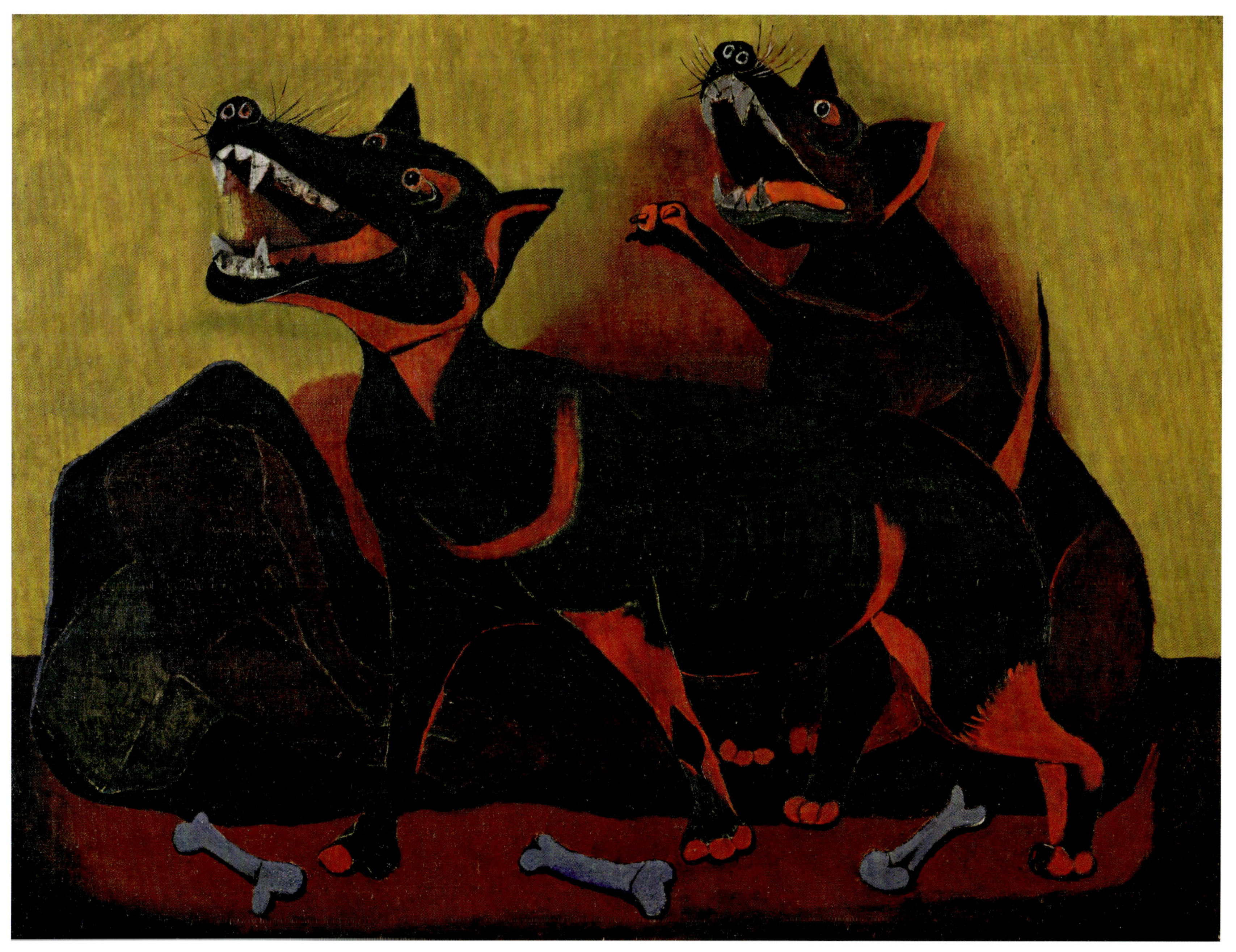

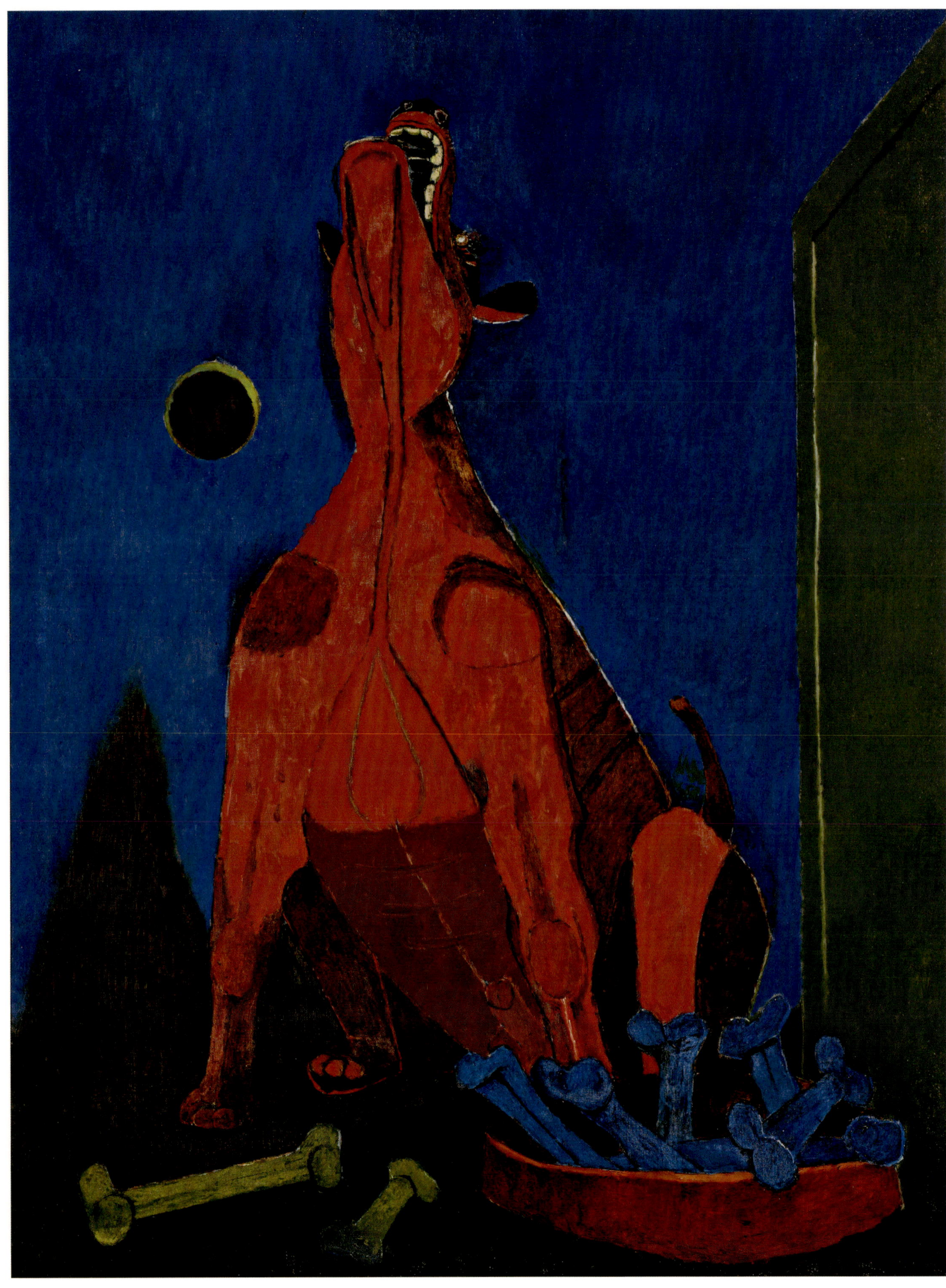

33

DOG BARKING AT THE MOON
[PERRO LADRANDO A LA LUNA]

1942
oil on canvas
47 1/4 × 33 7/16 in.

Private collection

34

MAD DOG
[PERRA RABIOSA]

1943
oil on canvas
32 × 43 in.

Philadelphia Museum of Art, Gift of Mrs. Herbert Cameron Morris, 1945

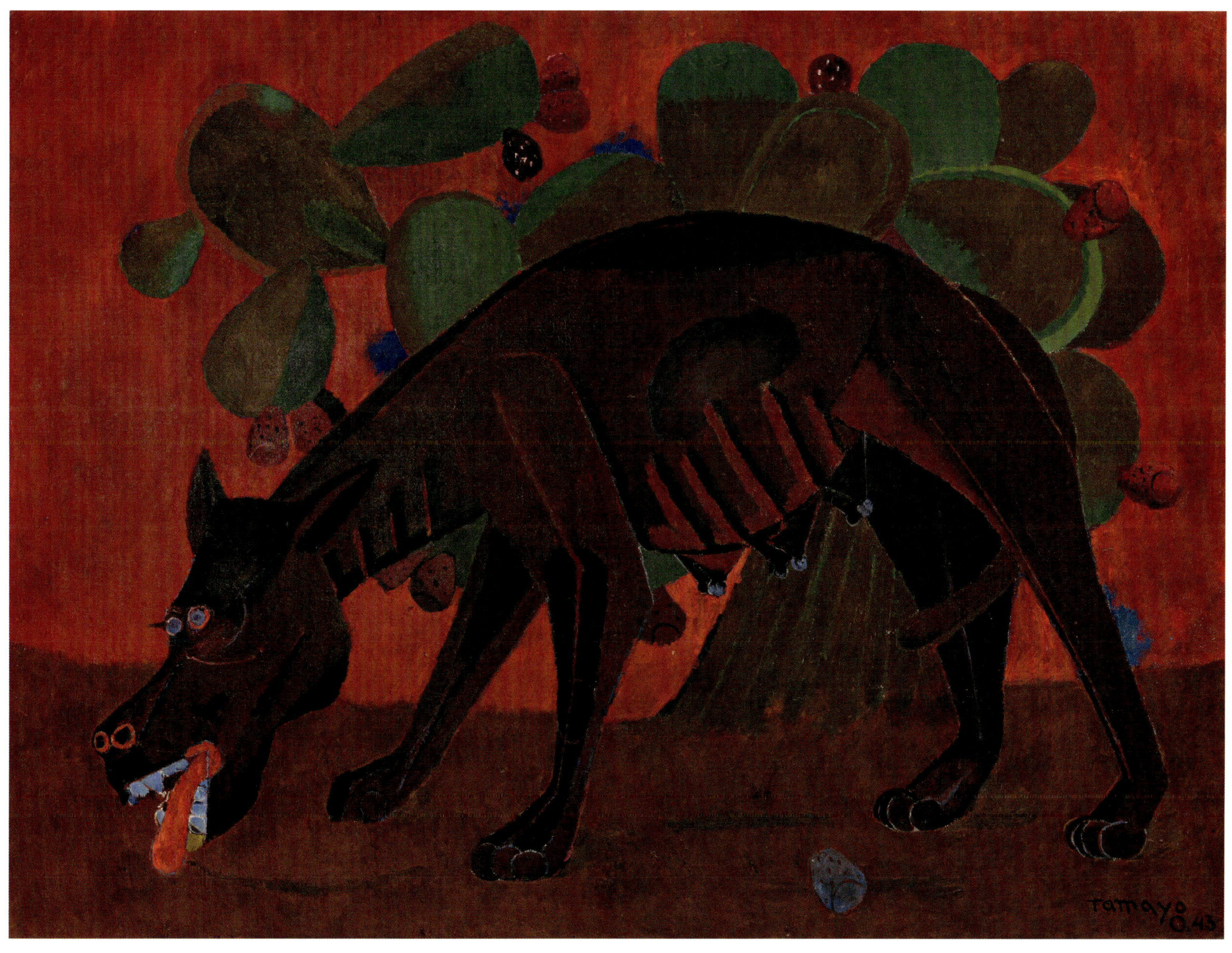

35

GIRL ATTACKED BY A STRANGE BIRD
[NIÑA ATACADA POR UN PÁJARO EXTRAÑO]

1947
oil on canvas
70 × 50 1/8 in.

The Museum of Modern Art, New York, Gift of Mr. and Mrs. Charles Zadok

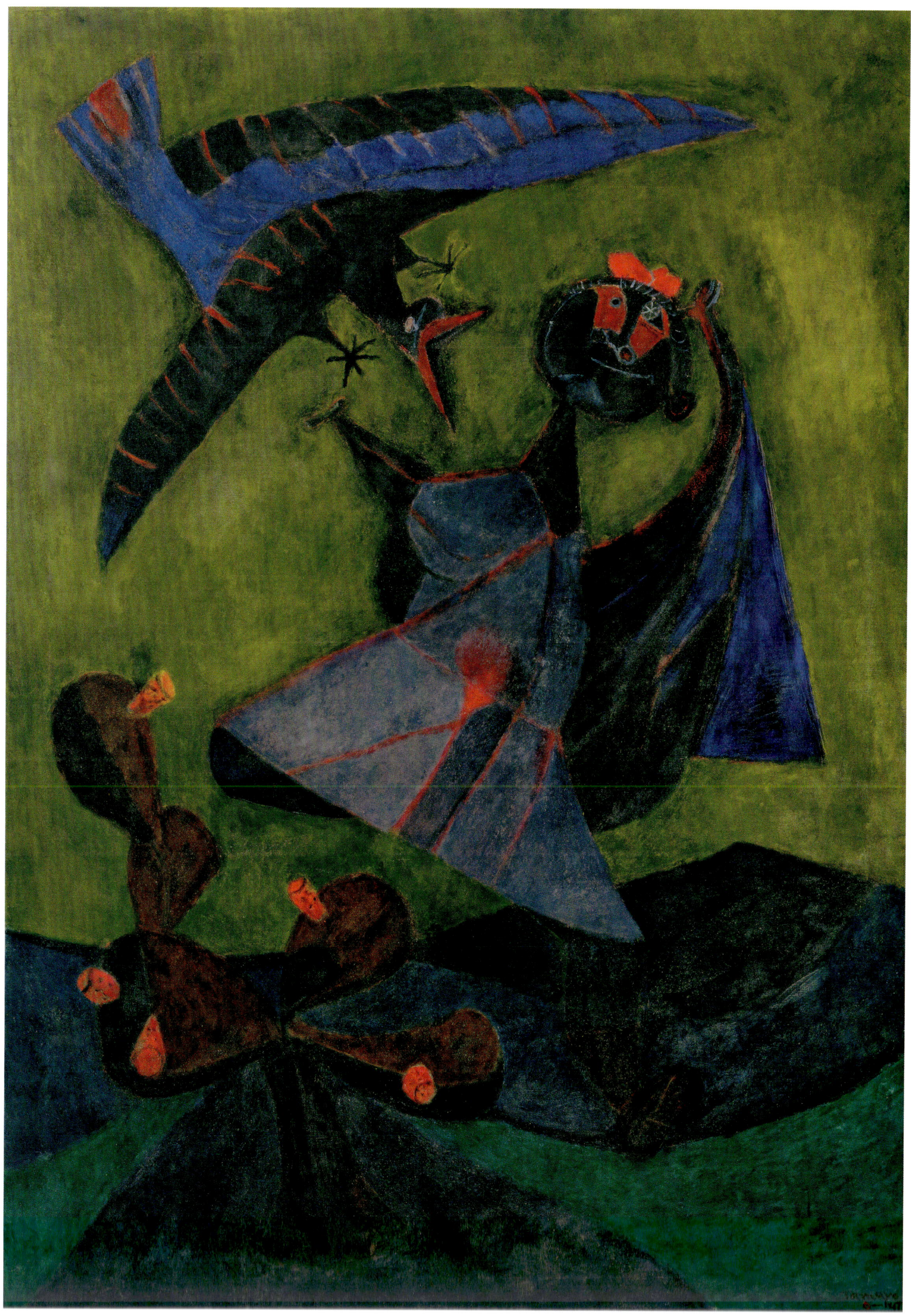

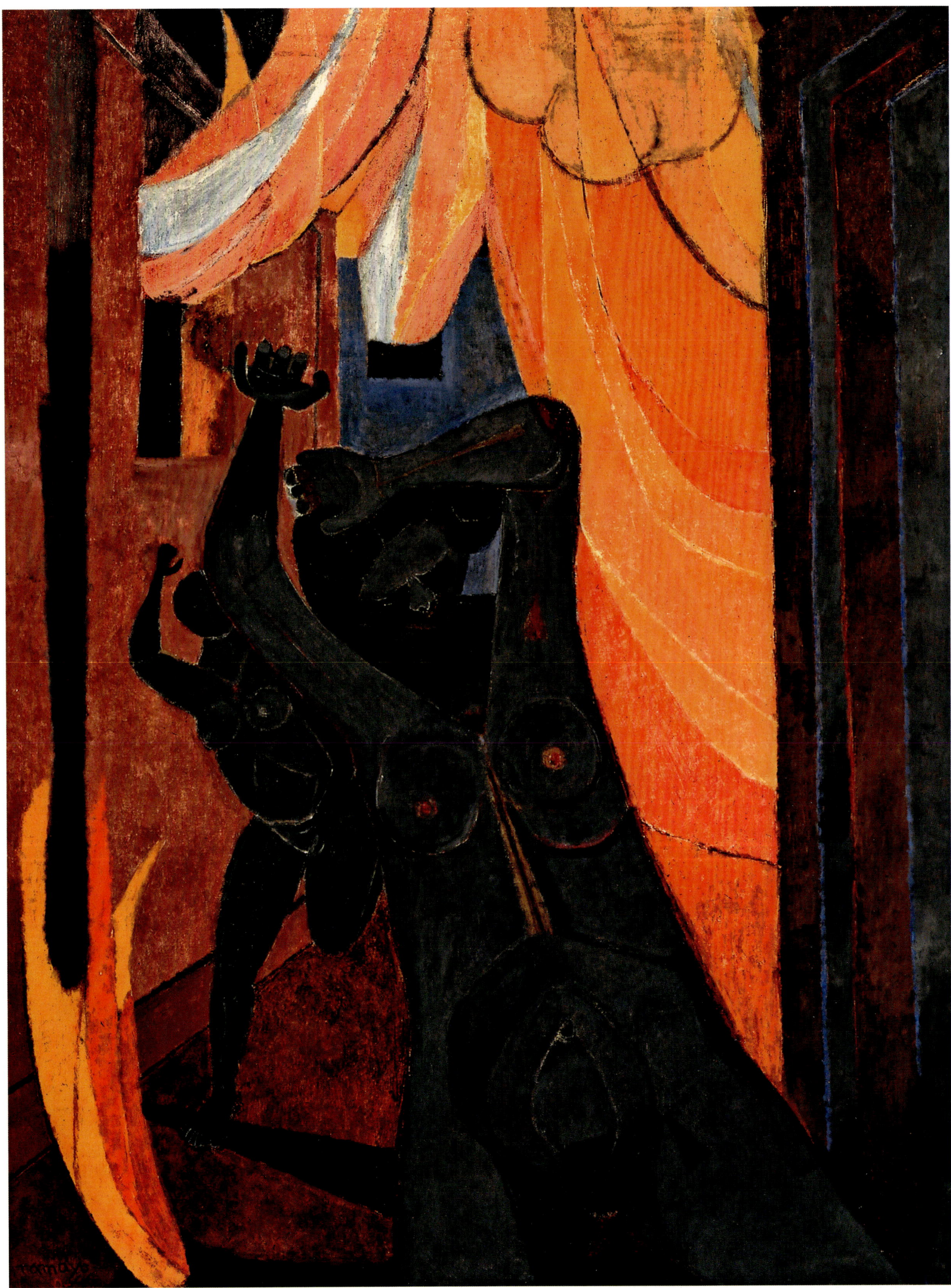
tamayo

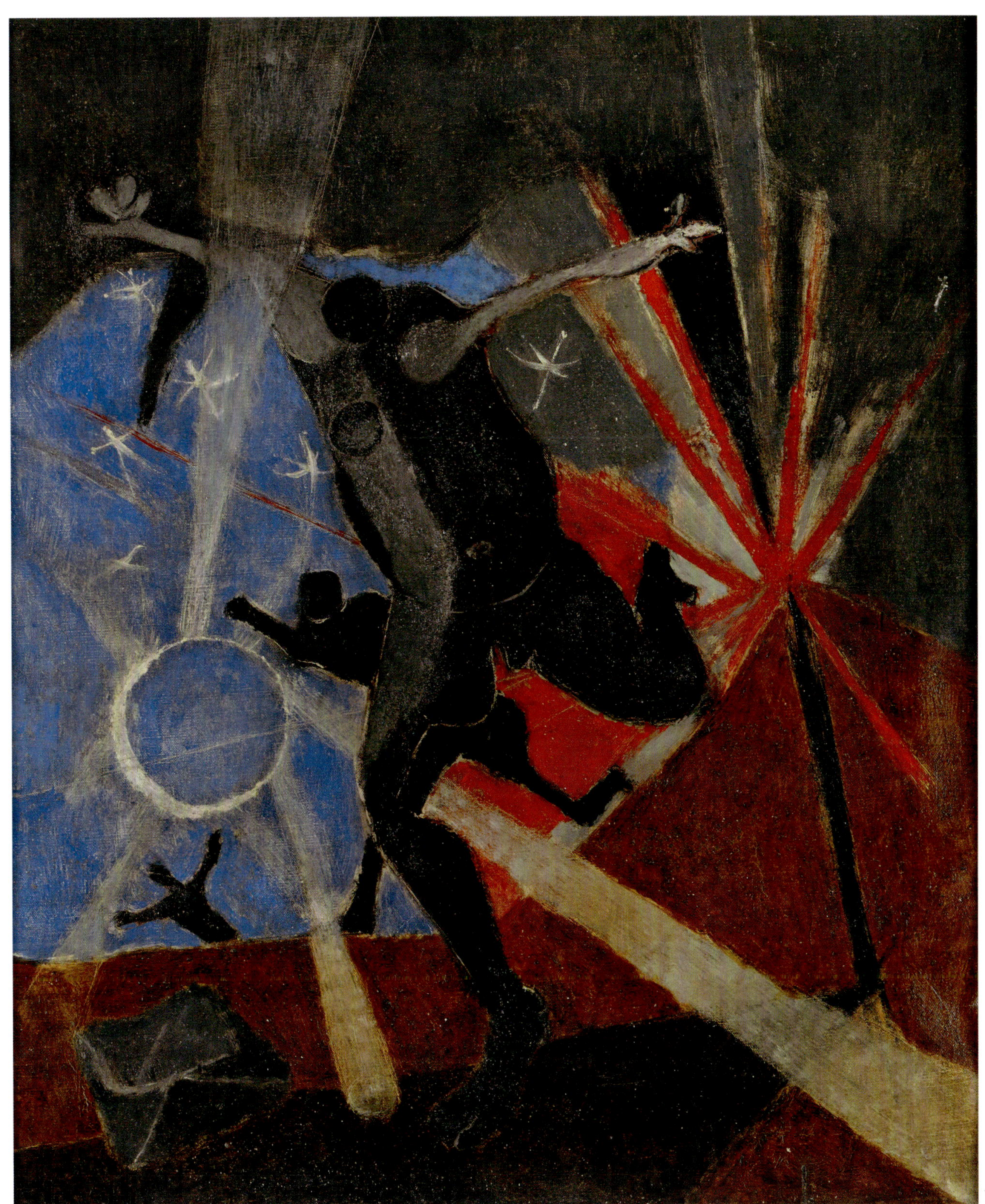

36

FIRE
[FUEGO]
1946
oil on canvas
44 × 34 in.
Collection of Mrs. J. Todd Figi

37

CATACLYSM
[CATACLISMO]
1946
oil on canvas
24 × 20 in.
Private collection

38

THE FULL MOON
[LA LUNA LLENA]

1945
oil on canvas
26 ¼ × 36 in.

Private collection

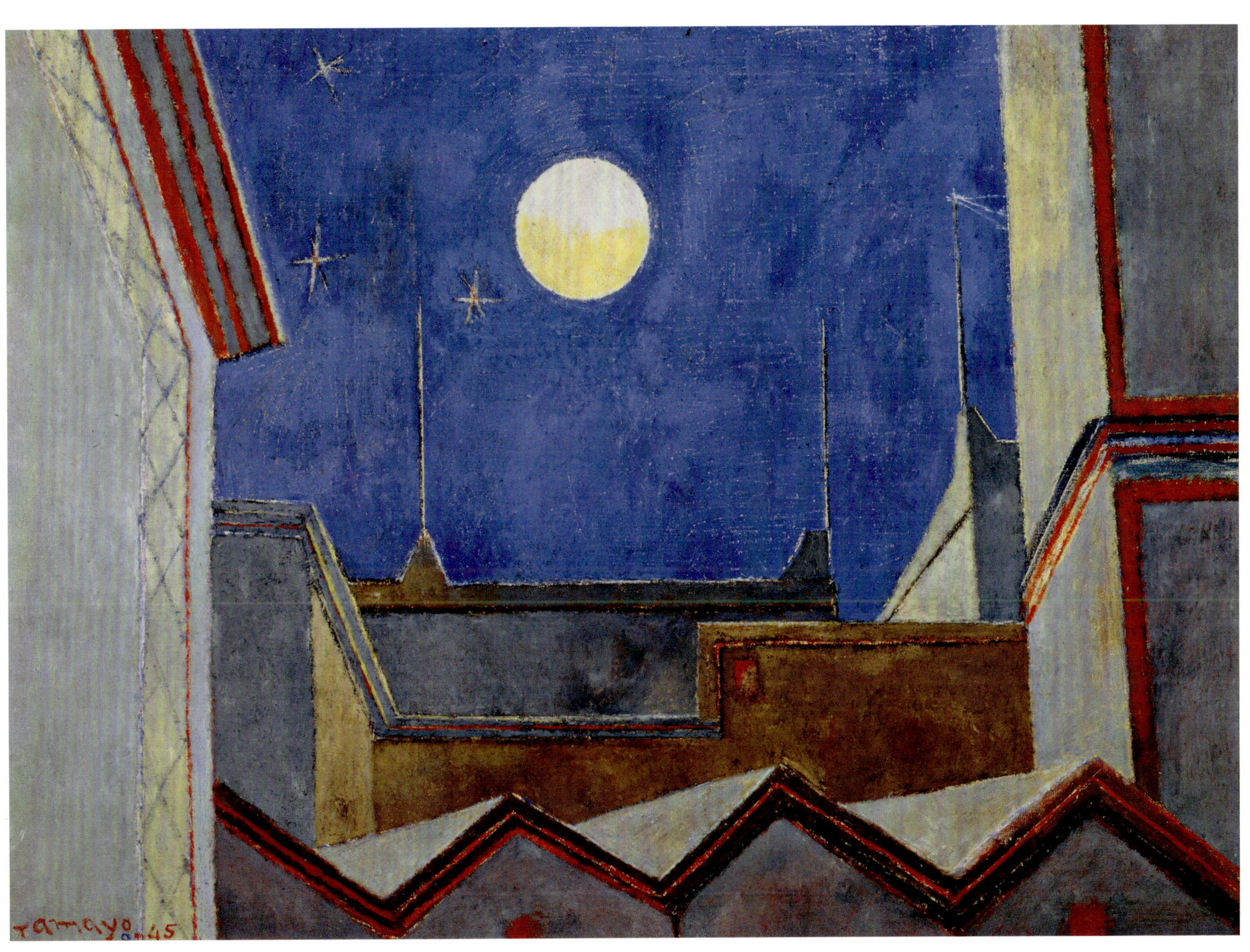

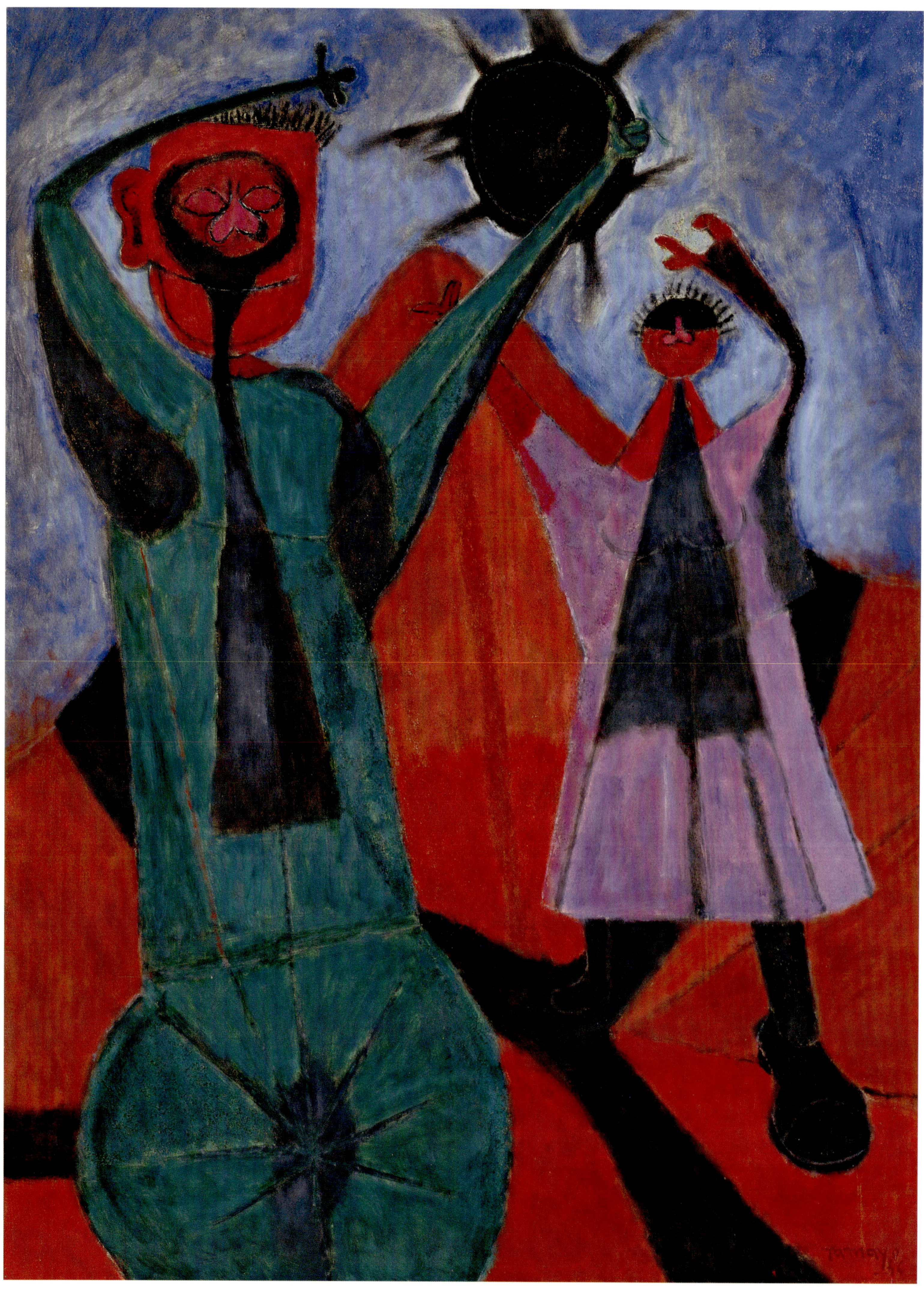

39

TOTAL ECLIPSE
[ECLIPSE TOTAL]

ca. 1946
oil with sand on canvas
39 7/8 × 29 7/8 in.

Harvard Art Museums/Fogg Museum, Gift of Mr. and Mrs. Joseph Pulitzer Jr.

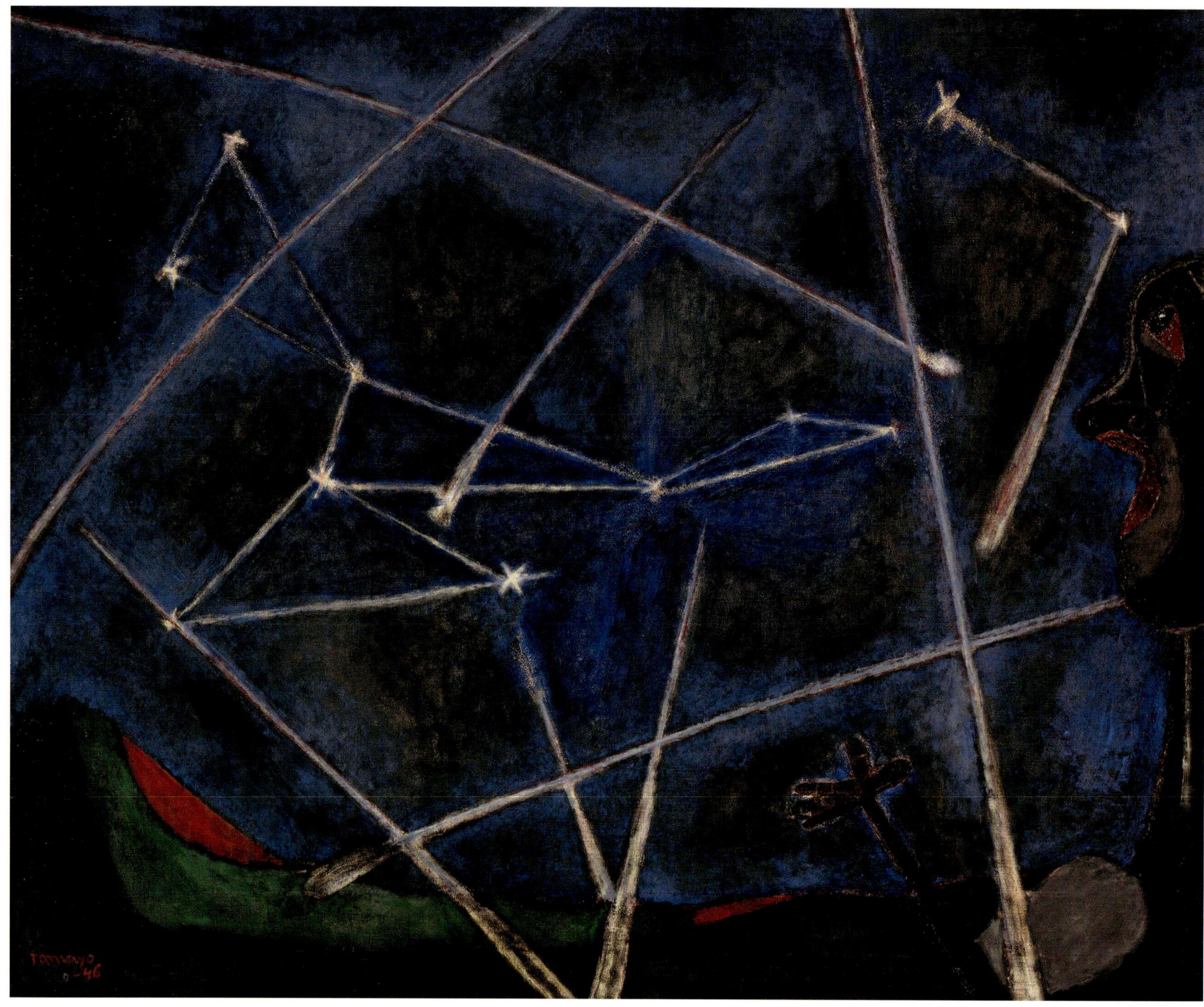

40

HEAVENLY BODIES
[CUERPOS CELESTES]

1946
oil with sand on canvas
34 × 41 5/16 in.

Peggy Guggenheim Collection, Venezia (Solomon R. Guggenheim Foundation, New York)

41

WOMEN REACHING FOR THE MOON
[MUJERES ALCANZANDO LA LUNA]

1946
oil on canvas
36 × 26 in.

Private collection, Courtesy of Christie's

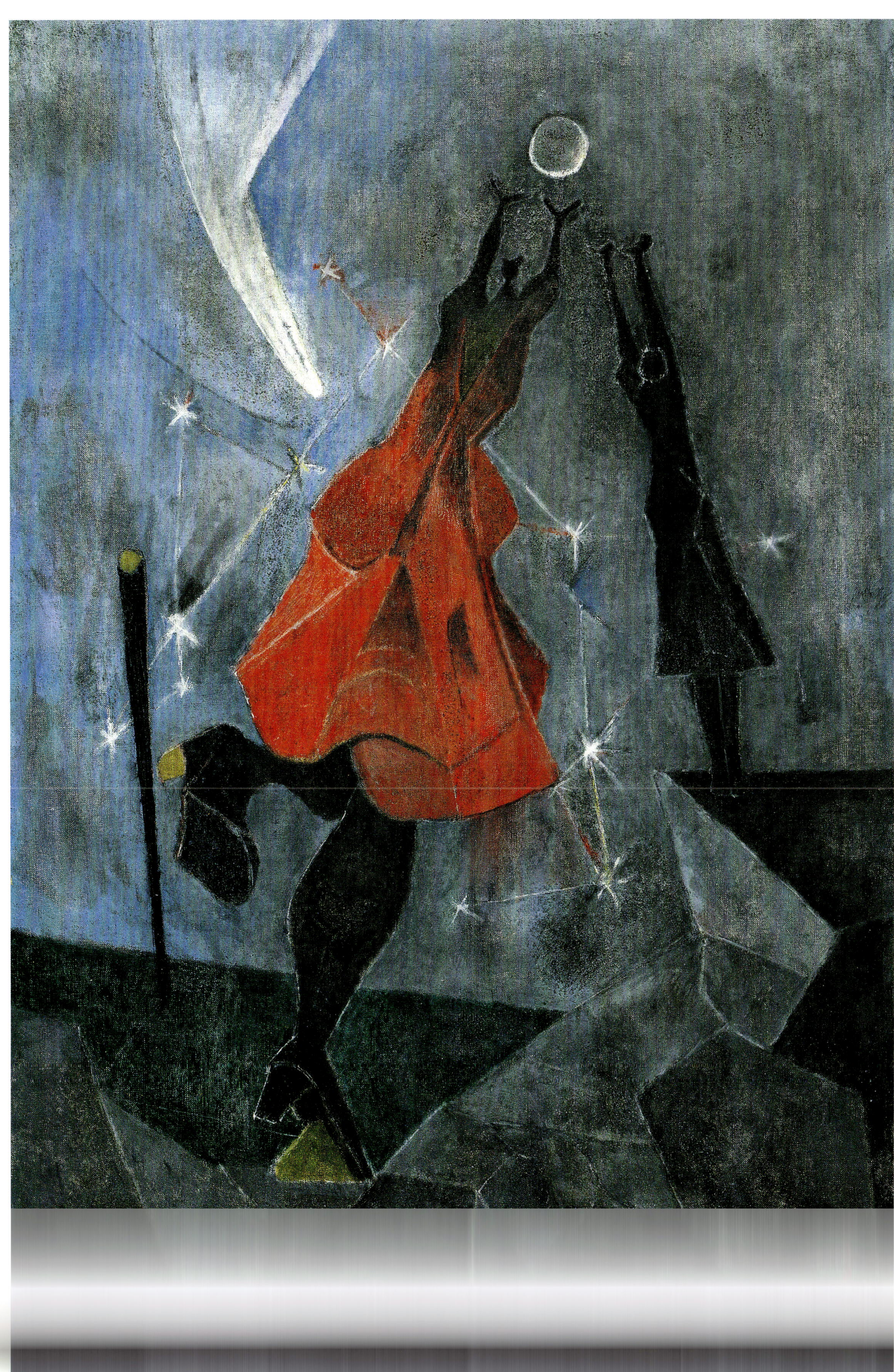

42

MAN SEARCHING THE HEAVENS

[HOMBRE ESCUDRIÑANDO EL FIRMAMENTO]

1949

oil on canvas

39 3/8 × 27 5/8 in.

Harvard Art Museums/Fogg Museum, Gift of Mr. and Mrs. Harold Gershinowitz

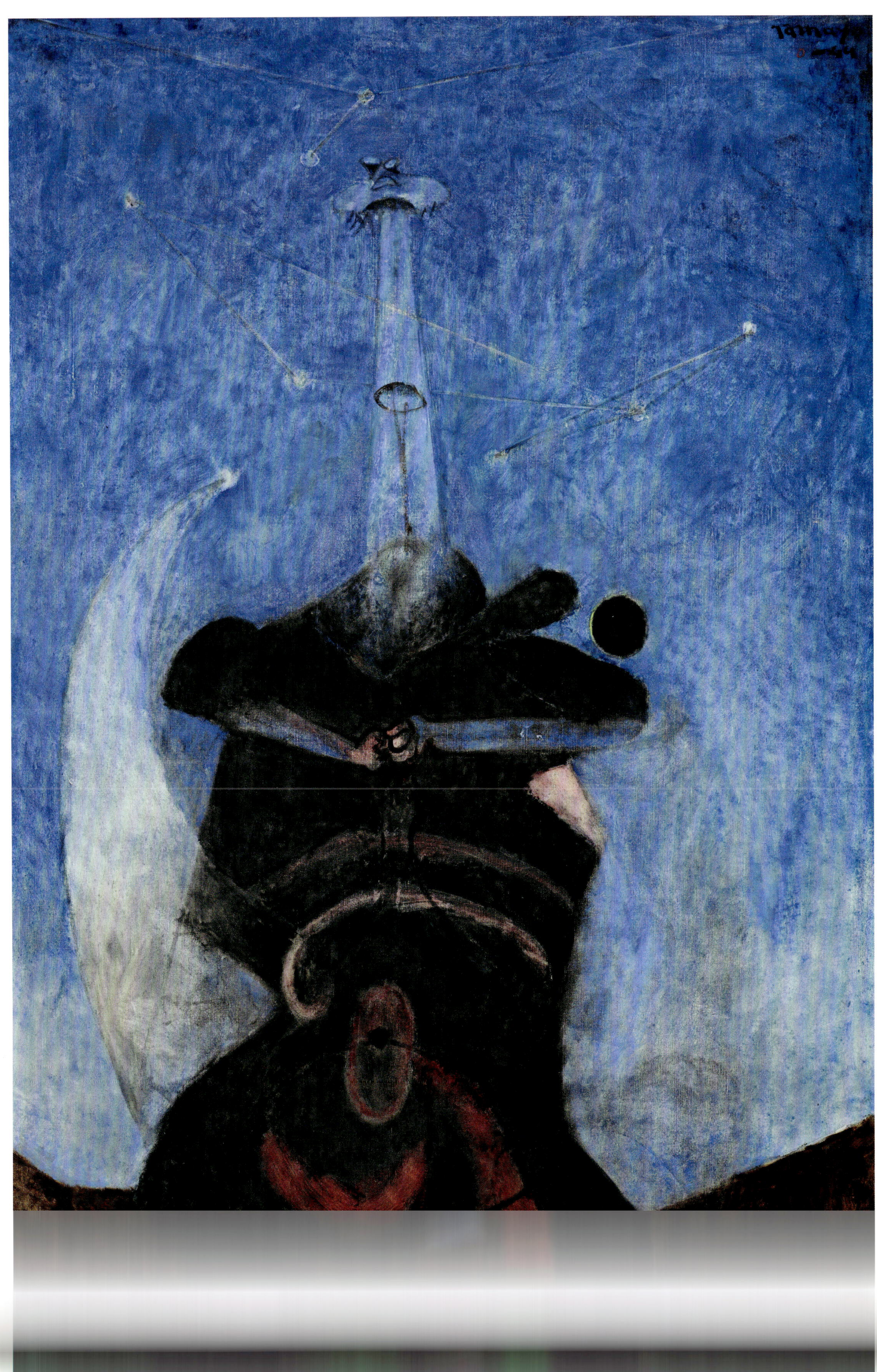

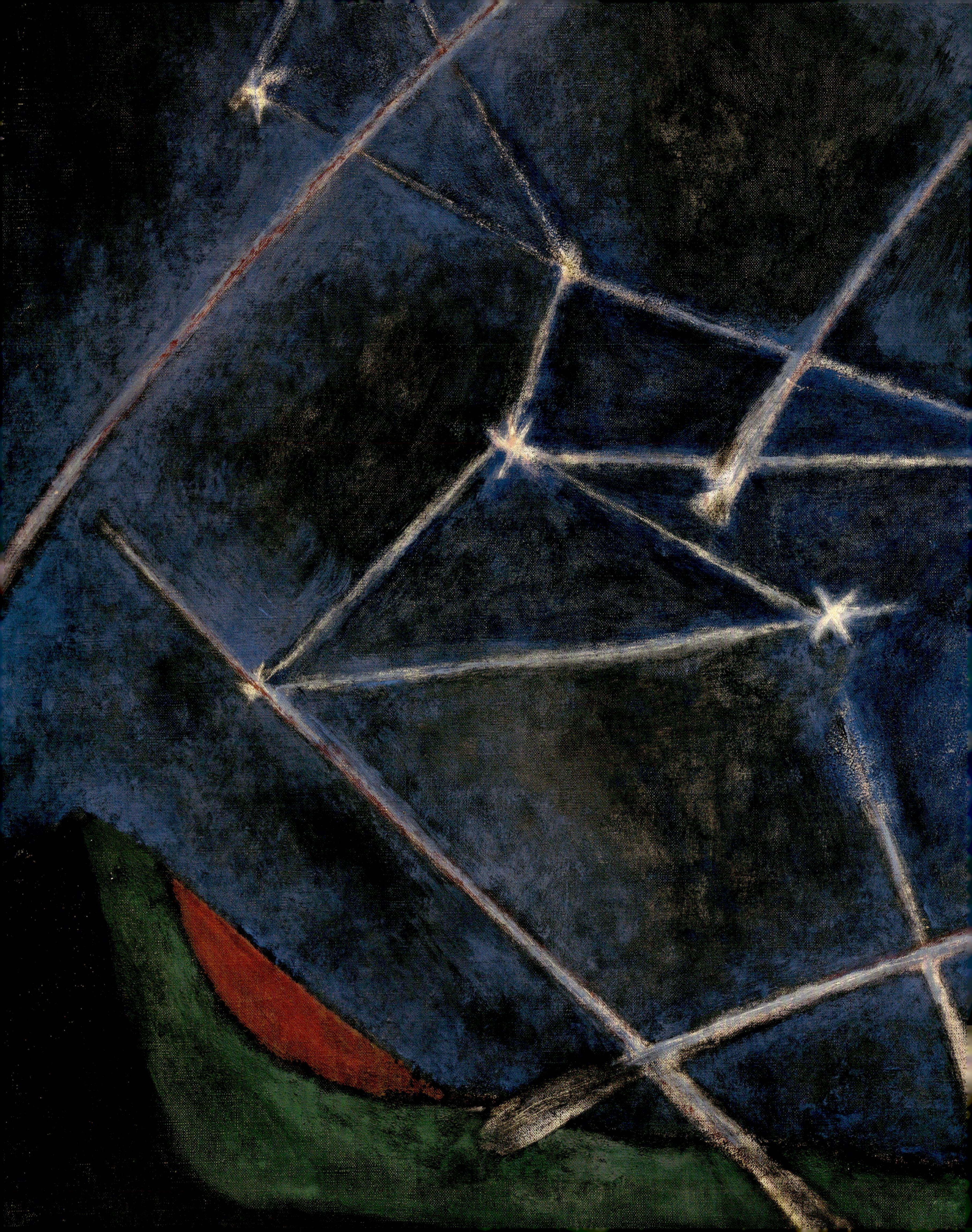

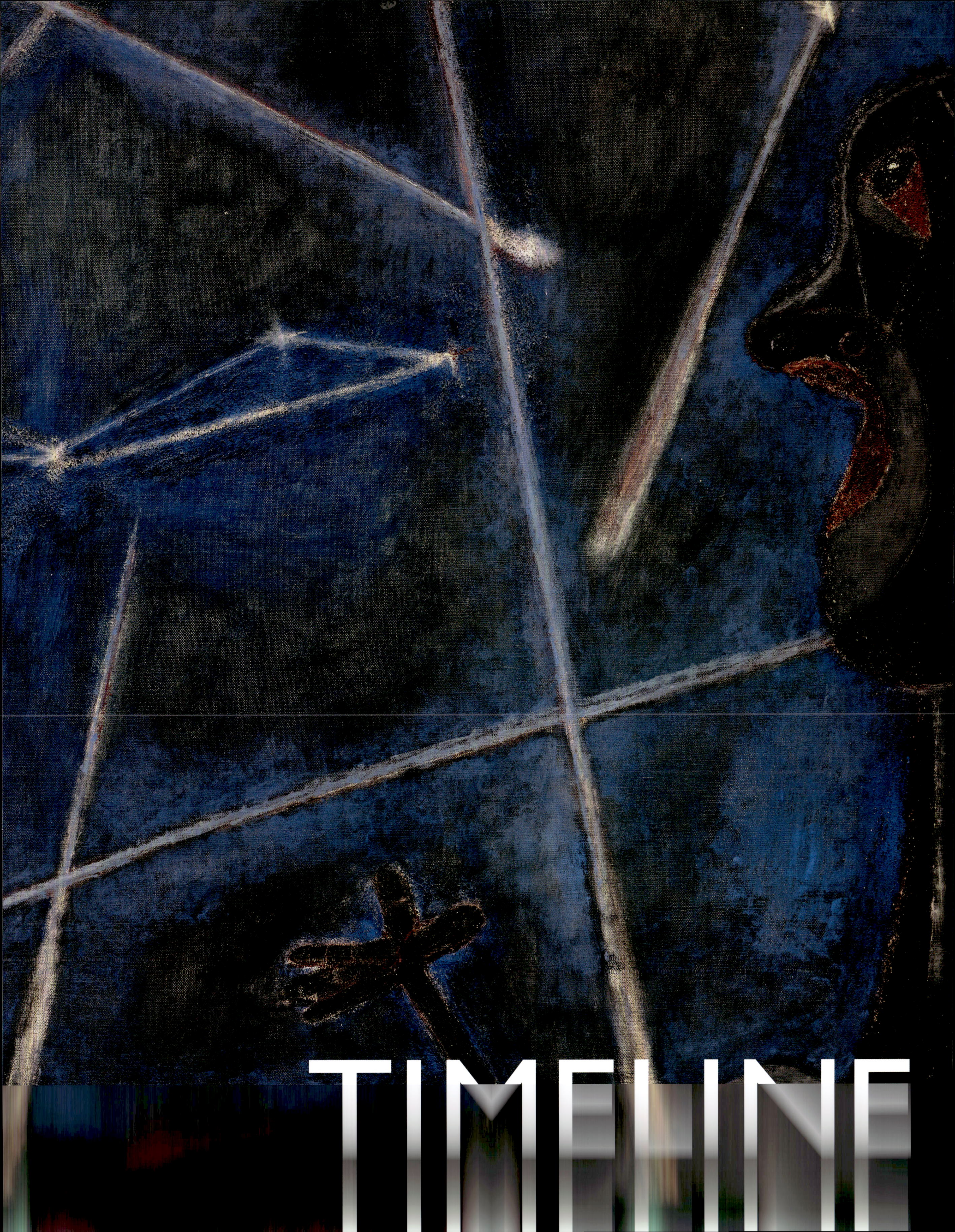

TIMELINE

Preceding pages:

Heavenly Bodies, 1946; detail.
See p. 132.

1899 RUFINO ARELLANES TAMAYO IS BORN IN MEXICO to Manuel Arellanes and Florentina Tamayo Navarro in the city of Oaxaca on August 25. His date of birth is mistakenly registered as August 26, the date of his baptism. He will eventually take his mother's name.

1910 Tamayo witnesses the appearance of Halley's Comet over Oaxaca on April 10:

> *I remember an object of dread in the town: the famous Halley's Comet, which... had a great tail, as long as two streets. It was an amazing thing and one would go out at night and in the early morning to watch it with profound terror, as it had been publicized that the tail of the comet was going to graze Earth on its last day.*[1]

\+ Months later, popular uprisings against longtime president Porfirio Díaz mark the beginning of the Mexican Revolution.

1911 Following the death of his mother, Tamayo moves with his maternal aunt Amalia Tamayo Navarro from Oaxaca to Mexico City, where she operates a fruit stall at Mercado La Merced, selling fruit grown by Tamayo's uncle in Veracruz.

1917 Tamayo enrolls in the Escuela Nacional de Bellas Artes (National School of Fine Arts), or ENBA, despite his family's wishes that he study accounting. His classmates include Julio Castellanos, Francisco Díaz de León, Gabriel Fernández Ledesma, Agustín Lazo, Leopoldo Méndez, and Antonio Ruiz—artists who will go on to form Mexico's major avant-garde groups during the 1920s and 1930s. One of Tamayo's early instructors is Saturnino Herrán, a prominent painter influenced by both symbolism and the indigenist movement. Tamayo will later call him a "genius," despite disagreeing with his outmoded teaching methods.

1920 Tamayo studies under painter Roberto Montenegro. Inspired by art reproductions circulated from Europe, Tamayo adopts an impressionist style around this time. He later notes that "it could be said that the first phase of my painting was Impressionism."[2]

\+ Álvaro Obregón is elected president of Mexico, marking the end of the Mexican Revolution.

1921 President Obregón places José Vasconcelos in charge of the new Secretaría de Educación Pública (Ministry of Public Education), or SEP. Vasconcelos will play a major role in the reformulation of Mexican cultural and artistic identity during the period known as the Mexican Renaissance.

\+ In June, Tamayo is hired as Primer Dibujante (First Draftsman) in the ethnographic drawing department of the Museo Nacional de Arqueología, Historia y Etnografía (National Museum of Archaeology, History, and Ethnography):

> *I went to the museum, where my little office was in the middle of the great pre-Columbian collections. There I was surrounded by objects that were a revelation to me. They made me realize that everything I had been taught in school was useless, at least for me.... I absorbed the new influence, almost subconsciously.*[3]

\+ In July, Diego Rivera returns from his travels in Europe and becomes a kind of mentor to Tamayo and his peers.

\+ In the fall, Tamayo sees the celebrated *Exposición de arte popular*, a traveling exhibition that had the dual nationalist objectives of showcasing the diverse art traditions of Mexico's indigenous cultures and commemorating the centennial of Mexican independence. He also participates in his first documented exhibition, an ENBA group show, which is reviewed unfavorably by Rivera in the publication *Azulejos* in October.

Around this time, Tamayo abandons art school.

1922 US artist and critic Walter Pach spends the summer in Mexico, where he writes for the bulletin of the Museo de Arqueología and teaches at the national university. Pach and Rivera help arrange for young Mexican artists including Tamayo to exhibit with the Society of Independent Artists in New York the following year. Rivera writes to Pach:

> *The boys are thrilled by the invitation from the society of [Independent Artists] of N.Y., which we owe to your generosity; they beg me to thank you most effusively and to advise you of our gratitude and our acceptance of the offer from the Society of Independent Artists of New York.*[4]

1923 Tamayo begins teaching drawing in Mexico City primary schools using the Best Maugard Drawing Method.

1926 Tamayo holds his first-ever one-man exhibition at an empty storefront at Avenida Madero 66 in Mexico City. The exhibition includes twenty oil paintings.

Tamayo quits his jobs and in early September leaves Mexico for the first time, traveling to New York City on SS *Monterey* with musician Carlos Chávez. He speaks no English. The two arrive on September 10 and rent a small apartment on Fourteenth Street in Greenwich Village, the artistic and literary hub of the city. In New York, Tamayo finds a tight-knit community of Mexican intellectuals that include the celebrated caricaturist Miguel Covarrubias, writer and cultural critic Octavio G. Barreda, and the poet José Juan Tablada, whose Spanish-language bookstore in Midtown Manhattan is popular among the city's Mexican intellectuals.

On Fourteenth Street, Tamayo also encounters a community of artists from the United States, Europe, and elsewhere, including Stuart Davis, Yasuo Kuniyoshi, Reginald Marsh, and Raphael and Moses Soyer.

The Société Anonyme, founded in 1920 by Katherine Dreier, Marcel Duchamp, and Man Ray, presents the *International Exhibition of Modern Art* at the Brooklyn Museum, which Tamayo likely attends.

Walter Pach introduces Tamayo to Carl Zigrosser, director of the Weyhe Gallery and an early champion of Mexican art. He and his assistant, Julien Levy, offer Tamayo his first New York one-man show, which takes place in October. Twelve of thirty-nine works included are sold.

1927 The leftist journal *New Masses* begins running illustrations by Tamayo on its covers, including two New York–themed illustrations, which appear on the covers of the April and July issues.

Despite periodic work, Tamayo struggles to make ends meet in the city. In March, he describes his difficulties to his friend in Mexico, the poet José Gorostiza:

> *Certainly the struggle is hard, don't think my perspective completely diaphanous. Often I have miserable days that I wouldn't wish upon anyone; then again, I think I've made some progress. This compensation makes it worth it.*[5]

Tamayo makes plans for additional exhibitions. On June 19, he writes again to Gorostiza:

> *I hope to do two exhibitions in the next season and naturally in two different galleries, one with things from Mexico and the other with the things I'm working on right now. I already have an agreement with the Art Center Gallery, which as you know is one of the most important in New York.*[6]

FIG. A Cover of *Contemporáneos*, no. 3, August 1928, Mexico City

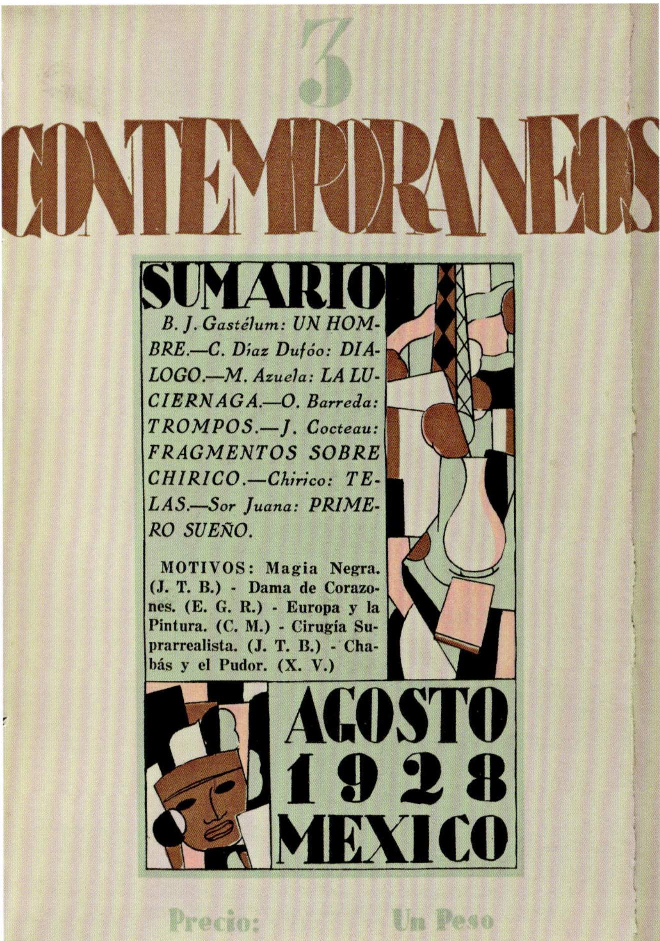

Covarrubias introduces Tamayo to an important connection: *Vanity Fair* editor Frank Crowninshield, an avid collector of African art. Tamayo and Crowninshield connect over a shared interest in "non-Western art." When Tamayo is given a one-man show at the Art Center in November, it is Crowninshield who writes the exhibition text.

November also marks the arrival of Mexican muralist José Clemente Orozco in New York.

Pleased by positive criticism following his second solo show, Tamayo writes to Gorostiza on December 26:

> *Finally the path is clearing and now it's just a question of a little time and a lot of English. . . . New York presents strong symptoms of* mexicanismo, *which hopefully works out in our favor.*[7]

In December, A. E. Gallatin's Gallery of Living Art (later called the Museum of Living Art) opens at 100 Washington Square East. It is the first public collection of contemporary art in the United States and, with its inaugural exhibition of European and US art, is likely a source of inspiration for Tamayo.

1928 Tamayo likely sees Giorgio de Chirico's exhibition at the Valentine Gallery early in the year, noting later that "of the young [artists], Chirico interests me."[8]

In April, Mexican writer Jaime Torres Bodet describes Tamayo as struggling financially and in poor health. That summer, Tamayo returns to Mexico City due to a stomach illness.

[FIG. A] On June 15 the first issue of the avant-garde journal *Contemporáneos* is published by the group of the same name. The journal will include illustrations by both Mexican artists and some of Tamayo's US peers like George Biddle and Yasuo Kuniyoshi. Tamayo, whose friends are among the founders of the group, participates in a Contemporáneos exhibition in December.

Around the same time, the radical ¡30–30! Group of Painters is established with the aim of opposing the academy and democratizing art.

1929 Tamayo is hired as an art teacher at ENBA in March. There he meets the artist María Izquierdo, and the two begin a nearly four-year-long romantic and intellectual relationship.

The civic action office of Mexico City places Carlos Mérida and Carlos Orozco Romero in charge of the Galería de Arte Moderno in the

Teatro Nacional (now the Palacio de Bellas Artes [Palace of Fine Arts]). Despite its state funding, the gallery comes to serve as an important avant-garde space over the next two years, emphasizing surrealism.

+ The i30-30! Group organizes several exhibitions, and Tamayo contributes paintings to at least one.

+ The US stock market crash in October signals the beginning of the Great Depression.

1930 Tamayo returns to New York via Veracruz, arriving on September 17 aboard SS *Orizaba*. A month later his work is included in *Mexican Arts* at the Metropolitan Museum of Art, a sweeping survey of Mexican art history organized by the American Federation of Arts. There, prominent Washington, DC-based collector Duncan Phillips sees Tamayo's *Mandolins and Pineapples* (1930) and purchases it soon after, writing, "It seemed to me about the best [picture] in the Mexican show at the Metropolitan."[9]

1931 Tamayo is in New York in the spring, where he is included in a two-person exhibition at the John Levy Galleries as part of Frances Flynn Paine's "Mexican Month." His works do not sell.

+ Tamayo returns to Mexico, where he illustrates the *Cancionero Mexicano* for *Mexican Folkways*, a bilingual publication edited by Frances Toor, a US writer and promoter of Mexican culture.

+ He is awarded a prize in the Tolteca Cement Company art contest in Mexico.

1932 Around this time, Tamayo designs a mural for the Museo Nacional de Antropología (formerly the Museo de Arqueología) called *Conquista* (Conquest) or *Conquista de México* (Conquest of Mexico). The work is rejected, possibly owing to disagreement over its lack of historical narrative. Tamayo will paint a new mural in its place in 1938.

+ Around this time Tamayo is appointed head of the Department of Fine Arts of SEP, where he is charged with evaluating the arts curriculum in public primary schools.

1933 In the spring, Tamayo is commissioned to paint a mural at Mexico's national conservatory, which he titles *El canto y la música* (Song and Music). While working on the project he meets a piano student named Olga Flores Rivas, and the two begin a relationship. The allegorical mural is protested and vandalized—according to Tamayo, the culprits include students and faculty from both the conservatory and the conservative Escuela Central de Artes Plásticas (Central School of Plastic Arts), formerly ENBA.

+ David Alfaro Siqueiros, Luis Arenal, Juan de la Cabada, Gabriel Fernández Ledesma, Leopoldo Méndez, and Pablo O'Higgins found the Liga de Escritores y Artistas Revolucionarios (League of Revolutionary Writers and Artists), or LEAR, whose mission is to advocate on behalf of the working class and combat fascism. In its first phase LEAR is hostile to so-called *artepuristas* like Tamayo; he is later welcomed into the group, though he is never a very active member.

1934 Early in the year Tamayo is named art professor at several secondary schools and at a night school for workers.

+ Less than a year after meeting her, Tamayo marries Olga on January 26, with a religious ceremony taking place on February 3. Olga soon abandons her career as a pianist to manage the sale and promotion of Tamayo's work.

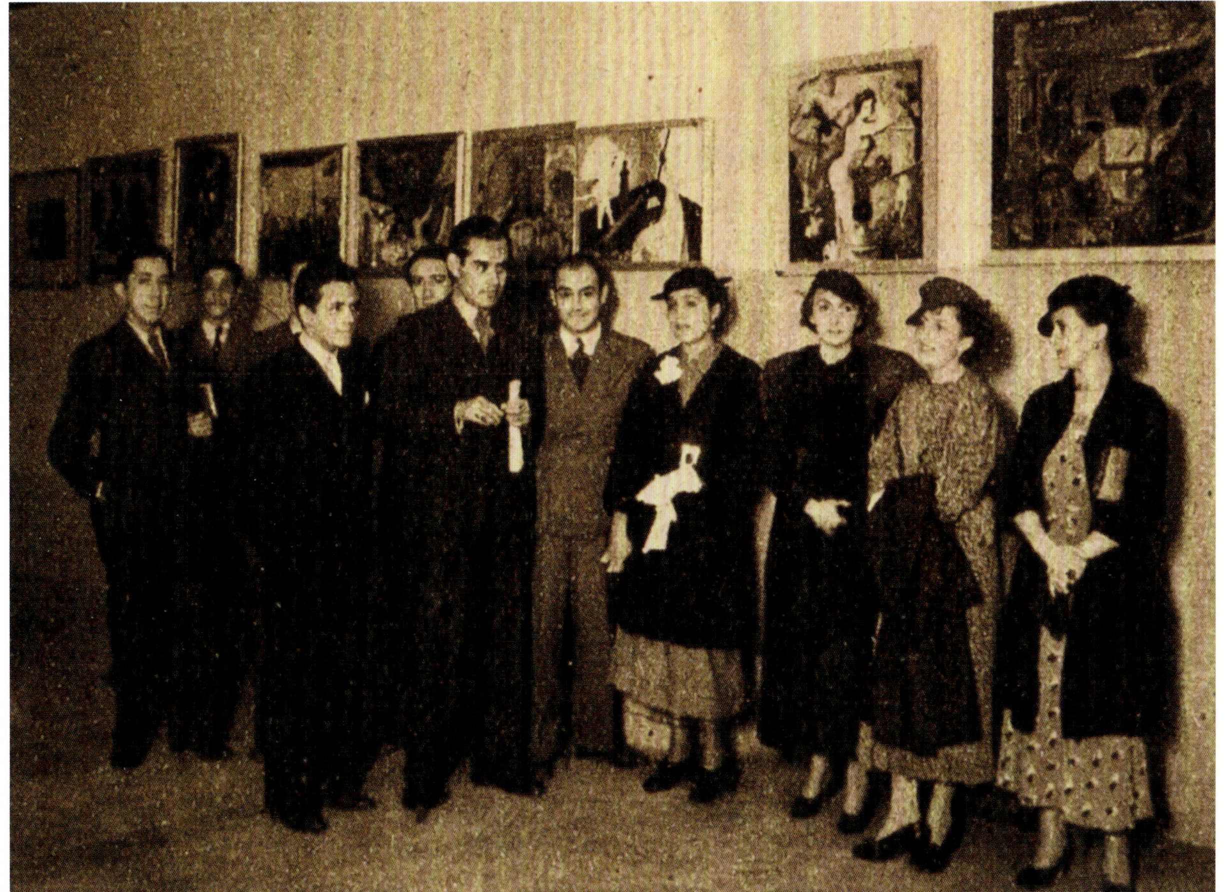

FIG. B Rufino Tamayo (sixth from left) attends the opening of his solo exhibition at the Galería de Arte Mexicano, November 1935. Tamayo Archive, Museo Tamayo, Mexico City

\+ On February 29 the Palacio de Bellas Artes opens in the Teatro Nacional building in Mexico City. It includes painting galleries and a museum of popular art that is managed by Roberto Montenegro.

\+ The administration of President Lázaro Cárdenas ushers in a new period of ideological alignment between the artist-intellectual class and the Mexican government. The mid-1930s mark Tamayo's most political period as an artist.

1935 Mexico's first private art gallery, the Galería de Arte Mexicano (GAM), is founded by Carolina Amor. The Tamayos attend the March 7 opening of GAM's inaugural exhibition, which features Tamayo's work. In a later interview, he notes:

> *When it occurred to [Carolina Amor] to found an art gallery, it never occurred to her how important it would be for the history of painting in Mexico. Before, there was no permanent place to exhibit, to sell. For us, those just starting out at that time, in 1935, it opened up doors, because we began to have contact with the public, something that had been difficult.*[10]

The title of director of GAM will soon be passed on to Carolina's sister Inés Amor. The Tamayos will come to form a close relationship with the Amor sisters.

\+ Tamayo receives an SEP employee ID card on June 4, indicating a public school teaching position.

\+ [FIG. B] In November, Tamayo is given a solo exhibition by GAM. He has so much new work that the show is relocated to a larger space.

1936 In February, accompanied by Olga, Tamayo travels to New York to represent Mexico's Asamblea Nacional de Productores de Artes Plásticas (National Assembly of Producers of Plastic Arts) as a delegate, along with Siqueiros, to the First American Artists' Congress against War and Fascism. Orozco attends as a delegate for LEAR. The Mexican artists are among ten delegates from Latin America. Tamayo's work is also included in a LEAR exhibition in Mexico City this summer.

+ Tamayo and Olga will reside in New York semi-permanently for the next decade and a half. According to Tamayo, "We were supposed to stay there for fifteen days, and we stayed for fifteen years."[11]

+ The two move into a studio apartment on Fifteenth Street near Union Square. In order to spend most of the year in the United States (while summering in Mexico), Tamayo takes a job as a low-level Mexican government employee tasked with observing and reporting on educational and artistic matters abroad.

+ [FIG. C] He also participates in the New York division of the Federal Art Project, under the umbrella of President Franklin D. Roosevelt's Works Progress Administration (WPA). In the fall, two of his watercolors are exhibited as part of *New Horizons in American Art* at the Museum of Modern Art (MoMA), an exhibition documenting the success of the program. He also submits designs for a mural at Kings County Hospital in Brooklyn, but the work is never completed.

+ This year Tamayo likely sees several major exhibitions: *Cubism and Abstract Art* and *Fantastic Art, Dada, Surrealism*, both at MoMA, and a Picasso retrospective at the Valentine Gallery.

1937 [FIG. D] Tamayo is given one-man exhibitions at the Julien Levy Gallery in New York and the Howard Putzel Gallery in Los Angeles, placing him in the company of major surrealist artists. This prompts one critic in Mexico to caution: "For us Tamayo is Tamayo and nothing more."[12] Tamayo had met Levy in 1926, when the latter worked as an assistant to Carl Zigrosser at the Weyhe Gallery.

+ *New Masses* illustrates *Ritmo obrero* (1935), one of Tamayo's labor-themed works from Mexico.

+ Mexican critics celebrate Tamayo's crossover success and positive reviews in New York, referring to him as a "Mexican celebrity" in New York.

+ US citizenship becomes a requirement for WPA participation, thereby ending Tamayo's relationship with the program.

1938 Tamayo travels back and forth between New York and Mexico, arriving in the United States via Laredo, Texas, in February and September.

+ [FIG. E] Having become close friends with Minister of Education Gonzalo Vázquez Vela when both were in New York, Tamayo is invited by the SEP to paint a mural at Mexico's Museo Nacional de Antropología. In its depiction of workers and peasants violently rebelling against the bourgeoisie, *Revolution* is Tamayo's most explicitly political mural. The work, however, is left unfinished due in part to officials' opposition to its lack of specific historical references.

+ Despite this disagreement, Tamayo requests that the SEP renew his position as a consular observer on educational and artistic activity in New York.

+ He also reaches out to art dealer Pierre Matisse seeking gallery representation. However, Inés Amor, Tamayo's dealer in Mexico, arranges for

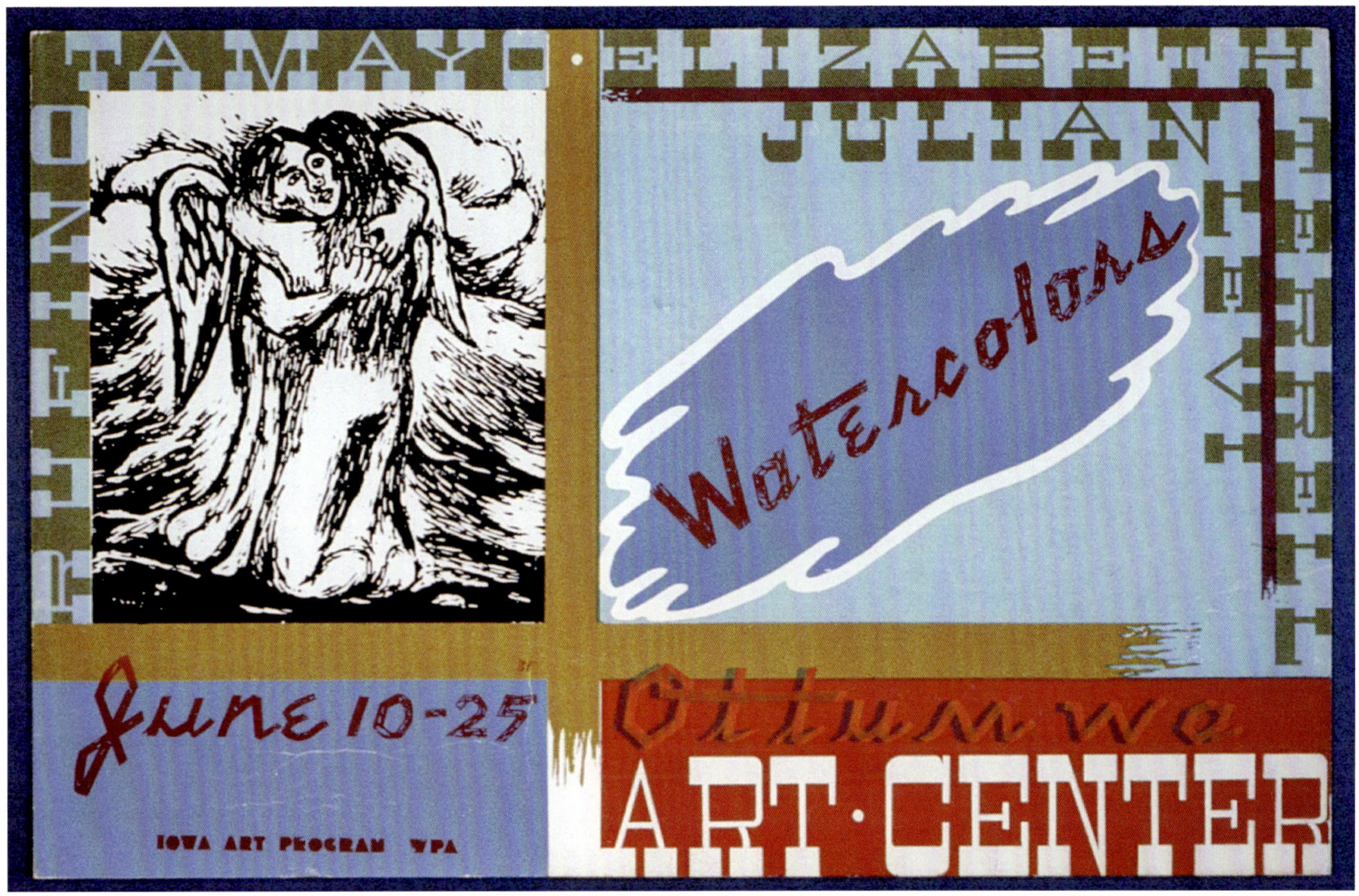

FIG. C Poster announcing Works Progress Administration exhibition of watercolors by Rufino Tamayo, Elizabeth Terrell, and Julian Levi at the Ottumwa Art Center in Iowa, ca. 1939–40

FIG. D Brochure for Tamayo's first solo exhibition at the Julien Levy Gallery, New York, in 1937

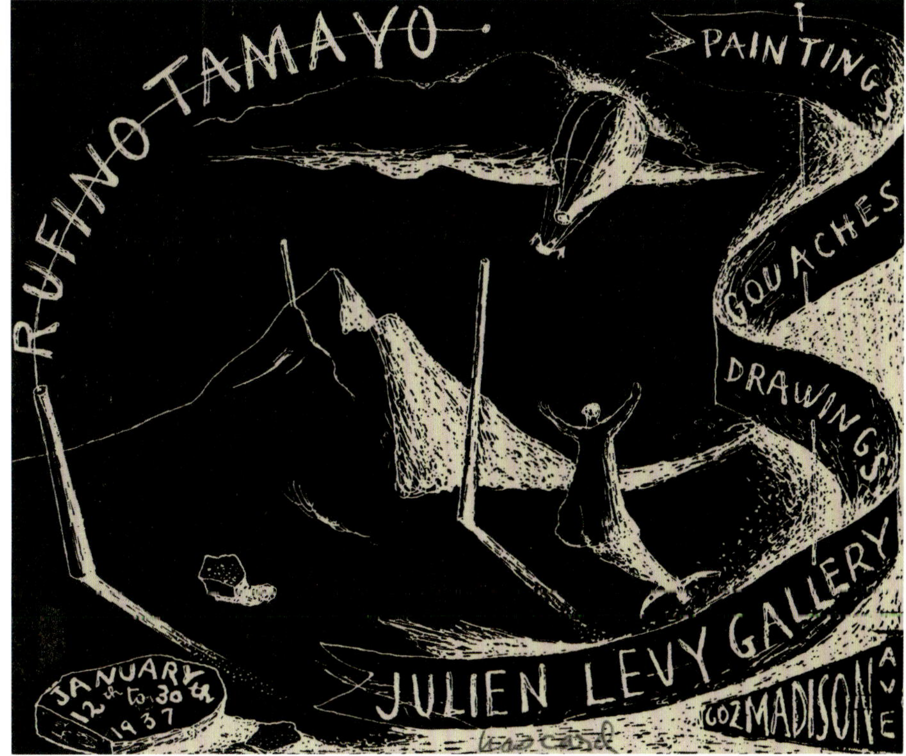

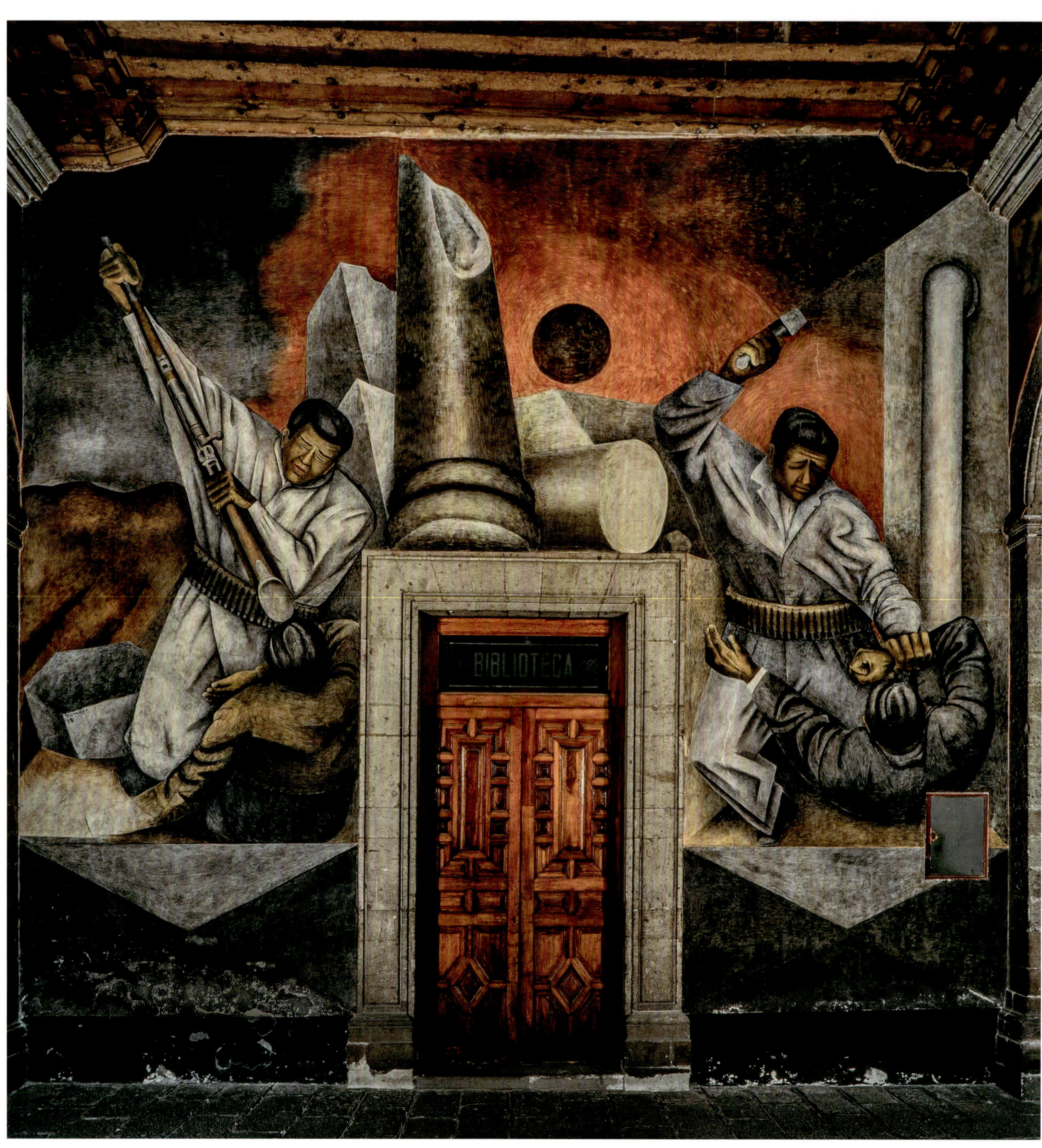
BIBLIOTECA

FIG. E Rufino Tamayo, *Revolution* [*Revolución*], 1938, fresco mural, Museo de las Culturas, Mexico City (formerly Museo Nacional de Antropología)

FIG. F Page from the 1941 Dalton School yearbook. Collection of the Dalton School

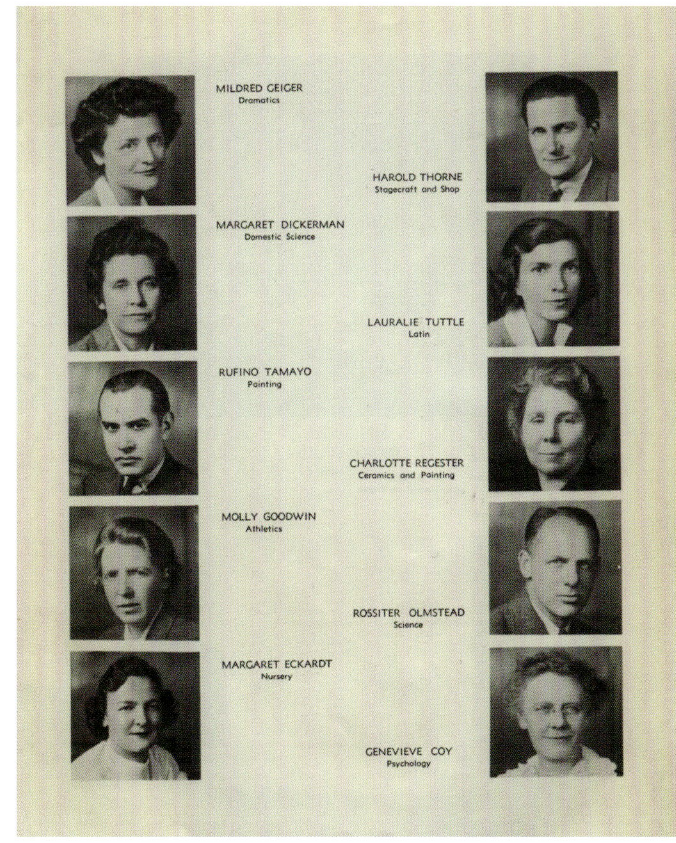

him to be taken on by Valentine Dudensing, another prominent dealer in New York. Tamayo begins exhibiting at the Valentine Gallery and continues to do so until 1947.

\+ [FIG. F] This year Tamayo also begins teaching part-time at the prestigious Dalton School, thanks in part to his connection to Carlos Dávila, former president of Chile and Dalton board member. Although he does not particularly enjoy teaching, the job allows Tamayo to finance his art making, and he continues teaching at Dalton into the late 1940s.

1939 Tamayo's first solo exhibition at the Valentine Gallery opens at the beginning of the year. His paintings garner positive reviews but don't sell.

\+ Tamayo first sees Picasso's *Guernica* and related drawings at the Valentine Gallery. This monumental painting will have a lasting impact on Tamayo's style and thematic interests, as well as those of the future abstract expressionists who also frequent the gallery.

\+ After touring the United States, *Guernica* returns to New York in the fall for the MoMA retrospective *Picasso: Forty Years of His Art*.

\+ World War II begins.

1940 Tamayo applies for a John Simon Guggenheim Memorial Foundation fellowship, but the Mexican awards are instead given to the painters Roberto Berdecio and Carlos Orozco Romero.

\+ [FIG. G] Tamayo's *The Pretty Girl* (1937) is included in MoMA's landmark exhibition *Twenty Centuries of Mexican Art*. The exhibition includes more than 150 objects and is accompanied by concerts, organized by Tamayo's friend Carlos Chávez, and a "traditional" Mexican marketplace outside the museum. Despite the inclusion of a new portable mural made on site by Orozco, for some US critics, like Henry McBride, the exhibition underscores the decline of muralism and the rise of a more universal art exemplified by Tamayo.

1941 Around this time, Tamayo befriends fellow teacher Ukrainian artist Alexander Archipenko.

\+ The Albright-Knox Art Gallery acquires Tamayo's *Women of Tehuantepec* (1939) in December from the Valentine Gallery.

FIG. G Tamayo's *The Pretty Girl* (center left) installed as part of *Twenty Centuries of Mexican Art* at the Museum of Modern Art, May 15–September 30, 1940. The Museum of Modern Art Archives, New York

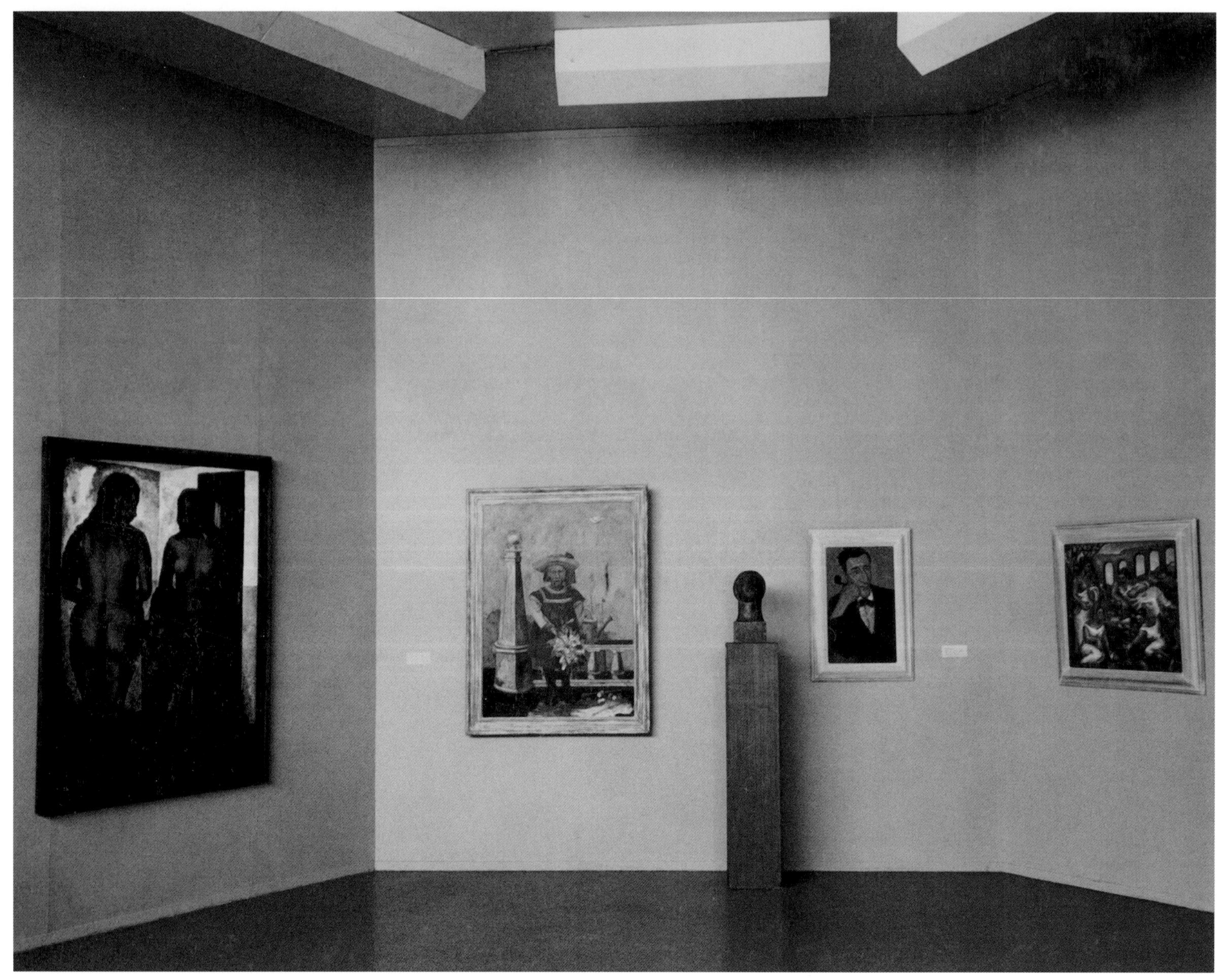

+ Tamayo likely sees Joan Miró's retrospective and the groundbreaking *Indian Art of the United States,* both at MoMA.

1942 In Mexican intellectual circles, rumors swirl about Olga's failure to bear children, with some questioning Tamayo's sexuality. Tamayo later attributes some of these rumors to Diego Rivera.

+ Olga's mental health subsequently begins to deteriorate. On November 22, Tamayo writes a desperate letter to his friend, the writer Carlos Pellicer, expressing concern about Olga's illness and requesting an extension of his official appointment so that he can avoid being drafted by the US Army.

+ The Art Institute of Chicago acquires *Woman with a Bird Cage* (1941).

+ MoMA acquires *Animals* (1941), the first work by Tamayo to be added to the museum's collection.

+ Tamayo's work is included in a Fogg Museum exhibition in Cambridge, Massachusetts, that juxtaposes work by Mexican painters with that of Picasso.

1943 Tamayo's *Photogenic Venus* (1934) is included in Henry Clifford's important *Mexican Art Today* exhibition at the Philadelphia Museum of Art.

+ MoMA acquires *Woman with Pineapple* (1941).

+ Helen Frankenthaler is one of Tamayo's Dalton students around this time. The young painter will come to be an important figure in the history of US abstract expressionism.

+ Jere Abbott, director of the Smith College Museum of Art and former founding associate director of MoMA, initiates a conversation with Tamayo about being an artist-in-residence at the college. The residency does not pan out, but Tamayo proposes to do a mural instead. While still teaching at Dalton, Tamayo spends his weekends painting a two-paneled fresco titled *La naturaleza y el artista: la obra de arte y el espectador* (Nature and the Artist: The Work of Art and the Observer) at Smith College's Hillyer Art Library in Northampton, Massachusetts. The allegorical painting will become his most well-known mural work in the United States.

+ Olga is hospitalized in early November in Mexico City, possibly due to a miscarriage. With *White Nude* of this year, Tamayo begins dedicating works to his wife by painting the prefix "O" before each work's date.

+ Tamayo likely sees Jackson Pollock's first solo exhibition at Peggy Guggenheim's Art of This Century gallery.

+ [FIG. H] Art patron and financier Roy R. Neuberger purchases *Woman Spinning* (1943) from the Valentine Gallery.

1944 The Tamayos spend much of the year in San Miguel de Allende, Mexico, returning to New York in September.

1945 An article by US painter and critic Barnett Newman comparing Tamayo and his contemporary Adolph Gottlieb is published in *La Revista Belga* in April.

+ The following month, Tamayo is included in *A Problem for Critics*, Howard Putzel's groundbreaking exhibition of US abstraction at New York's 67 Gallery, alongside Pollock and Gottlieb, among others.

+ Miró's *Constellations* paintings are smuggled out of Europe and exhibited at Pierre Matisse Gallery in New York, where Tamayo likely sees them.

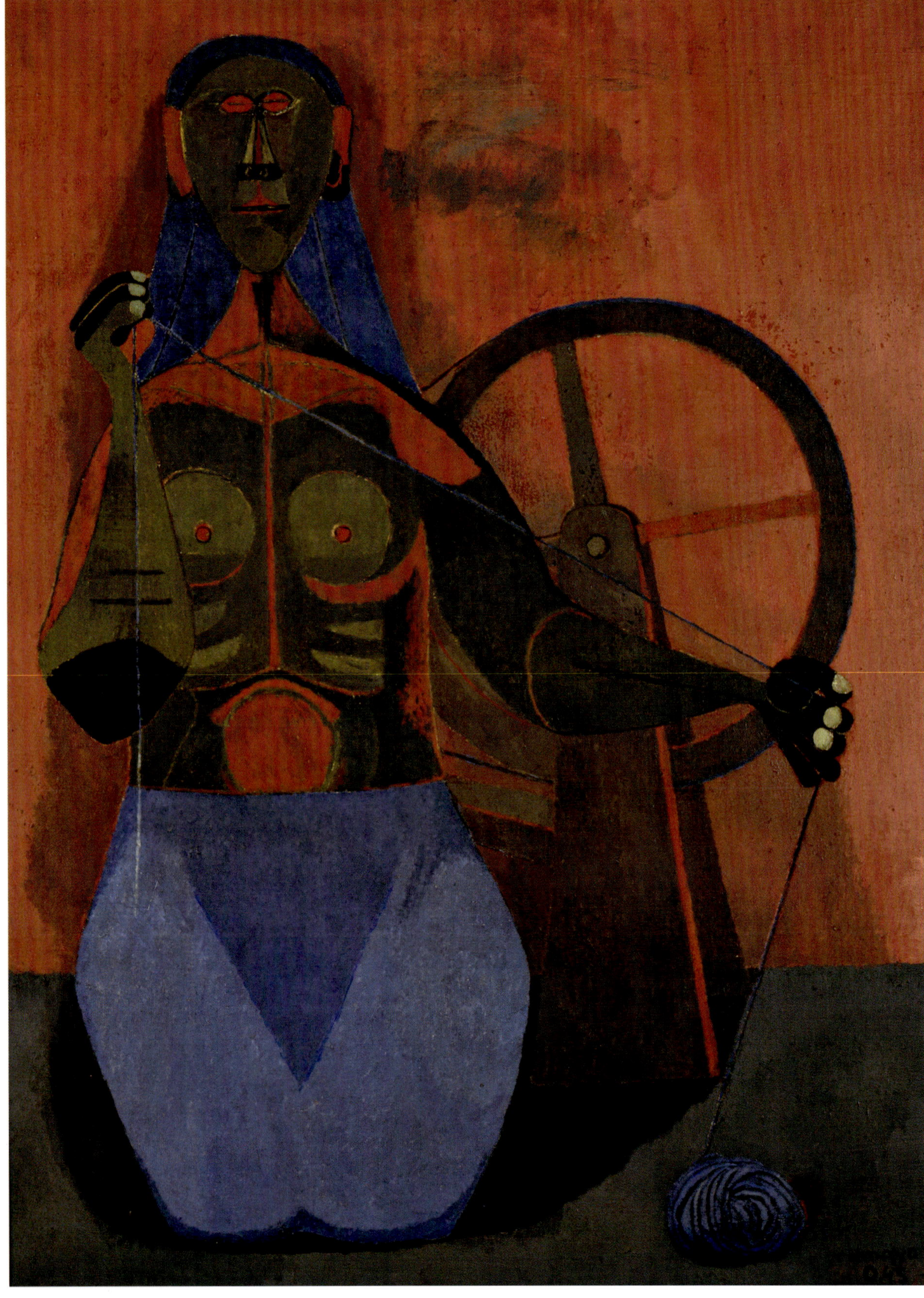

FIG. H Rufino Tamayo, *Woman Spinning,* 1943, oil on canvas, 43 x 32 in. Collection Friends of the Neuberger Museum of Art, Purchase College, State University of New York, Gift from the Estate of Roy R. Neuberger

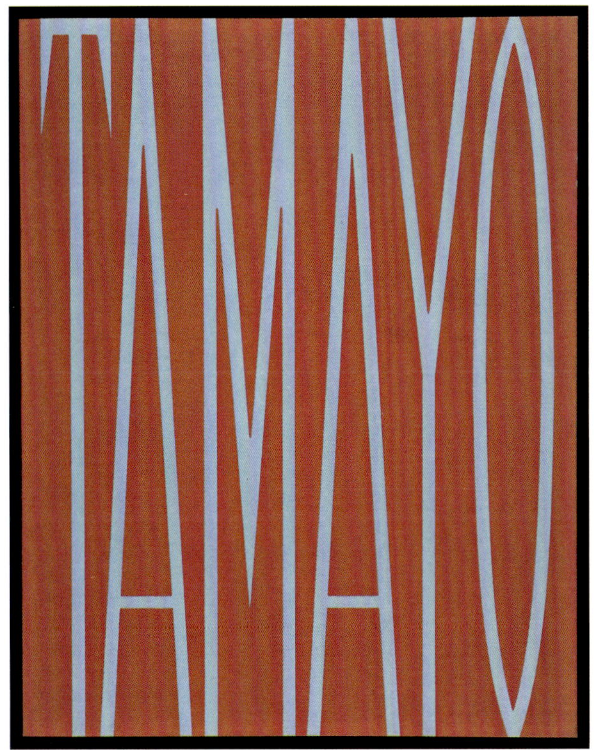

FIG. 1 Exhibition brochure for Tamayo's 1945 solo exhibition at the Arts Club of Chicago. Courtesy of The Arts Club of Chicago

+ [FIG. 1] In May, soon after presenting an exhibition of work by Jackson Pollock, the Arts Club of Chicago, one of the leading venues supporting international and US modern art in the United States, presents a Tamayo exhibition.

+ Nazi Germany surrenders to the Allied forces, marking the end of World War II in Europe.

+ In August, Hiroshima and Nagasaki are bombed. Tamayo later notes: "Immediately after World War II and the bombings of Hiroshima and Nagasaki, I started thinking about the implications of a new space age and did the first paintings of constellations shooting through space."[13]

1946 Tamayo is hired as an instructor at the Brooklyn Museum Art School, where he directs the "Tamayo Workshop" in the fall.

+ His work continues to shift thematically toward an emphasis on the cosmos, celestial bodies, and man's place in the universe.

+ H. W. Janson, art historian and curator, acquires *Lion and Horse* (1942) for the Washington University Art Collection (now the Mildred Lane Kemper Art Museum at Washington University in St. Louis), adding Tamayo's name to a roster of celebrated European and US modernists in the collection.

1947 In January the Cincinnati Modern Art Society presents the *Exhibition of Paintings by the Mexican Artist Rufino Tamayo* at the Cincinnati Art Museum.

+ Tamayo continues to receive major critical attention in the United States: Robert Goldwater completes his monograph on the artist, while Clement Greenberg, the most prominent critic of the postwar period, publishes a mixed review of Tamayo's work.

+ Several paintings by Tamayo are featured in *Tiger's Eye*, an avant-garde magazine of literature and art published in New York between 1947 and 1949.

+ In September, Tamayo becomes embroiled in a fierce debate about the state of Mexican painting with Siqueiros and Orozco in the pages of the Mexican daily *El Nacional*.

+ In December, he is given his first one-man show at Pierre Matisse Gallery, New York.

1948 In February, *Look* magazine publishes the results of a poll of leading museum directors, critics, curators, and artists ranking the best painters in "America." Artists rank Tamayo in the top ten.

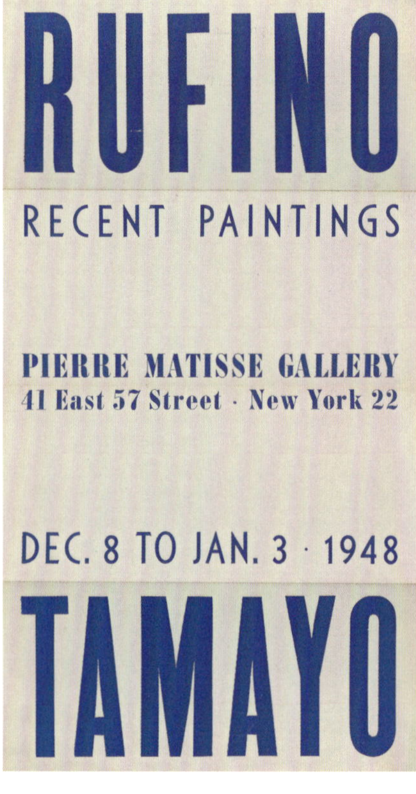

FIG. J Exhibition brochure (front and back) for Tamayo's 1947 solo exhibition at Pierre Matisse Gallery, New York. The Morgan Library & Museum, New York, Gift of the Pierre Matisse Foundation, 1997

\+ [FIG. J] Pierre Matisse officially becomes Tamayo's dealer.

\+ Fernando Gamboa organizes Tamayo's first major survey in Mexico at the Palacio de Bellas Artes, *Tamayo: 20 años de su labor pictórica* (Tamayo: Twenty Years of Artistic Labor), a project first proposed by Tamayo's old friend Carlos Chávez. He exhibits eighty-two works, most belonging to US collections. The exhibition is supplemented by a gallery of objects, including pre-Hispanic and colonial sculpture and contemporary photography.

\+ Tamayo begins to spend time in Europe, traveling to Paris in September.

1949 Tamayo returns to Europe at the end of the summer and spends several months in Paris painting. While they will continue spending time in New York and Mexico, by the next year he and Olga will have made Paris their primary residence.

\+ The American Federation of Arts circulates the exhibition *New Directions in Modern Painting*, which is organized by Pierre Matisse and includes works by Tamayo, Wifredo Lam, Roberto Matta, Joan Miró, and Yves Tanguy.

1950 Tamayo is in New York in April for the opening of his exhibition at the Knoedler Gallery.

\+ He is invited to participate in the Mexican Pavilion of the twenty-fifth Venice Biennale alongside Rivera, Siqueiros, and Orozco. Though he does not come away with any prizes, his work receives positive reviews and the Musée d'Art Moderne in Paris acquires *Singing Man* (1950), making Tamayo the first Mexican artist to enter the museum's collection.

\+ Tamayo is given his first European one-man exhibition at the Galerie Beaux-Arts in Paris in November. He exhibits the same works at the Palais de Beaux-Arts in Brussels soon after.

NOTES

Unless otherwise noted, all translated Spanish quotations are from Beth Shook.

1. Bambi (Ana Cecilia Treviño de Gironella), "Rufino Tamayo relata los pecados de su infancia," *Excélsior*, May 9, 1972, cited in Norma Ávila Jiménez, *El arte cósmico de Tamayo* (Mexico City: Praxis/Universidad Nacional Autónoma de México, 2010).

2. Cristina Pacheco, *La luz de México: entrevistas con pintores y fotógrafos*, 2d ed. (Mexico City: Fondo de Cultura Económica, 1995), 576.

3. Emily Genauer, *Rufino Tamayo* (New York: Harry N. Abrams, 1974), 30.

4. Diego Rivera to Walter Pach, December 7, 1922, Walter Pach papers, 1857–1980, Archives of American Art, Smithsonian Institution.

5. Rufino Tamayo to José Gorostiza, March 1, 1927, in José Gorostiza et al., *Epistolario (1918–1940)*, ed. Guillermo Sheridan (Mexico City: Consejo Nacional para la Cultura y las Artes, 1995), 122–23.

6. Rufino Tamayo to José Gorostiza, June 19, 1927, in ibid., 130.

7. Rufino Tamayo to José Gorostiza, December 26, 1927, in ibid., 167.

8. "Rufino Tamayo, pintor mexicano, nos habla de su arte," incomplete newspaper clipping, December 7, 1928, cited in Judith Alanís and Sofía Urrutia, *Rufino Tamayo: una cronología, 1899–1987* (Mexico City: Museo Rufino Tamayo, INBA/SEP, 1987), 19n1.

9. Duncan Phillips to Frances F. Paine, October 31, 1930, curatorial file, Phillips Collection, Washington, DC.

10. Delmari Romero Keith, *Historia y testimonios: Galería de Arte Mexicano* (Mexico City: Ediciones Galería de Arte Mexicano, 1985), 23.

11. Jacobo Zabludovsky, *Charlas con pintores: Dr. Atl, Siqueiros, Rivera, Tamayo, Cuevas, Dalí* (Mexico City: Costa-Amic, 1966), 82.

12. "Rufino Tamayo, otra celebridad mexicana en Nueva York," incomplete newspaper clipping, April 8, 1937, cited in Alanís and Urrutia, *Rufino Tamayo*, 31n3.

13. Genauer, *Rufino Tamayo*, 58.

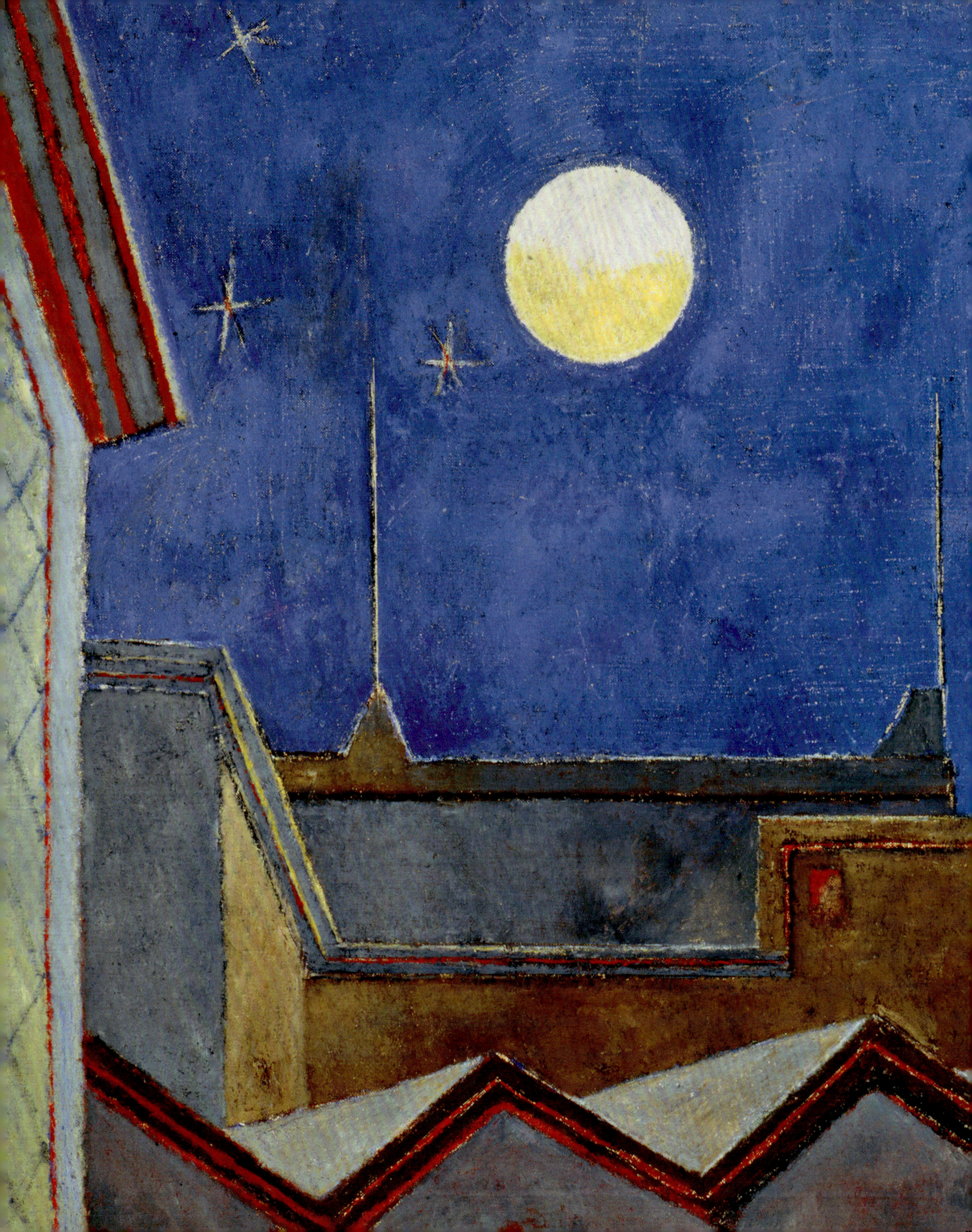

The Full Moon [*La luna llena*], 1945, detail. See p. 129.

CHECKLIST OF THE EXHIBITION

THE FAMILY
[LA FAMILIA]
1925
oil on canvas
28 3/4 × 33 in.
William and Christopher Brumder Collection

MAN AND WOMAN
[HOMBRE Y MUJER]
1926
woodcut
sheet: 12 1/8 × 12 in.
image: 9 7/8 × 9 7/8 in.
Smithsonian American Art Museum, Museum purchase, 1976.27

VIRGIN OF GUADALUPE
[LA VIRGEN DE GUADALUPE]
1926–27
woodcut
sheet: 9 1/2 × 12 1/8 in.
image: 7 1/4 × 9 9/16 in.
Museum of Fine Arts, Boston, Eleanor A. Sayre Fund

HEAD II (GRIEF)
[CABEZA II (PESAR)]
ca. 1926–28
woodcut
sheet: 16 × 12 15/16 in.
image: 10 × 9 7/8 in.
Museum of Fine Arts, Boston, Gift of W. G. Russell Allen

TWO MERMAIDS, ONE PLAYING A GUITAR
[DOS SIRENAS, UNA TOCANDO UNA GUITARRA]
ca. 1926–30
woodcut on Japan paper
sheet: 9 1/4 × 12 in.
image: 6 1/8 × 8 1/4 in.
The Metropolitan Museum of Art, New York, Gift of Jean Charlot, 1931

THE WOODCUTTER
[LEÑADOR]
ca. 1926–30
woodcut
sheet: 15 15/16 × 12 13/16 in.
image: 10 1/16 × 9 13/16 in.
The Metropolitan Museum of Art, New York, Gift of Carl Zigrosser, 1930
Alternate title: *Woodchopper*

SEASHELLS
[LOS CARACOLES]
1929
oil on canvas
23 1/4 × 24 13/16 in.
Private collection
Alternate titles: *Shells*, *Arrangement with Seashells*

THE YELLOW CHAIR
[SILLA AMARILLA]
1929
oil on canvas
29 7/8 × 25 1/8 in.
Private collection, Courtesy of Galería Ramis Barquet, New York
Alternate titles: *Naturaleza muerta con mangos*, *Frutero amarillo*

MANDOLINS AND PINEAPPLES
[MANDOLINAS Y PIÑAS]
1930
oil on canvas
19 3/4 × 27 1/2 in.
The Phillips Collection, Washington, DC, Acquired 1930

CONEY ISLAND
1931
gouache and watercolor
6 1/2 × 20 in.
Collection of Gianfranco Arnoldi

MAN WITH MAGUEY
[HOMBRE CON MAGUEY]
1931
linoleum cut
sheet: 9 × 6 1/2 in.
image: 8 1/4 × 4 7/8 in.
Smithsonian American Art Museum, Museum purchase, 1980.4.2
Alternate title: *The Revolutionist*

NUDE
[DESNUDO]
1931
oil on canvas
37 1/4 × 56 3/4 in.
Dallas Museum of Art, Dallas Art Association Purchase

HOMAGE TO JUÁREZ
[HOMENAJE A JUÁREZ]
1932
oil on canvas
23 5/8 × 29 1/8 in.
Museo de Arte Moderno—INBA
Alternate titles: *Monumento a Juárez*, *Juárez*

ACADEMIC PAINTING
[PINTURA ACADÉMICA]
1935
oil on canvas
25 3/4 × 21 7/8 in.
Hirshhorn Museum and Sculpture Garden, Smithsonian Institution, Washington, DC, Gift of Joseph H. Hirshhorn, 1966

FACTORY WORKERS' MOVEMENT
[MOVIMIENTO FABRIL]
1935
oil on canvas
22 1/4 × 26 3/8 in.
Collection of Brian and Florence Mahony
Alternate titles: *Motivo fabril*, *Factory Motif*

CARNIVAL
[CARNAVAL]

1936
gouache on paper
15 × 22 in.
Smithsonian American Art Museum, Museum purchase through the Luisita L. and Franz H. Denghausen Endowment, 2017.22
Alternate titles: *Clown, El bufón de la vida, Circus*

THE FAMILY
[LA FAMILIA]

1936
oil on canvas
31 7/8 × 47 5/8 in.
The Minneapolis Institute of Art, Gift of Noma and William Copley

SHOWER
[AGUACERO]

1936
watercolor and pastel on paper
12 3/8 × 8 11/16 in.
Blanton Museum of Art, The University of Texas at Austin, Deposit from the Work Projects Administration, United States Government, 1943

WAITING WOMAN
[MUJER ESPERANDO]

1936
watercolor on paper
15 × 20 3/4 in.
The Museum of Modern Art, New York, Extended loan from the United States WPA Art Program; Fine Arts Collection, Public Buildings Service, General Services Administration
Alternate title: *Woman Waiting*

NEW YORK SEEN FROM THE TERRACE
[NUEVA YORK DESDE LA TERRAZA]

1937
oil on canvas
20 3/8 × 34 3/8 in.
FEMSA Collection

THE PRETTY GIRL
[NIÑA BONITA]

1937
oil on canvas
48 1/8 × 36 1/8 in.
Private collection

STRAWBERRY ICE CREAM
[HELADO DE FRESA]

1938
oil on canvas
17 1/2 × 24 in.
Collection of John Fox and Sandy Allen

THREE ICE CREAMS
[TRES HELADOS]

1938
oil on canvas
17 7/8 × 23 3/4 in.
Collection of Mrs. J. Todd Figi
Alternate titles: *Naturaleza muerta con helado, Still Life with Ice*

WOMAN
[MUJER]

1938
oil on canvas
35 5/8 × 27 5/8 in.
The Museum of Modern Art, New York, Estate of John Hay Whitney
Alternate titles: *Mujeres tehuanas, Mujeres de Tehuantepec*

THE DOCTOR
[EL MÉDICO]

1939
oil on canvas
22 3/4 × 17 in.
Collection of Stanley and Pearl Goodman, a promised gift to the NSU Art Museum, Fort Lauderdale, FL
Alternate title: *El fumador*

TWO WOMEN
[DOS MUJERES]

1939
gouache on canvas
14 5/16 × 24 3/8 in.
Museum of Art, Rhode Island School of Design, Providence, Mary B. Jackson Fund

WOMEN OF TEHUANTEPEC
[MUJERES DE TEHUANTEPEC]

1939
oil on canvas
33 7/8 × 57 1/8 in.
Albright-Knox Art Gallery, Buffalo, New York, Room of Contemporary Art Fund, 1941

ANIMALS
[ANIMALES]

1941
oil on canvas
30 1/8 × 40 in.
The Museum of Modern Art, New York, Inter-American Fund

CARNIVAL
[CARNAVAL]

1941
oil on canvas
44 1/8 × 33 1/4 in.
The Phillips Collection, Washington, DC, Acquired 1942

WOMAN WITH A BIRD CAGE
[MUJER CON UNA JAULA]
1941
oil on canvas
43 1/4 × 33 in.
The Art Institute of Chicago, Gift of Joseph Winterbotham Collection

DOG BARKING AT THE MOON
[PERRO LADRANDO A LA LUNA]
1942
oil on canvas
47 1/4 × 33 7/16 in.
Private collection
Alternate titles: *Perro aullando, Dog Howling*

LION AND HORSE
[LEÓN Y CABALLO]
1942
oil on canvas
36 1/4 × 46 1/2 in.
Mildred Lane Kemper Art Museum, Washington University in St. Louis, University purchase, Kende Sale Fund, 1946

THE LOVERS
[AMANTES]
1943
oil on canvas
34 1/4 × 44 1/4 in.
San Francisco Museum of Modern Art, Purchase with the aid of funds from W. W. Crocker

MAD DOG
[PERRA RABIOSA]
1943
oil on canvas
32 × 43 in.
Philadelphia Museum of Art, Gift of Mrs. Herbert Cameron Morris, 1945

THE FULL MOON
[LA LUNA LLENA]
1945
oil on canvas
26 1/4 × 36 in.
Private collection
Alternate title: *Rooftops*

CATACLYSM
[CATACLISMO]
1946
oil on canvas
24 × 20 in.
Private collection

FIRE
[FUEGO]
1946
oil on canvas
44 × 34 in.
Collection of Mrs. J. Todd Figi

HEAVENLY BODIES
[CUERPOS CELESTES]
1946
oil with sand on canvas
34 × 41 5/16 in.
Peggy Guggenheim Collection, Venezia (Solomon R. Guggenheim Foundation, New York)

TOTAL ECLIPSE
[ECLIPSE TOTAL]
ca. 1946
oil with sand on canvas
39 7/8 × 29 7/8 in.
Harvard Art Museums/Fogg Museum, Gift of Mr. and Mrs. Joseph Pulitzer Jr.

WOMEN REACHING FOR THE MOON
[MUJERES ALCANZANDO LA LUNA]
1946
oil on canvas
36 × 26 in.
Private collection, Courtesy of Christie's
Alternate titles: *Woman Reaching for the Moon, Mujer tendiendo la mano a la luna*

GIRL ATTACKED BY A STRANGE BIRD
[NIÑA ATACADA POR UN PÁJARO EXTRAÑO]
1947
oil on canvas
70 × 50 1/8 in.
The Museum of Modern Art, New York, Gift of Mr. and Mrs. Charles Zadok

MAN SEARCHING THE HEAVENS
[HOMBRE ESCUDRIÑANDO EL FIRMAMENTO]
1949
oil on canvas
39 3/8 × 27 5/8 in.
Harvard Art Museums/Fogg Museum, Gift of Mr. and Mrs. Harold Gershinowitz

SELECTED BIBLIOGRAPHY

ARCHIVES

Albright-Knox Art Gallery Curatorial Files, Buffalo, NY.

Archives of American Art, Smithsonian Institution, Washington, DC.

Archivo Carlos Pellicer Cámara, Instituto de Investigaciones Bibliográficas, Biblioteca Nacional, Universidad Nacional Autónoma de México, Mexico City.

Archivo de la Galería de Arte Mexicano, Mexico City.

Archivo Histórico del Museo Nacional de Antropología, Mexico City.

The Art Institute of Chicago Curatorial Files.

The Arts Club of Chicago Archives, Newberry Library, Chicago.

Centro de Documentación del Museo Tamayo Arte Contemporáneo, Mexico City.

Dallas Museum of Art Curatorial Files.

The Frick Collection and Frick Art Reference Library Archives, New York.

Knoedler Gallery Archives, Getty Research Institute, Los Angeles.

The Museum of Modern Art Archives, New York.

The Museum of Modern Art, Paintings and Sculpture Curatorial Files, New York.

Philadelphia Museum of Art Curatorial Files.

The Phillips Collection Curatorial Files, Washington, DC.

Ryerson Library, The Art Institute of Chicago.

BOOKS AND PERIODICALS

A. E. Gallatin Collection: "Museum of Living Art." Philadelphia: Philadelphia Museum of Art, 1954.

Affron, Matthew, Mark A. Castro, Dafne Cruz Porchini, and Renato González Mello, eds. *Paint the Revolution: Mexican Modernism, 1910–1950.* New Haven: Yale University Press, 2016.

Alanís, Judith, and Sofía Urrutia. *Rufino Tamayo: una cronología, 1899–1987.* Mexico City: Museo Rufino Tamayo, INBA/SEP, 1987.

American Federation of Arts. *Mexican Arts.* Portland, ME: Southworth Press, 1930.

Anreus, Alejandro. *Orozco in Gringoland: The Years in New York.* Albuquerque: University of New Mexico Press, 2001.

Anreus, Alejandro, Diana L. Linden, and Jonathan Weinberg, eds. *The Social and the Real: Political Art of the 1930s in the Western Hemisphere.* University Park: Pennsylvania State University Press, 2006.

Anreus, Alejandro, Leonard Folgarait, and Robin Adèle Greeley, eds. *Mexican Muralism: A Critical History.* Berkeley: University of California Press, 2012.

Ault, Lee. *Rufino Tamayo.* Cincinnati, OH: Cincinnati Modern Art Society and Cincinnati Art Museum, 1947.

Ávila Jiménez, Norma. *El arte cósmico de Tamayo.* Mexico City: Praxis/Universidad Nacional Autónoma de México, 2010.

Baigell, Matthew, and Julia Williams, eds. *Artists against War and Fascism: Papers of the First American Artists' Congress.* New Brunswick, NJ: Rutgers University Press, 1986.

Brading, David A. "Manuel Gamio and Official Indigenismo in Mexico." *Bulletin of Latin American Research* 7, no. 1 (1988): 75–89.

Braggiotti, Mary. "No Little Donkeys for Tamayo." *New York Post Magazine,* February 3, 1947.

Braun, Emily, ed. *Giorgio de Chirico and America*. New York: Hunter College, 1996.

Bustard, Bruce I. *A New Deal for the Arts*. Washington, DC: National Archives and Records Administration in association with the University of Washington Press, 1997.

Cameron, Alison. "Buenos Vecinos: African-American Printmaking and the Taller de Gráfica Popular." *Print Quarterly* 16, no. 4 (December 1999): 353–67.

Caplow, Deborah. *Leopoldo Méndez: Revolutionary Art and the Mexican Print*. Austin: University of Texas Press, 2007.

Charlot, Jean. "Rufino Tamayo." *Magazine of Art* 38, no. 4 (April 1945): 138–41.

Chassen-López, Francie. "The Traje de Tehuana as National Icon: Gender, Ethnicity, and Fashion in Mexico." *The Americas* 71, no. 2 (October 2014): 281–314.

Chipp, Herschel B. *Picasso's Guernica: History, Transformations, Meanings*. Berkeley: University of California Press, 1988.

Cocteau, J[ean]. "Fragmentos sobre Chirico." *Contemporáneos* 1, no. 3 (August 1928): 261–64.

Coffey, Mary K. *How a Revolutionary Art Became Official Culture: Murals, Museums, and the Mexican State*. Durham, NC: Duke University Press, 2012.

Coffey, Mary K., Sharon Lorenzo, Lisa Mintz Messinger, and Stephen Polcari. *Men of Fire: José Clemente Orozco and Jackson Pollock*. Hanover, NH: Hood Museum of Art, Dartmouth College, 2012.

Conde, Teresa del, ed. *Tamayo*. Boston: Little, Brown, 2000.

Cooper, Harry. *Adolph Gottlieb: Pictographs 1941–1951*. New York: PaceWildenstein, 2004.

Cordero Reiman, Karen. "The Best Maugard Drawing Method: A Common Ground for Modern Mexicanist Aesthetics." Special issue, *Journal of Decorative and Propaganda Arts* 26 (2010): 44–79.

Cordero Reiman, Karen, Arely Ramírez Moyao, and Adriana Domínguez Velasco. *Construyendo Tamayo, 1922–1937*. Mexico City: Fundación Olga y Rufino Tamayo, AC, 2013.

Cullen, Deborah, ed. *Nexus New York: Latin/American Artists in the Modern Metropolis*. New York: El Museo del Barrio in association with Yale University Press, 2009.

Debroise, Olivier. *Figuras en el trópico, plástica mexicana, 1920–1940*. Barcelona: Océano, 1984.

———. "From Modern to International: The Challenges for Mexican Art." In *Collecting Latin American Art for the 21st Century*, edited by Mari Carmen Ramírez with Theresa Papanikolas, 61–97. Houston: Museum of Fine Arts, 2002.

Delliquadri, Lyn. "A Living Tradition: The Winterbothams and Their Legacy." *Art Institute of Chicago Museum Studies* 20, no. 2 (1994): 102–10.

Delpar, Helen. *The Enormous Vogue of Things Mexican: Cultural Relations between the United States and Mexico, 1920–1935*. Tuscaloosa: University of Alabama Press, 1992.

D'Harnoncourt, René. "The Loan Exhibition of Mexican Arts." *Metropolitan Museum of Art Bulletin* 25, no. 10 (October 1930): 210–17.

Dickerman, Leah, and Anna Indych-López. *Diego Rivera: Murals for the Museum of Modern Art*. New York: Museum of Modern Art, 2011.

Du Pont, Diana C., ed. *Tamayo: A Modern Icon Reinterpreted*. Santa Barbara, CA: Santa Barbara Museum of Art, 2007.

Eckmann, Sabine, with contributions by Bradley Fratello, George V. Speer, and H. W. Janson. *H. W. Janson and the Legacy of Modern Art at Washington University in St. Louis*. St. Louis, MO: Washington University Gallery of Art, 2002.

Fernández, Justino. *El arte moderno en México; breve historia, siglos XIX y XX*. Mexico City: J. Porrúa e hijos, 1937.

FitzGerald, Michael C. *Picasso and American Art*. New York: Whitney Museum of American Art in association with Yale University Press, 2006.

Fitzpatrick, Tracy, and Nicole Bass. *When Modern was Contemporary: The Roy R. Neuberger Collection*. Purchase, NY: Neuberger Museum of Art of Purchase College, SUNY, and American Federation of Arts, 2014.

Flam, Jack, and Miriam Deutch, eds. *Primitivism and Twentieth-Century Art: A Documentary History*. Berkeley: University of California Press, 2003.

Flores, Tatiana. *Mexico's Revolutionary Avant-Gardes: From Estridentismo to i30–30!* New Haven: Yale University Press, 2013.

Frank, Robin Jaffee, ed. *Coney Island: Visions of an American Dreamland, 1861–2008*. New Haven: Yale University Press, 2015.

Frost, Rosamund. "Tamayo: Ancient & Modern Savagery." *Art News* 42, no. 13 (November 15–30, 1943): 10.

García Morillo, Roberto. *Carlos Chávez: vida y obra*. Mexico City: Fondo de Cultura Económica, 1960.

Garza, Makedonio. "Los Mexicanos en Nueva York: Rufino Tamayo." *Revista de Revistas* (February 13, 1927): 7.

Genauer, Emily. *Rufino Tamayo*. New York: Harry N. Abrams, 1974.

Gibson, Ann Eden. *Abstract Expressionism: Other Politics*. New Haven: Yale University Press, 1997.

———. *Issues in Abstract Expressionism: The Artist-Run Periodicals*. Ann Arbor, MI: UMI Research Press, 1990.

Gilbert, Courtney. "Negotiating Surrealism: Carlos Mérida, Mexican Art and the Avant-Garde." Special issue, *Journal of Surrealism and the Americas* 3, no. 1–2 (2009): 30–50.

———. "The (New) World in the Time of the Surrealists: European Surrealists and Their Mexican Contemporaries." PhD diss., University of Chicago, 2001.

Goldman, Saifra M. *Contemporary Mexican Painting in a Time of Change*. Albuquerque: University of New Mexico Press, 1995.

Goldwater, Robert J. *Rufino Tamayo*. New York: Quadrangle Press, 1947.

González Mello, Renato, and Diane Miliotes, eds. *José Clemente Orozco in the United States, 1927–1934*. Hanover, NH: Hood Museum of Art, Dartmouth College, 2002.

Gorostiza, José, et al. *Epistolario (1918–1940)*. Edited by Guillermo Sheridan. Mexico City: Consejo Nacional para la Cultura y las Artes, 1995.

Greenberg, Clement. "Art." *The Nation*, March 8, 1947, 284.

Hagedorn, Dan. *Conquistadors of the Sky: A History of Aviation in Latin America*. Washington, DC: Smithsonian National Air and Space Museum, 2008.

Harten, Jürgen. *Siqueiros/Pollock, Pollock/Siqueiros*. Düsseldorf: DuMont, 1995.

Helms, Cynthia Newman, ed. *Diego Rivera: A Retrospective*. New York: W. W. Norton, 1986.

Hitchcock, Henry-Russell, and Miller Company. *Painting Toward Architecture*. New York: Duell, Sloan and Pearce, 1948.

Hodge, Frederick Webb, Herbert J. Spinden, and Oliver La Farge, eds. *Introduction to American Indian Art*. 2 vols. New York: Exposition of Indian Tribal Arts, 1931.

Hoving, Kirsten A. "Jackson Pollock's 'Galaxy': Outer Space and Artist's Space in Pollock's Cosmic Paintings." *American Art* 16, no. 1 (Spring 2002): 82–93.

Hurlburt, Laurance P. "The Siqueiros Experimental Workshop: New York, 1936." *Art Journal* 35, no. 3 (Spring 1976): 237–46.

Iduarte, Andrés. "Rufino Tamayo: un pintor mexicano en Nueva York." *Romance*, May 1, 1940.

Indych-López, Anna. *Muralism without Walls: Rivera, Orozco, and Siqueiros in the United States, 1927–1940*. Pittsburgh, PA: University of Pittsburgh Press, 2009.

Ittmann, John, ed. *Mexico and Modern Printmaking: A Revolution in the Graphic Arts, 1920 to 1950*. Philadelphia: Philadelphia Museum of Art, 2006.

Lader, Melvin Paul. "Peggy Guggenheim's Art of This Century: The Surrealist Milieu and the American Avant-Garde, 1942–1947." PhD diss., University of Delaware, 1981, 141–91.

Langa, Helen. "'At Least Half the Pages Will Consist of Pictures': 'New Masses' and Politicized Visual Art." *American Periodicals* 21, no. 1 (2011): 24–49.

Lee, Anthony W. *Painting on the Left: Diego Rivera, Radical Politics, and San Francisco's Public Murals*. Berkeley: University of California Press, 1999.

LeFalle-Collins, Lizzetta, and Shifra M. Goldman. *In the Spirit of Resistance: African-American Modernists and the Mexican Muralist School*. New York: American Federation of Arts, 1996.

Leja, Michael. *Reframing Abstract Expressionism: Subjectivity and Painting in the 1940s*. New Haven: Yale University Press, 1993.

Lola Álvarez Bravo: fotografías selectas 1934–1985. Mexico City: Centro Cultural/Arte Contemporáneo, 1992.

Madrigal, Érika. "Tamayo y los Contemporáneos: el discurso de lo clásico y lo universal." *Anales del Instituto de Investigaciones Estéticas* 30, no. 92 (2008): 155–89.

Marquardt, Virginia Hagelstein. "'New Masses' and John Reed Club Artists, 1926–1936: Evolution of Ideology, Subject Matter, and Style." *Journal of Decorative and Propaganda Arts* 12 (Spring 1989): 56–75.

McBride, Henry. *The Flow of Art: Essays and Criticisms*. Edited by Daniel Catton Rich. New Haven: Yale University Press, 1975.

McMahon, Audrey, and Virginia Nirdlinger. "A Perspective View of the New York Season (1930–1931)." *Parnassus* 3, no. 5 (May 1931): 6–44.

Mendoza, Miguel Ángel. "Artes plásticas." *Revista de América*, October 4, 1947, 38.

Mérida, Carlos. "La nueva galería de arte moderno/The New Modern Art Gallery." *Mexican Folkways* 4, no. 4 (October–December 1929): 184–91.

"Modern Art for New York University." *Art News* 26, no. 5 (November 5, 1927): 1–2.

Montaño, Jorge. "Rufino Tamayo: Leader of a New Mexican School of Painting." *Mexican Life* 5, no. 11 (November 1929): 23–27.

Montenegro, Roberto, Xavier Villaurrutia, and Ramón Mena. *Máscaras Mexicanas*. Mexico City: Talleres Gráficos de la Nación, 1926.

Muehlig, Linda. *Nature and the Artist: The Work of Art and the Observer*. Northampton, MA: Smith College Museum of Art, 1993.

Nash, Steven A., ed., with Robert Rosenblum. *Picasso and the War Years, 1937–1945*. San Francisco: Fine Arts Museums of San Francisco, 1998.

"The Native Expression." *Vogue*, likely 1927 or 1928.

Newman, Barnett. "The Painting of Tamayo and Gottlieb (1945)." In *Barnett Newman, Selected Writings and Interviews*, edited by John P. O'Neill, 71–72. New York: Knopf, 1990.

Odenheimer, Dorothy. "Woman with Bird Cage by Tamayo." *Bulletin of the Art Institute of Chicago* 37, no. 3 (March 1943): 34–35.

Oles, James. "Industrial Landscapes in Modern Mexican Art." Special issue, *Journal of Decorative and Propaganda Arts* 26 (2010): 128–59.

———. "Rufino Tamayo." In *Blanton Museum of Art: Latin American Collection*, edited by Gabriel Pérez-Barreiro, 395–98. Austin: Blanton Museum of Art, The University of Texas at Austin, 2006.

Oles, James, ed. *South of the Border: Mexico in the American Imagination, 1914–1947.* Washington, DC: Smithsonian Institution Press, 1993.

Ortiz de Montellano, Bernardo. "La obra expresiva de Rufino Tamayo." *Revista de Revistas* (April 4, 1926).

Pacheco, Cristina. *La luz de México: entrevistas con pintores y fotógrafos*. 2d ed. Mexico City: Fondo de Cultura Económica, 1995.

Parker, Howard. "Rufino Tamayo," *Mexican Folkways* 7, no. 2 (1932): 75–81.

Paz, Octavio. "Tamayo en la Pintura Mexicana (1951)." *Panorama* 1, no. 1 (1952): 55–56.

Pemberton, Murdock. "The Art Galleries." *New Yorker*, May 9, 1931, 40.

Polcari, Stephen. "Adolph Gottlieb's Allegorical Epic of World War II." *Art Journal* 47 (Fall 1988): 202–7.

Quintanilla Obregón, Lourdes. *Liga de Escritores y Artistas Revolucionarios (LEAR)*. Mexico City: Centro de Estudios Latinoamericanos, Facultad de Ciencias Políticas y Sociales, UNAM, 1980.

Ramírez, Mari Carmen, Héctor Olea et al. *Inverted Utopias: Avant-Garde Art in Latin America*. New Haven: Yale University Press, 2004.

Reyes Palma, Francisco. "Radicalismo artístico en el México de los años 30: una respuesta colectiva a la crisis." *Artes Plásticas: Revista de la Escuela Nacional de Artes Plásticas UNAM* 2, no. 7 (December 1988/89): 5–16.

Rivera, Diego. "La exposición de la Escuela Nacional de Bellas Artes." *Azulejos* 1, no. 3 (October 1921): 22–26.

Romero Keith, Delmari. *Historia y testimonios: Galería de Arte Mexicano*. Mexico City: Ediciones Galería de Arte Mexicano, 1985.

"Rufino Tamayo." *Universidad: Mensual de Cultura Popular* 4, no. 22 (November 1937): 48.

Rufino Tamayo: antología crítica. Grandes Maestros Mexicanos 13. Mexico City: Editorial Terra Nova, SA, 1987.

Rushing, W. Jackson. *Native American Art and the New York Avant-Garde: A History of Cultural Primitivism*. Austin: University of Texas Press, 1995.

S., J. "Tamayo." *Art Front* 3, no. 1 (February 1937): 17.

Smith, Elizabeth A. T., Colette Dartnall, and William Rubin. *Matta in America: Paintings and Drawings of the 1940s*. Chicago: Museum of Contemporary Art, 2001.

Stavitsky, Gail. "A. E. Gallatin's Gallery and Museum of Living Art (1927–1943)." *American Art* 7, no. 2 (Spring 1993): 46–63.

Suckaer, Ingrid. "Pocos años y muchos sucesos. Sobre Rufino Tamayo." *Saber ver* 2ª época 1, no. 1 (May–June 1999): 31–38.

———. *Rufino Tamayo: aproximaciones*. Mexico City: Editorial Praxis, 2000.

Tamayo, Rufino. "El nacionalismo y el movimiento pictórico." *Crisol: Revista de Crítica* 9, no. 53 (May 1, 1933): 275–81.

———. *Rufino Tamayo: Fifty Years of His Painting*. Washington, DC: Phillips Collection, 1978.

———. *Rufino Tamayo: pinturas*. Madrid: Centro Nacional de Exposiciones, 1988.

———. *Rufino Tamayo: 70 años de creación*. Mexico City: INBA/Museo Tamayo Arte Contemporáneo, 1987.

"36 Years of Matisse Shown at Dudensing's." *Art News* 25, no. 13 (January 1, 1927): 1.

Tibol, Raquel, ed. *Textos de Rufino Tamayo*. Mexico City: Coordinación de Difusión Cultural, Dirección de Literatura, UNAM, 1987.

Todd, Ellen Wiley. *The "New Woman" Revised: Painting and Gender Politics on Fourteenth Street*. Berkeley: University of California Press, 1993.

Torres, Ana. *Identidades pictóricas y culturales de Rufino Tamayo: ¿Un pintor de ruptura?* Mexico City: Universidad Iberoamericana, 2011.

Torres Bodet, Jaime. *Sedienta soledad: treinta y seis cartas a Bernardo Ortiz de Montellano*. Edited by Lourdes Franco Bagnouls. Mexico City: Universidad Nacional Autónoma de México, 2003.

"Una exposición de pintura moderna." *Revista de Revistas*, October 27, 1929, 17.

Vaughan, Mary Kay, and Stephen E. Lewis, eds. *The Eagle and the Virgin: Nation and Cultural Revolution in Mexico, 1920–1940*. Durham, NC: Duke University Press, 2006.

Villaurrutia, Xavier. *Tamayo: 20 años de su labor pictórica*. Mexico City: Instituto Nacional de Bellas Artes, 1948.

Wagner, Ann Prentice. *1934: A New Deal for Artists*. Washington, DC: Smithsonian American Art Museum in association with D Giles Ltd., London, 2009.

Westheim, Paul. *Tamayo: una investigación estética*. Mexico City: Artes de México, 1957.

Williams, Adriana. *Covarrubias*. Edited by Doris Ober. Austin: University of Texas Press, 1994.

Zabludovsky, Jacobo. *Charlas con pintores: Dr. Atl, Siqueiros, Rivera, Tamayo, Cuevas, Dalí*. Mexico City: Costa-Amic, 1966.

Zalman, Sandra. *Consuming Surrealism in American Culture: Dissident Modernism*. Farnham, Surrey: Ashgate, 2015.

Zavala, Adriana. *Becoming Modern, Becoming Tradition: Women, Gender, and Representation in Mexican Art*. University Park: Pennsylvania State University Press, 2010.

INDEX

Page numbers in *italics* refer to illustrations. Artworks are by Rufino Tamayo unless otherwise noted.

IMAGE CREDITS

Unless otherwise noted, photographs of works of art are provided by the owners/collections cited in the captions. Additional credits and copyrights:

Pl. 1 Photo by John R. Glembin, courtesy Milwaukee Art Museum

Pls. 2, 37; figs. 3, 32, "A" Photo by Mindy Barrett

Pls. 3, 7 Image copyright © The Metropolitan Museum of Art. Image source: Art Resource, NY

Pls. 4, 6 Photograph © 2017 Museum of Fine Arts, Boston

Pls. 8, 9, 13, 19, 23, 41; figs. 13, 29, 47, 59, "B" Image courtesy Colección Hemerográfica-Archivo Tamayo, Museo Tamayo

Pl. 12 Photo by Bill Orcutt

Pl. 14 Photography by Cathy Carver

Pl. 16 Photo by Greg Page/Page One Studio

Pl. 17 Photo by Rick Hall

Pl. 18 Photo by Roberto Ortiz

Pl. 21 Photo: Minneapolis Institute of Art

Pls. 22, 25, 32, 35; figs. 49, 50, "G" Digital Image © The Museum of Modern Art/Licensed by SCALA/Art Resource, NY

Pl. 24 Photography by Erik Gould, courtesy of the Museum of Art, Rhode Island School of Design, Providence

Pl. 26 Albright-Knox Art Gallery/Art Resource, NY

Pl. 28, fig. 17 The Art Institute of Chicago/Art Resource, NY

Pl. 30 Photo by Katherine Du Tiel

Pl. 34 The Philadelphia Museum of Art/Art Resource, NY

Pl. 37, fig. 39 Reproduced in Sotheby's auction catalogue, November 27, 1984; photo by Mindy Barrett

Pl. 38, fig. 10 Image courtesy Mary-Anne Martin Fine Art, New York

Pls. 39, 42 Photo: Imaging Department © President and Fellows of Harvard College

Pl. 40 Photo by David Heald

Fig. 1 Photo by Apic/Getty Images

Figs. 4, 5 Reproduced from Robert J. Goldwater, *Rufino Tamayo* (New York: Quadrangle Press, 1947), pp. 9, 26; photo by Mindy Barrett

Fig. 6 Reproduced from Erika Billeter, ed., *Images of Mexico: The Contribution of Mexico to Twentieth-Century Art* (Dallas: Dallas Museum of Art, 1987), p. 378; photo by Mindy Barrett

Figs. 7, 11 Digital Image © 2017 Museum Associates/LACMA. Licensed by Art Resource, NY

Figs. 8, 35, 43 © 2017 Banco de México Diego Rivera Frida Kahlo Museums Trust, Mexico, D.F./Artists Rights Society (ARS), New York; photo by Bob Schalkwijk Photography

Fig. 9 Foto: Martin Franken

Fig. 14 Art © Estate of Stuart Davis/Licensed by VAGA, New York, NY. Image copyright © The Metropolitan Museum of Art. Image source: Art Resource, NY

Fig. 16 © 2017 Succession H. Matisse/Artists Rights Society (ARS), New York; photography by: Mitro Hood

Fig. 18 Image © The Cleveland Museum of Art

Fig. 19 Reproduced from Miguel Covarrubias, *Negro Drawings* (New York: A. A. Knopf, 1927), pl. 19; photo by Mindy Barrett

Figs. 20–23, 25, 28 Reproduced under Creative Commons Attribution-ShareAlike 2.0 license from the Marxists Internet Archive, https://www.marxists.org/history/usa/pubs/new-masses/. Scans by Marty Goodman of the Riazanov Library Digital Archive Project

Fig. 24 © 2017 Estate of Reginald Marsh/Art Students League, New York/Artists Rights Society (ARS), New York; Digital Image © Whitney Museum, NY

Fig. 26 © 1925, Lee Lozowick; photo by Mindy Barrett

Fig. 27 © 2017 Estate of Pablo Picasso/Artists Rights Society (ARS), New York

Fig. 31 de Chirico © 2017 Artists Rights Society (ARS), New York/SIAE, Rome

Fig. 33 © Colette Urbajtel/Archivo Manuel Álvarez Bravo, SC

Fig. 34 © María Izquierdo Estate; photo by Rick Hall

Fig. 36 Photo by Francisco Kochen

Fig. 38 Reproduction authorized by the Instituto Nacional de Bellas Artes y Literatura, 2017

Fig. 41 Photo by Hulton Archive/Getty Images

Fig. 42 © 2017 Estate of Reginald Marsh/Art Students League, New York/Artists Rights Society (ARS), New York

Fig. 44 © 2017 Artists Rights Society (ARS), New York/SOMAAP, Mexico City

Fig. 45 Berenice Abbott/Masters Collection/Getty Images; photo: The Museum of the City of New York/Art Resource, NY

Fig. 46 © The Estate of Charles Green Shaw, courtesy D. Wigmore Fine Art, Inc., New York

Figs. 48, 52, 53 © 2017 Estate of Pablo Picasso/Artists Rights Society (ARS), New York; photo: Photographic Archives Museo Nacional Centro de Arte Reina Sofia

Fig. 54 © The Irving Penn Foundation

Fig. 55 Art © Adolph and Esther Gottlieb Foundation/Licensed by VAGA, New York, NY; photo by Jim Frank

Fig. 56 © 2017 The Pollock-Krasner Foundation/Artists Rights Society (ARS), New York; Digital Image © The Museum of Modern Art/Licensed by SCALA/Art Resource, NY

Fig. 57 © Successió Miró/Artists Rights Society (ARS), New York/ADAGP, Paris 2017

Fig. 58 © 2017 The Pollock-Krasner Foundation/Artists Rights Society (ARS), New York

Fig. C Library of Congress, Prints & Photographs Division, WPA Poster Collection, LC-USZC2-897

Fig. D Photograph courtesy of Ryerson & Burnham Libraries, Art Institute of Chicago

Fig. E Photo by Bob Schalkwijk Photography

Fig. F Courtesy of The Dalton School Archives, New York

Fig. H Photo by Jim Frank

Fig. I Photo courtesy of The Newberry Library, Chicago. Call # MMS Arts Club

Fig. J Photographic credit: The Pierpont Morgan Library, New York